PARIS 1918
The War Diary of the British Ambassador, the 17th Earl of Derby

Liverpool Historical Studies

1. Patrick J. N. Tuck, *French Catholic Missionaries and the Politics of Imperialism in Vietnam, 1857-1914: A Documentary Survey*, 1987, 352pp. (Out of print)
2. Michael de Cossart, *Ida Rubinstein (1885-1960): A Theatrical Life*, 1987, 244pp.
3. P. E. Hair, ed., *Coals on Rails, Or the Reason of My Wrighting: The Autobiography of Anthony Errington, a Tyneside colliery waggon and waggonway wright, from his birth in 1778 to around 1825*, 1988, 288pp.
4. Peter Rowlands, *Oliver Lodge and the Liverpool Physical Society*, 1990, 336pp.
5. P. E. H. Hair, ed., *To Defend Your Empire and the Faith: Advice on a Global Strategy Offered c. 1590 to Philip, King of Spain and Portugal, by Manoel de Andrada Castel Blanco*, 1990, 304pp.
6. Christine Hillam, *Brass Plate and Brazen Impudence: Dental Practice in the Provinces 1755–1855*, 1991, 352pp.
7. John Shepherd, *The Crimean Doctors: A History of the British Medical Services in the Crimean War*, 1991, 2 vols, 704pp.
8. John Belchem, ed., *Popular Politics, Riot and Labour: Essays in Liverpool History 1790–1940*, 1992, 272pp.
9. Duncan Crewe, *Yellow Jack and the Worm: British Naval Administration in the West Indies, 1739–1748*, 1993, 352pp.
10. Stephen J. Braidwood, *Black Poor and White Philanthropists: London's Blacks and the Foundation of the Sierra Leone Settlement 1786–1791*, 1994, 336pp.
11. David Dutton, *'His Majesty's Loyal Opposition': The Unionist Party in Opposition 1905–1915*, 1992, 336pp.
12. Cecil H. Clough and P. E. H. Hair, eds, *The European Outthrust and Encounter: The First Phase c.1400–c.1700: Essays in Tribute to David Beers Quinn on His 85th Birthday*, 1994, 380pp.
13. David Dutton, ed., *Statecraft and Diplomacy in the Twentieth Century: Essays Presented to P. M. H. Bell*, 1995, 192pp.
14. Roger Swift, ed., *Victorian Chester, Essays in Social History 1830–1900*, 1996, 263pp.
15. P. E. H. Hair, ed., *Arts · Letters · Society: A Miscellany Commemorating the Centenary of the Faculty of Arts at the University of Liverpool*, 1996, 272pp.
16. Susan George, *Liverpool Park Estates: Their Legal Basis, Creation and Early Management*, 2000, 176pp.
17. Alex Bruce, *The Cathedral 'Open and Free': Dean Bennett of Chester*, 2000, 304pp.

PARIS 1918

The War Diary of the British Ambassador, the 17th Earl of Derby

Edited by David Dutton

LIVERPOOL UNIVERSITY PRESS

Liverpool Historical Studies, No. 18
General Editor: P. E. H. Hair

Published 2001 by
Liverpool University Press
4 Cambridge Street
Liverpool
L69 7ZU

British Library Cataloguing-in-Publication Data
A British Library CIP record is available

ISBN 0 85323 517 1 cased
     0 85323 657 7 paperback

Typeset by Northern Phototypesetting Co Ltd, Bolton
Printed in Great Britain by Bell and Bain Ltd, Glasgow

In memory of Jean and Ronald George

Edward George Villiers Stanley, 17th Earl of Derby, 1924
(photograph by E. Chambré Hardman, reproduced by permission of the
E. Chambré Hardman Trust)

Contents

DIARY

Acknowledgements

I should like to thank the Right Hon. The Earl of Derby for encouraging me to produce this edition of his great-grandfather's diary, and also for granting me access to the original text held in the library at Knowsley, where I received much help and kindness from the Keeper of the Knowsley Collection, Miss Amanda Straw. The bulk of the Derby papers are held at the Liverpool Central Library Record Office, where the staff were unfailingly helpful and responsive to my needs.

Material of which they own the copyright is reproduced by kind permission of the Earl of Crawford and Balcarres, the Earl Haig, Sir Ian Hogg and Lord Robertson of Oakridge.

For assistance in elucidating references within the text I am pleased to thank Philip Bell, Charles Esdaile, Naomi Evetts, Michael Hughes, Gaynor Johnson, John Keiger, John Kentleton, William Philpott, and Robert Williams, none of whom of course bears any responsibility for remaining errors of fact, interpretation and assessment.

I am grateful to the Publications Committee of the School of History at the University of Liverpool for supporting this project, and particularly to Paul Hair, the General Editor of Liverpool Historical Studies, whose keen eye and tactful comments have saved me from many slips. Robin Bloxsidge has, as ever, proved an admirable publisher. Andrew Kirk oversaw the later stages of production.

A formidable feat of word-processing was carried out by Alison Bagnall, whose expertise commands the unstinting admiration of lesser mortals such as the editor of this text.

David Dutton
Liverpool, 2000

Abbreviations

ADC	aide-de-camp
AG	Adjutant-General
AJB	Arthur James Balfour
ASC	Army Service Corps
ASE	Amalgamated Society of Engineers
BEF	British Expeditionary Force
CIGS	Chief of the Imperial General Staff
CMG	Companion of (the Order of) St. Michael & St. George
DGT	Director-General of Transport
DH	Douglas Haig
DMI	Director of Military Intelligence
DSO	Distinguished Service Order
FO	Foreign Office
GBE	Knight Grand Cross (of the Order) of the British Empire
GHQ	General Headquarters
GOC	General Officer Commanding
GQG	Grand Quartier Général
GSO	General Staff Officer
MC	Military Cross
M of FA	Ministry of Foreign Affairs
OC	Officer Commanding
PLM	Paris–Lyon–Méditerranée (railway)
QMG	Quartermaster-General
RA	Royal Artillery
S of S	Secretary of State
YMCA	Young Men's Christian Association

Introduction

Edward George Villiers Stanley, seventeenth Earl of Derby, was born at Derby House in St James's Square, London, on 4 April 1865. He would not, in the normal course of events, have expected to inherit the earldom of Derby, but the failure of the marriage of his uncle, the fifteenth earl, to produce a child made him heir presumptive to a title which went back to the exploits of his ancestor at the Battle of Bosworth Field in 1485. Stanley entered the House of Commons as a Unionist member for South-East Lancashire (Westhoughton) in 1892 and was Financial Secretary to the War Office between November 1900 and October 1903, and Postmaster-General with a seat in the Cabinet from then until December 1905. In this latter post he earned notoriety by referring to his employees during a postal strike as 'bloodsuckers' and 'blackmailers'. But, like many other prominent Tories, he went down to defeat in the Liberal landslide general election of January 1906. Though declaring himself a free trader, Stanley suffered from his party's association with the Chamberlainite policy of tariff reform. From this experience he learnt an important lesson about the need of the Conservative (Unionist) party to ensure that it could carry sufficient popular support for any major policy initiative.

Stanley succeeded to the earldom of Derby upon the death of his father in June 1908. Though now out of the House of Commons, it was during the Unionists' long years of opposition after 1906 that he first came to national political prominence. His influence derived from the powers of patronage which he exercised in the party's affairs in Lancashire, in a manner, suggests Blake, 'reminiscent of a great territorial magnate of the eighteenth century'.[1] Whatever the problems experienced at this time by the British aristocracy as a whole, there were few signs of declining fortunes in the case of the earls of Derby. At the time of his succession the seventeenth earl owned land totalling nearly seventy thousand acres on estates which ranged from Witherslack in Westmorland to Fairhill House in Kent. According to his biographer, Derby was 'the last of those great English territorial magnates who exercised an effective and pervasive political influence based on the ownership of land and the maintenance of an historic association with it'.[2] But it was his Lancashire seat at Knowsley, sandwiched incongruously between the industrial conurbations of Liverpool and St Helens, which formed the basis of his territorial power. The Earl of Crawford and Balcarres, who owned a neighbouring estate near Wigan, has left a vivid picture of Knowsley in the last years before the outbreak of the Great War:

> What a place Knowsley is — within a stone's throw of Liverpool, cheek by jowl with Prescot, squeezed by St. Helens — and yet standing within a park of 3,500 acres. The park is dreary — vast expanses of smoke-laden grass, pastured by sooty red deer, but all the same its scale is so fine as to redeem many shortcomings. The house mercifully was only half rebuilt by a reforming grandfather, and a considerable portion of the handsome old structure was saved. The modern part is like a really first-class hotel.[3]

From this power-base Derby emerged as the conduit by which the Unionist leadership became acquainted with Lancashire opinion and by which that opinion influenced the party hierarchy. During and after the two general elections of 1910, which removed the Liberal government's massive parliamentary majority but failed to restore the Unionists to power, Lancashire was widely seen to hold the key to the political complexion of the Westminster government. Such thinking lay behind the decision to persuade the prominent tariff reformer, Andrew Bonar Law, to leave his safe seat at Dulwich and stand for North West Manchester, in the second of 1910's elections, in an attempt to sway the political allegiance of the whole country.[4] Part of Lancashire's significance lay in the contemporary practice of staggered elections, as a result of which it was believed that early polling declarations in the North of England would have the effect of influencing voting patterns in the rest of the country at the same election. At all events, it was generally held that, if the Unionists could not take control of Lancashire, they were unlikely to regain their national predominance.

Matters came to a head when the party began to rethink its policy on tariff reform after Bonar Law succeeded Arthur Balfour as party leader in November 1911. The latter had fought the general election of December 1910 under the commitment that a future Unionist government would not introduce the policy of tariff reform without first submitting it to the electorate in a referendum. Opinion was divided as to whether this pledge had helped Unionist fortunes at the polls or prevented the party from regaining office, and it was not until April 1912 that the shadow cabinet met to decide whether to abandon the referendum and thus revert to the full policy of tariff reform. Prior to the meeting at which the decision would be taken, Derby tried to use his influence to stop the shadow cabinet from taking this fateful step. 'Please believe me', he warned Law, 'whatever you hear to the contrary, that there is still as great an opposition to the food taxes in Lancashire as there was when the proposal was first brought forward.'[5] Inside the shadow cabinet, however, it was the intense pressure from the Chamberlainite faction which prevailed. The decision was finally made public by Lord Lansdowne, Unionist leader in the House of Lords, in a speech at the Albert Hall on 14 November 1912.

The reaction in Lancashire was both swift and predictable. In the Manchester cotton trade the response was one of despair 'followed in some by the complete political apathy of men who feel their cause lost and in others by rage at what they hold to be a betrayal'.[6] Derby's position was now extremely difficult. As president of the Lancashire division of the Unionist Association, which was due to meet on 21 December, he would have to chair a meeting at which motions critical of the leadership's new policy were bound to be proposed. Indeed, on the very eve of the meeting, Derby warned Law that the abandonment of the referendum pledge would have a 'very disastrous effect in this county unless some substitute is provided'.[7] He was convinced that a party committed to food taxes could never present itself effectively to a working-class electorate. Though warned that persistence on his part could lead to the resignation of both Bonar Law and Lansdowne, with no member of the front bench willing to take up the leadership in their place, Derby was ready to take the risk.[8] In the event, it was Law's nerve which failed. He proposed to summon a party meeting and resign — a prospect which panicked the party towards the well-known Memorial to the leaders, by which Law and Lansdowne stayed on while the party agreed to drop food taxes from its programme. Though his second period of cabinet office still lay some years in the future, this crisis marked in many respects the high point of Derby's political influence. Certainly, 'he never acted again either with the determination or with the self-confidence which he manifested on this occasion'.[9]

By this time Derby had developed a well established political persona. His image was that of a bluff, good-natured nobleman with no particular axe to grind, a picture confirmed by his increasingly ample physical dimensions. Many of his public speeches were embellished by the story of his 'speaking weighing machine' which responded to his presence with the muffled groan of 'one at a time, please'. He seemed better able than some to keep his political career in perspective. The turf was of at least equal importance to him. Indeed, a story was told that he had been obliged when Postmaster-General to deal with a bill in the Commons on the day before the Grand National. It was getting late and the last train which could get him to Liverpool in time left around midnight. Derby kept looking at his watch. The whole House understood the situation and amendment after amendment was moved to bait him. He got more and more worried until finally, at the last moment, a member rose to say that everyone realised that he had an important engagement and that the remaining amendments need not be taken. Beaming, Derby left to a roar of cheers from the whole House.

But there was more to Derby than many realised. Some saw him as the 'outstanding type of the "faux bonhomme"'.[10] According to Lord Riddell, the newspaper proprietor and friend of Lloyd George, 'Derby is much shrewder than appears — very observant, a good judge of character, and an intriguer of the first water. A proclivity which is aided by his bluff John Bull manner.'[11] Crawford confirmed that 'good fellow as he is', Derby was 'a born intriguer' and 'as shrewd as possible'.[12] 'Beneath this bluff and almost Falstaffian exterior, there runs a very marked vein of pessimism — the nervousness born in the intriguing outlook which is always present to him.'[13] Clementine Churchill was more scathing: 'People think he is bluff and independent and John Bullish but he is really a fat sneak'.[14] Such qualities served Derby well in the increasingly byzantine politics of the Great War.

Derby had a good war — or at least a good first half of the war. Person-ally committed since 1902 to the principle of compulsory national service, he rapidly emerged as 'England's best recruiting sergeant'. The war gave Derby the opportunity to offer the sort of local leadership which, histori-cally speaking, the aristocracy was expected to provide. His unique ability was to sustain an ideology of regional pride while encouraging patriotism in a local setting. As chairman of the West Lancashire Territorial Associa-tion, Derby devoted himself to army recruiting, speaking on innumerable platforms where he urged the country's young men to follow the example of his two sons, Edward and Oliver, by signing up for military service. Closely associated with the concept of the 'pals' battalions, he succeeded in raising three battalions for the King's Liverpool Regiment within a week of the start of recruitment by this system on 31 August 1914.[15] For his efforts he received the Knighthood of the Garter on 1 January 1915.

Derby seemed anxious to put aside domestic party squabbles, declaring to an audience in Liverpool that he would:

> look forward to supporting, and supporting with all my power, that party, whether composed of those who have been up to now Unionists or those who have been Liberals or have represented the Labour Party — if they can fuse in one great national party — a party that, having secured victory on land over the enemy and peace for ourselves and succeeding generations, will also take care that the fruits of our labours are not lost...[16]

In many minds Derby began to emerge as the sort of unequivocal patriot who could rise above the level of party political dispute which continued to disfigure the nation's war effort, and he was a natural choice for the post of Director-General of Recruiting in October 1915. His appointment was seen as the last hope for the maintenance of the voluntarist principle. In practice, however, his scheme represented a vehicle of transition between that and the principle of compulsion, since it showed that the available manpower would not come forward in sufficient numbers under the existing voluntary system.[17]

The Derby scheme was launched on 23 October 1915 through a royal message to the nation. 'In ancient days the darkest moment has ever produced in men of our race the sternest resolution. I ask you, men of all classes, to come forward voluntarily.' All physically fit men, between the ages of 18 and 41, not engaged in essential work on the home front, were asked to attest their willingness to serve when called upon to do so. Importantly, married men were assured that they would not be called up until the great majority of single men had enlisted. But the scheme enjoyed only limited success. When the cabinet discussed the figures just before Christmas it was clear that the scheme was not going to raise the numbers demanded by the generals. Enough bachelors had held back to persuade the government to introduce a first, limited measure of conscription in January 1916.

Opinions varied on Derby's own performance in the post of Director-General. He seemed at first unsure how to proceed. 'I must confess', he told the War Minister, Lord Kitchener, 'the more I look at it the more puzzled I am with regard to what is expected of me.'[18] C. P. Scott, editor of the *Manchester Guardian*, left an unflattering picture:

> Lord Derby hopelessly muddled and with no grasp whatever of the essential points, merely declaring, in his good-natured way, that all would be well, that he had various (perfectly vague) ideas for improving the scheme in his head, that the matter was difficult and must evolve by degrees. Mean-

while he goes on making one mistake after another...When I expressed to Asquith a doubt whether Lord Derby was equal to his task he merely remarked that he had the best intentions, but unfortunately was short of brains.[19]

But H. A. Gwynne of the *Morning Post* drew a very different conclusion. Still sceptical at the end of 1915 as to whether Derby would be 'strong enough for a fight', Gwynne soon decided in the New Year that he was the man to head a new National Party which would rescue the country from the indecision and blunders of Asquith's government. To Derby he wrote on 20 January:

> I had hoped and believed that this war would have thrown up a man in whom the public would have faith and confidence, not only in regard to his honesty, but also in regard to his statesmanship. So far nobody but Carson and yourself have appeared. Carson is a great big strong man and perfectly honest. But sometimes I begin to incline to the belief that he is too old to throw himself into such a job as the creation of a new party. There remains yourself. You have got more energy than any public man I know. You have the saving grace of immense common sense which, after all, is the rarest of gifts. But above all this, you have the faith and trust of the people.[20]

Derby's apparently apolitical stance had a particular appeal for the army high command, increasingly concerned that the country's war effort was at the mercy of the latest sordid party intrigue. By March the British Commander in France, Sir Douglas Haig, was urging upon Derby 'the necessity of *you* taking on yourself the complete control of the Government as long as war lasts'.[21] Whether Derby's own ambitions ran to such heights is unclear, though it was often said that his two ambitions in life were to win the Derby and to become Prime Minister.[22] More realistically, he clearly nurtured the hope of becoming War Minister. It was, he confessed in June 1916, 'the one office I have ever really wanted'.[23] The evident decline by the end of 1915 in the standing, at least among his ministerial colleagues, of the existing incumbent, Lord Kitchener, inevitably encouraged Derby's interest in this post.[24] He seems to have hoped that Kitchener might be appointed Commander-in-Chief of the British army, thus freeing up the ministerial position.[25] In the event, the Field-Marshal clung to office, albeit with reduced powers. Not until Kitchener's death by drowning in June 1916 did the political situation open up to Derby's advantage.

After protracted negotiations it was David Lloyd George who took over as Secretary of State and, although some had expected the under-secretaryship to be offered to Arthur Lee, Derby emerged as Lloyd George's junior minister.[26] The appointment involved a clear political calculation on the Welshman's part. As civil–military relations became increasingly strained, it was recognised that no one was better equipped than Derby to act as a buffer between the government and the military. 'His general disposition, his talent for bringing opponents together, his distaste for forcing things to an issue were all of service in this useful task.'[27] Be that as it may, Derby quickly fell under Lloyd George's spell, admiring the latter's resolute determination to bring the war to a successful conclusion. 'Lord Derby is quite devoted to D[avid]', recorded Frances Stevenson, Lloyd George's secretary and mistress. 'He has unbounded admiration for him, and I know is absolutely loyal.'[28] Their differing political backgrounds did not make the two men natural allies. But traditional political divisions seemed increasingly irrelevant to Derby and he looked forward to the formation of a new party at the end of the war 'which shall break down all the old Party ties'.[29]

Such thinking made him as impatient as his new master at the uninspiring leadership offered by Prime Minister Asquith, and by the autumn the War Office had become the main focus of criticism within the government of Asquith's premiership. Not surprisingly, the crisis of December 1916 which resulted in Lloyd George's elevation to 10 Downing Street also marked a further step up in Derby's career. Though he did not play a leading role in the manoeuvres which brought Asquith's government to an end, his promotion was inevitable. His loyalty to Lloyd George would be rewarded but, more importantly, the new Prime Minister, whose power-base was now largely divorced from his own political roots, needed to fill the vacant War Office with an appointment which commanded the support of both the Conservatives and the army. Derby was the obvious candidate. The support of Sir William Robertson, the Chief of the Imperial General Staff, was probably decisive: 'He knows the ropes of the office. The country believes in him as a good, honest man. The Army likes him.'[30]

Secretary of State for War at the height of the greatest military conflict in which Britain had ever been engaged was a post of no little importance. Yet Derby was never as prominent within Lloyd George's government as his nominal status might suggest. For one thing, he was not a member of (though he regularly attended) Lloyd George's new War Cabinet, designed as the small executive body for the management of the British war effort. More importantly, his own relationship with the Prime Minister now began to decline. Derby believed that his first task as War Minister was to offer support to his professional subordinates in the army. This naturally suited the generals. 'Derby is very good and helpful', noted Robertson as 1916 drew to a close, 'and all the office is very satisfactory now.'[31] But this took no account of Lloyd George's inflexible determination to win back civil control of the war, which had increasingly passed into the hands of the military, and especially Robertson, in the last year of Asquith's premiership. Derby's relationship with the Prime Minister was therefore never likely to be as easy as when the two men had served together inside the War Office. Elevating Derby to the Secretaryship of State, Lord Beaverbrook later reflected, 'wasn't worth the price'.[32]

Moreover, his new office revealed deficiencies of character in Derby which made it unlikely that he would, in the last resort, be able to resist the Prime Minister's will. Even in the crisis of December 1916 he had displayed a certain weakness. As the editor of *The Times* recorded:

> I was surprised to find him in a thoroughly flabby state of mind. After committing himself during the last day or two to thoroughgoing support of Lloyd George, and if necessary to resignation with him, he was now full of every kind of qualification.[33]

Now, as 1917 showed, it needed a man of higher intellectual capacity and firmer purpose than Derby possessed to cope with Lloyd George's machinations. The Secretary of State's irresolution became a by-word. As Douglas Haig once famously put it, Derby was 'a very weak-minded fellow ... and, like the feather pillow, bears the marks of the last person who has sat on him!'[34] Though Derby had nailed his colours firmly to the mast of the High Command, even the military hierarchy soon became sceptical of his ability. In May 1917 Haig noted:

> I spoke to Lord Derby ... for at least an hour. He havers a good deal now, but is a nice gentlemanly fellow. I can't think how he can get through his work if he wastes so much time talking on matters of secondary importance.[35]

Derby seemed to believe that the threat of his resignation, if Lloyd George interfered too blatantly in the affairs of the army, would be enough to keep the Prime Minister at bay. In practice, however, such a strategy earned him Lloyd George's growing contempt. His position within the government was always going to be vulnerable just as soon as the premier felt that his services had become dispensable.

The limitations to Derby's authority became clear when, on 24 February and in the War Minister's absence, the War Cabinet discussed plans to place the British army in France under the operational control of the newly promoted French Commander, General Robert Nivelle, for the duration of the forthcoming allied offensive. These plans owed as much to Lloyd George's desire to reduce Haig's authority as they did to his commitment to the principle of unity of command on the Western Front. To the dismay of Haig and Robertson, the new arrangements were finalised at an Anglo-French conference in Calais three days later when Nivelle produced a detailed written plan for unified command. Back in London Lloyd George did his best to convince the War Cabinet that the initiative for the new command structure had come from the French. Derby was 'furious and disgusted' and talked of resignation.[36] At his insistence and in what amounted to a rebuke to Lloyd George, the government sent Haig a letter expressing their full confidence in him. At the end of the day, however, Derby had to accept the Prime Minister's judgement that the Calais decision could not be reversed. 'I don't see how we can go back on the agreement — for the present offensive', he told Haig, 'without infuriating the French and risking the alliance.'[37] Pressure upon Derby not to resign came from Buckingham Palace. More important, however, was his own continuing conviction that Lloyd George, whatever his faults, remained the one indispensable figure in the British war effort. As he later explained to Lord Northcliffe:

> I am just as convinced now as I was in December that Lloyd George, although he has his failings, is the only man to be Prime Minister at the present moment. His energy is something extraordinary... and as long as he sticks to the main theatre of War and assists [sic: ?resists] the arguments of the armchair strategists I am sure all will go well.[38]

Notwithstanding Nivelle's disastrous spring offensive and subsequent dismissal, Lloyd George's personal war of attrition with the military high command was far from over. As Derby's appointment to the Paris Embassy — a post for which he had few obvious qualifications — was inextricably bound up with this ongoing struggle, its development must be outlined here. The Prime Minister's case was greatly enhanced by the military setbacks of the autumn of 1917. As Lloyd George explained, he 'meant to take advantage of the present position' to secure 'control of the War'.[39] While Haig's Passchendaele offensive failed to produce its promised results, news came through at the end of October of the disaster at Caporetto, where the Italians suffered 800,000 killed, wounded or captured. At the subsequent conference at Rapallo it was agreed to set up the Supreme War Council at Versailles, a significant landmark on the road to a unified command structure. This body would have the task of co-ordinating the allied military effort for 1918 and its practical effect would be to undermine Robertson's authority. The key feature was the selection of Sir Henry Wilson as Britain's Permanent Military Representative at Versailles and Lloyd George's insistence that the new man should not be subordinated to Robertson in London. For Derby this change seemed to involve a point of principle which would impel his resignation:

> There was a most disagreeable incident at this morning's Cabinet. Lloyd George was in a towering rage. He was most sarcastic and abusive and tried to attribute the whole of the Italian trouble to our General Staff. It was no good arguing with him and I left the room telling George Curzon and Arthur Balfour ... that I proposed to send in my resignation at once. They begged me not to do so ... I have therefore withheld my resignation but I personally do not see how I can possibly remain.[40]

A draft constitution for the Supreme War Council was approved by the War Cabinet on 2 November, leaving Robertson convinced that Derby had 'let the Army down badly'.[41] Once again, in fact, Derby, at a low ebb following the death in action in Palestine of his son-in-law, Neil Primrose, proved no match for the Prime Minister's wiles. Lloyd George insisted that no proposals would be placed before the new body without the War Cabinet having seen them and heard Robertson's opinion of them. Derby now felt able to assure Haig that he had created 'a sufficient safeguard against any wild cat scheme'.[42] He was no doubt constrained by the fact that he was in principle in favour of the sort of body which had now been created. 'I am low about my position', he told Lord Esher:

> I feel I have let the army down by not resigning as a protest against this Inter-Allied Staff, but if it were not for the various personalities interested in the matter, I should really approve of it, and I don't quite see what good I should have done by resigning.[43]

In all probability Lloyd George had decided by the end of 1917 to remove Haig, Robertson *and* Derby from their offices.[44] But to do this in one move was probably not possible. After all, at least two of the three men enjoyed the active backing of the King. So the Prime Minister was prepared to proceed slowly, taking advantage of situations as they arose and removing those who stood in his way one by one. General Allenby's triumphal entry into Jerusalem on 9 December seemed to open up a first opportunity by throwing into relief the lack of success enjoyed by the army in France. Two days later Lloyd George proposed that Haig and

Robertson should be 'promoted' to high-sounding but relatively power-less posts. Derby once again threatened resignation and Lloyd George drew back from precipitating a crisis. The War Minister did, however, agree to press Haig to dismiss his chief intelligence officer, Brigadier-General Charteris, who was held responsible for feeding Haig with unduly optimistic military assessments.[45]

The Prime Minister now seems to have concluded that he should focus his attention on Robertson. 'He said he could do with Haig, but not with Robertson, and of the two Robertson would be the easier, as Haig was a great friend of Lord Derby.'[46] Immediately after Christmas, in fact, Lloyd George persuaded the War Cabinet that Robertson should be replaced. Once more, Derby used the threat of a governmental crisis to thwart the Prime Minister. As Haig recorded:

> [Derby] first told me of Lloyd George's decision to change Robertson. This was only abandoned when Derby told him that he (D) would also resign if either R or myself were moved. The Prime Minister apparently was afraid of a Cabinet crisis and that his Government would be forced to go.[47]

As in his moves against Haig the previous spring, Lloyd George was always going to be in a stronger position if he could enlist the support of Britain's French allies and present Robertson's removal or demotion as vital to the allied war effort. The massing of German troops on the western front, following the collapse of Russian resistance in the east, brought into prominence the question of how Anglo-French reserves might be quickly deployed in the event of a German breakthrough. At a meeting of the Supreme War Council at Versailles on 1 February 1918 it was agreed that an inter-allied reserve should be created and placed under the command of a committee consisting of the Military Representatives of all the allied nations. General Foch was to take the place of General Weygand and become president of that committee. Foch's status meant that these changes would represent a significant step towards the appointment of an allied 'generalissimo'.

Robertson quickly understood what this meant for his own position and looked to Derby for support. 'The Army, the Army Council, the CIGS and the Cs-in-Chief will look to you, their Minister, to see that they are not placed in an impossible, unfair and unpractical position.'[48] Derby too seemed ready to let matters come to a head:

> There is a certain gang who want to get rid of Robertson, not you [Haig], and they think that I stand in the way of their doing so, which is quite true. I do stand in their way and I mean to as long as I have the confidence in him

that I now have, and I see no reason whatever for changing my view of his work.[49]

To the Prime Minister Derby complained that he might as well have been a 'dummy' for all the advice that had been asked of him.[50]

But Lloyd George seemed so reasonable and ready to compromise that it was difficult for Derby to maintain his position of uncompromising opposition. The premier was apparently ready to allow Robertson and Wilson to change places and also suggested that, if the British Permanent Military Representative was made a member of the Army Council in London, this would get round any constitutional problem resulting from the command of British soldiers being removed from the War Office's remit. The Prime Minister saw that he could isolate Robertson if he could only break down the Derby-Haig-Robertson axis which had appeared so solid at the outset of the crisis. Two entries in the diary of Sir Frederick Maurice, the Director of Military Operations, chart the weakening of Derby's resolve. On 5 February Maurice recorded: 'Derby says he will stand by W.R. and resign if Government insist on Versailles proposals'. By the following day, however, 'G has talked Derby round and proposes to get over difficulty by making the Versailles representative an Army Councillor'.[51]

What really undermined Robertson's position, however, was an apparent waning in Haig's support for him. The latter complained that the CIGS had 'not resolutely adhered to the policy of "concentration on the Western Front". He has said that is his policy, but has allowed all kinds of resources to be diverted to distant theatres at the bidding of his political masters.'[52] This assessment did less than justice to the struggles in which Robertson had engaged against Lloyd George for most of 1916 and 1917, but it cannot have encouraged Derby to make a firm stand at this time.[53] Haig's comment that a general reserve was 'desirable' but that he did not 'concur in [the] system set up for commanding it' failed to give the impression that this was an issue upon which he was prepared to go to the stake. 'From that point', concludes one recent historian of these events, 'Robertson's fate was sealed.'[54]

Over the next few days Derby failed to sustain any consistent line. At one point he tried to revive an earlier idea that Robertson should remain as CIGS with Wilson as his deputy, but he was not prepared to support Robertson's own claim that the same man could occupy the two posts of CIGS and Permanent Military Representative.[55] Failing to secure the backing of the War Cabinet, by 16 February Derby seems once more to have determined upon resignation. Lloyd George even got to the point of consulting the Unionist leader, Bonar Law, about a successor and decided to appoint Austen Chamberlain to Derby's post. Chamberlain motored to London only to find that Derby, having spoken to Bonar Law and Haig, had yet again changed his mind.[56]

The outcome of this protracted crisis was thus the removal of Robertson from the power-base from which he had exercised a sometimes dominant influence over British strategic policy for more than two years. Haig and Derby remained in their posts, but there was widespread agreement that the latter had left himself seriously, if not mortally, weakened. His conduct over the previous fortnight had not been impressive. A leader in the *Morning Post* of 20 February charged him with deserting Robertson when the cock crowed. Robertson himself considered that he had not been 'quite straight'.[57] After lunching with the former CIGS, the *Post's* editor, H. A. Gwynne, once an admirer of Derby, had a clear view of the War Minister's responsibility for what had occurred:

> I am afraid that the man who comes out of it worst of all is our friend Lord Derby. Nobody ever accused Lord Derby of being clever or able, but everybody thought he was a straight man. I am afraid we shall have to alter our opinion.[58]

But more significant was the Prime Minister's assessment:

> Derby has been the chief difficulty. He has been resigning twice a day. He has no courage, and funk is often equal to treachery. I can see why they call him 'Genial Judas'. First he sold Robertson; then he sold me; then he resold Robertson; then he resigned and now he wants to know if we really wish him to resign. He is frightened to death of criticism.[59]

Derby had certainly exhausted the weapon of his threatened resignation. Drained of credibility through over-use, it had earned only Lloyd George's contempt, just as would be the case a few years later with another of his ministers, Lord Curzon, who was equally fond of this device. When, almost exactly twenty years later, Derby's son, Oliver Stanley, failed to resign from Neville Chamberlain's government alongside Anthony Eden and Lord Cranborne, the latter's wife may well have had this episode in mind in declaring contemptuously that the Stanleys had 'been trimmers since Bosworth Field'.[60] The judgement of Robertson's biographer is harsh, but has much to be said for it:

> Having threatened all along to resign if anything was done to break up the partnership of Wully [Robertson] and Haig, he teetered and tottered at the

very moment when he should have taken the plunge. True, he was in torture as to where his duty lay. But by going round and asking everyone — the King included — whether he should resign or not, he only made himself ridiculous. Eventually he did stay, but by that time everyone was laughing at him.[61]

It was probably in Lloyd George's interests to leave a decent interval between Robertson's departure and that of his political mentor in the War Office. Nonetheless, Whitehall insiders now understood that Derby's resignation had only been postponed and that he would not long remain in his present position.[62]

As it happened, there had been serious discussion of Derby's possible removal from the War Office for some time before the Robertson issue became critical. At least since January, Lloyd George had been toying with the idea of sending Derby as ambassador to Paris and replacing him at the War Office with Lord Milner. The performance of the elderly incumbent in Paris, Lord Bertie, had been giving cause for concern for several months. As early as May 1917 the influential Lord Esher began urging upon both Lloyd George and Derby the case for Bertie's removal.[63] More recently, Lloyd George had seen that shunting Derby abroad might remove a serious impediment to his plans to reorganise the British high command.[64] Derby himself was well disposed to the idea of a change at the Paris embassy and, though writing in the third person, evidently did not rule out his own claims to the post:

> I think also that he probably would be more able to get in personal touch with all political sections in Paris than Bertie has been able to do and by entertaining be able to bring the British Embassy in Paris more, what I may call, 'into the picture' than it is at the present moment.[65]

Haig did nothing to discourage Derby from thinking in such terms. Indeed, he suggested that Derby's appointment might be a positive advantage for the British army in France.[66] From inside the War Cabinet secretariat Leo Amery suggested that the War Office was in need of new leadership and Lloyd George developed this theme in discussions with Maurice Hankey at the beginning of February.[67]

For most observers Derby's performance during the Robertson crisis merely underlined the case for a change of personnel at the War Office. Thomas Jones judged him a 'public danger'. 'So long as you have Derby as Secretary of State', confirmed F. S. Oliver, 'you will have misunderstanding, friction, chaos.' Milner, the likely beneficiary of Derby's removal, was even more emphatic:

Derby has been the curse of this thing from the beginning. He has clung to us like a shirt of Nessus, and will continue to cling until he has poisoned the whole body.[68]

But Lloyd George viewed the matter somewhat differently. Though he had apparently told the King on 16 February that he intended to transfer Derby to Paris, he seems on reflection to have concluded that the War Minister's dismissal, coming hard on the heels of that of Robertson, would merely offer his parliamentary critics a stick with which to beat him. For the moment, therefore, Lloyd George was prepared to bide his time in the expectation that a more favourable moment would soon present itself to effect the changes he wanted.

The opportunity was not long in coming. Events in France, military and personal, came to the Prime Minister's aid. On 21 March the Germans launched a heavy bombardment on a front of 80 kilometres from the Scarpe to the Oise. It was the beginning of the enemy's most dangerous offensive of the whole war and the one which came closest to success. Lloyd George later recorded that the events of that day convinced him that Derby was 'not an ideal War Minister':

He was not at his best in a crisis. In an emergency leaders who sweat despondency are a source of weakness. I then made up my mind that the Ministry of War in the supreme trial of a tremendous struggle was not the role for which he was best fitted, and that he would render greater service to this country in a position where it would not be obvious that his bluffness was only bluff.[69]

At the same time a serious decline in Bertie's health made the nomination of a replacement ambassador to Paris a matter of urgency. In this way Lloyd George was able to present Derby's transfer less as a demotion and more in terms of a key appointment at a critical moment for the Anglo-French alliance, while also securing, as he had wished for some months, the services of Lord Milner at the War Office in London. The Prime Minister made sure that he had the backing of the Foreign Secretary, Arthur Balfour — the political figure for whom Derby felt most regard[70] — to ensure the latter's acceptance of this proposal.

Derby was understandably anxious that his new appointment should appear in the best possible light. He wanted it made 'perfectly clear' that he was being endowed with greater powers than those given to an ambassador in normal circumstances — a claim which had its precedent in the recent appointment of another political figure, Lord Reading, as ambassador in Washington. Furthermore, 'I must stipulate to be kept very fully informed, not only on the diplomatic, but on the military situation, and to have the right, if necessary, to return to this country and represent in person my views to the War Cabinet'.[71] The Prime Minister did his bit to sustain the illusion. At the War Cabinet on 16 April he explained that experience had shown that

> what was needed was some representative who was in active touch with the views of the British Government on the innumerable questions, mainly of a military character, that were arising between the two countries.[72]

It was therefore agreed that Derby would be head of Britain's War Mission, with the same powers recently accorded to Reading, namely that he did not have to confine his activities to diplomatic issues but had full authority to discuss matters relating to the War with the French government on behalf of the War Cabinet.[73]

Yet Derby himself viewed his removal to Paris —'in my wildest moments I have never looked upon myself as a diplomat' — with some apprehension and he was certainly reluctant to leave his existing post.[74] In private he admitted that he had been 'pushed out'.[75] To the Cabinet Secretary he confided:

> How I hate leaving the War Office but the PM was determined really for some time to press Milner... into my place. I can't help feeling very bitter, but I look on A.J.B[alfour] as my master ... and for his sake I shall do all in my power to assist. I daresay the present 'soreness' will wear off, but it is very sore at the moment.[76]

Derby's misgivings about his new posting were shared by many others. The reaction of the *Morning Post* was brutal and to the point: 'If we cannot congratulate the Foreign Office upon this appointment, we may at least congratulate the War Office, which is doubly fortunate in losing Lord Derby and gaining Lord Milner.'[77] His erstwhile admirer, H. A. Gwynne, believed that, in accepting the post, Derby had fallen victim to 'the bribery and corruption of modern politics'.[78] Lord Hardinge, Permanent Under-Secretary at the Foreign Office, who might normally have expected to have some input into this most senior of ambassadorial appointments, was shocked at Bertie's unceremonious dismissal after more than half a century in the public service, a sentiment shared by Paul Cambon, the French ambassador in London.[79] Not surprisingly, the French themselves objected to the notion that the Paris embassy should be used as a waste-paper basket for discarded politicians.[80]

For all that, Derby's appointment was announced on 19 April. His formal title was clearly designed to soothe his sensibilities. Derby was described as 'His Majesty's Ambassador Extraordinary and Plenipotentiary on a special mission to the Government of the French Republic'. Not surprisingly, his initial reception was somewhat frosty, with the French premier, Georges Clemenceau, refusing to speak English at his first meeting with the new ambassador.[81] Derby claimed to be able to understand French, though not to speak it, confessing to Bonar Law that he would have to go to bed with a dictionary.[82] Yet, against all the odds, Derby proved to be an effective and successful ambassador. By early May he was 'getting quite reconciled to my work which might be interesting'.[83] Two-and-a-half years later, as his embassy came to a close, *The Times* published this tribute:

> The retiring Ambassador, when he first came to Paris, declared that, so far as he could see, the only reasons why he had been offered the post were that he did not speak French and was not a diplomatist. Lord Derby has demolished whatever truth there may have been in this joke. He does now speak French, and he has become a diplomatist — and one who will be affectionately remembered in France for many years to come.[84]

Derby succeeded in making himself popular with all sections of Parisian society. Notwithstanding his initial reception, he soon developed an easy relationship with Clemenceau, recognising in the French prime minister the only man who really counted when it came to important decisions in Paris.[85] The French responded well to his qualities of bluff geniality and forthrightness while, in addition, Derby revealed acute powers of observation which had not hitherto been apparent.[86] Whereas Bertie had derived most of his information from an intimate circle of close associates and had never strayed beyond a strictly diplomatic role, Derby determined to extend the scope of the ambassador's contacts.[87]

As a result, during Derby's time in Paris, the British embassy operated on an unprecedented scale. His lavish hospitality became legendary and it was said that six footmen were brought over from England for special functions.[88] This was not just self-indulgence on Derby's part but an intrinsic element in his attempt to collect as much useful information as possible. As he explained towards the end of his time in Paris, 'the French take very much the idea of cutlet for cutlet, and if you don't entertain then they don't get to know you and they don't entertain you'.[89] The ambassador's entertaining was 'National business'.[90] Indeed, it may fairly be said that, had Derby not run the embassy as extravagantly as he did, his diary would not have been as important an historical record as it is.

It is not totally clear for how much of his life Derby kept a diary. The surviving document covers the years 1918–1927, but becomes increasingly fragmentary for the latter part of this period. In all probability he only took up the habit upon arrival in Paris. It was written 'for my private information and in order that in after years I may recall what happened'.[91] The diary was used by Derby's biographer, Randolph Churchill, and also by Robert Blake in the preparation of his life of Andrew Bonar Law.[92] By the 1970s, however, it was believed to have been lost, with the finger of accusation pointing clearly at Churchill's cavalier treatment of archival material.[93] In fact, as there are no quotations at all from the diary for 1918 in Churchill's book — nor in Blake's for that matter — it seems more likely that this part of Derby's journal was not available to him and that it may have become mixed up with the papers of earlier earls which remained in private hands when the bulk of the seventeenth earl's papers were transferred to the Liverpool Central Library in 1971. At all events the diary was deposited at the Library in 1980 along with the papers of the fifteenth and sixteenth earls. It thus remains — at least as far as 1918 is concerned — a largely untapped historical source.[94]

The diary for 1918 is extremely full, running to about seven hundred typed pages. 'Derby was far from a pithy writer', comments Randolph Churchill, 'indeed, he was inclined to be diffuse.'[95] Derby seems to have dictated his diary on a daily basis and, not having to produce a typescript himself, was not particularly mindful of its length. It was, he once admitted, his habit to 'put down *everything*'.[96] It is not, however, an account of the inner thoughts of the British government. Lloyd George never made use of Derby in the way that he had suggested, as an extension of the War Cabinet in Paris. Indeed, the ambassador once complained that he had become a 'mere cipher'.[97] What we have is an extremely detailed record of the last months of the First World War, highlighting in particular continuing tensions in Anglo-French relations, complicated now by the intrusion of the United States; the intrigues of French domestic politics; and the ongoing war situation. Derby's account of the last is particularly interesting. By the time that he arrived in Paris, the main thrust of the German spring offensive had probably peaked, halted at the rail centre of Amiens on 4–5 April. The German High Command, we now know, had put all its resources into a final effort to achieve victory before American troops arrived in full force on the Western Front. But this was not immediately apparent. The British army had suffered over 200,000 casualties between 21 March and 15 April, a figure which exceeded losses in any comparable earlier period of the war. During June 1918, as the diary makes clear, plans were being made for the possible evacuation of Paris. As Derby reported to Balfour on 14 June:

> There is no doubt the Germans have only a very little further to go before being able to bombard, at all events the outskirts, of Paris and I am afraid of a panic and everybody wanting to get away at once.[98]

Similarly, the diary captures the surprise with which the final collapse of the enemy in the autumn confronted contemporaries. Allied planning had been on the basis of a decisive campaign in 1919 once the full weight of the American war machine was in place.

In the context of Anglo-French relations the diary shows how, after nearly four years of warfare, the two countries remained deeply suspicious of each other's intentions and critical of their contributions to the common war effort. 'If we were alone in this War', Derby once reflected, 'matters would be comparatively easy but Allies complicate things in more ways than one.'[99] In particular, the amount of the front line held by the British army and the numerical contribution of British manpower remained, as they had been throughout the conflict, significant bones of contention.[100] Relations between the two Prime Ministers, Lloyd George and Clemenceau, were often difficult if not openly antagonistic, and Derby with his easy-going manner and genial disposition played an important part in reducing tension. As the ambassador wrote in August 1918:

> We must make Lloyd George decently civil to Clemenceau. I am all for his sticking up to him in anything in which he has to be stuck up to but there are two ways of doing that and LG has so far taken the wrong way and it does an infinity of harm not only in the relations of the two Governments but incidentally in the relationships between the two countries.[101]

As regards French domestic politics, the diary reveals that, at least as far as contemporaries were concerned, Clemenceau's position at the head of the government was less secure during 1918 than history has tended to assert. Certainly there were, as Derby records, several rivals in the wings, typical examples of the intricate politics of the Third Republic, who would have been ready to replace him in the event of a significant military reverse.[102]

Derby sent his diary to England on a weekly basis, where it was carefully locked away. But he soon got into the habit of sending extracts to trusted colleagues in London, especially Arthur Balfour. Lloyd George, however, with whom Derby's relations never fully recovered, was not favoured in this way. The ambassador clearly intended such extracts to be read in conjunction with his political letters, and these have been included where appropriate. Balfour once described Derby as 'a past master in the art of political letter-writing', while his successor as Foreign Secretary, Lord Curzon, declared that he received better information from Derby than from any other ambassador.[103] The first part of the diary covering the period until the Armistice of November 1918 is now presented largely as it was composed.[104]

Derby returned from Paris in November 1920. At the fall of Lloyd George's coalition government in October 1922 he began his third and final period as a cabinet minister, serving again as Secretary of State for War under Bonar Law and Baldwin until January 1924. This was a period of considerable flux in the upper reaches of the Conservative party and there were those who, once again, mentioned Derby's name as a possible contender for the premiership. In fact, however, the fall of Baldwin's first government marked the end of his ministerial career. Thereafter he retired to the Lancashire base which had always perhaps been his preferred milieu, continuing to exert a powerful influence over the party's affairs in the county. Over the next two decades he only rarely intervened in national politics. Derby died at Knowsley on 4 February 1948.

Notes to the Introduction

1. R. Blake, *The Unknown Prime Minister: The Life and Times of Andrew Bonar Law 1858–1923* (London, 1955), p. 66.
2. R. Churchill, *Lord Derby: King of Lancashire* (London, 1959), pp. 94–95.
3. J. Vincent (ed.), *The Crawford Papers* (Manchester, 1984), p. 293. As a trustee of the National Gallery and art connoisseur, Crawford's opinion merits some attention.
4. D. Dutton, *'His Majesty's Loyal Opposition': The Unionist Party in Opposition 1905–1915* (Liverpool, 1992), p. 87.
5. London, House of Lords Record Office (hereafter HLRO), Bonar Law MSS 25/3/32, Derby to Law 14 March 1912.
6. HLRO, Bonar Law MSS 27/4/57, G. Bowles to Law 27 November 1912.
7. HLRO, Bonar Law MSS 28/1/65, Derby to Law 20 December 1912.
8. Dutton, *Loyal Opposition*, p. 191.
9. Churchill, *Derby*, p. 183.
10. A. Clark (ed.), *A Good Innings: The Private Papers of Viscount Lee of Fareham* (London, 1974), p. 174.
11. J. McEwen (ed.), *The Riddell Diaries 1908–1923* (London, 1986), p. 312.
12. Vincent, *Crawford*, p. 409.
13. *Ibid.*, p. 543.
14. M. Gilbert, *Winston S. Churchill*, vol. 4, companion pt. 1 (London, 1977), p. 71.
15. K. Grieves, *The Politics of Manpower, 1914–18* (Manchester, 1988), p. 10. Though Derby is often given the credit for the idea of encouraging recruitment by allowing men to serve with their friends and workmates from the same locality, there is some evidence that the

idea itself was conceived inside the War Office. But Derby did discuss such a proposal with Kitchener on 24 August 1914. P. Simkins, *Kitchener's Army: The Raising of the New Armies, 1914–16* (Manchester, 1988), p. 83.

16. K. Wilson (ed.), *The Rasp of War: The Letters of H. A. Gwynne to the Countess of Bathurst 1914–1918* (London, 1988), p. 160.

17. Grieves, *Politics of Manpower*, p. 73. For the suggestion that the government intended the Derby Scheme to fail in order to justify the introduction of conscription, see R. J. Q. Adams and P. Poirier, *The Conscription Controversy in Great Britain, 1900–18* (London, 1987), p. 121.

18. J. Osborne, *The Voluntary Recruitment Movement in Britain, 1914–1916* (New York, 1982), p. 102.

19. T. Wilson (ed.), *The Political Diaries of C.P. Scott 1911–1928* (London, 1970), p. 154.

20. Wilson, *The Rasp of War*, p. 159.

21. Churchill, *Derby*, p. 348.

22. Derby's horses won the race which bears his name on three occasions: *Sansovino* in 1924, *Hyperion* in 1933, and *Watling Street* in the restricted wartime race of 1942.

23. R. A. Barlow, 'Lord Derby and the Paris Embassy', MSc Dissertation, University College of Wales, Aberystwyth, 1976, p. 5.

24. C. à C. Repington, *The First World War 1914–1918*, vol. 1 (London, 1920), p. 66.

25. *Ibid.*, p. 86.

26. C. Addison, *Four and a Half Years*, vol.1 (London, 1934), p. 228.

27. Churchill, *Derby*, p. 219.

28. A. J. P. Taylor (ed.), *Lloyd George: A Diary by Frances Stevenson* (London, 1971), p. 128.

29. Derby to Lloyd George 19 August 1916, cited M. Gilbert, *Winston S. Churchill*, vol. 3, companion pt. 2 (London, 1972), p. 1545.

30. HLRO, Lloyd George MSS E/1/5/5, Robertson to Lloyd George 6 December 1916.

31. Repington, *First World War*, vol. 1, p. 419.

32. Wilson, *Scott Diaries*, p. 313.

33. *History of the Times*, vol. 4, part one (London, 1952), p. 299.

34. R. Blake (ed.), *The Private Papers of Douglas Haig 1914–1919* (London, 1952), p. 279. See also Lord Beaverbrook, *Politicians and the War* (London, 1960), p. 252.

35. Blake, *Haig Papers*, p. 232.

36. Edinburgh, National Library of Scotland (hereafter NLS), Haig MSS 3155/110, Robertson to Haig 28 February 1917.

37. Churchill, *Derby*, p. 254.

38. Liverpool Record Office (hereafter LRO), Derby MSS 920DER (17) 27/3, Derby to Northcliffe 5 September 1917.

39. D. Woodward, *Field Marshal Sir William Robertson: Chief of the Imperial General Staff in the Great War* (Westport, 1998), p. 191.

40. LRO, Derby MSS 920DER (17) 27/2, Derby to Haig 29 October 1917 (not sent).

41. NLS, Haig MSS 3155/119, Robertson to Haig 4 November 1917.

42. Woodward, *Robertson*, p. 193.

43. Churchill, *Derby*, p. 297. See also McEwen, *Riddell Diaries*, p. 207.

44. For Lloyd George's desire to remove Derby, see S. Roskill, *Hankey: Man of Secrets*, vol. 1 (London, 1970), pp. 474–75.

45. LRO, Derby MSS, 920DER (17) 27/2, Derby to Haig 12 December 1917.

46. Wilson, *Scott Diaries*, p. 321.

47. Blake, *Haig Papers*, p. 276.

48. LRO, Derby MSS 920DER (17) 27/7, Robertson to Derby 2 February 1918.

49. LRO, Derby MSS 920DER (17) 27/2, Derby to Haig 30 January 1918.

50. LRO, Derby MSS 920DER (17) 27/7, draft memorandum 4 February 1918.

51. N. Maurice (ed.), *The Maurice Case* (London, 1972), p. 69.

52. NLS, Haig MSS 3155/149, Haig to wife 5 February 1918.
53. D. Dutton, 'The "Robertson Dictatorship" and the Balkan Campaign in 1916', *Journal of Strategic Studies*, 9/1 (1986), pp. 64–78.
54. LRO, Derby MSS 920DER (17) 27/2, Haig to Derby 8 February 1918; J. Turner, *British Politics and the Great War* (New Haven, 1992), p. 274.
55. V. Bonham-Carter, *Soldier True: The Life and Times of Field Marshal Sir William Robertson* (London, 1963), p. 345; A. Gollin, *Proconsul in Politics* (London, 1964), p. 480; Turner, *British Politics*, pp. 275–76.
56. University of Birmingham Library (hereafter UBL), Austen Chamberlain MSS AC 18/2/1, note by A. Chamberlain 18 February 1918.
57. Blake, *Haig Papers*, p. 286. Derby later defended his own conduct: 'If only people knew that in this particular instance of Robertson's the man whose advice I acted on in staying was Sir Douglas Haig's, I think they would have a different opinion as to one's loyalty'. (LRO, Derby MSS 920DER (17) 28/3, Derby to Violet Markham 10 May 1918.)
58. Wilson, *Rasp of War*, p. 253.
59. McEwen, *Riddell Diaries*, p. 218.
60. A. Roberts, *The Holy Fox: A Biography of Lord Halifax* (London, 1991), p. 85.
61. Bonham-Carter, *Soldier True*, pp. 350–51.
62. Addison, *Four and a Half Years*, vol. 2, p. 488; UBL, Austen Chamberlain MSS AC 5/1/63, Chamberlain to H. Chamberlain 2 March 1918.
63. K. Hamilton, *Bertie of Thame: Edwardian Ambassador* (London, 1990), p. 359; P. Fraser, *Lord Esher* (London, 1973), p. 364.
64. Addison, *Four and a Half Years*, vol. 2, p. 465.
65. Churchill, *Derby*, p. 337.
66. NLS, Haig MSS 3155/123, Haig to Derby 26 January 1918.
67. HLRO, Lloyd George MSS F/2/1/15, Amery to Lloyd George 3 February 1918; D. Woodward, *Lloyd George and the Generals* (Newark, 1983), p. 260.
68. T. Jones, *Whitehall Diary*, vol. 1 (London, 1969), p. 52; Gollin, *Proconsul*, p. 487; Turner, *British Politics*, p. 277.
69. D. Lloyd George, *War Memoirs*, 6 vols (London, 1933–36), vol. 6, p. 3406. It should be noted that, by the time he published the final volume of his memoirs, Lloyd George's opinion of Derby had been adversely influenced by revelations from Haig's diary published in Duff Cooper's biography of the British commander: A. Duff Cooper, *Haig*, 2 vols (London, 1935–36).
70. When Bonar Law had replaced Balfour as Unionist leader in 1911, Derby had written to the King: 'six months from now ... the party will want [Balfour] back and wonder at their disloyalty to him and I hope be ashamed of themselves' (R. J. Q. Adams, *Bonar Law* [London, 1999], p. 87).
71. Churchill, *Derby*, pp. 349–50.
72. London, Public Record Office, CAB 23/6/394, War Cabinet 16 April 1918.
73. LRO, Derby MSS 920DER (17) 28/2/1.
74. Churchill, *Derby*, pp. 349–50.
75. K. Jeffery (ed.), *Military Correspondence of Field Marshal Sir Henry Wilson, 1918–22* (London, 1985), p. 39.
76. Roskill, *Hankey*, vol. 1, p. 526.
77. *Morning Post*, 19 April 1918.
78. Wilson, *Rasp of War*, pp. 266–67.
79. Lord Hardinge of Penshurst, *Old Diplomacy* (London, 1947), p. 226; P. Cambon, *Correspondance 1870–1924*, vol. 3 (Paris, 1946), p. 251.
80. Repington, *First World War*, vol. 2, p. 299; Paris, Service Historique de l'Armée de Terre, Archives de Guerre, 15N42 [d]7, La Panouse to Foch 20 April 1918. I am grateful to Mrs Elizabeth Greenhalgh for this reference.

81. Hamilton, *Bertie*, p. 385.
82. Repington, *First World War*, vol. 2, p. 276.
83. LRO, Derby MSS 920DER (17) 28/2/5, Derby to Hankey 11 May 1918.
84. *The Times*, 20 November 1920.
85. 'The principal outstanding fact in political life here is that Clemenceau is everything...': LRO, Derby MSS 920 DER (17) 28/2/1, Derby to Balfour 24 May 1918.
86. Barlow, 'Lord Derby', p. 23.
87. Hamilton, *Bertie*, p. 360.
88. C. Gladwyn, *The Paris Embassy* (London, 1976), p. 181.
89. LRO, Derby MSS 920DER (17) 28/3, Derby to Sir G. Grahame 7 September 1920.
90. *Ibid.*, 920DER (17) 28/1/1, diary 2 July 1918.
91. *Ibid.*, 920DER (17) 28/2/1, Derby to Balfour 12 October 1918.
92. Churchill's book was intended to display his credentials to take on the altogether greater task of writing his father's biography, the overriding ambition of his last years. B. Roberts, *Randolph: A Study of Churchill's Son* (London, 1984), p. 312; A. Leslie, *Randolph* (New York, 1985), p. 124; W. Churchill, *His Father's Son* (London, 1996), p. 316. According to Paul Johnson, writing in the *New Statesman*, Randolph's *Lord Derby: King of Lancashire* marked a return to the life and times style of political biography which presented the 'raw material of a man on which future historians can work at leisure': Roberts, *Randolph*, p. 337.
93. See, for example, C. Hazlehurst and C. Woodland (eds), *A Guide to the Papers of British Cabinet Ministers 1900–1951* (London, 1974), p. 138.
94. I am grateful for information from Mrs Naomi Evetts of the Liverpool Record Office which forms the basis of this interpretation.
95. Churchill, *Derby*, p. xi.
96. LRO, Derby MSS 920DER (17) 28/2/1, Derby to Balfour 6 July 1918.
97. *Ibid.*, 1 September 1918.
98. *Ibid.*, 14 June 1918.
99. LRO, Derby MSS, 920DER (17) 28/3, Derby to Le Roy Lewis 27 August 1918.
100. *Ibid.*, 920DER(17) 28/2/1, Derby to Balfour 1 May 1918: 'As I have told you before, there is no doubt a very strong undercurrent of feeling existing in this country against us, and it is based on the idea that we are not doing all that we can in the way of man power'.
101. *Ibid.*, 4 August 1918.
102. See, for example, LRO, Derby MSS 920DER (17) 28/2/1, Derby to Balfour 28 May 1918.
103. *Ibid.*, Balfour to Derby 15 January 1920; Vincent, *Crawford*, p. 413.
104. A handful of inessential passages (mainly phrases referring to or cross-referencing unpublished material) have been omitted and obvious typographical errors corrected. Inconsistent spellings, particularly of names, have, when misleading, been silently amended and the idiosyncratic punctuation of Derby's secretary has sometimes been modified in the interests of clarity. However, minor and inconsequential inconsistencies such as Sackville-West/Sackville West, Du Puy/Dupuy/du Puy, and Czecho-Slovaks/Czecho Slovaks have been allowed to remain, as has the use of contemporary conventions with respect to abbreviations, for instance the use, after Mr and Mrs, of the full point. In the interests of the flavour of the original, commas have only very occasionally been introduced into the many rather breathless sentences. It follows that there are slight style inconsistencies between the text and the scholarly apparatus.

Persons Mentioned
Frequently in the Diary

The reference is to the note where each is more fully identified (e.g. 10/5/1 = 10 May, Note 1).

POLITICIANS/OFFICIALS
French
Briand 24/5/7
Caillaux 7/6/7
Clemenceau 17/5/1
Klotz 21/5/5
Loucheur 10/5/8
Malvy 2/8/2 (letter)
Mandel 2/6/4
Margerie 4/6/9
Painlevé 19/6/3
Pichon 10/5/1
Tardieu 4/6/8

British
Asquith 19/6/7
Balfour 20/5/8
'Bobbe(r)ty' see next
Cecil/Cranborne 17/5/4
Esher 17/5/2
Milner 26/5/3
Reading 3/8/4
Trenchard 16/5/7

USA
Wilson 23/5/2

SOLDIERS
French
Foch 11/5/1
Franchet-d'Espérey 22/6/2
    (letter)
Joffre 28/5/7
Pétain 25/5/11

British
'Charlie' see Sackville-West
Delmé-Radcliffe 19/5/2
Du Cane 25/5/12
Grant 25/5/9
Haig 23/5/6
'Johnny' see Du Cane
LeRoy-Lewis 16/5/2
Robertson 26/5/5
Sackville-West 16/5/1
Wilson 25/5/1

USA
Pershing 20/6/3

DIPLOMATS, etc.
Bertie 10/5/6
Bliss 21/5/7

Capel 18/5/2
Cohn 23/5/3
Grahame 17/5/5
House 3/7/4
Maclagan 25/5/6
Murray of Elibank 10/5/9
Spiers 20/5/7
Zaharoff 21/5/1

FAMILY
'Portia' (daughter-in-law) 25/7/1
Alice (wife) 29/6/10
Cynthia (de Trafford) 19/9/3
Edward (son) 20/5/5
Oliver (son) 20/5/4
Victoria (daughter) 25/7/2

SOCIETY
B., Lady see Pembroke
Castéja 11/5/5
D'Aubigny 9/7/1
De Castellane 18/5/1
De Polignac 21/6/4
De Trafford 10/7/1
Dolly (Rothschild) 10/5/7
Du Bos 11/5/2
DuPuy 7/7/3
Hartington 17/5/3
Hennessy, Jean 28/5/3
Lowther, Jack 3/8/3
Pembroke, Beatrice 6/10/1
Rodney, Lady 22/5/4
Tweedmouth 29/6/11

May 1918

Friday, 10th May

PARIS

Attended luncheon at the M of FA given in honour of the American Mission. Found myself sitting next one of the women from the Mission who had originally come from Lancashire.

4 o'c. Had interview with M. Pichon[1] on 3 subjects.

(1) Question of exchange of French and German prisoners. Found treaty had already been ratified. I protested most strongly but M. Pichon said they had been forced to do it by the Country who insisted on this return of prisoners. He disputed the effect of such exchange which the English Government had put as being equivalent to 12 Divisions and as the French were responsible for the rate at which the exchange was made gave me an assurance that the rate of 8,000 per month should not be exceeded. I gave him to understand pretty clearly that I thought it was a direct breach of faith with the English Government which might very easily have serious consequences and I told him I must have a definite assurance in writing that the 8,000 would not be exceeded. He promised me that this should be done.

(2) I also handed him a Memorandum stating the Government's policy with regard to the Bolshevists. Asked him to kindly let me have in return a statement of his Government's views. He gave me very clearly to understand that he would have nothing whatever to do with Trotsky;[2] that he was in favour of immediate Japanese intervention but of course it could not be done unless Russia agreed.[3] The question as to whether the Japanese were invited or not by Trotsky to intervene did not in any way affect him as he was certain Trotsky was nothing but a German agent.

[1]

I gave him a copy of Lockhart's[4] telegram conveying the resolutions which were supposed to have been passed by all the Military representatives as conditions under which such interventions should take place. He had never seen them before. They had not been telegraphed by his Government's Military representative. He promised to telegraph them out to Russia and to ask whether their Military Representative agreed with them.

(3) I spoke to him with regard to the question of sharing with us the expenses of the Russian Ambassador now in Madrid. He definitely declined to in any way participate in the expense. He said they were already paying the Russian Diplomatic and Consular Authorities in this country and he was not prepared to do so anywhere else.

Saw Lady Algy[5] in the evening. She tells me that the consultation with regard to Bertie[6] not at all satisfactory. She fears an operation will certainly be necessary and that he is really most seriously ill.

In the evening Dolly Rothschild,[7] Loucheur,[8] Murray of Elibank[9] and Sir John Simon[10] came to dinner. Quite an amusing dinner. Loucheur in very good form. From all I can hear he is the dark horse of French politics and might come to the front at any time.

Notes to 10 May

1. Stephen Pichon (1857–1933). Long-term political associate and loyal follower of Georges Clemenceau, he served as Foreign Minister in the latter's wartime government, as he had done 1906–10. Derby soon came to realise that he was not the source of executive authority in the making of French foreign policy. In some pithy advice offered soon after Derby's appointment to the Paris embassy, Lord Esher suggested that among the 'governing blokes' Pichon would 'never get half round the course at Aintree'. R. Churchill, *Lord Derby: King of Lancashire* (London, 1959), p. 356.
2. Leon Trotsky (1879–1940). Soviet commissar for foreign affairs.
3. The British request in December 1917 for large-scale Japanese intervention in Siberia was an indication of their desperation to maintain an Eastern Front. In the event the Japanese, after much delay, landed only a small force and refused to operate beyond eastern Siberia.
4. Robert Bruce Lockhart (1887–1970). British representative to the Bolshevik government.
5. Lady Algernon Gordon Lennox (d.1945). Close friend of Lord Bertie during his years at the Paris Embassy and subsequently the editor of his diaries.
6. Francis Bertie, from 1915 Lord Bertie of Thame (1844–1919). British Ambassador in Paris, 1905–18. Known in the Diplomatic Service as 'The Bull'.
7. Dolly Rothschild, married (1913) James de Rothschild, son of Baron Edmond de Rothschild.

8. Louis Loucheur (1872–1931). Appointed French Minister of Armaments in September 1917. One of the new breed of managerial politicians who rose to prominence during the war.
9. Alexander Murray, Lord Murray of Elibank (1870–1920). Government Chief Whip, 1910–12. In 1912 he became director of S. Pearson and Son at the invitation of the Liberal industrialist, Weetman Pearson, later 1st Viscount Cowdray.
10. Sir John Simon (1873–1954). Liberal MP for Walthamstow, 1906–18. Home Secretary, 1915–16. Intelligence Officer with Royal Flying Corps, 1917–18.

Saturday, 11th May

Président du Sénat came to see me in the morning. Evidently not very enthusiastic about Foch[1] but I gather his real feeling is that he is not kept fully informed by the Government of what is going on.

Luncheon with Monsieur Dubos.[2] Murats[3] there.

Afternoon, Dutch Minister called to see me. Frankly pro-Entente.[4] Thinks that things will be satisfactorily arranged with Germany and it does not look now so much as if Germany was picking a quarrel with Holland. At the same time thinks that if we have really successfully blocked Zeebrugge and Ostend it may be that they will make another attempt to coerce Holland to let them use Antwerp.

Leaving for G.H.Q. 3.30 taking Castéja[5] with me.

Notes to 11 May

1. Ferdinand Foch (1851–1929). Was created chief of staff to the French Army in May 1917 and was elevated to the post of Supreme Allied Commander in France following the Doullens Conference of March 1918.
2. Of the French Jockey Club.
3. Descendants of the sister of Napoleon Bonaparte.
4. Holland remained neutral throughout the war.
5. Marquis de Castéja (b.1875). A neighbour of Derby's from Scarisbrick Hall, Ormskirk. Interpreter with the French Military Mission attached to the British armies in France, 1914–19.

[NO DIARY FOR THE PERIOD OF A VISIT TO ENGLAND]

Thursday, 16th May

PARIS

Left London 9.25 a.m. Crossed with Charlie,[1] Leroy-Lewis,[2] Geddes (First Lord),[3] Admiral Hope,[4] Simon Lovat,[5] and his brother in law Lindley,[6] Trenchard,[7] and F. E. Smith[8] all on the same boat. Brought Rolls Royce over with me.

Left Boulogne 2.45. Punctured every tyre and every inner tube on the way. Luckily got another inner tube from the French at Beauvais, arriving here 10.30 p.m.

Notes to 16 May

1. Major-General Charles Sackville-West (1870–1962). British military representative to the Supreme War Council at Versailles. Known as 'Tit Willow'. Derby stayed at his home in Paris during his first weeks as Ambassador.
2. Herman Le Roy-Lewis (1860–1931). Appointed military attaché to the Paris Embassy in January 1916. Derby later wrote: 'I suffered in the early part of my time here through having as Military Attaché, Le Roy Lewis, who though he had my confidence was detested and distrusted in French political and military circles'. (LRO, 920DER (17) 28/3.)
3. Sir Eric Geddes (1857–1937). Moved from railway management to become First Lord of the Admiralty in July 1917.
4. Rear-Admiral George Hope (1869–1959). Served at Dardanelles, 1915. Deputy First Sea Lord, 1918–19.
5. Major-General Simon Lovat (1871–1933). Served in Gallipoli, France and Flanders.
6. Francis Lindley (1872–1950). Appointed Counsellor to the British Embassy in Petrograd in 1915. HM Commissioner in Russia, June 1918.
7. Hugh Trenchard, Viscount Trenchard (1873–1956). Appointed Major-General in command of the Royal Flying Corps in France in 1915. The RFC became the world's first independent air force in 1918 with Trenchard as its first professional head.
8. F. E. Smith, 1st Earl of Birkenhead (1872–1930). Conservative MP for Liverpool (Walton), 1906–18. Attorney General, November 1915–January 1919.

Friday, 17th May

I went with Geddes and Admiral Hope to see Clemenceau[1] on subject of Naval control in the Mediterranean. Geddes absolutely satisfied. Clemenceau in very good form. Quite evident he agreed to our wishes more because he hoped it would put Italians in a hole than that he really liked our proposition.

Spoke to him afterwards about Exchange of Prisoners and told him that I thought he had behaved very badly indeed about it and it was likely to cause very considerable trouble. He assured me he could not help it. It was forced on him by the country but he admitted that he had done it without any consultation with us and that he knew it was against our wishes. He pointed out that the number to be exchanged was entirely at the option of the French Government and whereas we talked of thousands being exchanged he only thought of exchanging in hundreds. He told me there would be an official note sent to me on the subject but when I asked that the number to be exchanged should be limited to hundreds and a notification of such should be in the note, he told me that though he gave me his word of honour it would be so, it was impossible to do this as that would undo all the good that had been done in this country by announcing the fact of the exchange.

Afternoon. Swedish Minister called upon me. He married an English-woman and is I believe thoroughly pro-entente, at all events there is no doubt he hates the Germans, if what he told me was true.

Went to see Frank Bertie. Thought him looking very ill. Really it is rather a trial seeing him now as from beginning to end it is nothing but abuse of Leroy Lewis, Esher[2] and [blank]. His memory is going and as soon as he has finished telling me the whole tale once he starts it afresh.

Dinner in the evening. Hartington,[3] Cranborne,[4] Madame Castéja, Madame de Jauzé, and Madame Montesquieu and Grahame.[5]

Alert at 10.30. Nothing came. French believe barrage drove aeroplanes off. As a matter of fact it was the thunderstorm.

Notes to 17 May

1. Georges Clemenceau (1841–1929). French Prime Minister, 1906–09 and 1917–20. Failed to secure election as President of the Republic in 1920 and retired to private life. The 'Tiger'.
2. Reginald Brett, 2nd Viscount Esher (1852–1930). A powerful behind-the-scenes figure in the first two decades of the twentieth century. As an unofficial liaison officer his reports from Paris did much to undermine the position of Derby's predecessor, Lord Bertie.
3. Edward William Cavendish, Marquess of Hartington (1895–1950). Heir to the Duke of Devonshire. Served in the British Mission in Paris and in the 1919 Peace Delegation.
4. Robert Gascoyne-Cecil, Viscount Cranborne (1893–1972). Fifth Marquess of Salisbury, 1947. Known as 'Bobbe(r)ty'. Won Croix de Guerre before being invalided

home in September 1915. Personal Military Secretary to Derby when War Minister.
5. Sir George Grahame (1873–1940). Minister Plenipotentiary to France, 1918–20.

Saturday, 18th May

Nothing but departmental work in the morning.

Luncheon with Madame de Luart. Afterwards received returned visit from Italian Ambassador. He informed me that he was quite certain that a big attack was going to take place in Italy but they were perfectly prepared for it.

Went to see Pichon again about exchange of prisoners but it was beating a dead donkey and nothing would induce him to give me an assurance that only a very limited number of prisoners should be exchanged each month. At least he was ready to give me the assurance but not put it in writing.

I forgot to say that yesterday Boni de Castellane[1] came to see me bringing various papers. He took exactly the same line as he did before, namely that England ought to take full control of the diplomacy of the Allies and again urged that nothing should be done that would put Austria in the position of feeling that we were trying to break up her Empire.

Dined in the evening with Capel,[2] Madame Jeanne Jennessy [?Hennessy], Madame de Ludre, the Robert Rothschilds, Mill Fitzgerald[3] and Grahame. Very pleasant party. Just as we left the usual alarm, and the raid lasted for about an hour. They certainly dropped one very heavy bomb.

Notes to 18 May

1. Comte Boni de Castellane. Like Derby a prominent patron of the turf. His divorce from the American heiress, Anna Gould, in 1906 had scandalised foreign opinion. See *Confessions of the Marquis de Castellane* (London, 1924).
2. Arthur Capel. English intelligence officer living in Paris who became a friend of Clemenceau. He died soon after the war ended.
3. Millicent, Duchess of Sutherland, who married Lieutenant-Colonel Percy Fitzgerald (b.1873) in 1914.

Sunday, 19th May

Departmental work in morning up to 11.30 when I went to Versailles.

Discussed several matters with Sackville-West who is very helpful with regard to the formation of our new Committee. Had luncheon with him, Lady Hadfield, Mrs. Kinnaird Storr and young Macready.[1] Afterwards went to Mrs. Wolff's house. Met several people, Carters, others whose name I do not know and Madame Edwina and Coleporteur, a young American who has been refused by the American Army on account of his health and has joined the Foreign Legion. They both sang rag time — very amusing. Gloriously hot day.

On return went to see Bertie who is evidently getting steadily weaker. He was in his sitting room but I saw a great change.

Evening Delmé-Radcliffe[2] dined with Charlie and me. He is very interesting but as usual cocksure of everything he says being right. Very confident that the propaganda work now being done with the Yugo-Slavs and Slovaks will have great effect and will gradually disintegrate Austrian army. He says he has got Lloyd George's[3] consent and approval but as he has not got it in writing I very much doubt whether this policy will be kept to. Quite impossible to have the two policies running at the same time, the one trying to make arrangements with Austria on a basis that she should not be disintegrated and arranging with these various nationalities to give them independence which necessarily means the disintegration of Austria.[4] It is just the same in this case as with Russia. Our Government never seems to be able to make up its mind which horse to ride and the result is confusion and distrust by all parties.

Notes to 19 May

1. Captain John Macready (1887–1957). DSO 1915.
2. Brigadier-General Charles Delmé-Radcliffe (1864–1937). Military Attaché, Rome, 1906–11; Chief of British Military Mission to Italian Army, 1915–19.
3. David Lloyd George (1863–1945). British Prime Minister, December 1916–October 1922.
4. For the complexities of British policy towards Austria at this time see H. Hanak, *Great Britain and Austria-Hungary during the First World War* (London, 1962).

Monday, 20th May

Routine work in the morning.

Saw Delmé-Radcliffe who had been to see Clemenceau which personally I think entirely wrong and have written to complain to London about it. He put forward his own memorandum on the Yugoslav question.

Clemenceau will naturally take it as being the Government's point of view although Delmé-Radcliffe had no authority for putting it forward. I have got to see Clemenceau about it and I have telegraphed to London to know which policy they intend to pursue, backing the Yugo-Slav or making love to Austria. This habit of Lloyd George of employing the last man he comes across to undertake business with a Foreign Nation regardless of what has gone before seems to me to be fatal.[1]

Luncheon, Lady Hadfield, Mrs. Kinnaird and Alan Fletcher.[2]

After luncheon paid return visit to Swedish Minister. Talks English perfectly. Married to an English woman the daughter of Plunkett[3] who was our Ambassador at Vienna. Lady Plunkett also there. Afterwards picked up Oliver[4] and Edward[5] in the Bois. Blazing hot day.

Sir Arthur Duckham[6] and Stoner came to see me and very anxious I should do all I could to help Italy with regard to coal, or rather to help Fiat works in Italy to get more coal allowed to them than at present as it is keeping back output of Fiat Engines. Duckham very hopeful about output of aeroplanes, both heavy bombing and new scouts which according to his account are wonderful.

Dined with Spiers.[7]

Had a long talk with Boni de Castellane who is making his influence considerably felt. He is very strong on the subject of trying to get the Pope on our side, making Austria into a much stronger state than she is and, as she is really bitterly opposed for the most part to Germany, form her into a buffer state between Germany and the East. Strongly opposed to giving way to Yugo-Slav pretensions. Reported all this in a letter to Arthur Balfour.[8] After others had gone stayed behind talking with Dumesnil[9] the French Aviation Minister who was most interesting. He is very satisfied with his arrangement for the defence of Paris and thinks he will be able to keep the raiders off but of this I have my doubts.

Notes to 20 May

1. An early example of Derby's sensitivity about his own position and authority. He was determined to hold Lloyd George to his promise that he should have full powers to represent the British point of view to the French government. On 3 May he had already written angrily to Balfour: 'I was sent out here on a distinct understanding, and if Lloyd George ... does not fulfil his part of the bargain, I am certainly not going to fulfil mine'. (London, British Library, Balfour MSS, Add. 49743.)
2. Lieutenant-Colonel Alan Fletcher (b.1876). DSO 1915.
3. Sir Francis Plunkett (1835–1907). Ambassador in Vienna, 1900–05.

4. Oliver Stanley (1896–1950). Derby's younger son. He rose to cabinet rank in the 1930s and was Colonial Secretary, 1942–45.
5. Edward Stanley, Lord Stanley (1894–1938). Derby's elder son. MP for Liverpool (Abercromby), 1917–18. He became Dominions Secretary in May 1938, but died in October of that year.
6. Sir Arthur Duckham (1879–1932). Chairman of the Advisory Committee, Ministry of Munitions since 1917.
7. Edward Louis Spiers (1886–1974). In 1918 he changed his name to Spears. Head of the British Military Mission in Paris, 1917–20.
8. Arthur James Balfour (1848–1930). British Foreign Secretary, 1916–19.
9. Jacques-Louis Dumesnil (1882–1956). French Under-Secretary of State for War, 1917–19.

Tuesday, 21st May

Luncheon. Charlie, Oliver, M. Zaharoff,[1] General Thornton,[2] M. Geraud, Colonel Leroy Lewis, Mr. Bridgeman[3] and Mr. Adam.[4]

Dinner. Duchess Camastre, M. Klotz,[5] Madame Klotz, Mrs. J. Rothschild, Mr. Lambton, Mr. Phipps,[6] Mrs. Phipps, Mr. Bliss,[7] Charlie and Oliver.

Air raid in evening.

Notes to 21 May

1. Sir Basil Zaharoff (1849–1936). Armaments magnate and financier, of Greek parentage.
2. Major-General H. W. Thornton (1871–1933). Assistant Director-General of Movements and Railways since 1917.
3. Reginald Bridgeman (1884–1968). Second Secretary in Diplomatic Service since 1911.
4. George Adam. *The Times* correspondent in Paris.
5. Louis-Lucien Klotz (1868–1930). French Finance Minister, 1917–20.
6. Eric Phipps (1875–1945). First Secretary at the Paris Embassy since 1916. British Ambassador in Paris, 1937–39.
7. Tasker H. Bliss (1853–1930). American Military Representative on the Supreme War Council, 1917–19.

Wednesday, 22nd May

Angela Forbes came to see me and asked me to write to Cambon[1] to secure her a Pass to work with the French and told me that she had put the matter in Hugo's hands and half threatened that if it was not granted her case would have to be opened afresh. I took no notice of that and informed her that if her Pass was not granted all I would do would be to draw M. Cambon's attention to what I said in the House of Lords; that I certainly should not press her claim. It must be for the French to decide whether she is to have a Pass or not.

12 o'c. Had first meeting of our new Board. On the whole a success and I am sure that I shall be able to make something of it. It was extraordinary that after the first question had been broached, how other questions cropped up one after the other. They all had luncheon with me afterwards.

3.15. A deputation from the British Chambers of Commerce came to welcome me.

Afterwards went to see Clemenceau on the subject of Mediterranean Command which Geddes had discussed with him. Most energetic man I have ever seen. He could not get hold of Leygues,[2] Minister of Marine, on the telephone as they said he had gone down to the Chamber so took me in his motor and hunted Leygues up. Result most satisfactory.

I also mentioned to him that Delmé-Radcliffe had had no authority whatever to speak to him on the subject of the Yugo-Slavs and I begged for the future, before any of these people came to see him, he would find out from me what their credentials really were. I think he will do this.

I also spoke to him and asked him to get the French papers to make quite clear that some of the sneering remarks that had been made with regard to our Staff did not emanate from him or from anybody in authority. He promised to do this.

He spoke to me about the employment of the Czechs in Russia about which Lord Robert Cecil[3] had written to him privately explaining our policy. He entirely disagreed with that policy but is going to write a letter and will send me a copy.

Afterwards taken by M. Du Bos to the Jockey Club and introduced to all the members. Most lengthy proceeding.

Went to see Bertie. Found him considerably weaker. Dinner in the evening. Ganays, Lady Rodney,[4] Mrs. Ward (Muriel Wilson), Vicomte d'Harcourt, Mr. & Mrs. Addison[5] from the Embassy.

Alerte sounded about 11.30. Raid was soon over. Later and heavier raid about 2.30 in morning.

Notes to 22 May

1. (Pierre) Paul Cambon (1843–1924). French Ambassador in London, 1898–1921.
2. Georges Leygues (1857–1933). Minister of the Marine in eleven different governments, including 1917–20.
3. Lord Robert Cecil (1864–1958). From 1923 Viscount Cecil of Chelwood. Parliamentary Under-Secretary of State for Foreign Affairs, 1916–19. One of the founding figures of the League of Nations.
4. Lady Rodney, wife of 8th Baron Rodney whom she married in 1917.
5. Joseph Addison (1879–1953). Acting First Secretary, Paris Embassy, October 1917; Commercial Counsellor, August 1918. Nevile Henderson judged him 'one of the best brains in the whole of the Diplomatic Service'.

Tursday, 23rd May

Morning. Saw Alan Fletcher before he went back to G.H.Q.

Estonian Government representative to France and friend came to see me. Why I do not know as there is nothing they wanted me to do.

Afterwards luncheon given to me by Americans. Spoke in answer to the toast of my health. Think it went all right.

3.30. Count D'Aunay[1] came to see me. He and his wife great friends of Clemenceau. He is however himself an interminable bore who promised he would drop in and see me whenever he had anything of interest to say. Judging by today's conversation that will not be often.

Afterwards Mr. Roy Commissioner General for Canada whom I had met in England came. He brought two gentlemen with him here interested in a case in regard to wagons they had contracted to supply to the P.L.M. They made a shocking bad contract, so bad that it has practically broke the Company. They have not got a leg to stand on and admit it but think that out of common fairness the French Government ought to see that they do not lose by it. An impossible position as I told them. We are doing our best to get some mitigation of the contract which undoubtedly was very hard. It is quite certain if it had been the other way they would have asked for their pound of flesh.

Then Japanese Ambassador. He tells me no further advancement in the question of the intervention of Japan. President Wilson[2] is still thinking over it. He has thought over it already for 6 months and personally I believe now it is too late, whereas if it had been done 6 months ago I think we could have calculated on many of the Divisions which now have come to the Western front having been obliged to remain on the Eastern front. It is a serious position out there and especially for us as the German and

Austrian prisoners are gradually getting armed and they might make a very formidable attack on India. The Ambassador told me that he thought there were something like 1,400,000 of them but many of these of course were Austrians who would not fight.

Went for a walk with Charlie afterwards to see Bertie. He is very pleased with himself as he slept through the raid. Of course he does not realise that he is having narcotics. He is now unable, except with difficulty, to take even milk and there is no doubt it is a case of gradually sinking but luckily he suffers no pain. I have never seen him once yet that he has not referred to the Cohn[3] affair.

Sloggett[4] to see me to say good-bye. He is very bitter at having to give up and says it is all due to personal spite on the part of Macready.[5] He thinks that his going is going to create an uproar amongst the civilian doctors and nurses and says that Haig[6] is furious at his recommendation that he should be kept on being turned down. I do not think myself there will be the least trouble or any row at the change.

Dined with Mr. and Mrs. Toulmin.[7] Not a particularly interesting evening. They are essentially second rate people. He is the Manager of Lloyds Bank and has built up an enormous business for that Bank during the War. He is a friend of Andrew Weir and it was really at Andrew Weir's[8] request I went there.

Notes to 23 May

1. Comte d'Aunay. Former French Ambassador to Denmark, whose American-born wife had once been Clemenceau's mistress.
2. Woodrow Wilson (1856–1924). Twenty-eighth president of the USA, 1913–20.
3. Jefferson D. Cohn (1881–1951). Son-in-law of Horatio Bottomley. Worked for British Red Cross in France, but came under surveillance because of stories about his pre-war connections with the German royal family. Bertie regarded Cohn as an agent of Esher's campaign against him and was dismayed when Cohn was made an Honorary Captain in the British Army. For the 'Cohn Affair' see K. Hamilton, *Bertie of Thame: Edwardian Ambassador* (London, 1990), pp. 345–51.
4. Surgeon-General Sir Arthur Sloggett (1857–1929). Director-General Army Medical Service, 1914–18.
5. Major-General Nevil Macready (1862–1946). Adjutant-General to the Forces, 1916–18; Commissioner of the Metropolitan Police, September 1918–April 1920.
6. Douglas Haig (1861–1928). Succeeded Sir John French as Commander-in-Chief, British Expeditionary Force, December 1915. Field Marshal, January 1917.
7. E. M. Toulmin. Of Swiss origin, he held the position of General Manager, Paris, Lloyds and National Provincial (Foreign) Bank until 1931.
8. Andrew Weir (1865–1955). Baron Inverforth, 1919. Surveyor-General of the Army, 1917–18; Minister of Munitions, 1919–21.

Friday, 24th May

In the morning went to see Clemenceau to tell him that Lloyd George wished the Supreme War Council to meet on June 1st at Versailles. Also spoke to him with regard to Northcliffe's[1] request for M. Moysset to be attached to our Propaganda Department.

Clemenceau in a violent temper over this and said he would not have Northcliffe's interference. It is evident he means to get rid of Moysset altogether and I gathered he is going to make a complete sweep of their Propaganda Department, getting rid amongst others of Franklin Bouillon.[2] That will flutter the dovecotes at home as he is a great friend of Lloyd George and his surrounders and was the great correspondent of Sir Henry Norman[3] who in my opinion is a most pernicious pest and I am glad to see he has been sacked from the Air Board. I spoke to him with regard to cooperation between General Trenchard and General Duval.[4] He is sending instructions to Duval to do all that he can to help in long distance bombing. Clemenceau also told me then that he had received an answer from the Italian Government going back on everything they had previously said and refusing to entertain the idea of an Admiralissimo. He is heart and soul with us on that subject but says that he will not come into the arrangement unless the Italians are made to as well. He is quite prepared to put pressure on them and suggests that it should be done at the Supreme War Council.

Had a visit from M. Géraud[5] who is the moving spirit under the title of Pertinax of the *Echo de Paris*. He was attached to the Embassy in London for some time and now connected with the Irish Department in the French Foreign Office. He wanted permission for 3 Abbés (two brothers Flynn and Abbé Logan) to visit Ireland for propaganda work. They are I believe quite sound and one Abbé Flynn has just returned from America. Géraud himself was also in Ireland at instance of Irish Government directly after the rebellion[6] and did propaganda work amongst the clergy. Think it might be of advantage for these 3 abbés to go but communicated with Balfour to know if he can find out more about Géraud's credentials.

Count de Fels came to luncheon. Great friend of Briand's.[7] Told me that there was no doubt Briand meant to wait his time and get Clemenceau out. At the present moment Clemenceau was too strongly in the saddle. If however there came any opportunity of attack, he would not hesitate to make use of it.

Then went to the meeting L'Effort Naval Britannique at the Sorbonne.

Had to read a French speech which terrified me. I think it is the only time I have really been nervous when speaking. Had a very excellent reception and on the whole things went off well though I felt more than I have ever felt before my handicap of not speaking French fluently.

In the evening dined alone with Charlie and Oliver.

Notes to 24 May

1. Alfred Harmsworth, Viscount Northcliffe (1865–1922). Newspaper proprietor. Director of Propaganda in Enemy Countries, 1918.
2. Henri Franklin-Bouillon (1870–1939). Minister of Propaganda under Painlevé in 1917.
3. Sir Henry Norman (1858–1939). Liaison officer of Ministry of Munitions with Ministry of Inventions, Paris, 1916. He acted as an agent for Lloyd George. Liberal MP 1900–10 and 1910–23.
4. General Maurice Duval (1869–1958). After the Armistice he became France's Director of Military Aviation.
5. André Géraud (Pertinax) (1882–1956). Foreign affairs editor of the *Echo de Paris*, 1917–38.
6. The Easter Rising, 1916.
7. Aristide Briand (1862–1932). Ubiquitous figure of the Third Republic. Prime Minister eleven times (including 1915–17) and Foreign Minister on seventeen occasions. He was, as Adamthwaite has put it, 'the archetypal figure of the regime; middleman and conciliator, ceaselessly forming and reforming coalitions' (A. Adamthwaite, *Grandeur and Misery: France's Bid for Power in Europe 1914-1940* [London, 1995], p. 112).

Saturday, 25th May

Morning. Routine business.

Heard Spiers had got Mumps. We must put somebody else in there but he resents it very much and I shall have to speak to Henry Wilson[1] about it when he comes next week as Spiers won't be free from infection for a month.

Luncheon with Comtesse de Jean de Castellane.[2] Her first husband was Carl Egond of Furstenberg. Knew her before when she came to Chatsworth and also she had been at Palace House in the old days for racing. Briand who is a great friend of hers was there. I did not get any chance of speaking with him. He is however coming to luncheon. Also met Maître Robert the head of the Paris Bar who struck one as a most able man. Amongst others there were Duc D'Elchingen who has been with our army as Liaison Officer. Very full of praise of it. He of course is the direct descendant of Marshal Ney.[3]

Afternoon. Had meeting with regard to propaganda. Onslow[4] and Lytton[5] from G.H.Q., Maclagan[6] and Leroy Lewis. They all agreed that something more wants doing than is being done at the present moment and that the co-operation between civil and military is not good. After Maclagan went I had a private talk with Lytton and Onslow. Personally I think the best way would be to put Lytton in supreme charge as I do not think Maclagan is any good. He would be able to keep in personal touch with G.H.Q. and with the correspondents there with whom he is on excellent terms. All that part of the work is well done. Where the failure takes place is that the Editors and the Chief newspaper proprietors here are not sufficiently well posted with our views. Maclagan cannot do it as the matters are entirely military of which he is absolutely ignorant. Lytton and Onslow are going to draw out a scheme, I shall then submit it with any alterations I think necessary to London. I think I shall have no difficulty in getting the Military authorities into line but I may have some difficulty with Beaverbrook[7] though I think he would be quite keen to help as I think he recognises that things are not going as smoothly as they ought to.

Persian Minister came to see me. Talks French very well and one would never take him for an Eastern. He has lived most of his life in Europe. As far as protestations go entirely pro-entente and especially pro-English and hates the Germans. He is very much afraid that the force we are sending into Persia is too small. He says unless we have a really effective force it is worse than useless. He tried to pump me as to how strong the force was and naturally I told him I hadn't the least idea and pretended I didn't even know that a force was going. He seems to take no objection whatever to our sending troops.[8]

Went to tea with Lieutenant Hermann who is one of Clemenceau's Military Secretaries. Very nice fellow.

Evening. Dined with Ralph Lambton and came back early to have a talk with Charlie Grant[9] who had just come in from Foch's Headquarters. He was very interesting on several points.

First of all the mixing up of French Divisions with ours as opposed to their taking over more line. Foch's contention is that the Germans do not mean to attack the French if they can help it. They mean to try and crush our Army and if our Army is altogether [sic] in one section they know precisely where to go for it. On the other hand if our Divisions are mixed up it is not the English Force they attack but an Allied Force when the losses will fall equally on English and French and the burden be mutually shared. Charlie thinks that he has no thought of sacrificing English for French but that this is the only way of getting a really Allied Army much as the Germans did by putting German and Austrian Divisions mixed up on the Russian Front. Charlie evidently agrees with this.

We then started talking about Spiers and there is no doubt there is a great deal of animosity against Spiers which to a certain extent I understand but which I am sorry for as he is no doubt a very capable fellow.[10] It is a matter of fact that Spiers cannot go either to Petain's[11] or Foch's headquarters and that Foch has said very definitely that if any information he gives to Du Cane[12] or Charlie Grant is transmitted to Spiers he will never tell them anything further and the reason for this is that Spiers undoubtedly mixes too much with the politicians and in order to get certain information out of them he gives them information, or hints information, which neither Foch nor Clemenceau want the ordinary politician to have.

I think Charlie is very disgruntled with the position he holds and I do not wonder at it and really he would be an excellent man to take Spiers' place. I should like to try the experiment while Spiers has got the mumps. I made the suggestion but Spiers I hear is up in arms against it.

Notes to 25 May

1. General Sir Henry Wilson (1864–1922). Chief of the Imperial General Staff, 1918–22. Assassinated by the IRA.
2. Sister-in-law of Comte Boni de Castellane.
3. Michel Ney (1769–1815). French marshal, described by Napoleon as 'the bravest of the brave'.
4. Richard W. A. Onslow, 5th Earl of Onslow (1876–1945). Colonel Assistant Director Staff Duties, BEF, 1918; British War Mission, Paris, 1918–19.
5. Hon. Neville Lytton (1879–1951). Fourth son of the 1st Earl of Lytton. Wounded in France, 1916. Served thereafter on the General Staff. See N. Lytton, *The Press and the General Staff* (London, 1920).
6. Eric R. D. Maclagan (1879–1951). Ministry of Information, Head of Paris Bureau, 1917; Controller for France, 1918.
7. William Maxwell Aitken, Baron Beaverbrook (1879–1964). Canadian-born newspaper proprietor. Britain's first Minister of Information, 1918.
8. See F. J. Moberly, *The Campaign in Mesopotamia*, vol. 4 (London, 1927), pp. 172–73.
9. Lieutenant-Colonel Charles Grant (1877–1950). Brigadier-General, General Staff, 1918–19.
10. For Spiers' mounting problems with his French hosts, see M. Egremont, *Under Two Flags* (London, 1997), pp. 79–81.
11. Philippe Pétain (1856–1951). Replaced Nivelle as commander of the French armies on the western front in 1917 and re-established the morale of the French

troops. Created a marshal in 1918.
12. Major-General Sir John Du Cane (1865–1947). Liaison officer between Foch and GHQ 1918.

Sunday, 26th May

Attended the Empire Day Service at the Embassy Church. Packed full. Most uninteresting sermon by Bishop Brent the American Chaplain General. Never heard a sermon with less sequence in it.

Sidney Clive[1] who is the Liaison Officer with Pétain's Army came to see me. He is very anxious to come to our weekly meetings. He thinks they would be very useful to him. Of course I am delighted he should do so. He then got on the subject of Spiers just as Charlie Grant did the night before and his words with regard to Pétain's relationship to Spiers were precisely the same as Charlie Grant's with regard to those of Foch.

To luncheon at Versailles. After luncheon had a long talk with Nash[2] on the subject of the mixing up of French and English Divisions as looked on from the transport point of view. He tells me he saw the king who is deadly opposed to this mixing of divisions and spoke very strongly against it and says that it means a loss of our National effort. I cannot help thinking there is the other side to be looked at and that is our National effort may be lost far more effectually if our army is concentrated on one part of the line and on that part of the line falls the concentrated attack of innumerably superior German Divisions. Nash himself thinks that it is essential there should be this mixing up so as to get the roulement for our troops in quiet places of the line but he says that if this practice is adhered to it must mean a pooling of more than men and that all stores etc must be equally pooled. That of course is bitterly opposed by Q.M.G. and C.I.G.S. at home and I think with reason. Nash however says that it is quite impossible to work the show unless there is such pooling.

Nash tells me there is considerable trouble at home as Milner[3] has now decided to put the whole of the transportation branch under the Q.M.G. and Lloyd George agrees with him. I think it was the right thing to have done in the first instance if we had changed the Q.M.G. but considering that Lloyd George himself set up this separate Department under Eric Geddes,[4] which he claims to have been such an enormous success — as it has been — it seems an extraordinary idea to now make a change. There is however one thing which I agree with Nash ought to be gone into at once and that is that now we are on the defensive the whole question of the personnel of this Branch should be looked into as it was based on an offensive in which we might have to build railways in Belgium to the extent of 50 miles a day. That I think is not a likely contingency and I should think we could get at least 20,000 men out of transportation.

Sidney Clive dined with me in the evening. Very interesting talking over things. I am afraid there is no doubt there is a great deal of feeling between Pétain and Haig and he tells me also a good bit against Henry Wilson now and Pétain says openly that he wishes he had Robertson[5] back.

Notes to 26 May

1. Brigadier-General George Sidney Clive (1874–1959), DSO. Became Military Governor of Cologne in 1919.
2. Major-General P. A. M. Nash (1875–1936). Director General of Transportation to the British Expeditionary Force, 1917–18.
3. Alfred Milner, Viscount Milner (1852–1925). Member of Lloyd George's War Cabinet, December 1916–April 1918, when he succeeded Derby as War Secretary, a post he held until December 1919.
4. Derby is presumably mixing up Eric Geddes, the First Lord of the Admiralty, with his brother Auckland (1879–1954), who was Minister of National Service, August 1917–August 1919.
5. Sir William Robertson (1860–1933). CIGS 1915–18. Rose from the rank of Private (1877) to Field-Marshal (1920).

Monday, 27th May

The Bertha[1] began at 6.15. Fired rounds fairly regular every quarter of an hour for some considerable time. Have not heard yet what damage done. Everybody tells one bombs fell in different parts of the City but I believe most of them fell by the War Ministry and in that direction.

Presented a Military Cross to a French Officer and at 11 o'c Milner came to see me. We had an hour's talk. He was very interesting about things and quite nice. I think he is finding his difficulties at the War Office very great, much more than he had expected. They have however done very well in the way of raking out men. He told me he had just got word that the big attack had begun, but later in the day his opinion was that it was not a big attack although it was on a 55 kilometres front.[2] Unfortunately our wretched tired divisions came right into the middle of it and I am afraid they got very much knocked about. They were taken out of the Somme and sent to a quiet part at Kemmel only to get knocked about there and now had a third doing, all within 2 months. I am afraid if they give way, as I fear they have done, it may make a nasty feeling again.

The attack north at Kemmel seems to have been held but down south the whole line seems to have been driven back a bit chiefly by gas shells. No very reliable information at present. 3 o'c.

At luncheon I had Colonel Georges,[3] Colonel Herchere and Capitaine Barbier. Colonel Georges is a most amusing man. He is the man who really carried out, and carried out most successfully, the deposition of King Constantine.[4] The other two men are the very Private Secretaries of Clemenceau and are quite delightful. Herchere has been shockingly wounded. It really was a very pleasant luncheon.

After luncheon saw Mr. Fletcher, President of the Chamber of Commerce. Not very much impressed with him. He is full of complaints about the way our people are treated here and he says that it has been gradually getting worse the whole of this year and has got more particularly worse since our Army was put under Foch. He tells me the French people were very offensive about it and says we ought to have done it two years ago. He is agitated about a Commercial Attaché and I sounded him about Addison. He seemed to have a good opinion of him but I think he soars very high in his choice of a man to be Commercial Attaché here as he wants a man who has been a Diplomatic Minister somewhere and says he ought to rank next to the Ambassador which is I think rather extravagant.

Did various routine work in the afternoon. Went to see Bertie who I am sorry to say is decidedly worse. I saw a great change in 48 hours. He tried to get out of bed but failed and the nurse told me that the son had at last telegraphed for his mother to come.

Dined in the evening with the Italian Ambassador. By far the nicest dinner I have been to. Met the Duchesse de Tremouille who is most amusing though not in the least pretty.

Got back to find the news not at all nice and I am afraid two of our Divisions must have lost very heavily. As yet they seem undecided whether it is the big attack. Personally I think there will be three attacks, one up in the North, one at Arras and one where they are fighting now, and probably simultaneously within the next week.

Notes to 27 May

1. The Germans used massive pieces of ordnance to bombard Paris from March 1918. The 42cm Mörser was nicknamed 'Big Bertha'.
2. The third battle of the Aisne began on 27 May when the German 1st and 7th

armies attacked the British 9th Army Corps and the 5th French Army. By 30 May
the Germans claimed 50,000 prisoners and around 800 captured guns.
3. Colonel Alphonse-Joseph Georges (1875–1951). Assistant to the Allied High
Commissioner in Greece, 1917.
4. Constantine I, King of Greece (1868–1923). Reigned 1913–17 and 1920–22.
Deposed by the Allies in June 1917. See D. Dutton, 'The Deposition of King Constantine of Greece, June 1917', *Canadian Journal of History*, XII/3 (1978), pp.
325–45.

Tuesday, 28th May

Princesse de Pois came to see me to ask me to telegraph about her son the
Duc de Mouchy who is liaison officer with Milne[1] and whom she hears is
very seriously ill.

Afternoon. Saw Chancery people.

Jean Herbedde Foreign Editor of the *Temps* came. Anxious to know
about Ireland.[2] Assured him I did not expect any trouble there at all.
Talked to him about the relationship between the two countries. He told
me that although undoubtedly after the retreat of the 5th Army there was
a feeling amongst some of the soldiers it never existed in the country and
that the feeling towards England was excellent.

Saw Capel who had no good news. Tells me that Clemenceau told him
last night that our Divisions had fought magnificently considering how
weak they were. Asked Capel to see that this was put in *The Times* and the
fact emphasised that these battalions were supposed to be resting. Fear
from what I hear they have been almost exterminated.

Dined with Madame Jean Hennessy.[3] Quite a small dinner. Only two
ladies present being Comtesse de Clermont Tonnerre[4] and Mme [blank].
Grahame, Joseph Reinach,[5] and De Mun[6] a brother of Mrs. Hennessy, and
Deputy for Rheims.

Reinach full of talk. Bitter against Clemenceau whom he accused of
being a bad judge of men and in every way unsuitable for a Prime Minister. I believe there is a great deal of personal feeling between the two.
When I asked him at the end who he proposed to substitute he admitted
quite frankly that that was a question he could not answer and that for the
moment undoubtedly Clemenceau was the only possible Prime Minister
but from what he afterwards said there is no doubt that he is a supporter
of Briand. Reinach great admirer of Joffre[7] whom he claimed to be the
biggest soldier of the War. I think he greatly exaggerated Joffre's doings
in the beginning of the War. He is also a great supporter of Haig's. He

knew absolutely to a letter what had happened with regard to the taking over of more line and his bitterest talk of Clemenceau was on this account. He says that that is the cause of all our present misfortune and that alone is sufficient to condemn Clemenceau.

News tonight not at all good. Reinach however says that the French are very loud in praise of the behaviour of 3 out of 4 of our Divisions. The fourth did not do very well. They were completely overwhelmed by tanks.

Notes to 28 May

1. General George Milne (1866–1948). Field-Marshal 1928. Commander of the British forces based on Salonika, 1916–18.
2. Probably a reference to the recent disclosure of a plot between Sinn Fein and the Germans.
3. Madame Jean Hennessy (Comtesse Marguerite de Mun). Wife of one of the leading proprietors of the famous cognac firm, she became a close and valued friend of Derby soon after his arrival in Paris. Their correspondence continued until his death.
4. Comtesse de Clermont-Tonnerre. Formerly Madeleine de Juigné.
5. Joseph Reinach (1856–1921). Journalist and politician. He campaigned for Dreyfus and wrote a history of the affair.
6. Bertrand de Mun. Deputy for Reims, 1914–19 and 1924–28.
7. General Joseph Joffre (1852–1931). Commander of the French armies on the Western Front until December 1916, when he was created Marshal but removed from day-to-day control.

Copy of letter sent to Mr. Balfour to be attached to Diary 28 May 1918

I hope I may see you at the end of the week as Milner told me yesterday you are likely to come over but I have heard nothing definite from you. This letter is only in case I do not see you.

There is very little to tell you. I told you I think in one of my letters that I was going to meet Briand at luncheon. I met him but unfortunately did not have a chance of talking to him afterwards as he had to go off, but he is coming to luncheon with me this week. Charlie Montagu[1] however did have a long talk with him and he was very communicative on the subject of the famous Emperor Charles letter[2] and very bitter about it too. He says that although it is no good crying over spilt milk, still they will have to attack the Government on the subject: that he knew for an absolute fact that the Kaiser had seen the letter before it was signed and had approved of it. The Germans had a very bad knock at Verdun and they were very much frightened about our offensive and it would have been perfectly easy at that time to have arranged some terms of Peace. He says that our diplomacy has always made a mistake throughout in refusing to even consider any terms of Peace and that in his opinion it would have been perfectly possible, at times other than the latter, though he did not mention what times, to have arrived at some understanding. I am certain that he is biding his time to attack Clemenceau and of course Clemenceau's position depends entirely on successful resistance to the big offensive. If yesterday's action is any pointer I am afraid that we are going to have a very nasty time within the next fortnight. I do not see how we are going to help being driven back everywhere simply by weight of numbers. The only question is how quickly can we bring the advance to an end and what price shall we make the Germans pay for it.

I find people are very jumpy and I think the Big Bertha beginning yesterday morning has only made them more so. I was at Dinner with the Italian Ambassador last night and was told there that a great many people who went away for Easter remained away and a great many more went for Whitsuntide and although they talked of coming back, now that Big Bertha had started there was little chance of their doing so and really except for officials Paris is a City of the Dead. All this I think is rather demoralising to the people who cannot get away and I am afraid the result will be reaction against Clemenceau.

Meanwhile the fact that it was our Divisions, poor tired fellows who had been both in the retreat from the Somme, and at Mount Kemmel[3] – who had to bear the brunt of this fighting and gave way owing to force of numbers, will mean a restarting of recrimination between French and English which was very bad when I came here though to a great extent has died down.

Now to look at another picture. I have had a long talk with Albert Thomas[4] who was very interesting. He is rather cross with Lloyd George whom he said has deserted him; very bitter against Clemenceau, but recognises that his Government is very popular at the present moment and the only possible one.

With regard to the publication of the Emperor Charles letter he takes an entirely different view to Briand but condemns its publication. He says that he is perfectly certain it would never have led to anything. He thinks that it was written with all sincerity but that when written the Emperor Charles did not realise what a hold Germany had got over his country and he is certain that the Kaiser knew nothing about it. With regard to the second pourparler in Switzerland when Colonel Armand[5] was sent, he thinks it was a very different pair of shoes. By that time the German

Emperor[6] had got to hear of the letter and the meeting in Switzerland was simply used as a meeting to carry off the indiscretion of the previous letter. It was never meant to come to anything but afforded the Emperor Charles an opportunity of telling the Kaiser that the first letter was written with extreme loyalty to Germany. He does not believe in detaching Austria from the War. He does think a great deal can be done in the way of stirring up revolution and he is all for the policy of getting hold of the Yugo-Slavs and thinks that a revolution there is very probable and comparatively easy to get. I asked him how soon he knew of the original letter and apparently he knew of it at once which shows that the loyalty of Lloyd George in the matter of maintaining secrecy was not a loyalty which was kept in this country.

He then went on to talk to me about the state of the War. He says that there have been very serious strikes. He is doing his best to control them but that the under-current in the Country generally is very strongly in favour of peace. They are War weary to a degree which we do not understand and that if we were now to have a reverse, especially if that reverse fell on French troops, he is very doubtful whether it would be possible to really go on with the War. He thinks Clemenceau would fall and be replaced by somebody else who might be in favour of making the best Peace possible. He pretended that of course he would have nothing to do with such a Government but incidentally he let out a little later when talking about coming to England that he did not mean to come till he was again in the Government and he hinted that would not be very long. On the other hand I hear that as a matter of fact he has lost a great deal of ground with the Socialists and is not in the least likely to come into power. He is very strongly in favour of Japanese intervention and I pointed out to him that we were all strongly in favour of that but to a great extent it depended on the co-operation of America which could not be obtained. He evidently knows nothing of what is going on because he said he does not think we have put enough pressure on at present and he said if the President would not agree we ought to go on without him. He is very afraid of the influence the President may have at a Peace Conference because he says he seems to treat the question of the retention by Germany of Alsace and Lorraine just in the same way as he would treat the retention of Armenia by Turkey, and I should think that the visit of the American Labour Party the other day has considerably disturbed the socialists here. They are disagreeably deceived to find that the socialism of America is not the anarchy which a great many in this country would like to produce.

He then spoke to me about the League of Nations. He said when President Wilson first mentioned it there was a genuine enthusiasm in this country for the proposal but they began to think that Wilson is now weakening on it. He is very anxious that Lloyd George should take up the question. I could not quite follow his argument when he said that he had all the material now in England to form a League of Nations outside the Central Powers and he instanced the fact that we now have bureaux controlling raw materials, etc. and we ought to begin to make a definite policy with regard to the control of these materials after the War and their distribution in fair quantities to all the Allied Nations. That was getting quite outside my depth and I simply let him make his statement.

He was most friendly and has promised to come and see me again whenever I ask him to. I shall keep in touch with him because he represents a certain sentiment in this country, although there is no doubt, as I said before, he has lost caste a great deal with the socialist party proper.

Notes to letter of 28 May

1. Lord Charles Montagu (1860–1939). Son of 7th Duke of Manchester.
2. Charles (Carl) I (1887–1922). Last Emperor of Austria. Abdicated 1918. During 1917 he launched a number of peace feelers, none of which bore fruit.
3. The Germans had captured this pivotal position on 25 April.
4. Albert Thomas (1878–1932). Socialist politician who held posts of junior War Minister and Armaments Minister between May 1915 and September 1917, during which time he formed a close association with Lloyd George.
5. In August 1917 Count Revertera, a retired Austrian diplomat, carried on tentative peace talks with a French friend of his, Colonel Abel Armand, who was serving with the military intelligence. The talks were resumed, without result, in February 1918.
6. Wilhelm II (1859–1942). German Emperor and King of Prussia, 1888–1918. He fled to Holland when Germany became a republic.

Wednesday, 29th May

Meeting in the morning of Heads of Missions. They all had luncheon with me afterwards. One thing not mentioned in the Agenda which I shall keep private is that of all stupid things today the War Office telephoned here to know exactly where all the shells from Bertha had fallen. As it is the one thing you are not allowed to talk about and as it can be of no possible interest to the Cabinet — unless it means they are frightened to come here — I told Capel who is acting for Spiers that he had better not send any reply.

In the afternoon Roumanian Deputation came to see me to protest against the Treaty.[1] Nothing of course for me to do except meet them sympathetically and let the Government in London know that I had done so. Dined with Mr. Hyde an American and think I made a great mistake in doing so as he is a great bounder. His wife had left Paris for Versailles as she was afraid of the gun and Gothas[2] and perhaps with reason as one of the Shells had hit the house next door to them in the morning. Met Otto Kahn who was at one time a candidate for a Lancashire constituency.[3] Notwithstanding the fact of his name and that he is a German Jew he has been extraordinarily loyal to us in America. Sat next to Princess Murat. Most extraordinary woman. She is a daughter of the Duc de Rohan. Married to a man who lives in Russia where he has big property from his mother. She went with him when he first went to Russia but soon got bored with it and has since been out there for 3 days every 8 years. She has been everywhere, India, Afghanistan, walked through Persia, is thoroughly Bohemian and most amusing and notwithstanding her various eccentricities still received everywhere. On the other side the young Madame de Jaucourt whose mother is a sister to Mrs. Hartmann. Curiously enough they have got property at Clitheroe in Lancashire. Great friends of the Castéjas. Madame Viel Castel there also and a lady whose name I did not catch but who it appears nobody meets so the dinner was somewhat of a frost.

Notes to 29 May

1. In March 1918 the Germans imposed the Treaty of Bucharest upon Romania, bringing the war between the Central Powers and Romania to an end.
2. Gotha. German twin-engined biplane bomber. It was the principal strategic bomber of the German air force from 1917.
3. Though Max Aitken, the future Lord Beaverbrook, had negotiated with the Unionist party in the Gorton constituency on behalf of his friend, the American banker, Otto Kahn, the latter did not in fact contest the constituency.

Thursday, 30th May

Went to the American Church celebration of their Decoration Day when they decorate all their graves. Glad I went as I was the only Ambassador there. It pleased Sharp[1] very much indeed. I sat next to him and I think he was grateful to me for coming. Welsh Guards Band was sent over specially for service.

Afterwards had luncheon given to me at the Inter-Allied Club by the Committee. Quite nice. Made the acquaintance of M. Arthur Meyer,[2] the leading man of *Gaulois*. Most interesting little Jew. Old and knows everything.

Afternoon M. Paul Cambon came to see me. It is the only time I have ever got him to talk English to me. Afterwards Trenchard and Sykes[3] came in and we had a long discussion with regard to future arrangements for bombing and especially in regard to chief command. They agreed on a policy to be pursued and telegraphed it to Sir William Weir.[4] They both seem glad to have someone to come to help them in their difficulties.

Then on a round of official calls.

News today bad and wildest rumours going about. The French Government for the first time really anxious.

Notes to 30 May

1. William G. Sharp (1859–1922). United States Ambassador in Paris, 1914–19.
2. Arthur Meyer. Editor of *Le Gaulois*.
3. Lieutenant-Colonel Frederick Sykes (1877–1956). Major-General and Chief of the Air Staff, 1918–19.
4. Sir William Weir (1877–1959). Created Baron, 1918. President of the Air Board, April 1918–January 1919.

Friday, 31st May

This morning heard Arthur Balfour coming here to stay. Saw Mr. H. Bone of *The Times* who has been sent out on a special propaganda Mission by Beaverbrook. Told me all about the south and how bad the feeling there is against us and gave as the reason exactly what I had heard, that people had made an enormous amount of money and wanted to have peace so as to prevent their money being taken. Feeling against us very high indeed. I think he a little exaggerates but still there is a great deal of truth in what he says. He submitted a scheme home to Beaverbrook which seems to me very sound provided that it all is linked up with a Central Board here and put on a proper basis.

Luncheon today. Duchesse de Clermont Tonnerre, Madame Jean de Castillane, Madame Caracciclo who is the daughter of Crosby[1] the American finance Minister, Lady Rodney, the American Ambassador, General Bliss and Briand.

After luncheon walked round the garden with the latter. I asked him point blank whether he meant to attack Clemenceau and he told me "No". He was a great believer and a strong supporter of Foch. That he would have employed Foch instead of Nivelle[2] last year only Foch happened to be ill at the time. He says Clemenceau must be supported and is evidently prepared to play a thoroughly patriotic role. At the same time he thinks his position is considerably shaken in the country. He came in on the plea the War was not being prosecuted sufficiently energetically and these two serious reverses have made people wonder whether they were wise in making the change. He thinks a great mistake was made in publishing the Emperor's letter but a still greater mistake in not making more use of it when it was received. Nivelle had just had his big offensive which he claims was a great success. We had just had a successful offensive. The state of Germany and Austria were both very bad and though there could have been no question either then or now of detaching Austria from Germany he feels certain that the internal condition of Austria was so bad that they would have practically forced Germany to give a Peace very favourable to us.[3] He, Briand, knew at the time that Russia had broken down and he evidently feels that probably the best chance of the whole of the War of making a good peace was lost.

I also had a talk with Bliss. He tells me that at Versailles they were perfectly convinced that the attack was going to come exactly where it did and Haig was entirely of the same opinion and warned Foch that he was putting our tired Divisions in the very centre of the next attack but the French would not believe him. Bliss says the whole situation is very anxious. He does not think they will press on much towards Paris but straighten out the right of their line from their present push to Montdiddier and then put in a big attack. That I think is contrary to what our people think. They think it is the real big attack which has succeeded far beyond any German anticipation and they will exploit it to the full.

Johnny Ward[4] came in for a minute or two after luncheon. He tells me all London is very much amused at Lady Randolph's marriage.[5]

After luncheon nothing very much. Saw various people from the Embassy. News still bad.

Arthur Balfour and Eric Drummond[6] came just before dinner and with Capel dined with us.

Usual air raid in evening.

Notes to 31 May

1. Oscar T. Crosby. United States Assistant Secretary of the Treasury.
2. General Robert Nivelle (1856–1924). Replaced Joffre as Commander-in-Chief in December 1916. Dismissed in favour of Pétain, May 1917, following the disastrous spring offensive.
3. This issue is discussed in C. J. Lowe and M. L. Dockrill, *The Mirage of Power*, vol. 2 (London, 1972), pp. 256–60, and Z. A. B. Zeman, *A Diplomatic History of The First World War* (London, 1971), pp. 132–61.
4. Sir John Ward (1870–1938). Assistant Private Secretary to Derby when he was Financial Secretary to the War Office.
5. Lady Randolph (Jennie) Churchill (1854–1921). Mother of Winston S. Churchill; married her third husband, Montagu Porch, 23 years her junior, in 1918.
6. Sir (James) Eric Drummond (1876–1951). Earl of Perth, 1937. Private Secretary to A. J. Balfour, 1916–19, after which he became the first Secretary-General of the League of Nations.

June 1918

Saturday, 1st June

Long talk with Arthur Balfour. He did not tell me much that I did not know already. He seems to think that they are getting into a great mess over the Irish Home Rule Bill[1] and it will be a long time before it will be able to be produced. It has not even yet been circulated to the Cabinet.

Had talks with various people in the morning. Nothing of any interest. Wild rumours of Cabinet changes including the substitution of Barthou[2] for Pichon. Cannot find out if there is any truth in it and think it extremely unlikely as Barthou is a great friend of the President[3] who of course hates Clemenceau. I feel all the more convinced if there is to be a change that either Briand will come back or else, what to my mind is even more likely, Loucheur who is I am sure playing a double game, will become a sort of figure-head Prime Minister with Briand in the Government really pulling the strings and probably Albert Thomas as well. I do not say that this would be a pacifist government but there is no doubt that they would be prepared to turn a ready ear to any offer of peace.

Went round with Arthur Balfour to see Frank Bertie who had had a good night and was rather better but the sister says there are several very disturbing complications.

After luncheon McDonough[4] and Onslow came to see me with regard to Propaganda work. I read them my letter to Beaverbrook and I am glad to say they are entirely in accord with it. McDonough is to see Beaverbrook on his return to England and try and get his consent.

Every sort of wild rumour going about and there is no doubt Paris is for the moment very rattled but as yet no talk of the Government and Diplomatic Staffs leaving the place.

A.J.B. did not get back till late. He was I think rather dissatisfied with the way business had been arranged and said he was kept waiting the whole afternoon and his business was not even touched.

Dinner. Party in the house, Ian Malcolm,[5] Hartingtons,[6] Dolly Roth-schild and Madame de Viel Castel.

Notes to 1 June

1. An attempt by Lloyd George to achieve Home Rule, following the Easter Rising, foundered on the question of partition. On 9 April 1918 Lloyd George announced the so-called dual policy which involved extending conscription to Ireland com-bined with the pledge of 'a measure of self-government'. By the end of 1918 the whole Irish question had been transformed by the emergence of the Sinn Fein movement which refused to accept a limited settlement based on Home Rule.
2. (Jean) Louis Barthou (1862–1934). Ministerial career extended from 1894 until his death. Minister of Foreign Affairs under Painlevé, October–November 1917. Assassinated, October 1934.
3. Raymond Poincaré (1860–1934). Held cabinet rank from 1893. President of the Republic, 1913–20, after which he returned to active politics.
4. Major-General George McDonough (1865–1942). Director of Military Intelli-gence, 1916–18; Adjutant-General, 1918–22.
5. Sir Ian Malcolm (1868–1944). Parliamentary Private Secretary to A. J. Balfour, 1916–19.
6. Major-General Charles Hartington (1872–1940). Deputy CIGS, 1918–20.

Sunday, 2nd June

PARIS

Haig came to see me and we had a long talk about various things. It is quite evident that they did try to get him out as, though he did not say Home Command had been offered to him, he asked me why Henry Wilson was so keen to get him there. He says Henry Wilson behaved quite straight about it and I should gather therefore that Haig having refused Henry Wilson was now supporting him. I thought D.H. very anxious and tired but at the same time he evidently has great confidence in Foch and the relationship between the two is excellent which I think is more than it is between Pétain and Foch. D.H. is most anxious that Foch should take his G.H.Q. away from Pétain and form a regular Staff, having four groups of Armies, two French under Pétain and Castelnau,[1] a third English group under Haig and a fourth under the Belgians. He said he is certain that is the only way the supreme command will really work properly. There are all sorts of stories going on about the Chemin des Dames fight.[2] It appears that General Duchesne, who was in command, was actually leaving Paris at the time although he had been warned there would be an attack. Whether this is true or not I do not know. Many rumours of Ministerial crisis but I do not believe in them except as far as Pams[3] is concerned. There is no doubt he and Clemenceau have had a row in which Clemenceau was very rude to him and I think it very likely that he may go, especially as Mandel,[4] Chef de Cabinet to Clemenceau, is working very hard to get somebody else put in Pams' place. There is a story that Briand had been asked to be Foreign Minister in Pichon's place but I think that is only one of the numerous wild rumours.

Went to luncheon at Versailles where the whole gang was. Had a walk and talk with Lloyd George who seems to me not to realise in the very least what the great danger here is, namely that favourable terms will be offered to France and she will accept them and it will be we who will have to be called upon to pay the price. As long as Clemenceau is in power I do not think there is any fear of a separate peace but still at the same time if Germany does make a favourable offer to France I do not believe we could afterwards get the French soldiers to fight or the French Nation to continue the War as they would say it would be simply and solely to fight for our interests. What will happen then Heaven only knows.

Dinner. Henry Wilson, Hartingtons, Lady Rodney and Princesse Lucien Murat. I think I did mention about her before and what an extraordinary career she has had having travelled all over the world, Persia, Afghanistan, and one of her most recent exploits was to visit Rasputin.[5] She told us all about it — most interesting. She says there was no question of his being in German pay. He was thoroughly patriotic and at the same time though very clever absolutely uneducated. Everybody thought that once he was murdered everything would go well with Russia. There was a genuine fear of his influence over the Czar and Czarina which she did not think was really bad and it really was confined to having some sort of healing power which had a great effect on the Czarevitch.[6]

Henry Wilson looked rather low and depressed but he seems to think that this present push will be held up. It appears that so far all the French reserves that have gone in had to go in without any artillery to support them but they have now got their guns up.

Notes to 2 June

1. General Edouard de Castelnau (1851–1944). Prominent Catholic general. Commanded Eastern Group of Armies under Pétain, 1917–18.

2. Chemin des Dames. Ludendorff launched the third Battle of the Aisne on 27 May. On the French sector of the Chemin des Dames front the Germans drove through to a depth of twelve miles, annihilating four French divisions.

3. Jules Pams. Contested presidential election of 1913 against Poincaré. Minister of the Interior, November 1917–January 1920.

4. 'Mandel'. George Louis Rothschild (1885–1944). As Clemenceau's Chef de Cabinet Mandel controlled French domestic politics during a decisive period. Became a Deputy in 1919.

5. 'Rasputin'. Grigory Efimovich (1871/2–1916). Russian 'holy man' who enjoyed great influence under the last tsar until his assassination in December 1916.

6. A reference to his apparent success in alleviating the haemophilia of the heir to the Romanov throne.

Monday, 3rd June

Saw Toulmin and Ralph Lambton who are anxious to remove all the securities at Lloyds Bank and want to get a special railway truck for the purpose. I told them they must try and get it for themselves. If they fail then I might intervene but for me to ask for a truck for them to move their securities would probably make the French think we were in a panic here, whereas if they do it showing letters from their clients which they say they have, asking that their securities should be removed, nobody could say anything to them.

Afterwards saw Captain [blank] who has come over here to review exemptions. I do not think myself he will be able to get many but needless to say he requires the whole of one floor of a building and new Committees. I had met him before. He seems a quiet fellow but it adds yet one more to the many Missions here.

In the afternoon went about paying official calls which I have now nearly completed.

In the evening apart from those in the House, the Edouard Rothschilds, Dolly and Mlle Saint Sauveur dined.

Tuesday, 4th June

A.J.B. & Co. left by motor at 8 o'c in the morning. He tells me that on the whole they settled things satisfactorily but I cannot find anything on which they did really arrive at an agreement.

Sir Thomas Barclay[1] came to see me. He was radical member for Blackburn in the short 1910 Parliament. He claims to have laid the ground for the Entente but as a matter of fact the one thing that he was working for was an entente between ourselves and Germany, he having married a Boche. He gave me a certain amount of political news all of which I have since discovered to be totally inaccurate. He was at one time head of the Chamber of Commerce here which only confirms my low opinion of the Chamber in the past whatever it may become in the future.

Winston[2] came to see me. Quite nice but says what is very true and that is that War Cabinets never do anything until forced by circumstances to do it.

Went to luncheon given by Sir Charles Ellis[3] on getting into the new Munitions Building. Winston there made a speech and I had to. Nothing of any consequence. Sat next to Furse[4] who rather gives me the impression that there is a certain amount of friction at the War Office and that as a matter of fact Milner does nothing there. Macpherson[5] is to all intents and purposes Secretary of State for War. Milner is entirely engaged on War Cabinet business or coming over here. I am bound to say that Milner here has got a high reputation and as a business man they evidently think more of him than they do of Lloyd George. Talking to some of the Ministers yesterday during my visit they all mentioned Milner's name with a certain amount of respect.

In the afternoon went to the Interpellation in the Chambre des Députés.[6] They tell me it was a comparatively quiet sitting but I never saw such a bear-garden in my life, everybody talking at the same time, everybody running about the house, shaking fists in other men's faces and shouting at them. Clemenceau seemed to me old and tired and certainly at the commencement of the Debate did not at all get hold of the House. Later he did and appealed to them not to press the question of an Enquiry but he did not deal with it in the least on its merits. He dealt with it more from a personal point of view. Grahame who was there does not agree with me but I think that Clemenceau rather lost feathers and though he was assured of a majority the extreme left has become a very coherent body and very articulate and strongly in opposition to him and any further reverses I think would shake his position considerably.

News again not at all good and as the Germans are doing this push without employing very many new Divisions I do not at all like the prospect when they put in their next and what will probably be their biggest attack and which in my opinion will be on a front from Arras to Noyon.

Went to see Bertie whom I found better but I think it is only a flash in the pan. Lady Bertie had arrived and told me she considered the accounts of his illness much exaggerated. I hope that she is correct but I think when she sees him on one of his bad days she will realise they are not exaggerated.[7] Evidently she is very angry at having been brought back and he is not at all pleased at her being there. I spoke to her however about moving because he announced the other day that if the Embassy had to move he intended to go with it and that of course is out of the question. I believe he now wishes to go to Treport where there is an English Hospital. I offered to get an ambulance to have him moved there but Lady Bertie was very casual about it and says she will let me know in a few days time when of course it may be too late. If the push is on I cannot get the ambulance.

Dined in the evening with M. & Mme Klotz. He is Minister of Finance. Both very nice people. Had a most pleasant dinner. Italian Minister and his wife; Serbian Minister and his wife, she was an American and he was a very nice fellow and has lived in France many years. M. Tardieu[8] who was the man sent to America at the same time as, or rather before, Arthur Balfour — quite nice to talk to and very plausible but I know of his doings of old and nothing can have been meaner than the way he behaved towards us in America. He deliberately put out several false statements about our troops and was always magnifying France at our expense. In addition M. & Mme Gouin. He is a very big manufacturer with enormous interests in Russia. She is a very nice woman. Sat next to her at dinner. The Margeries.[9] He is Chef de Cabinet to M. Pichon. I know him very well. He always is present when I see Pichon in order to act as interpreter if that is required. He was talking to Charlie after dinner and told him that he felt perfectly certain that if anything happens to Clemenceau the President would send for M. Barthou to form a Government and he thought he would be able to do so. He has been Chef de Cabinet to both Briand and Barthou as well as the present man and he has a much higher opinion of Barthou than of Briand whom he says is very lazy and an opportunist. I do not quite know what Barthou's ideas are but I believe he is quite sound about the War.

On return found despatch rider bringing a letter from Raw[10] to say that they had fearful casualties in the Hospitals, over 1,000 in a fortnight, although luckily our Hospital had entirely escaped. Still it had made it necessary to evacuate the whole place and he wants to come and see me to try and arrange for the Hospital to be put elsewhere. All the personnel has returned to England.

Notes to 4 June

1. Sir Thomas Barclay (1853–1941). President of the British Chamber of Commerce in Paris, 1899–1900; Liberal MP for Blackburn, January–December 1910.
2. Winston S. Churchill (1874–1965). Minister of Munitions, July 1917–January 1919.
3. Sir Charles Ellis (1852–1937). Director-General of Ordnance Supply, Ministry of Munitions.
4. Major-General Sir William Furse (1865–1953). Master-General of Ordnance since 1916.
5. (James) Ian Macpherson (1880–1937). Baron Strathcarron. Parliamentary Under-Secretary at the War Office, 1916–19.
6. The 'interpellation' procedure gave any deputy the right to initiate a debate, and the vote on it could easily become one of confidence or censure.
7. In fact Bertie made a surprising recovery once he returned to England. However, he became ill again in the summer of 1919 and died that September.
8. André Tardieu (1876–1945). High Commissioner for Franco-American Affairs in 1917 and Clemenceau's chief personal assistant during the Paris peace negotiations, 1919.
9. Pierre de Margerie (1861–1942). Directeur Politique at the Quai d'Orsay, though for much of the War his influence was eclipsed by that of the nominally subordinate Philippe Berthelot.
10. Nathan Raw (1866–1940). Senior Physician, Liverpool Hospital, BEF.

Wednesday, 5th June

Usual meeting of the Board at 12 o'c. Nothing much to discuss except the question as to what would happen if we had to leave Paris. Difficult subject to deal with as we do not know where we should go to and we cannot ask for fear of giving rise to rumours. We put the whole thing in the hands of General Thornton who has promised to make all arrangements to get people away. I am endeavouring to get the members of the Missions who have their wives out here to send them home but it is a little difficult to do without giving rise to a suspicion.

After luncheon Furse came in.

Afternoon. Nothing of importance and in the evening we three with Lady Rodney dined at the Ambassadeur.

Thursday, 6th June

Busy morning seeing various people including Maklakoff[1] the Russian Ambassador who brought various telegrams to me which he had received all of which were to the effect that if intervention did not hurry up it would be out of the question. Apparently the Russians blame us but as a matter of fact it is entirely the Americans and if we have to fight for our lives in India we have got nobody to thank but the Americans.[2]

Luncheon we had Arthur Lawley[3] and an elder sister of his who is married to an Italian. Marlborough[4] and Winston. Toulmin who is the head of Lloyds Bank here. Caillaut the racing man and a M. Bunan-Varilla who is the Chief proprietor of the *Matin*, a great friend of Esher's who had asked me to invite him and a man with great power but I do not think a very desirable sort of friend. They look upon him here very much as they look in England upon Northcliffe. He is an out and out supporter of Briand's.

Greek Minister came to see me afterwards. He told me the most extraordinary thing was the change that took place in King Constantine and the Queen with reference to their feeling towards England. They had both been tremendously pro-English before the War, so much so that the Queen and the Kaiser had quarrelled over it but that they were both very weak people and the Kaiser had gradually managed by means of German agents to turn them round to his way of thinking.[5] As the Minister said to me if only Greece had come in at the beginning of the War, small as she is, what a difference she might have made to you as Gallipoli would then have been a success.

Mme St. Aldegorde and her daughter came to tea. Old friends of Charlie. The girl is extremely pretty and very rich.

Oliver and I dined together at the Ambassadeur.

Notes to 6 June

1. M. Maklakoff (b.1870). Russian ambassador in Paris, appointed by the Provisional Government. Stranded in Paris after the Bolshevik Revolution, he tried to persuade the Allies not to recognise the Soviet regime.
2. There was considerable apprehension at this time that Germany might launch a great offensive against India during 1919. See V. H. Rothwell, *British War Aims and Peace Diplomacy* (London, 1971), p. 189.
3. Sir Arthur Lawley (b.1860). Governor of Madras, 1906–11.
4. Charles Spencer-Churchill, 9th Duke of Marlborough (1871–1934).
5. King Constantine's lack of sympathy for the allied cause helped to undermine the Anglo-French expedition which arrived at Salonika in October 1915 and led ultimately to his deposition two years later.

Friday, 7th June

Saw various people in the morning. Thornton with reference to possible evacuation of Paris. Sir Charles Ellis with reference to a Clearing House here and in London for the payment of accounts as between ourselves and the French. He has drawn up a minute with which I entirely agree and I am forwarding it to Hankey[1] to put before the War Cabinet. It is perfectly monstrous the charges that the French make against us. Whereas we only charge them 5% on the goods for headquarter charges, transport, etc. they charge us 20%.

General Crookshank[2] D.G.T. came to see me with reference to Railway Wagons where the French are behaving most unfairly. Although our proper complement is 40,000 we have given them 55,000 notwithstanding that we are now short of trucks which they keep for their own people. I advised him to see the Under-Secretary of Railways and he is going to put the matter strongly before him. If it is not remedied at once he is to see me next week and when I go to G.H.Q. I will see Claveille.[3]

Had luncheon with Prince and Princess Murat. Most delightful house I have seen in Paris with a lovely garden. They are both perfectly charming. One subject of conversation was our friend Cohn and the bitterness of feeling was something beyond belief. It really is disgraceful Sloggett with Arty's connivance having given him a Commission.[4]

In the afternoon Haig with Fletcher and Philip Sassoon[5] came round here. Haig tells me his difficulty with Foch has been satisfactorily arranged and I hope it is so but from what I heard subsequently I am not so sure. It is a question of moving reserve Divisions and especially American Divisions from behind him and I think as usual the French have rather done us. I thought Haig very well. Much less tired but extremely anxious. He told me a very interesting thing about our Divisions who are fighting with the French. He told Foch he wished to take them out of the line so as to give them a real rest and refit them. Foch remonstrated strongly and perfectly frankly said that if the English leave the line the line will go, but after a certain amount of argument he agreed with Haig it was essential they should be taken out and rested but he made a stipulation, which in view of all that is said by our own War Cabinet is very interesting and that is that our Corps Commander, Hamilton Gordon[6] and the Divisional Generals with their Staffs should be allowed to remain and have French troops put under them, as he told Haig that he had none of his own that he could trust. Considering that our own War Cabinet, primed I think by Henry Wilson, have always abused our Staff and praised up the French it is a very remarkable thing to have happened.

I afterwards went to see Bertie who is certainly much better. It really is an extraordinary change. He is able to eat and has certainly gained strength and from my own part I begin to think now that this recovery is not a flash in the pan and it may be that he really is on the high road to a complete recovery. I am making arrangements for him to go on Monday night or Tuesday morning. He is not in the least grateful for anything one does in this way — at least he does not show it and he is extremely diffi- cult to manage as anything you ask him to do he always wants to do some- thing different.

In the evening, Haig, Fletcher and Sassoon dined with me and we sat talking quietly in the garden about every sort of thing but the War. Haig told me that Henry Wilson had again told him that he (H.W.) had begged the Government to appoint him to command the Home Forces as he thought that was his proper place. D.H. is extraordinary about it and keeps on asking why H.W. should have proposed this. He thinks it is very straight of him telling him he had done so. He does not seem to see that of course the real reason is that there was an opportunity of getting rid of him from the Command in France and that H.W. was trying to do this acting of course under superior orders. However it has been defeated and I do not think, at all events for the present, they will attempt to alter the command.

There are very curious peace rumours about and apparently the Cham- bre des Députés was full of people yesterday and today talking about them. I do not believe there is any truth in them although there is so much smoke that there may be a little fire and apparently the German newspapers are also alluding to it. One theory that I have heard is this, that they are put about by Caillaux[7] and that they generally coincide with an offensive in order to try and convince people, who are certainly very war weary, that the only way to get peace is to give a certain freedom to Caillaux and that Clemenceau is not likely to fall in with. I hear also that there is no doubt that Briand's friends are taking advantage of the rumour to suggest if peace offers are made that Clemenceau is the wrong man to deal with them and that Briand ought to be in power but I cannot find out that Briand is in any way mixed up in this. At the same time there is a very general feeling that if anything approaching a peace offer is made that it ought to be considered and not turned down in the way the one was last year.

There is a rather amusing story about Clemenceau and the Préfet of the

Seine area. The latter is a strong supporter of Caillaux. The other day Clemenceau sent for him and said you have got to give up. I want your place. The man protested. Clemenceau said it is no good your protesting. You have got to give it up and I have appointed you our Ambassador in Tokio. Again the man protested and asked for 24 hours to consider it. This Clemenceau absolutely refused — which incidentally reminds me of the incident in my own case. The man said he must have 24 hours to consult his friends. Oh, No, said Clemenceau, that is useless. All your friends are in prison for treason. The man had not a word to say and immediately accepted the position and was sent off to Tokio where I believe he will probably find he is not appointed Ambassador but only some subordinate position. The incident however has given rise to trouble as apparently Clemenceau did this without saying a word to Pichon who is very angry, not that that matters as he is absolutely a tool of Clemenceau's.

Notes to 7 June

1. Colonel Maurice Hankey (1877–1963). Secretary to the War Cabinet, 1916–19 and to the Cabinet, 1919–38.
2. Major-General Sidney Crookshank (1870–1941). Director-General of Transport, BEF.
3. Albert Claveille (1865–1921). Minister of Public Works and Transport, 1917–20.
4. With the backing of Sloggett, the Director-General of the Royal Army Medical Corps, Cohn had been granted an honorary captaincy in the British army in December 1916.
5. Sir Philip Sassoon (1888–1939). Conservative MP, 1912–39. Private Secretary to Douglas Haig, 1914–18.
6. Major-General Alex Hamilton Gordon (b.1859). Director of Military Operations, General Staff in India, 1910–14.
7. Joseph Caillaux (1863–1944). A pre-war Finance Minister and Prime Minister, he was accused of treason for his support of a compromise peace and was tried before the Senate in February 1920. Condemned to the loss of political rights for five years, he returned to high office later in the decade.

Saturday, 8th June

Lady Algy Gordon Lennox came to luncheon. She also is surprised at the extraordinary improvement in Frank Bertie's health.

After luncheon Captain Heaton Ellis[1] came to see me. He is the head of the Naval Mission. We had a long talk about various matters. Nothing of any special interest but he is very much opposed to General Phillips'[2] appointment which he thinks quite unnecessary and very extravagant.

He is a great friend of Patrick Acheson[3] and was on the Inflexible with him for a long time.

Afterwards Bennett-Goldney[4] came to see me with a telegram about Angela Forbes. It was a confidential telegram which I was not supposed to see from the French Embassy in London to the authorities out here with regard to Lady Angela's pass. They did not wish to employ her but said that of course if we pressed it they would give the necessary permits. He wanted to know what my views were. I told him that I did not wish to be brought into the matter at all. It was entirely a matter for the French themselves to decide and they must take the responsibility for either accepting or refusing her services. They could turn up my speech in the House of Lords on the subject. I would neither add nor take away a single word of what I said there and under no circumstances would I interfere in this particular instance.

Charlie, Oliver and I went to Versailles.

Notes to 8 June

1. Captain Edward Heaton Ellis (1868–1943). Assistant Director of Intelligence Division, Admiralty War Staff, 1914–15; Naval Liaison Officer, Paris, 1917–19.
2. Brigadier-General George Phillips (1863–1921). Member of the Allied Military Control Mission, Athens, 1917; Commandant, Paris Area, 1917–18.
3. Patrick Acheson (1883–1957). Awarded DSO for conduct when the *Inflexible* was struck by a mine at the Dardanelles in 1915.
4. Francis Bennett-Goldney (1865–1918). Independent Conservative MP for Canterbury, 1910–18.

Sunday, 9th June

VERSAILLES

Lovely hot morning. We three went for a walk.

Luncheon, Princesse d'Arenberg, the Neuflizes, Madame Roger and Colonel Buzzard.

After luncheon we all went to the Palace at Versailles and were shown over that part which is now closed to the public. Not so interesting as it might have been as so many things have been taken away for purposes of safety. The gardens looked lovely but of course all the fountains and statues are covered up to protect them against bombs.

Afternoon. Came back to Paris to see Clemenceau whom I found in very good form. I wanted to see him to explain that Sir George Cave's[1] going to the Hague had no political significance whatsoever as reports were being spread about that he was going to discuss peace. I also had a communication on the subject of the Czecho-Slovaks to show him and I then asked him what the meaning of this Committee for the Defence of Paris meant — whether he was at all desirous that we should move our women and any English people who were not engaged on Government work from Paris. His answer was thoroughly characteristic. He said he hopes everybody would go who was afraid but nobody else. For his own part he had no intention of moving and he was perfectly certain the necessity for doing so would never arise. The big attack had begun in the morning and they were very pleased with the result so far.[2] The major portion of the line had been held and only a small pocket made in the centre which they thought they could easily retake. The Germans had attacked in great masses and had had enormous losses all of which is good. He thinks that in addition to this there will be another very big attack on our front within the immediate future.

Dinner. Only ourselves.

Notes to 9 June

1. Sir George Cave (1856–1928). Viscount, 1919. Conservative lawyer and politician. Home Secretary, 1916–19. Cave had gone to The Hague to discuss prisoners of war, but was approached by the Germans with regard to peace terms. See Sir C. Mallett, *Lord Cave: A Memoir* (London, 1931), pp. 207–10.
2. The Germans launched the Montdidier-Noyon offensive (Operation Gneisenau) on 9 June. The French countered with a barrage of mustard gas.

Monday, 10th June

Wet morning. Went round to see Bertie who is much better.

Luncheon. Neuflizes, Austin Lees,[1] Admiral Fournier[2] who is the President of the Inter Allié Club and entertained me at luncheon the other day. M. Martin[3] the head of the Protocol and M. Dubos.

Sevastopoulo[4] came to see me in the afternoon. His is a miserable position. He tells me he has not had a penny from Russia for over a year. I believe however they do get paid something by the French Government and he knows nothing of what is going on and apparently things are going from bad to worse. He likes his Ambassador Maklakoff who he says is quite the right sort of class man for an Ambassador.

Sir Park Goff[5] an F.O. Messenger came to see me also. I knew him in the political world. He is very much in with Walter Long,[6] Hayes Fisher[7] and Co. He tells me there was a great difficulty over the appointment of French.[8] That the Cabinet decided one day that French should be appointed but that Lloyd George's Radical friends protested very strongly against the appointment and that Dillon[9] on behalf of the Irish opposed the appointment most bitterly. They had a long discussion at one of the Cabinets but in the end it was decided to make the appointment and Lloyd George behaved very well about it. I gather that the Home Rule Bill is going extremely badly. That any question of Home Rule in itself must fall to the ground and that the only possible solution is a Federal system. That seems to me to be a possible solution but not one that could possibly be put in operation during the War and I think that Lloyd George will have many difficulties in front of him on this subject and that it is quite possible the Government may fall over it.

Dined with Margeries. He is the Chef de Cabinet of Pichon and really represents a sort of Charlie Hardinge.[10] He is in the Diplomatic Service, has been all over the world and is extremely ambitious. His great wish in life is to become Ambassador in London. They are both very nice people. I met there again Tardieu who was and still is the French High Commissioner in America and the more I see of him the more I dislike him. He has got a villainous face and I am sure he is very anti-English.

The news was not at all good and there is a great deal of anxiety.

Frank Bertie left for home about 10 o'c. I had seen him in the afternoon to say good-bye. He was very nice about all one has been able to do for him and I think it is a great relief to him to go home. I saw Lady Bertie again. I do not think I have met a more odious woman. She contends there is nothing wrong with Bertie. That he is not really nor ever has been dangerously ill and evidently resents having had to leave the south of France. She said that it had been difficult for her to make excuses to come away from the south of France to see him when her son telegraphed for her. She is I am glad to say going with her son and daughter-in-law back to England on Thursday. I have never heard a good word said for her here.

Notes to 10 June

1. Sir Henry Austin Lee (1847–1918). Commercial Attaché, Paris Embassy.
2. Vice-Admiral François-Ernest Fournier (1842–1934). Headed French diplomatic missions to Romania and Russia during the War.

3. William Martin. Director of Protocol at the Quai d'Orsay.
4. M. Sevastopoulo, Chargé d'Affaires in Paris of the Russian Imperial Government.
5. Sir Park Goff (1871–1939). Appointed honorary King's Foreign Service Messenger, September 1914. Conservative MP for Cleveland, 1918–23 and 1924–29 and for Chatham, 1931–35.
6. Walter Long (1854–1924). Viscount Long, 1921. Secretary of State for the Colonies, 1916–19.
7. William Hayes Fisher (1853–1920). President of the Local Government Board, June 1917–November 1918.
8. Sir John French (1852–1925). Viscount, 1916; Earl of Ypres, 1922. Commander-in-Chief, Home Forces, 1915–18; Lord Lieutenant of Ireland, 1918–21.
9. John Dillon (1851–1927). Became Leader of the Irish Nationalists at Westminster in February 1918, but lost his seat at the General Election in December.
10. Charles Hardinge, Baron Hardinge of Penshurst (1858–1944). Permanent Under-Secretary of State at the Foreign Office, 1906–10 and 1916–20. Succeeded Derby as Ambassador in Paris in 1920.

Tuesday, 11th June

Uneventful day. Only routine work.

In the evening Mme St. Aldegonde, her daughter and Dolly Rothschild and Bullock[1] dined.

Notes to 11 June

1. Sir Malcolm Bullock (1890–1966). Military Secretary to Derby. In 1919 he married Derby's daughter, Victoria.

Wednesday, 12th June

Sir John Pilter[1] came to see me. He is the head of the British Colony here. He is very disturbed on the subject of the permits for English people. He is just one of those men who are most tiresome to deal with although there is something to be said on his side. He claims all the rights of a British Citizen and yet when it comes to anything that he does not like he wants to be treated as a Frenchman. They all seem to think that a war is not on and as far as going backwards and forwards into the Army Zone is concerned they ought to be allowed to go as they like. At the same time there are grievances which I hope to get right.

Usual meeting of Missions at 12 o'c.

[43]

Left in the afternoon at 2.45 for G.H.Q. with Oliver. Took us just 5 hours, good going considering that we had 3 punctures on the way. Nobody staying at G.H.Q. Winston and Marlborough having been got rid of with difficulty in the morning. Winston cannot have much to do in his office as he has now been away for 10 days and as far as I can see joy-riding. He asked for a House to be taken for him in the Army Zone. When this was done he was very angry about it because naturally he has been told he must pay for it himself. He has no official standing out here whatsoever.

Bacon[2] dined in the evening. He is now the American Officer on Haig's staff, a most charming fellow who was Ambassador here about 5 years ago and very popular. Haig had been to see an American Brigade and told me they were some of the most splendid men he had ever seen and very well drilled. They were National Guard Troops and therefore correspond to our old Militia. They find the Americans pick up the work very quick and are able to go into the line much sooner than was anticipated which is a good thing.

Heard how poor Lumsden, V.C.[3] had been killed. It appears it was entirely his own fault. He was warned that there was a sniper about yet would not go down the communication trench and was shot dead. He is a great loss although like so many other gallant fellows they lose half their value when they get a Brigade and therefore get out of contact with the actual fighting line.

Notes to 12 June

1. Sir John Pilter (1848–1935). President of the British Chamber of Commerce in Paris.
2. Colonel Robert H. Bacon (1860–1919). Chief of the American Military Mission at British GHQ.
3. Major Frederick Lumsden, VC (1871–1918). Awarded VC, April 1917.

Thursday, 13th June

Oliver and I went down to the Headquarters in Montreuil. Had a long talk with Fowke[1] on many matters in which I think I shall be able to help him. He is only too ready to get into closer touch with the Embassy as is Haig and the whole of the Staff. Saw Travis Clegg afterwards and then had a long talk with Ruggles Brise.[2]

Hear that Etaples shelling was very bad but we really have not got a leg to stand on when talking of the brutality of the Germans. We had every conceivable military supply both of men and munitions all round the Camp and the Germans can make a really good case for having bombed although there was no doubt that the Hospital bombing on the second occasion was a very deliberate affair.

Reports of the bombing at Abbeville as told by Bobby Ward[3] are proved to be most exaggerated. Bobby gave long descriptions the other day of the hairbreadth escapes he himself had of being bombed and of the utter devastation of Abbeville. I did not motor through the centre of the town and the way we went we only saw one place where a bomb had fallen so I made enquiries with the above result.

Very sad saying good-bye to Oliver. I don't know who hated going back the most, he or Middleton, and I hated leaving them. The Brigade is in G.H.Q. Reserve which means that one never will know where they are but it also means that they won't be regularly in the line.

The 30th Division is after all to be reconstituted and made up with drafts.

Got back under 5 hours and should have been here sooner only happened to take a wrong turning.

Notes to 13 June

1. Lieutenant-General Sir George Fowke (1864–1936). Adjutant-General in France, 1916–19.
2. Major-General Harold Ruggles Brise (1864–1927). Grenadier Guards. Served in France and Flanders, 1916–18.
3. Robert Arthur Ward (1871–1942). Son of the Earl of Dudley. Conservative MP, 1895–1900.

Friday, 14th June

PARIS

Ordinary routine work all the morning.

Discussed generally with Leroy Lewis and Grahame the question of English honours to French Civilians. The whole affair in great muddle but as Military Authorities at G.H.Q. are ready that all their recommendations should come to me to be examined, if only I can get the Civil Authorities at home to do the same, feel that we shall be able to get some order and the fearful mistakes that have been and are being made will be obviated. Decided to put Bridgeman in charge.

Leveson Gower[1] who is newly attached to the office had luncheon. He is I think the son of the people from whom Louise Gosford took Titsey. Very nice fellow who had been out in Greece and previously had been a sort of Controller of the Household to Grey.[2] He is going to take on the position of Liaison Officer with the Poles.

Also at luncheon Captain Van Baerle who has been sent out by the National Service Department to go through the list of exemptions of English people living in France. I believe he is a very good man at his work but he is a fearful bounder and reminds me both in appearance and the way he talks of Carnaby Foster.

Spiers came at tea time looking still very ill and very shaky. I was rather horrified by his appearance and still more by his talk. There is no doubt he realises that after the row he had at Abbeville Clemenceau places no more confidence in him and will not only not give him information but is gradually trying to oust him from everything including rooms in the Ministry of War. I think he exaggerates a good deal but he was evidently in a very excited state about it. He ended up by telling me I was in Clemenceau's bad books owing to my interference in the internal politics of France which amuses me as I know nothing and care nothing about their internal politics and have never interfered in any way. I think this, with many of the other statements that he made, were the creation of a fertile imagination on his part.

In the evening Terry and Alec Russell dined. They are dealing with propaganda. Hugo Baring[3] also came. He is Staff Officer to General B[blank] who is our Liaison Officer with the Czecho-Slovaks whatever that office may be.

Notes to 14 June

1. Major Lord Alastair Leveson-Gower (1890–1921). Royal Horse Guards. Heir presumptive to the Duke of Sutherland.
2. Edward Grey, Viscount Grey of Fallodon (1862–1933). Foreign Secretary, December 1905–December 1916.
3. Hugo Baring (1876–1949). Son of Lord Revelstoke. Wounded at Ypres. Served with British Mission in Siberia, 1918–19.

Saturday, 15th June

Went to Ministry of Foreign Affairs to see Margerie on the subject of presentation by the President of Flags to the Czecho-Slovaks and the Poles.
Our Government think it advisable that in any speech the President may
make he should also pat on the back the Yugo-Slavs who think they are
being badly used. Find that both Ceremonies are postponed but Margerie
entirely agrees with view of our Government and will represent same to
the President.

Afterwards had talk with M. Marsillac a man to whom I have given an
interview before for *Le Journal*. He is writing an interview but I have
telegraphed home to know whether they would like me to give an interview or not. It is on the subject of our effectives in England. Afterwards
saw M. Métin[1] a Deputy who is proceeding on an official Mission to Australia. He did not strike me as a man who would impress the Australians
very much.

Maclagan came to see me with reference to my giving the interview to
Le Journal. He is very anxious I should do so. Grahame whom I spoke to
afterwards is rather opposed as *Le Journal* had rather an awkward connection with the Bolo scandal.[2] If this is so it just shows that Maclagan is
not the right man to be the head of the propaganda here. I am making further enquiries.

Went to luncheon with Sharp. His daughter, quite a nice girl, does hostess. People there were the Pichons, Austin Lees, Spiers, and a man whose
name I think was Croset. He is the biggest lawyer in America but just one
of the most offensive of Americans — very bumptious and with an awful
voice. Had a talk to Pichon after luncheon. Very pleased with the message
that has come from the Government with regard to the extra troops that
they are sending out.[3] Heaven knows what they are sending and I expect
most of them are crocks. The French however hold tremendously to our
sending out B men and even lower categories as they say they are quite
competent to hold a quiet part of the line but as no part of our line is quiet
and when they put them down in what they think is a quiet part of their
sector and they tumble up against the biggest attack the French have ever
had to meet it seems to me only sending food for Hospitals. Pichon says
it is much more hopeful about the Americans agreeing to Japanese intervention but in my opinion he is too sanguine and I think now it is too late.
If it had been done as we wanted and as the French wanted 6 months ago
I believe it would have been quite possible to have forced the Germans to

keep a great many troops on the Eastern Front. They talk of our being too late but it is a joke to what the Americans are although the men are coming over very well now.

Spiers came back with me and talked over various matters. Then Mr. Roye came. He is the Canadian High Commissioner out here. Very nice sort of fellow a French Canadian. We had to discuss a matter of business where a Canadian Company made a contract with the P.L.M. by which they managed to lose £500,000 and they are very angry because the French Government won't make it good to them. They are also rather indignant with me because I have not been able to persuade the Government to do so. Roye agreed with me that they had no case whatsoever but he would not have taken it up except that the firm has got political influence in Canada.

Notes to 15 June

1. Albert Métin. Held several ministerial posts under Doumergue, Briand, Ribot and Painlevé between 1913 and 1917.
2. Paul Marie Bolo (Bolo Pasha). Fraudulent purveyor of German gold for the subversion of France, who was shot for treason on 17 April 1918.
3. For details, see K. Grieves, *The Politics of Manpower, 1914–18* (Manchester, 1988), pp. 196–99.

Sunday, 16th June

PARIS

Various routine work in the morning. News of the Italian offensive came in.[1] I could not get much news till I went out to luncheon at Versailles where all the reports we had were on the whole quite favourable.

Afternoon. Went for a few minutes to St. Cloud Golf Course which is perfectly lovely. Then back to Paris and went to tea with Princesse Marie Murat a wild creature who has been everywhere but who is most interesting. There is no part of the globe she has not visited. She hears all the gossip but is in with politicians of both sides. Quite hopeful about the present but very gloomy as to what will happen after the War and she thinks that unless the Allies can all hold together France will be crushed economically by Germany.

Notes to 16 June

1. The Austrians launched an offensive on the Piave on 15 June. They were thrown back by an Italian counter-offensive on 2 July.

Monday, 17th June

Routine work. Saw Mrs. Henshaw, Canadian Red Cross lady who is doing good work in helping to evacuate French people from the shelled areas. She comes from Victoria B.C. and knows Annie and Victor[1] well.

Luncheon. Pichon and wife. Dumesnil and wife, both very nice people. He is the Minister for Aviation. Paul Reinach, the Greek Minister, also nice, and Grahame. Very amusing discussion after. Poor Reinach of course likes to hear himself do all the talking and tries to do it but met more than a match in Madame Pichon who is [a] most amusing old thing and chaffed him unmercifully. Really a very pleasant luncheon.

After luncheon saw Horodyski[2] who is I think a sort of secret agent with the Poles. I thought him one of the most villainous fellows I had ever come across. Could not look you straight in the face and I should be very much surprised if he is straight. He is the nephew of the General of the Jesuits and for that reason I think is backed up by Eric Drummond who is a Catholic. Personally I cannot help thinking this Catholic clique will get us into trouble because all that is done goes straight to the Pope[3] and we all know he is in direct contact with the Austrians.

Charlie and I went to tea at the Tiraux Pigeons with Mme de Montescieu. Lot of nice people there but these sort of teas are abominable institutions. I believe they are extremely popular here but I mean to avoid them for the future. Charlie and I dine alone together. News from Italy seems quite good.

Notes to 17 June

1. Victor Stanley (1867–1934). Derby's brother, who married Annie Bickerton in 1896.
2. Count Jean Marie de Horodyski. A Galician Pole who from 1915 worked as a British agent under the direction of Sir Eric Drummond. He was involved in attempts to initiate negotiations with Austria-Hungary for a separate peace.
3. Benedict XV (1854–1922). Pope, 1914–22.

Tuesday, 18th June

Routine work. Saw Sir John Pilter who is the head of the British Colony here in reference to petrol questions. He is an old gentleman who tries it on and somehow managed to square the General here to give him petrol to run between Paris and his house near Trouville. I have put a stop to that.

Luncheon. Some of the Chancery had luncheon. Saw Spiers after that. News from Italy quite good except for Montello which is the most important place where the Italian counter-attacks have failed. But on the whole I think things are good and there is nothing approaching a débâcle.

Afternoon. Went with Sir John Pilter to see the Richard Wallace Hospital. Most delightful building and beautifully kept and run. Also went to the office of the British Charitable Association which again seems to be run on extraordinary good lines.

Charlie Grant came to tea and says that Foch seems quite satisfied with regard to the Italian Front. Charlie, Dolly Rothschild and I went out to a bagatelle. Extraordinarily pretty and we were just in time as the roses are beginning to go off. Masses of them but of course the whole place is now not so well kept up during the War and many of the rose trees are dead.

Wednesday, 19th June

Meeting in the morning of the Board. Studd came instead of West on leave and Dillon in place of Clive who was not able to come.

Murray of Elibank came and we went for a walk together. He is most friendly but somehow one does not quite trust him and I am sure he is a born intriguer though evidently his one wish is to help me here as much as he can.

Have embodied all that I have heard recently in a letter to Arthur Balfour, copy attached.

In the evening Charlie and I dined at the Jockey Club.

Copy of letter sent to Mr. Balfour 19 June 1918

I am extremely sorry to have telegraphed to you the "canard" with regard to the King of Spain[1] but Le Roy-Lewis was so emphatic as he got his information through the Police I thought it worth letting you know. They now say that there is a man who is exactly like the King who does come backwards and forwards to Paris.

There was an article in the *Matin* this morning from the Deputy who represents the Seine area, strongly advocating that all women and children should if possible be sent out of Paris and when General Guillaumat[2] came as he did to see me this afternoon I asked him point blank whether that represented his views, he now being the Governor of Paris, and he said they did and that he was quite expecting a bombardment of Paris and he gave me to understand we should really be doing a favour to him by getting people out. I have made all arrangements here for getting rid of people in case there was a sudden evacuation but of course this makes it much easier and I am having a small meeting tomorrow morning to insist on people on whom we can put pressure going at once. This includes all the people who are on the books of the Charitable Association here and I think we shall get them all down somewhere into the country. It may however strain the resources of the Charitable Association almost to breaking point and I presume that if any expense has to be incurred in this removal I may rely upon the Government at home giving some assistance to them. Everybody is leaving Paris and taking away any valuables and packers are making a fortune. Of things political I hear very little except the question of effectives both here and in England which is the main topic of conversation and there is no doubt that Clemenceau's enemies are trying to make of this a stick to beat him with but I am perfectly certain his position is quite secure.

Painlevé[3] is very indignant at the suggestions that are going about that he stopped Nivelle's advance last Spring year and that if it had not been for that Nivelle would have won a great victory.[4] I believe he is going to take some steps, probably by writing an article in one of the papers to put his version of the matter before the public. On the other hand Murray of Elibank who I have just seen and who has seen a great deal of Nivelle in Algeria[5] tells me that Nivelle is equally determined to have his view of the case put forward, so I see the makings of quite a nice row. I do not think there is any truth in the rumour that Nivelle was going to be given a command over here. I think it probably originates from the fact that Nivelle is probably leaving Algeria but not as far as I can make out to take up any other post.

Guillaumat was very interesting on the subject of Salonika. He apparently got on very well with Milne. He praised the British troops very much but seemed to think that we did not seem to realise at home how decimated they are with malaria. He was very anxious if possible something should be done to relieve these men. I told him that we knew all about it but relieving them was easier said than done. He told me that he was agreeably surprised with the Greek troops[6] and that they had fought really magnificently and he has great hopes of those who are still to come into the line but in his opinion the great thing will be to always keep them fighting. He says without this their morale will go down. Their fighting so well has had a very good effect on the Serbians and he thinks that the spirit of emulation will greatly improve the latter troops. Of the Italians he spoke very slightingly. I asked him what sort of troops they were. He said they were very good troops indeed for Italians. He is very keen about our assuming the offensive there in August or September and it is quite evident he is going to press this view for all he is worth on Clemenceau. He thinks that the Bulgarians have got very little fight left in them now and that a big attack on our part might put Bulgaria out of the War. We have heard that so often that I do not feel sanguine. At the same time I give you his statement for what it is worth. He impresses me very much as a very smart level-headed fellow who is very anxious about his new task, as he said if there was a sudden bombardment begun there would undoubtedly be a panic here and he does not quite know what that would lead to.

Murray of Elibank was very anxious that Asquith,[7] who through his identification with the Maurice case[8] had got rather the reputation of being an opponent of the unified control, should give an interview to some French journalist. I have written this to the Prime Minister. I wish you would rather press it as I think it would be of good service as showing the unity of our country. I am not sure that perhaps the best thing would not be for Asquith to pay a short visit here and see some of the principal people. I do not know whether he would do this but of course I should be very glad to put him up if he did.

No news today from Italy which makes one a little anxious but I hope all is going well. I am probably going down tomorrow to stay with our Mission attached to Foch just for one night as Foch has been good enough to ask me to go and see him.

Notes to letter of 19 June

1. Alfonso XIII (1886–1941). King of Spain, 1886–1931.
2. General Marie-Adolphe Guillaumat (1863–1940). Commander of the Armée d'Orient based on Salonika from December 1917 until June 1918 when he was recalled to take over the military governorship of Paris.
3. Paul Painlevé (1863–1933). Mathematician and politician. Minister of War, March–November 1917; Prime Minister, September–November 1917.

4. For Painlevé's version of these events see his *Comment j'ai nommé Foch et Pétain* (Paris, 1923).
5. After the failure of his spring offensive, an Army court of inquiry largely exonerated Nivelle and he was made military commander in French North Africa at the end of 1917.
6. Prime Minister Venizelos brought Greece into the war after the deposition of King Constantine in June 1917.
7. Herbert Henry Asquith (1852–1928). Prime Minister, April 1908–December 1916, when he was replaced by Lloyd George.
8. Major-General Sir Frederick Maurice (1871–1951). Director of Military Operations, 1915–18. The Maurice Case arose in May 1918 when he sent a letter to the leading newspapers claiming that Lloyd George had wilfully misled parliament about the strength of the British army in France. See N. Maurice (ed.), *The Maurice Case* (London, 1972).

Thursday, 20th June

Letter from Lady Hardinge (Arthur Hardinge's[1] wife) in which she hints that I was lacking in my duty in not having time to see her when passing through Paris. I am told she is always like this and talks of her rights and thinks that everything ought to be done for her. Considering that I sent somebody from the Embassy and lent her my car I thought that was sufficient. So very amusing, so very unlike her sister Molly Sneyd.

Newspapers announce Tardieu's appointment as High Commissioner for Franco-American affairs. I foresee trouble over this as though very clever he is I am sure very tricky and anti-English. There is no doubt whatever the French are very jealous of the way we get on with the Americans and are anxious in every way to prevent this. They are a funny people and with the exception of Clemenceau and a few others they think much more of playing the game for themselves than for the whole side.

Colonel Statham came to see me. He is the Medical Officer here — a very nice fellow. I wanted to arrange that our cases should go to the Hertford Hospital instead of the new Hospital which we have started with 5 nurses and 20 orderlies in what were offices and which cannot under any circumstances be a good hospital. He is anxious for the moment at all events we should keep that on though eventually I think we should close it and use only the Hertford Hospital.

Received a very interesting letter from Edward on the subject of the fighting in Italy. Can anything exceed the folly of the Italians in giving the defence of what was almost an impregnable place, Montello, and the key of the whole position to the newly constituted 8th Army which is made up of the Divisions who ran away last autumn.

Luncheon Simon Lovat and Charlie Grant. Were amusing because they represent two such very opposite schools. Charlie being extremely intelligent, recognising what the War is and what a necessity there is for playing up to the French. Simon on the other hand imagining himself much cleverer than he is, thinking himself a born soldier, being thoroughly British and therefore ready to abuse everything that the French do.

Afterwards motored with Charlie to our mission with Foch's Headquarters. Johnny Du Cane is the head of it. Got a nice Staff. Charlie Winn[2] who lost an eye being one of his A.D.C.'s — a very nice boy indeed.

After Dinner had a long talk with Du Cane. It really is extraordinary to me the intense jealousy that the French have of the good feeling that exists between our troops and the Americans. To give an instance. The next American Divisions were by agreement to have come to us for training to help to make up our cadres. Foch had agreed to this and supported it when he found that they could not be taken by the French, but Pershing[3] has now put forward a request that they should go straight to him as he had got ample instructors to train them himself and Foch has supported him although he knows it is not correct; that they will not be so well trained, but the fact that they will be away from the pernicious influence of the British is quite sufficient to make him agree.

Notes to 20 June

1. Sir Arthur Hardinge (1859–1933). British Ambassador to Madrid, 1913–19.
2. Charles Winn. Younger son of Lord St. Oswald.
3. General John Joseph Pershing (1860–1948). Commander of American troops in France.

Friday, 21st June

Went to see Foch at 9.15. His Chateau, a lovely old place, is about 3 or 4 miles from our headquarters. On the way we passed a motor which we afterwards discovered contained Clemenceau. He had been out already to talk to Foch which meant that he must have left Paris at about 6.30. It shows his wonderful energy but I am very glad that our Prime Minister is not able to do the same thing with Haig. I do not think that would work very long.

Foch was charming and I had a very long talk with him. He is full of confidence and says that he thinks all will go well. That the Germans have made two fatal mistakes for themselves. First of all not to press on after the battle of the 21st March when they would undoubtedly have separated our two armies, and secondly to have made the attack which led to their getting to Chateau Thierry, as it has done them no real good, used up a certain number of troops and given them a salient which it is difficult and dangerous to hold.[1] He is very pleased with our troops and he says he presses them very hard to do far more work in the way of digging than they have ever done before – I believe that is true – and he is now satisfied that there are many lines of defence which they would be capable of holding if they were driven out of the first. He says he does not like the mixing up of French and English Divisions and as I told him he might be quite sure that our people did not like it either. As a matter of fact it is Henry Wilson and Milner who adhere to this plan because they believe it is the only way by which the French troops can be brought into the battle and if we hold separate parts of the line the Germans will go on concentrating against us so as to smash us and leave the French alone. Foch gets on very well with Du Cane and has a very high opinion of his capability in addition to which he says he is one of the very few men he has come across who can carry opinions from one man to another accurately and have such knowledge of the views of each that he is able to propose some middle course which is acceptable. He is also very fond of Charlie Grant whom of course he has known for a long time but naturally he does not put him on the same level as Du Cane. I asked if he thought the German losses lately had been heavy and he told me that as far as the Chemin des Dames attack was concerned, No. He says it was a bad business for the French, and he gave me to understand that it was more than a bad business, it was a disgraceful business which he had not got to the bottom of yet. On the other hand in the Montdidier and Noyon attack the Germans had made little progress and had had very heavy losses, more heavy perhaps than at any time. He looks upon the present crisis as being over but of course we must expect several more but he is quite confident as to the result and given another week he would be absolutely prepared. It poured with rain all right [*sic*: ?all night] and if it did the same up at Ypres it is all so much to the good. We discussed Robertson. He told me that he had a high opinion of him in some ways but that he would have been quite impossible under the present circumstances. That he was very difficult to deal with and very inflexible and I could see that on the whole he did not regret his having gone, although he wished more use could be made of his services than are made at the present.[2] On the other hand he spoke very highly of Maurice. He thought he had wonderful military ability and that though of course nothing could have been done except what was done with him,[3] his loss to the Army was a very great one and he had done his best to arrange before Maurice wrote the article to secure his being taken on to our G.H.Q. but Haig would not have it. He has evidently a very poor opinion of our G.H.Q. and does not like them at all, though he is very fond of Haig and a great believer in him. I was with him for ¾ hour and it was really most interesting.

It is perfectly extraordinary the loathing French people, civilians and soldiers, have for the Italians and I think they would sooner see them beaten than win. The soldiers because they have got a contempt for them as soldiers, and the civilians because they think that last year they prevented Peace being made and even Foch could not resist having a sneer at them. The news from Italy was not good. At least Foch said it would be good for any other Nation except Italy but that with them you never could tell whether there would not be a débâcle at any moment.

Returned to Paris. It takes one just 1½ hours.

The British Charitable Association came to see me. I am trying to induce them to send all their beneficiaries – all the old and infirm – out of Paris. They are making endless difficulties and the Committee is mostly composed of clergymen of various denominations who do not see further than their noses and they say it is their duty to go on paying these allowances and they cannot use it as a lever to get these people away. However I clinched matters at the end by telling them that I had a list of all the people they assisted and that after this week I could no longer be responsible for them and in the case of a sudden evacuation each man would have to take the responsibility for his own congregation. Of course when it comes to that none of them are willing to do so and I hope they will get them away. I see their difficulties but in these times they have got to do many things which in ordinary times they would not care to do.

Mendl came to luncheon. He is a good sort of Jew who lived for a long time in the Argentine. The worst thing against him is that he is a partner of Cohn. He is very clever, in with all the politicians and gives us most valuable information.

Dined with the Edouard Rothschilds. Quite an amusing dinner. Met the Polignacs.[4] She was an American, a Mrs. Eustis. He was with Tardieu in America. I had a long talk with her after dinner. She evidently reflects her husband's views but was very anxious to make me think that they were her own. Great respect for Tardieu who is a very clever man, but extremely conceited. Always ready to talk about himself. No ambition in the Diplomatic and much in the political world and would like to put himself in the position of being a possible successor to Clemenceau.

Notes to 21 June

1. The Germans began their spring offensive on 21 March when they launched the Second Battle of the Somme. Their third attack (Operation 'Blücher') launched on 27 May reached the Marne in the region of Château-Thierry.
2. After his dismissal as CIGS, Robertson accepted the unimportant Eastern Command before succeeding Lord French as Commander-in-Chief Home Forces.
3. Maurice's controversial letter ended his military career. He later entered the academic world.
4. François de Polignac. Deputy for Maine-et-Loire, 1928–42.

Saturday, 22nd June

Norwegian Minister called. He married Mme Vanandre. He has just come back from 6 weeks in Spain. Says that there is no doubt whatever that the country generally is pro-German and thinks that Germany is certain to win.[1] Even the King thought so till about a fortnight ago when his views suddenly began to change. He always was pro-Entente but he now has less confidence in the success of Germany. He is very much down on our propaganda work and says that it is bad but that the Germans' is equally bad. Both of us try and force our views down the Country and the amount of propaganda that is going on is exasperating everybody against us but equally against the Germans although they are much cleverer than we are at the game.

Albert Thomas came to luncheon alone with Charlie and me and talked very freely and openly. I think the best thing is to put in my Diary a copy of a letter I am writing to Arthur Balfour on the subject.

Went to see Clemenceau with regard to the conduct of the Bolsheviks to the Czecho-Slovaks in Siberia.[2] Quite friendly but he still adheres to his opposition to Arthur Balfour's proposal to retain them in Siberia rather than bring them to France. I am to see him again on Tuesday. Had a slight breeze with him. As I was going out I asked him how he was. He said much better than some of your friends would wish me to be. I resented his remark and I asked him to explain. He was quite friendly and evidently sorry that he had said it. He would not tell me whom he was referring to though I concluded it was my having had Briand and Thomas to luncheon. I therefore asked him point blank whether he objected to my having into my house for luncheon or dinner people to whom he was politically opposed and he at once jumped at a way of getting out of it; begged me not to think for one minute that he could have any such objection and said that he had only meant it as a joke and he asked me to consider the joke had never been made. I told him it was a sort of joke I did not care for and we parted the very best of friends, but it just shows that everything one does here is known.

Henry Wilson, Duncannon,[3] Hardresse Lloyd,[4] had dinner here at 7 o'c. en route to Italy. I did not think Henry Wilson was in very good spirits and although quite satisfied with the way everything had gone so far in Italy thought that the Italians were really not doing all that they might do and I gathered he was going out at the urgent request of Cavan[5] to endeavour to get them to make some offensive. He told me that he thought the political situation at home was not good especially with regard to Ireland, the difficulty there being accentuated by George Curzon[6] making a speech diametrically opposed to the line which the Cabinet had laid down. They were determined to have conscription and had practically settled the date. The only person who objected being Barnes[7] who says that he cannot agree to conscription without some form of Home Rule but the Home Rule Bill is in a hopeless state. The Committee have gone entirely to pieces and it looks as if they had utterly failed to bring out any workable scheme.[8]

Dined in the evening with Madame de Montesquieu. A very agreeable dinner. Sat between her and Princesse Marie Murat whom I have mentioned before. Extremely amusing. Very well informed. Amongst others there were Princesse D'Arenberg who was very pleasant and also Mme Viel Castel. There was a sort of Party afterwards — quite amusing.

Notes to 22 June

1. Dependent on Britain and France in economic terms and militarily weak, Spain was never in fact likely to enter the war on Germany's side.
2. A Czech legion, crossing Siberia for France by way of Vladivostok — Clemenceau's price for supporting the claims of the Czech leader, Benes, to be regarded as an ally — was blocked by the Bolsheviks at Irkutsk.
3. Viscount Duncannon (1880–1956). Conservative MP for Dover, 1913–20. Serving with General Staff in France since March 1916. Personal Assistant to Sir Henry Wilson, 1916–19.
4. Captain Hardress Lloyd (1874–1952). Brigade Commander, April 1917.
5. Lieutenant-General Earl of Cavan (1865–1946). Thought by many to be the best corps commander in the BEF. In charge of operations of the Tenth Italian Army on the Piave front, 1918. Known as 'Fatty'.

6. George Nathanial Curzon, Lord Curzon of Kedleston (1859–1925). Member of War Cabinet, December 1916–October 1919; Foreign Secretary, October 1919–January 1924.
7. George Barnes (1859–1940). Labour MP; Minister without Portfolio, 1917–20.
8. See S. Hartley, *The Irish Question as a Problem in British Foreign Policy, 1914–18* (London, 1987), pp. 174–92.

Copy of letter sent to Mr. Balfour

Confidential & Personal

22 June 1918

Albert Thomas came to luncheon with me today. Charlie Montagu was at luncheon but he went away and we were alone afterwards. Thomas talked most openly. I will try and give you the various points of his conversation. He goes to England next week to attend the Workmen's Conference but evidently that is only a minor consideration with him and his real object is to get into touch again with political life in England.

The question of the effectives is the one to which he apparently means to devote most attention and his attitude is changed to that which he showed to me when last I saw him on the subject. He has rather dropped the idea that we are keeping too many men in England but is taking up more the idea that we have too many men in the Auxiliary Services and that a very large percentage could be sent into the firing line if we, as he puts it, would do away with some of the luxuries of War. I think it would be as well that every facility should be given him to see the various figures and to have them explained to him. What the French people will not understand is that we have men in this country who are doing auxiliary work and who are wearing uniform and are soldiers but who the French, being in their own country, do not put into uniform. There is one particular service that he wanted to make enquiries into and that was the Flying Corps and here again it is impossible to tell him the truth. He complains that with practically the same number of machines England requires twice as many men as France. I did not like to tell him the answer which I conceive to be that while one may have twice as many men in France who do 4 times the amount of work, we expose our machines much more than the French do – they never go over the line if they can help it – and the consequence is that our repair work is infinitely greater than theirs is.

We then began to talk about various politicians. He is bitterly antagonistic to Clemenceau and told me that there were no circumstances that he could possibly think of which would induce him to serve, either under

Clemenceau or with Clemenceau. He says Clemenceau must reckon on the undying opposition of the Socialist Party. That he had a great opportunity to make a National Party on the 21st March but that old animosities prevented him from even making the attempt, but the moment has now gone by and it is quite impossible. He agrees that Clemenceau at the present moment is in a strong position but it entirely depends on his having Military successes. That another failure would inevitably put him out of office. I asked him who could possibly succeed if Clemenceau fell and put the question directly to him as to whether he thought he could form a Government. He said "No" that he did not think he could. That his time would come later but that there would certainly be somebody in between Clemenceau and him but that his time would come and when it did the man who would be associated with him would be Tardieu, an old friend of Caillaux's but at the present moment a lukewarm supporter of Clemenceau. As to the immediate successor in case of anything happening to Clemenceau he thought it would lie between Barthou and Briand and that circumstances alone would decide which it was. If the change took place owing to some military defeat and it was necessary to still further rouse the country and keep them together for the War, Barthou would be the man and he would do it very well but that nobody really trusted or liked him and as he put it, he is a man from the South who has the same method with regard to political people he wants to get rid of as his compatriots have in private life, namely he would stab them in the back. On the other hand if it was a question of making Peace it would unquestionably be Briand but Briand did not want to come in now but was perfectly determined if possible to be the Prime Minister who made Peace. I asked him whether there was any chance of a reconstituted Government with Briand serving under Clemenceau and he said, none whatever, that although it was nominally concealed there was bitter enmity between the two men.

He pooh poohs the idea of Loucheur being Prime Minister! He says he knows he wants to be and is working hard but that everybody knows Loucheur and he will have no following.

Painlevé he looked upon as completely done. I then led him on to telling me what the real truth was with regard to the statements now being made that Painlevé stopped Nivelle's offensive. He says it is not in the least true to say that Painlevé actually stopped the offensive in so many words but that as a matter of fact he created such an atmosphere of mistrust with regard to the offensive, both during the offensive and still more before the offensive, that Nivelle had no alternative but to stop.

Painlevé apparently was violently opposed to the offensive and only agreed to it under compulsion. That all the Army people were opposed to it and that Nivelle therefore started with practically everybody's hand against him. The result was that adequate preparations were not made and that the whole morale and discipline of the Army had deteriorated to such an extent that failure was inevitable though he believes if Nivelle had been properly supported it might have been a success.

He says that Clemenceau would like to bring Nivelle back and give him a Command in France and is sounding his way to do so but that at the present moment he realises it would create a political storm which it is certainly not in his interest to create.

On the subject of Military authorities generally Thomas was not enthusiastic and all I could get him to say about Foch was that perhaps he was the least bad of the lot. I think though he has got a high opinion of Guillaumat and he is very much down on Clemenceau for bringing him back from Salonika. He says that it is the one place that he thinks (if Germany fails in her offensive) we might be able to produce a real effect. He understands Guillaumat is very sanguine, and I can confirm this from what Guillaumat himself told me, of an offensive there.[1] That the Bulgarians are very half hearted. That the Greek Army is much better than it was thought possible it could ever be and that we might get almost decisive results. He conceives it to be utter folly to bring away English troops from there and to change the Commander in Chief at such a moment like this especially when it is to send a Commander in Chief who had absolutely failed in France.[2] He says that the French are considering whether they will bring away some of their troops but he thinks public opinion would be very much opposed to it.

I asked him what the general opinion of the country was with regard to the War. He says they are quite sound but very tired and that the slightest whisper of Peace negotiations would be at once seized on. They still think we could have had Peace last year with which sentiment he does not agree and it makes them very bitter against the Italians as they consider it was the latter who prevented it.

My general impression of Thomas' attitude is rather that he is like a mad dog who thinks that every hand is against him and who is snapping at everybody. I do not think he has strengthened his position by joining Varenne[3] which he has done within the last few days and I know that Varenne does not at all welcome him but it amused me to hear him when I asked his opinion of Varenne, he said "Varenne is one of my followers". I think he feels that at the present moment he has lost his hold, that he has got no real Party to follow him and he cannot quite make up his mind what line he will take in order to secure a following. It certainly will not be by assuming an anti-English attitude. Far from it. He tells me that both at Lyons and Marseilles there is a somewhat anti-British feeling and he has volunteered to go down with me and speak in both those places in favour of the English. I should like to do this but of course it is a little difficult and I do not want to get Clemenceau's back up. I think Clemenceau rather looks upon me with some sort of suspicion at the present moment because he knows that I see Thomas, Briand, and all these other people who are really in opposition to him, but I equally see and invite to this house all his own people so I do not propose to discontinue seeing men who will inevitably come to the front one day and from whom I can get really a better impression of the general state of the country than I can ever do from officials.

To sum up however I am certain from all I have seen and heard there is no question of France really weakening in the struggle. That there will never be any question of a separate peace; that Clemenceau is as strongly in the saddle now as he ever has been but he owes it to the confidence that the soldiers and the country generally have in him and I should never be surprised if some day the Chamber, which is at heart antagonistic to him, gave him a sudden downfall. I do not think it will come yet but I think that within the next few months you can certainly anticipate a political crisis. This is not a very brave prophecy to make because as we well know no Government in this country ever enjoys confidence for more [than a few] weeks at the outside.

Notes to letter of 22 June

1. On 22 June Clemenceau informed the newly installed General Franchet d'Espérey that the general military situation required the assumption of offensive action by the Armée d'Orient.
2. Louis Franchet d'Espérey (1856–1942). Commander Army Group of the East, 1916, and of the North, 1917; Allied Commander-in-Chief, Salonika front, June 1918. As commander of the Army Group of the North, d'Espérey was something of a scapegoat for recent setbacks in France.
3. Alexandre Varenne. Socialist politician on the right of his party. Made Governor-General of Indochina by the Cartel des Gauches government of 1924.

Sunday, 23rd June

PARIS

Motored to Versailles. Picked up Sackville-West and Caslett and went on to Maintenon to luncheon. The Duchesse de Noailles[1] there — great friend of Queen Mary's.[2] Rather low, poor woman, as her only son had gone back to the front yesterday, as she said after a very severe illness and quite unfit for duty. He is only a private soldier. It is the most lovely place I have ever seen. The stone part of it dates from about 1180, the brick part about 200 years later. Madame de Maintenon's[3] room is just as she lived in it with all her things about. The house itself stands in a lovely position with a river which divides before it gets to the house and runs round the house as a moat and then runs as a broader river down the front. There are remains of the big aqueduct begun by Louis XIV[4] to take water to Versailles which is about 20 miles. It is impossible to imagine that anybody could have contemplated such a work. There is a big aqueduct and it was to be doubled in two tiers. They only got as far as the one and even that is certainly as high as Derby House. A huge work and the ones that cross in front of the house about ¾ mile off were all to have been covered with marble. It does not sound like a pretty thing for a foreground but as a matter of fact it is lovely because it looks like old ruins and when you get past it and look back at the house through it is the most wonderful view I have ever seen.

Notes to 23 June

1. Duchesse de Noailles. Sister of the Duc de Luynes.
2. Queen Mary (1867–1953). Queen Consort of George V.
3. Madame de Maintenon (1635–1719). Second, but unacknowledged, wife of Louis XIV, who married her secretly in 1684.
4. Louis XIV (1638–1715). 'Le Roi Soleil'. King of France from 1643.

Monday, 24th June

Routine work morning. Got a message from Philip Sassoon to say Oliver had got slight attack of influenza.

Luncheon American Ambassador and his daughter. Duchesse de la Tremouille, Princesse Lignes, General Belin,[1] French representative at

Versailles and his Aide-de-Camp Colonel Descombes and Lady Rodney.

Henry Simond who is the Chief proprietor of the *Echo de Paris* came to see me. He is very nice. A supporter of Clemenceau's, a great lover of England and we had an hour's talk. Unfortunately he does not speak English but I find now I can get on perfectly well in French. We talked generalities. He tells me that he thinks that the country here is very sound but everything depends on Clemenceau. If he went or if anything happened to him there would be undoubted trouble. He was in every way friendly to me and is going to keep me fully posted with any things of interest. Afterwards went to call on the Governor of Paris, General Guillaumat, but found him out.

Dined at the Cerole Agricol with Madame Roger. Not a very amusing dinner and very mild baccarat afterwards. I was rather bored as there were no counters, only matches. Half of the people did not know the game and the remaining half did not care about playing.

Notes to 24 June

1. General Emile Belin (1853-1937). Chief of Staff to Joffre in 1914. Replaced Weygand as French military representative on the Supreme War Council, April 1918.

Tuesday, 25th June

Went to St. Cloud to see the English wounded in the Canadian Hospital. Curiously enough they were almost all Lancashire men except one who was a boy who says his name is Field. He enlisted from the Gardens at Coworth.[1] He is not badly wounded and hopes soon to be home. He says he is very keen to go back to the gardens again.

Luncheon with Stanislaus de Castellans. She was a Cuban. He is very nice and is in Clemenceau's Secretariat. Dolly de Castellan was there too but rather a dangerous woman. Very much in with Briand and repeats everything that is said.

M. Roman Dmowski[2] the head of the Polish Committee here came to see me. The substance of his conversation embodied in attached letter to Arthur Balfour.

Various other business. Ronnie Hamilton[3] came to see me on his way back to Switzerland where he is Assistant Military Attaché. Dined alone with Charlie.

Notes to 25 June

1. Coworth Park. A house near Sunningdale which was bought by the sixteenth earl in 1895 and where Derby's widow lived until her death in 1957.
2. Roman Dmowski (1844–1939). Head of the Polish National Committee in Paris and subsequently chief of the Polish Delegation to the Peace Conference.
3. Ronald J. Hamilton (b.1872). Assistant to the Military Attaché at The Hague from May 1915.

Wednesday, 26th June

General Goodwin[1] and General Burtchaell[2] came to see me. We discussed the question of the Hospitals here which to my mind are not satisfactory as we have plenty of vacant beds in the Hertford and St Cloud Hospitals and yet they have started a small hospital in a dingy street for 40 beds and have got 4 nurses and 15 orderlies for it. They both agreed with me and are taking the matter up. We also discussed the question of the Liverpool Hospital. Not quite sure what to do about it as it appears that Raw is most unpopular, especially with the big consultants and the consequence is they rather ignore the Hospital. As the two Generals both said, it therefore does not get the reputation which it ought to have because it really does excellent work. They are thinking of finding Liverpool doctors now in the army and putting them in but as they say the difficulty may come if these men decline to serve under Raw and I am writing confidentially to Bateson[3] on the subject as a new site has been found in Trouville which is in every way an excellent one.

Ordinary Meeting of Board. No particular business except question of Paris leave for officers. It seems to us very incongruous that while we are ordering the wives of members of Missions to leave Paris that wives should be allowed to come to Paris to meet Officers on leave. We have suggested conditions to the War Office under which permission should be given.

Marconi[4] and his wife came to see me after luncheon. He is going to England on some special Mission. She wanted to go to Boulogne to see her brother who is in the Irish Guards and has been badly wounded. Arranged it for her. The amount of red tape connected with such visits is extraordinary owing to the fact that though she was an Englishwoman she is now an Italian having taken the nationality of her husband.

Afterwards, Sir William Morrison who is a distinguished Indian Official and is now second in command of the Ordnance here, came to see me and I am very much alarmed at the amount of Clothing etc that is collected in this City to be cleaned and which could certainly not be moved if there had to be an evacuation. I think there has been an extraordinary want of foresight during the last 6 weeks with regard to this. Wrote to Haig on the subject.

Before Dinner went to meet the Duke of Connaught[5] who has come out with 500 decorations to give to the French Army. A very popular move. He seemed very well indeed.

Dined in the evening with Madame Sancay. Only Princesse Marie Murat, an Italian whose name I did not catch but who is apparently well known. Very clever, very excitable, talks English perfectly but is occasionally shut up. The other member of the Party Judge Perry, an American, very nice fellow indeed who has lived all his life in Paris. Practised at the Bar here and made his fortune. A great book lover and I am going to get him to help me to gradually pick up a certain number of French books for the Library at Knowsley. Madame de Sancay is an American and I think an extremely stupid and dull woman and very tactless.

I asked Clemenceau to dine to meet the Duke of Connaught but as he never dines out I told him I should understand a refusal. I have had a very charming note from him since, but refusing.

Notes to 26 June

1. Major William Goodwin (1875–1958). Royal Army Medical Corps. In command of Casualty Clearing Station, BEF.
2. Colonel Charles Burtchael (1866–1932). Royal Army Medical Corps. Assistant Director-General Medical Services.
3. Major John Bateson (1880–1956). Serving with General Staff.
4. Guglielmo Marconi (1874–1937). Scientist and Italian Senator. Married Hon. Beatrice O'Brien in 1905.
5. Duke of Connaught (1850–1942). Son of Queen Victoria. Served for many years in the army before becoming Governor General of Canada, 1911–16.

Copy of letter sent to Mr. Balfour

Confidential 26 June 1918

I am going to write to you a rambling sort of letter but there may be some news in it which may be of use to you.

Topic 1. The Polish question. I am not quite sure whether I ought to write you a confidential despatch, if so please let me know and I will at once do it. Monsieur Roman Dmowski, who is the head of the Polish Army Committee here, came to see me yesterday and had a long talk on the subject of his work. In the first place he is extremely grateful for the appointment of Leveson-Gower to act as Liaison Officer and I think it will turn out to be a happy appointment as he tells me that Leveson-Gower knows more about Polish Affairs than almost any man he has come across and as he is a very keen fellow I think that good will come of it. Dmowski has got a grievance against the Americans and the Canadians and that is that Poles are not allowed to go into what he calls his army. I told him that as far as the Americans are concerned he must talk to somebody else, but with regard to the Canadian Army I would see what could be done. His contention is that there are a great many Poles in Canada and even in the Canadian Army but they are not being made use of for fighting purposes as owing to their want of knowledge of the English language they are simply being used as Labour Battalions and he wants them transferred to his fighting forces. I pointed out that the scale of pay was so vastly different between Canada and France, the pay of which latter army his men get and that it might be very difficult to get men to transfer. He did not agree and said that a great many of these men would transfer even with the loss of pay as they want to fight. I do not know how this would be, but it might be worth your while saying something to Borden[1] on the subject and I do not see that any harm could come of volunteers from the Canadian Army, and especially from troops which are non-combatant, being called for to join the Polish Force here which apparently from all I hear is a very efficient one.

We then went on to talk on the subject of the Baltic. Of course as he says Poland as a separate State is impossible if it does not have access to the sea[2] and that must always be borne in mind when the subject of Poland's independence is under consideration but he tells me from what he hears in the Scandinavian Countries they are genuinely alarmed at the hold Germany is getting on the Baltic and they look upon it as likely to become nothing but a German Lake. I asked him what he thought Scandinavian Countries could do as to my mind they were so terrorised by Germany they would not make any effort to resist. He said he was not quite sure whether this was the case. He was getting a small committee together here and apparently he is on his own account going to undertake propaganda work in Scandinavian Countries. His ideas are not formulated to such an extent as to be able to put forward a definite scheme but he has promised to come and see me again and let me have some scheme in the working out of which he might perhaps require your assistance. He is an agreeable man. Talks English very well and is evidently very keen.

Topic No. 2. I am a little afraid what results will arise from Tardieu being High Commissioner for Franco-American Affairs. He is a very ambitious man, very pushing and I think brilliantly clever. Talks English quite well and has got the ear of Clemenceau who is I fancy a little afraid of him.

I do not know whether it was brought to your notice the other day that Clemenceau went down to see Pershing and took with him Foch and Tardieu and the newspapers said the result of their interview was most satisfactory. What the interview was about I have not been able to discover though I undoubtedly shall do so, but I think you will find it will be the thin end of the wedge for the pooling of all supplies. Tardieu will work for all he is worth to get French and American goods pooled and then will say to us you can come in or stay out, just as you like, and of course with the demands we have to make on America we should have to come in, with the result that France would get many things at our expense. I may be wrong in all this but I only give it to you as my impression, but I tell you in order that you may warn Milner and, if you think right, the P.M. to watch Tardieu's actions.

Topic 3. The rumoured visit of the King of Spain to Paris is still the great subject of gossip here. Personally I do not think he ever was here but you cannot convince the ordinary French public that one sees that he was not and that he did not bring with him some definite statement as to Germany's War aims and proposals of Peace. It is curious that from the day that he was supposed to have come here that we have neither had a bombardment of Paris by Bertha nor a raid. It may just be chance but of course it is something that gives colour to the rumours. He is supposed to have gone to the private house of the Spanish Minister here. There is as you know no Ambassador, he having died a few months ago, and the Minister is supposed to have turned out of his apartment for him. Again there is colour for such a rumour because there is no doubt the Minister did turn out of his house at that time and was living at a hotel. He said he was there because something had to be done to his apartment but I have seen nobody who ever saw the King and as I say I think all the evidence proves that he was not here; but to show you how widespread is the belief that he was Berthaulat who is the chief man of the *Liberté* and a personal friend of Clemenceau's told LeRoy-Lewis yesterday that he knew that he had been here; that he knew he had shown conditions of Peace and that Leygues to whom he had spoken had told him privately that this was the case. Berthaulat gave LeRoy-Lewis also another piece of gossip which was that Pichon is going to retire on the ground of health within the next fortnight and his place will be taken by Briand as Foreign Minister as they think that Briand would be the right man with Clemenceau to undertake consideration of any Peace terms. To my mind this second bit of gossip shows the inaccuracy of the former as I do not believe that Briand under any circumstances would serve under Clemenceau and I think what has given rise to this further bit of gossip is something which I know to be true and that is that Briand has given instructions to his friends that they are not to attack Clemenceau and to stop sniping.

Topic 4. I have telegraphed to you about Mr. Robert Dell's[3] article. It is a most mischievous one and I do not think represents the views of this Country. It is simply an outburst of spite on the part of a man who has been expelled from his country. I wish something could be done to stop such articles. In connection with this I should be very much obliged if you would let me know whether you think I might go to Lancashire in the middle of July and speak simply on the subject of France to the Lancashire Branch of the National Union. I hope I am not conceited in saying that I think it might do good as I feel sure Lancashire people would probably believe me sooner than a discredited journalist.

Notes to confidential letter of 26 June

1. Sir Robert Borden (1857–1937). Became Prime Minister of Canada in 1911 and led his country through the First World War.
2. It was this problem which the peacemakers of 1919 tried to resolve through the Polish corridor, giving access to the sea at the 'Free Port' of Danzig.
3. Robert Dell. Journalist and writer. Author of *My Second Country* (London, 1920).

Thursday, 27th June

The American Chaplain General for Paris came to see me in the morning. Wants me to attend the Concert they are giving on July 3rd. I suppose I shall have to do so.

I afterwards went to what is known as the Lighthouse — organised by an American Miss Holt for the care of blinded officers and men — had lunch with them all, the American Ambassador and many others there. They called on me for a speech afterwards and I had to make an impromptu one and in French. I do not know in the least what it was like but they all said it did quite well.

Nothing much in the afternoon till tea-time when I went to tea with Princesse Marie Murat. Met her mother who is a dear old lady, the

Duchesse de Rohan. She is acting as a nurse in a Hospital. Has got rather a look of Tess but much tidier and kinder looking. Amongst others who were there were Jules Cambon[1] whom I had much wanted to meet and Madame D'Aunay an American Lady of about 60 who is a great friend of Clemenceau and the only person in whom he really confides.

In the evening Dinner here for the Duke of Connaught. He and Malcolm Murray[2] came and they fitted in very well with a Dinner I had already invited. The Murats and their son who is a very nice boy who has lost his leg flying. Princesse D'Arenberg, Madame Hennessy. The Spanish Minister who is charming. He is acting as Ambassador, the Spanish Ambassador having died two or three months ago, and everybody hopes he will be appointed as Ambassador. He assured me there was not one word of truth in the King having been here. The Biche de Castellans. He is very nice, in Clemenceau's Secretariat. She is a Cuban. Grahame and Bobberty and Betty[3] made up the Party. Everything went very well and the Duke seemed very pleased. Dinner was broken up by an Alerte about ¼ to 11. It was a biggish raid. Charlie and I watched it from the window. Here in Paris you can see so much better than in London. You could see clearly where the shells were bursting. If the lights from the searchlights were really properly on the aeroplanes they were making extremely good practice. Got the news that the Czar had been assassinated. It is not confirmed but everybody seems to think it is certainly the case.[4]

Notes to 27 June

1. Jules Cambon (1845–1935). Secretary-General of the French Foreign Ministry, 1915–17. In 1919 he became one of the five-man French delegation to the Paris Peace Conference.
2. Lieutenant-Colonel Sir Malcolm Murray (1867–1938). Comptroller of the Household to the Duke of Connaught since 1906.
3. Betty Cranborne (née Vere). Married Lord Cranborne in 1915.
4. It is now generally accepted that the tsar and his family were murdered on the night of 16 July.

Friday, 28th June

Hear this morning that bombs last night fell in the Place Vendôme and on the Ministry of Justice which is next door to the Ritz. It has wrecked the former building and a good bit of the latter and there appears to have been several people hurt, but no English people. Bobberty and Betty were all right. I have sent round to ask them whether they would like to come and stay here as I think probably with so much open space round us we are in a better position than the Ritz is. Le Roy Lewis the Military Attaché who lives there has his room completely destroyed. One bit of shell going right through both walls so it evidently was a very big bomb.

Luncheon the Consul General[1] and Mrs. Hearn. He is a very able fellow. Was in Hamburg at the outbreak of War and has done really good service here. She also a nice woman. Mr. & Mrs. Howard. He does for me Harry Milner[2] sort of work. She was an Australian. Lady Rodney, Dubos and Blunt the Chaplain here who seems a very good sort of fellow indeed. I have never met him before but I have heard a good bit about him.

Ordinary work in the afternoon, then went with Charlie to see old Mrs. Standish, who of course Charlie knew very well before I had ever seen her. A delightful old lady, but it amused me to see, what everybody told me I should see, the way in which she tries to imitate Queen Alexandra.[3]

In the evening Betty, Bobberty and Bullock dined with me. We had the usual alarm but it did not come to very much though some machines came over.

Charlie and I went down in the cellar, really for inspection purposes but if there is a big raid again I think we shall both go down there as I have been shown very confidentially the returns of the previous night's bombardment and in every case where people were killed in the house it was in the upper stories whereas other people who had gone to the cellars were safe. It seems therefore ridiculous not to take any ordinary precaution in a really bad raid.

Notes to 28 June

1. Walter Risely Hearn (1853–1930). Consul-General, Paris, since 1914.
2. Marcus Henry Milner (1864–1939). Controller to Lord Derby; ADC, GOC, 55th Division.
3. Queen Alexandra (1844–1925). Queen Consort of Edward VII.

Saturday, 29th June

This morning presented a Military Cross to a French Officer. Afterwards had a meeting with Mr. Clipperton,[1] from the Foreign Office, General Thornton, General Phillips and Le Roy Lewis, all with regard to evacuation. It is a most complicated matter to deal with, especially in view of the two facts, one that you cannot make anything public and the other that you are in an absolute uncertainty as to the numbers of people who have to be evacuated. There is one happy result from it and that is that we are getting a correct list of all English people living in Paris. It is extraordinary that no such list should have existed up to now. The only list is the Police List and that is absolutely inaccurate in every way.

Henry Wilson came in for one minute on his return from Italy. Very pleased with what he has seen there. The Italians apparently have got their tails well up but as usual have begun to funk the idea of German Divisions coming against them. I was told one day this week rather an amusing thing about the Italians who of course are much exaggerating what they have done. They have hitherto had no nickname for their private soldiers and they say that the English call theirs "Tommy", the French "Poilu" and Americans "Sammy" and so they must have one, and they have christened their men "il terribili" which is the last thing that they are though some of them seem to have fought very well.

Got a line from Edward which Henry Wilson brought with him. He (H.W.) says Edward looking very fit and well.

Had luncheon with Duchesse de Camastra whose husband, an Italian is on the Staff of the Duc d'Aosta.² The house is some way away but it only takes a quarter of an hour in a motor and without exception the most beautiful house I have ever seen either here or in London. Lovely things in it and the Garden which is about half as big again as Devonshire House,³ perfectly lovely. Full of roses, fountains etc. She is a sister of Princesse Murat and so one had the whole of the Buonapartist people there. Duchesse Muchy who is very old, well over 80 and a great personal friend of the Empresse Eugénie.⁴ Princesse de la Moscowa, Princesse Demidoff⁵ whose husband now is the Russian Minister in Greece and who was very interesting on the subject of Greece as also Russia. She thinks that we managed our affairs very badly with Constantine. That neither he nor his wife were really pro-German and might, if we had treated them properly, have been kept well on our side. She has the same high opinion that I have of Jonnart⁶ and says if only he had gone there 6 months earlier all would have been well. Elliott⁷ was good but no real power and the French Ambassador⁸ bad and very mischievous and with no pretensions to be a gentleman. The others of the party were the little Duc and Duchesse de Leynes. She is a grand-daughter of Duchesse de Muchy. Then there were 3 Italians, De Robiland, the Italian Representative at Versailles and his Aide de Camp Siccany, and there was another Italian a very nice fellow who talks English well. Was on Robiland's staff in Italy and was attached to me when I was there. Also General Balfourier[9] who is the man who really managed the Defence of Verdun although many other Generals have claimed to be *the man*. Pétain was jealous of all the praise he got and put him on the retired list, and perhaps he was right because he seems old, but there is no doubt he was a very popular figure in the Army. Altogether it is a luncheon I have enjoyed more almost than any other luncheon I have been to. I am sure Alice[10] would thoroughly appreciate both the house and the garden.

Afternoon. Went to see a performance given by Miss Lena Ashwell's Company. Quite good but I am afraid it is going to be a disappointment to her. She deserves tremendous credit for sending out a Company simply to amuse troops but as they are to play only in Paris I fear her audiences will be very small as when English Officers and men come on leave they like going to see the Paris plays. Du Cane came to see me at 5 o'c and we were joined by Henry Wilson and discussed the whole question of the Spiers Mission. Things are getting very difficult thanks to Clemenceau's autocratic ways and unless our Government put their foot down with regard to it we are simply going to be pushed aside altogether. He has taken a dislike to Spiers and as he is backed up by both Foch and Pétain, who have always disliked him, the result is that Spiers' whole occupation is gone. He gets practically no information given to him at all. Clemenceau is angry with Spiers because the latter finds out and tells our Government a great many things which he (Clemenceau) does not wish [them] to know, but of course his whole position as Head of Mission has been changed by the fact that a Generalissimo has been appointed and that that General alone can really give full military information. My suggestion, and I think it is one they will eventually come to, is to make Du Cane, who is now head of the Mission with Foch the superior of Spiers (or somebody else in Spiers' place). Allow the latter officer to collect all the information that he possibly can, send it to Du Cane and let Du Cane send it on to England together with all such other information as he is able to gain from Foch. I think this system would work but of course it would be a come down for Spiers who has been on his own as far as France is concerned, except that he is nominally under me, and he has done such invaluable service that I hope nothing will be done to hurt his feelings.

Du Cane is staying for dinner with me and has brought with him Charlie Winn his A.D.C., the St. Oswald boy. I have got a thoroughly British dinner. The Hartingtons, Cranbornes and Tweedmouth[11] and Dolly Rothschild. I must say that I like the way that all these people when they come over here now always come and see one, and seem only too glad to come here for luncheon or dinner.

Notes to 29 June

1. Charles Chipperton (b.1864). Consul-General, Rouen since 1906.
2. Emmanuel-Philibert, Duke of Aosta (1869–1931). Italian military commander against the Austrian forces.
3. Devonshire House. Duke of Devonshire's London home in Piccadilly.
4. Empress Eugénie (1826–1920). Spanish-born wife of Emperor Napoleon III, whom she married in 1853.
5. Prince E. Demidov. Russian minister in Greece until 1917; stayed on after the Revolution, accredited to Athens by the anti-Bolshevik forces.
6. Charles Jonnart. Former French minister and Governor-General of Algeria who, as Allied High Commissioner, carried out the deposition of King Constantine of Greece in 1917.
7. Sir Francis Elliot (1851–1940). British Minister in Athens, 1903–17.
8. Jean Guillemin. French minister in Athens, recalled 1917.
9. General Balfourier. Commander 20th Corps, French Army, 1916.
10. Lady Alice Derby (1862–1957). Married Derby in 1889.
11. Dudley Marjoribanks, 3rd Baron Tweedmouth (1874–1935). CMG, 1915. Royal Horse Guards.

Sunday, 30th June

PARIS

Went round to see De Crespigny who had been taken very ill the night before. Found him much better but still ill. He was thinking of getting off on Monday but I stopped him and have telephoned to say that he won't arrive back till Wednesday or Thursday. Also saw young Wodehouse,[1] Kimberley's[2] son in the 16th Lancers. He lost a brother about 8 months ago and poor boy is in great distress as he has just heard that another brother was dying at Boulogne after a motor accident. He wanted me to try and arrange to get him a motor but it was impossible.

Went out to luncheon at Versailles. Usual party. Neuflizes, Madame Roger, the only additions being the St. Aldegondes and M. Manuel, and Frazier[3] the very clever Minister under Sharp at the Embassy. He tells me Kerensky[4] has arrived and he is going to see him. I have not made up my mind yet whether I will or not as after all the whole of our Russian troubles are due to him and I do not therefore care much about seeing the brute.

Sackville West told me something which shows to what extent Clemenceau now exercises what really is an autocratic hand and which will have to be checked. He sent a message to Sackville West to say there would be nothing for Sir Douglas Haig at the Supreme War Council and therefore there was no necessity for him to come. Sackville West replied that he noted what Clemenceau said but it was for our Prime Minister to say whether he wanted our Commander in Chief to be present and he could only take instructions from him. I hear too Clemenceau is now very bitter against Henry Wilson. I knew this would not take long in coming. Henry Wilson did everything that the French wanted when he was out here and now when he finds in another position he has to resist, then he is not as popular as he was. I must say I think Lloyd George and Co. are very inconsiderate. They refuse to come by train which after all would take them but 8 or 9 hours and insist on coming by motor car bringing a lot of friends with them. Lloyd George won't have our motors and so the French Government have to supply them with 20 motor cars and 3 motor lorries to bring them. As I say it is a very strong order and very inconsiderate considering how badly motor cars are wanted at the present moment.

Garstin[5] came to see me when I got back. He says he has been suffering from suppressed influenza and I never saw a man so changed in my life. He has got to look very very old and haggard but seems in fairly good spirits though for him that is not saying very much.

In the evening Henry Wilson, Sackville-West, and Tweedmouth dined. Had a long talk generally on every sort of subject. I had a few words privately with Henry Wilson on the subject of this grasping of everything by Clemenceau and Foch and I hope and believe they will put their foot down and decline to move Spiers at the dictation of the French Headquarters. Henry Wilson agreed with me in this but at the same time he equally agreed that if they said that Spiers was personally distasteful to them it would be very difficult to retain him.

Notes to 30 June

1. John Wodehouse (1883–1941). 3rd Earl of Kimberley, 1932. Captain, 16th Lancers; Liberal MP, 1906–10.
2. 2nd Earl of Kimberley (1848–1932).
3. Arthur H. Frazier (b.1868). Secretary at the American embassy in Paris since March 1915.
4. Alexander Kerensky (1881–1970). Head of Russian Provisional Government from July 1917. Overthrown by Bolsheviks in November and exiled.
5. Sir William Garstin (1849–1925). British Government Director of the Suez Canal Company since 1907.

July 1918

Monday, 1st July

Grahame saw Mme D'Aunay yesterday. She was alone and he had a long talk with her and she told him that she thought I was a Briandist. He I am glad to say completely dispelled that view. It is quite evident therefore that Clemenceau had been under the impression that I was supporting Briand against him which is the very opposite to what I would wish to do.

Sir Joseph Maclay[1] came to see me and had a long talk. He is very satisfied with the position in England and says that it is infinitely better than it has been any time during the last 18 months and they have got everything extremely well organised. He thinks there is not a sufficient grip being kept over the coal question and if we are not careful we shall have a very serious shortage in the winter. He tells me that it is very difficult to get the exact facts about the Americans as their reports vary from day to day but he is hopeful within the year they may get 2½ millions which is about the amount they promised would be ready at the beginning of this year. They are very difficult to deal with as they want us to do everything for them but he is gradually getting that right. Another of his troubles is one which I know of and that is shortage of wagons at Ports, but that is entirely French mismanagement which is being gradually remedied. Altogether things seem from this point of view most satisfactory.

Attended Luncheon given by Mr. Philip Roy, Canadian Commissioner in honour of Dominion Day. I had to make a short speech. I sat next to Viviani[2] at luncheon. Interesting man and I believe a real born orator. It was very interesting talking to him about Joffre. He is a tremendous believer in him. Thinks he has been very hardly used and it is quite evident if he had his way he would put him back in Foch's place. Has a high opinion of Foch but considers that Foch's proper place, where he would do the best work, is as subordinate to Joffre. He tells me that a very great number of people are of the same opinion and I believe that to be correct.

Afterwards went to the new little hospital in the Rue Christophe Colomb. There are only slight cases there mostly influenza,[3] but 5 or 6 cases of dog bite. They send everybody bitten by a dog to be treated for it at the Pasteur Institute. They have had a considerable number of cases. The Matron was curiously enough the Sister who had been sent by the Army to look after Frank Bertie.

Saw Spiers who had come back looking better but still seedy and Maclagan who is very anxious that we should make some sort of show on the 14th July. He wants a Scotch Battalion to march in the procession but I do not know if that can be arranged.

M. Jean Hennessy[4] came to see me. He is the brother of the racing one. Was attached to our Army at the beginning of the War. Is a Député but is looked upon as being a "défaitist". He did not give me quite that impression. He talked very freely. Said a year and a half ago or even a year ago he thought Peace was possible and that we ought to have taken it, but that now it was quite impossible and that we must go on fighting although he could not see what the end would be as in his opinion each Country was asking for more than it could possibly expect to get. My impression is that he is not at all keen about Alsace and Lorraine[5] for the simple reason that he says it is no use getting those provinces unless you can make them thoroughly French and he does not see how with the diminishing population, and with a population likely to still further diminish,[6] that that is possible. He is not at all one of those who wish to make love to the Americans. On the contrary he is very much afraid of them and thinks that after the War they will have established a tremendous hold on this country. Even now they are buying up all the land that they can. They are also buying up Companies giving a good price, putting in a few Frenchmen with a few shares as the Founders of the Company so as to make the Company appear to be still French. I should think there is a great deal in what he says from all I hear. But he talks in an extraordinary way about the population after the War and speaks even of settling English people on the land here. He also thinks that the law of primogeniture will have to be established here and that a great cause at the present moment of small families is that properties are divided equally amongst all the children, each knows what he will get and the younger ones make no effort to go away and make their fortunes elsewhere. They simply live on till they succeed to their small inheritance.

Haig, Lawrence,[7] Fletcher and Sassoon dined. Also Cranbornes, Hartingtons and Bullock. Haig is considerably mystified about the Germans.

He says that the prisoners they have taken all tell him that their Divisions are decimated by this influenza which they have apparently got in a badish form. I suppose it comes from their being underfed but the prisoners that they have taken say that their bread is quite uneatable and from some they had with them it is obviously true. He also told me another curious thing which seems almost too good to be true and that is that they have taken prisoners from 5 separate divisions who have been out resting and refitted but that during that time they did not receive a single reinforcement and the consequence is they have come back into the line exactly the same strength as they left it. This is not our idea of refitting. He also told me the 30th Division is going to be made up by troops coming from Salonika. He also spoke to me about the Air Service. He tells me it is not what it was in Trenchard's time and that Salmond[8] is nothing like as good as he was. I told him that as at the present Trenchard is practically unemployed as the French object to this bombing squadron being an independent command I should ask to make an exchange and let Trenchard come back to his old post and let Salmond go to where Trenchard is now. It would not in the least matter a junior officer being there. He is reluctant to do this because he says that it might have political consequences. I really do not understand his frame of mind in such matters as this and I told him so. What on earth are political consequences compared to Military consequences. I am certain as a matter of fact there would be no political consequences as Weir is a great admirer of Trenchard and would I know do anything to help him to get back into the position for which he is most fitted, namely a real active command. I must say I was disappointed with Haig's attitude on a question of so grave importance as this. I am going to see him again today and impress upon him the absolute necessity of making a change if he thinks it desirable. I offered to speak to Milner myself but he does not wish me to do so and there perhaps he is right. I did not think him in very good spirits. He talked very frankly about the French. He says that they are most difficult people to deal with as with the exception of Foch they never seem to think it necessary either to consult him even if they are under his orders or even when ordered to do anything to carry out these orders.

After we had finished dinner Arthur Balfour, Drummond and Ian Malcolm arrived. They had come at the most fearful pace as may best be shown by the fact that they arrived at 10 past 10 and their luggage which was certainly in a slower car but not a lorry, did not arrive till ¼ past 1. They had averaged 47 miles an hour which personally I think a ridiculous thing to allow. Even Arthur himself said that he had never been at such a pace in his life and it was a little too fast even for him. He seems in extraordinary good spirits and I think is quite happy and comfortable here. They are all rather amused with regard to this position. It appears there was an animated discussion at the War Cabinet before they started as to whether he or Milner should be considered Minister in addition to the Prime Minister.[9] It has been decided that Arthur is to be the Minister and Drummond tells me that Milner is very disgruntled at the decision. Nobody knows what they are going to discuss but at the present moment the Prime Minister has got Aliens on the brain and he can think of nothing but how severely to deal with them. It seems rather amusing after 4 years of War and after he has been Prime Minister for 15 months. They told me all that he suggests, though he has kept most of his plans to himself, but as far as I can see the first persons to be interned if he does bring in these new regulations will be Milner and Smuts.[10]

Arthur does not bring any news with him. Most amusing on the subject of George Curzon's party. He tells me that the real cause of trouble was that Winston of all George's colleagues was the only man who was permitted to bring his wife.[11]

Notes to 1 July

1. Sir Joseph Maclay (1857–1951). Baron Maclay, 1922. Minister of Shipping, December 1916–March 1921.
2. René Viviani (1863–1925). Prime Minister of France, June 1914–October 1915 when the power of General Joffre was at its height. Subesquently Minister of Justice under Briand and Ribot.
3. This first wave of influenza was relatively mild and most patients recovered after three days. Between October 1918 and January 1919, however, a pandemic killed something like 21 million people worldwide. See R. Collier, *The Plague of the Spanish Lady* (London, 1974).
4. Jean Hennessy. Minister of Agriculture under Poincaré, Briand and Tardieu, 1928–30.
5. The recovery of these two provinces, lost to Prussia after the war of 1870, had become the leading declared French war aim.
6. The French had been concerned about their falling birth rate before the outbreak of the Great War. War-time casualties inevitably exacerbated the problem. 1916 saw the lowest annual number of births in the recorded history of the French population. See C. Dyer, *Population and Society in Twentieth-Century France* (Sevenoaks, 1978).
7. General Sir Herbert Lawrence (1861–1943). Soldier, banker and industrialist; Chief of General Staff, BEF, 1918–19.
8. John Maitland Salmond (1881–1968). Major-General commanding the Royal Air Force in France, 1918–19.

9. The Supreme War Council allowed for each Great Power to be represented by its head of Government and one other political member, together with the Permanent Military Representative.
10. Jan C. Smuts (1870–1950). South African Minister of Defence, 1910–19; Minister without Portfolio in the War Cabinet, June 1917–January 1919. Milner had been born and had his early education in Germany.
11. Curzon gave a huge banquet 'in true viceregal style' to the representatives of the Dominions on 26 June. According to Hankey, 'there were a few ladies present'. S. Roskill, *Hankey: Man of Secrets*, vol. 1 (London, 1970), p. 158.

Tuesday, 2nd July

Another Alerte last night but nothing came of it. It is even rumoured that the cause was the car bringing Arthur's luggage which made the most infernal noise and only got [here] at ¼ past 1.

Had a talk with Eric Drummond upon certain matters here one of which is the question of my Allowances on which the Government at home charge income tax. I have protested against that and he tells me he thinks it will be settled in my favour and that no income tax will be charged. I do not in the least mind expending all the money that I get here but I strongly object to spending money on one's own entertaining which after all is National business.

Luncheon, besides people in the House, Marquise de Polignac, Madame Roger, Madame de Janze, Mr. & Mrs. Bliss, M. De Sillac. Quite an amusing luncheon. Madame de Polignac is an American.

After luncheon Sevastopoulo came in looking more dismal than ever. Poor wretch he has got every reason to be so. He talked very freely about Kerensky who he says [is] a very common sort of man but talks quite sensibly and is evidently very much sobered by his experiences. He still thinks he could be made use of in Russia where his presence might have some effect. Personally I do not think anything would do any good. I doubt now whether the Japanese would be ready to intervene, or at all events if they did intervene, to go any distance which would be of use and all this thanks to the American President who gets a reputation for wisdom which I am certain will not be justified when history comes to be written.

The Naval Attaché tells me that of the Black Sea fleet the Russians have sunk one Dreadnought and 6 Destroyers but the Germans have got the newest and best Dreadnought and 6 destroyers which might make things very awkward in the Mediterranean.

After luncheon, Macdonogh, Director General of Military Intelligence, came to see me. Had a long talk with him. He says that he sees no hope now of getting Austria out thanks to our having adopted the policy of supporting the Czecho-Slovaks and Yugo-Slavs. On the other hand he has great hopes that it might be possible to get the Bulgarians out. He believes the only way to do it would be to make a Central Macedonian State which would mean taking away something from Turkey, Greece, Bulgaria and Serbia and placing that under a Government of its own, but guaranteed by the Allies. He says that the Bulgarians he knows would be absolutely ready to accept that in the terms of Peace. Once Bulgaria was out Turkey would go out too as they are very much afraid of the Bulgarians. He says that the present policy with regard to the Yugo-Slavs is not the policy of the War Office but is the policy dictated by Northcliffe's lieutenants, Steed[1] and Co. who are bitterly anti-Bulgarian and are doing everything they can to prevent us coming to terms with Bulgaria. It really is criminal that perhaps the fate of our country should be decided by such men.

We also talked about propaganda work. It is very difficult to get anything done as Beaverbrook, though inclined himself to make an alteration, is very much in the hands of Arnold Bennett[2] and I do not think I shall get any move on till I have been home myself and discussed the question with them.

Dinner. Loucheur, General Guillaumat, the Governor of Paris who was recently at Salonika, and Alfred Capus[3] the academician, with Grahame and Capel. Loucheur is supposed to be extremely silent but he certainly was not so at Dinner and very communicative. He told us all he was a great friend of Albert Thomas and also that Briand was his greatest friend and had been staying with him Saturday to Monday. It only the more confirms my view that he is trying to keep in with both sides. I must say with regard to Albert Thomas he spoke only of him as having been his first Chief and having done marvellous work in Munitions. He did say however it was impossible to forgive his attitude to Painlevé when the latter was Prime Minister.[4] He behaved abominably. After Dinner we sat out under the umbrella and Guillaumat was most interesting on the subject of Macedonia and Greece. He says that the people of Athens are certainly pro-Constantine, not because they particularly like him, though they liked her, but they liked having the Court which brought a lot of money to them. Now there is nothing of the kind at all but the King[5] is quite a nice sort of man, not very intelligent and certainly not prepared to take any action. He said quite openly the other day "It does not in the least matter to me which way the War goes. If the Allies win they will give me what I want. On the other hand if the Germans win they will give my father what he wants, and we both want the same." Guillaumat further says that Venizelos[6] is gradually getting complete hold of the country and that the recent successes of the Greek troops did a lot of good. He is far more anxious about the Serbians and said that only a few months ago there was a time when he believed at any moment the whole of the Serbian Army might have gone over to the other side. The Crown Prince is querulous and no good. He thinks however things are rather better now and the Greeks having come in has made the Serbians more ready to fight as they realise that if they don't fight part of their country will be given up to the Greeks. Guillaumat is strongly in favour of an offensive. On the other hand I hear Hereward Wake,[7] who was sent out there on behalf of our War Office to enquire, has come back dead against any offensive as he says that no offensive would be possible there. I somehow would back Guillaumat's opinion especially as he says that he knew that the Bulgarians would willingly lay down their arms if only they could get anything approaching decent terms. He is very full of praise for our Army but says what I know only too well and that is it is absolutely decimated by malaria.[8] We stayed up till quite late and altogether I think Arthur Balfour enjoyed himself and was very much interested.

At the Supreme War Council today they seem to have got through their business very well and they have sent a very long telegram to President Wilson which gave the unfortunate Chancery here a terrible time. They began to Cipher the telegram at 6 o'c and did not finish till 1 o'c in the morning which was very hard on them. I hope the telegram will move Wilson but I am afraid not and if he delays even another week goodbye to any success in Siberia.

Notes to 2 July

1. Henry Wickham Steed (1871–1956). Foreign Editor of *The Times* since 1914. Editor, 1919.
2. Arnold Bennett (1867–1931). Novelist and playwright. During the war he served under Beaverbrook at the Ministry of Information and wrote powerful articles describing conditions at the front.
3. Alfred Capus (1857–1922). Journalist and playwright. Editor-in-chief, *Le Figaro*.
4. Thomas's Socialist Party refused to support Painlevé's ministry in September 1917. As a result, Painlevé's proved to be the weakest government of wartime France and the only one which fell as a result of an adverse vote in the Chamber of Deputies.
5. Alexander (1893–1920). King of Greece from 1917. He died from blood-poisoning after being bitten by his pet monkey.

[82]

6. Eleutherios Venizelos (1864–1936). Pro-Entente Prime Minister of Greece, 1917–20.
7. Lieutenant-Colonel Sir Hereward Wake (1876–1963). Made several tours of inspection to the Balkans in 1918 on behalf of the British government.
8. During the whole campaign ten times as many British soldiers entered hospital with malaria as with wounds from enemy action.

Wednesday, 3rd July

Had a talk with Eric Drummond on the subject of the President. He is a great believer in him and thinks he is a very clever far-seeing man. It is a view I confess I do not take but I hope he is correct.

Went round for a moment to see Haig. Think he was a little disturbed at the news. There has been pretty severe fighting and we have lost all that we gained on June 30th. I do not think he thinks it is the big attack but still it is rather awkward they should so very easily be able to take back all that we gained. Lloyd George came here before luncheon. We had a talk about several things. I can see he is very much anti-Clemenceau and it is not to be surprised at as both of them are men who like to be top dog. I think there will be a row this afternoon as apparently the change of Command in Salonika from Guillaumat who is decidedly a good man to Franchet d'Espérey who was unstuck for really bad work at the Chemin des Dames was done without any reference to our people at home and now he has received an order to take the offensive equally without any reference to our people at home and in direct contravention to what had been settled at the last Versailles Conference. It is rather interesting to me to think that at the meeting yesterday my prophecy has come correct. I warned Arthur Balfour and through him Lloyd George that they would find Tardieu a dangerous man to deal with. Yesterday he put forward a proposal dealing with our shipping and supplies from America and he said that it had been considered and accepted at Versailles. He was given the lie direct by both Bliss the American and Sackville West. I hear Lloyd George went for him. He was so hopelessly in the wrong that Clemenceau could not stick up for him for a minute. All this makes me think that the feeling between the two Governments is going to be a little strained.

Lloyd George stayed for luncheon and was in very good form. Nobody else here except people in the House which now include Betty Cranborne and Macdonogh. We did not discuss politics at all but various other matters of Home affairs. I see that Lloyd George is very anti-George Curzon. I asked him about the Dinner and he told me he did not think any man could offer a bigger insult to colleagues than George Curzon did by not asking their wives and if it had not been for the Colonial Premiers being there he would not have stayed. Luncheon was very amusing but it was a general talk upon old days in the House of Commons etc. They recalled an incident which I had completely forgotten, of days when I was a Whip. Arthur Balfour was taking the Education Bill through the House of Commons and Bryce[1] was talking and I was sent across to Lloyd George who was fighting the Bill, from Arthur Balfour, to say that he (A.J.B.) would give any amendment that Lloyd George wanted if he would only guarantee Bryce not speaking again. Lloyd George said he thoroughly appreciated A.J.B.'s feelings on that occasion.

It is rather interesting to note the complete revulsion of feeling there is now with regard to ourselves. The French people see that they are overdoing it with the Americans and are afraid we may be hurt and they are therefore doing everything they can now to bring us into this show tomorrow. Haig told me Pershing told him that he was absolutely fed up with the French and his only wish was to get back close to us to co-operate with us.

Afternoon. Charlie and I, with the Military Attaché and Naval Attaché, went to the presentation by Sir Robert Borden of a French Canadian Hospital to the French Government. The President was there to receive it. I must say he is a most insignificant man with rather an evil face and I can quite understand his not awakening any enthusiasm. The Hospital is a very good one but they have selected a site which is next door to one of the anti-aircraft batteries which does not seem a very wise thing to have done. Borden seems in great form. He tells me recruits are coming in splendidly. He is sending 18,000 across this month and will send 20,000 next.

Simon Lovat arrived before Dinner. Arthur Balfour and Co. did not get back till past 8.30. The only other people dining were the Edouard Rothschilds and Borden and Mr. Philippe Roy the High Commissioner in France for Canada. Not a particularly amusing Dinner. When we went to bed I went to talk to Arthur Balfour and found out what had gone on at the Conference. Apparently there had been not only one but many breezes and Lloyd George had been rather offensive to Clemenceau and Clemenceau had more than got his own back on the subject of Salonika Command. The result of all this however is that they settled nothing and have got to meet again today.[2] I was horrified to find that L.G. was contemplating telling Clemenceau he ought to take Albert Thomas into his Cabinet. A.J.B. asked me if I did not agree with him that Clemenceau would very much resent this. Of course he would. It is exactly the same as telling Lloyd George that he ought to take Henderson[3] back into his. I am afraid there is no doubt there is rather bitter feeling between Clemenceau and Lloyd George and what astonished me more than anything else was to hear from Arthur Balfour that although he has never seen him President Wilson cannot bear Lloyd George either and that House[4] when he was over, and who really represents the President, disliked him enormously. It is not a very happy augury for a Peace Conference if you have our Prime Minister disliked by President Wilson and by Clemenceau.

I told Arthur Balfour something that I had heard privately and which I think requires investigation. It appears that Prince Sixte[5] has been in Spain and whilst there received letters in which it is said he received definite terms of Peace from the Emperor of Austria. He showed them to the King of Spain and went straight off to the King of the Belgians. He passed through Paris but naturally after what happened before he was not going to see Clemenceau or tell any of the Government about this letter. He has communicated the terms under the seal of secrecy, solely to the King of the Belgians. I further have heard that the King of the Belgians is weakening very much on the War, hence the reason of his getting rid of Brockfield.[6] I think it is quite possible that some sort of talk is going on between Austria and Belgium.

Notes to 3 July

1. James Bryce (1838–1922). Viscount Bryce, 1914. Liberal Cabinet minister under Gladstone, Rosebery and Campbell-Bannerman.
2. See Roskill, *Hankey*, vol. 1, pp. 569–70.
3. Arthur Henderson (1863–1935). Labour member of the War Cabinet, December 1916–August 1917.
4. Colonel Edward House (1856–1938). Special representative of the United States at the Supreme War Council (1917) and in the Armistice negotiations (1918).
5. Prince Sixte of Bourbon. Brother-in-law of Emperor of Austria. Acted as intermediary during 1917 peace talks.
6. Possibly Charles de Broqueville (1860–1940). Belgian Prime Minister, 1911–June 1918.

Thursday, 4th July

Went to the naming of the Rue President Wilson. Not an extremely impressive ceremony. Several very long speeches but the allusions in almost all of them to England being particularly well received which was satisfactory. There were two regiments of Americans. First a very strong regiment and a fine lot of men. The second was the American Battalion which had done so well at Chateau Thierry. They equally were a very fine lot but you saw how decimated they had been in that last fight where they certainly saved the situation together with the French dismounted cavalry.

All the Colonial Premiers were there but their arrangements have been very tactlessly made. In the first place L.G. has taken Hughes[1] with him and ignored the rest who live in Paris. Then nothing was done about their going to this Ceremony but luckily I had some spare tickets and got them to them last night. Townroe is attached to the New Zealanders, Sir Joseph Ward[2] and Massey.[3] He came round to see me and he is very distressed this morning as Massey had been ordered to go to Versailles to meet Foch at 9 o'c and Sir Joseph who has been with him was ignored. Nobody had taken the trouble to ask Ward to go as well as Massey and they never let them know that the meeting had been postponed till 3 o'c this afternoon. However I was able to put everything all right.

I am sure the more I see of the President the more unsympathetic he appears to be. He never smiles and his greeting to everybody is frigid in the extreme.

Went to the American Chamber of Commerce to luncheon. Very hot and lengthy affair but from the point of view of England most successful. Every one of the speakers made a very nice allusion to England and an allusion to myself was extraordinarily well received. The last speech was made by Sharp who frankly announced that he was not going to speak of anything except England and England's part in the War. He was really most enthusiastic about us and was extraordinarily well received. The result was in the end I had to get up and say a few words which I think went all right but it was rather a trying ordeal. Tardieu's speech was a lamentable failure, although speaking as he did a few words in English at the end he was much applauded for that and it is really remarkable. He spoke very well and he did not know a word of English a year ago.

Dined in the evening with the Duchesse de la Tremouille. Quite a small dinner. Marie Murat, Biches de Castellans, Berckheims, Jules Cambon and two men whom I know but whose names I can't remember. Very pleasant. Got back fairly early and then had long discussion with Arthur Balfour and Eric Drummond on Bulgarian question. The whole question of attempting to eliminate Bulgaria from the War is to be discussed by two representatives of England, France and Italy. I am anyhow to be one of the English representatives. The question is whether I should be the principal one assisted by some junior Foreign Office official, or whether Bob Cecil should come out and be the British representative with me in attendance. I am strongly in favour of the latter course. I know nothing of the ins and outs of the Bulgarian situation whereas he has made a special study of it, and after hearing all I had to say Arthur Balfour was entirely of my opinion. Bob Cecil therefore is to be asked to come out as soon as possible but I am afraid that he will not be able to do so next week in which case I shall have to postpone coming home until after he has been out and finished. I do not think it would take more than a couple of days, perhaps not that.

Looking back on the day the more I think of it the more impressed I am with the good feeling of America towards England as represented by Americans out here and this 4th July meant to be a glorification of French and American unity has I think turned out to be one of Anglo-American.

Notes to 4 July

1. William Morris Hughes (1862–1952). Australian Prime Minister, 1915–23.
2. Sir Joseph Ward (1856–1930). Prime Minister of New Zealand, 1906–12. He returned to office in 1915 in coalition with his opponent, W. F. Massey.
3. William Ferguson Massey (1856–1925). Prime Minister of New Zealand, 1912–25.

Friday, 5th July

Saw Mr. Lorenzo Kihlman, the unofficial representative of the Finnish Government here who laid before me his views on the political situation in Finland.[1] Sent a despatch to London in following terms.

I think it right to say in the beginning that he seems to have had very little recent information or instructions from that Country, his last telegram from there being dated the 21st May and I should doubt his having any real authority to speak for that country, at all events at the present moment. He is however very friendly disposed towards the Entente and is proceeding to Finland next week and hopes to be able to influence that Country to a better understanding with the Entente.

The last telegram he received, that of the 21st May, assured him that the one wish of the Finland Government was to maintain strict neutrality and he is convinced that the presence of German soldiers is accounted for simply by the fact that they have been admitted with a view to defending Finland against the Bolshevik Government, and if Finland could be assured by the Entente of its independence the Government of that country would have no hesitation in asking the Germans to withdraw their troops. He admitted however in answer to a question of mine that although the Finnish Government might ask them to withdraw it was extremely unlikely they would do so, but he thinks that the mere fact of a request being made would make the Germans hesitate before taking any extreme action.

He observed that France is the only Country that has recognised the independence of Finland and has accepted its Government.

He is anxious to receive assurances on certain points as follows:—

(1) If the Germans remove their troops from Finland will England and the United States recognise the independence of Finland? He pointed out to me that if it were known in Finland that the sole obstacle to their recognition by England and the United States was the presence of German troops it would create a strong revulsion of feeling against the latter.

(2) In the event of the German troops being withdrawn would the Entente be prepared to send a force, which he thought should be from about 20 to 30,000 men to be landed at Alexandrowsk, remain there and only advance if called upon by the Finnish Government to assist them in fighting the Bolsheviks.

(3) Would the Entente be prepared to give provisions, both of food and War material, to the Finnish Government always presupposing that the German Force was withdrawn?

I was very careful to express no opinion on the subject except to say that it seemed to me that what he was asking us to do was to replace German troops by Entente troops and I asked him whether he felt certain that that was a change which would be agreeable to his Country, but I could get no definite answer out of him.

He is passing through London next week on his way to Finland and it might be advisable for somebody in authority to see him, but my personal opinion is that he has no real knowledge of the intentions of his Government and even if such assurances as he asks for were given I do not think it would mean either the evacuation of the Country by German troops or the securing of the good-will of the Finnish Government.

Lunch. Italian Ambassador and his wife. Klotz's, Danish Minister and Mme Vidal (she was Mme Venandré), Leygues, the Minister of Marine, and M. Desbordes a most amusing man. Vidal told me he was just back from Spain. That the feeling there is not very nice for us but is equally not very nice for the Germans. It is really entirely pro-Spanish. He had had a talk with the German Ambassador who was an old friend of his and who was stupefied at all he told him with regard to the position of the Entente. Vidal thinks that they get absolutely no information at all except cooked information which is made as favourable to them as possible. He also talked to the Austrian Ambassador and he said he had only one sentiment and that was absolute hatred of the Germans.

Had a meeting of the Board which ought to have been held on Wednesday. Nothing of very great interest.

Had a few words with Capel who tells me he spoke to Clemenceau on the subject of our little disagreement. Clemenceau assured him that it was really meant as chaff and that there was nothing behind it at all. He has not the least objection to my seeing whoever I like and that he has the friendliest possible feelings towards me. Clemenceau talked to him very fully about the Versailles Conference and said that he and Lloyd George had quite made it up at the end. He said to Lloyd George "Well it does not matter our quarrelling as it only leaves us better friends afterwards". I must say I think the air has been cleared and Clemenceau recognises that he cannot do things without consulting us.

I shall be curious to see what the English papers think of Wilson's speech.[2] To my mind it is utter twaddle from end to end.

Simon Lovat and I dined alone together. He tells me Ross is back again at Struy but he does not think he will be fit to go on the Hill and he is rather at his wits' end to know what to do about it. At the present moment his idea is to bring Macdonald down to Struy, if he is unable to let Braulen as he has been up to the present moment. Capel goes home on Sunday and Simon thinks they will be married almost directly and honeymoon at Struy.

Notes to 5 July

1. After the Russian Revolution the Finns declared their independence. Following a five-month civil war in 1918, right-wing forces emerged victorious.
2. In an address at the grave of George Washington on 4 July 1918, Wilson spoke of war aims in the most general and idealistic terms, calling for the 'settlement of every question ... upon the basis of the free acceptance of that settlement by the people immediately concerned, and not upon the basis of the material interest or advantage of any other nation or people which may desire a different settlement for the sake of its own exterior influence or mastery'.

Saturday, 6th July

Luncheon given by Les Amis de France. A very dull affair although there were interesting people there. Luckily no talking. The people there were M. Barrès,[1] M. Claveille, M. Doumer,[2] M. Leon Bourgeois,[3] Marquis de Pommeren, Mr. Carter, Mr. Bliss, M. Sembat.[4] There are several that I wanted to know and I shall now be able to get them to come quietly here to luncheon. Barrès struck me as far the most intelligent of the lot.

Du Cane came to see me. Tells me the French are very disturbed about the last Supreme War Council. Nothing of any importance was discussed and the whole thing resolved itself into bickering on minor points. Lloyd George is evidently rather jealous of Clemenceau's position and is determined to have a scrap with him but I think came off rather second best, though at the same time sounded a note of warning to Clemenceau that he must not try and get hold of everything. I think there is a great deal of soreness in Pétain's camp. Foch, but of course it is Clemenceau, has just dismissed Anthoine[5] who was his Chief of the Staff at a moment's notice. I asked Clavet today, whom I sat next to at luncheon what the reason was. He told me that Anthoine had been indulging in défaitist talk. Lloyd George is trying to set Versailles on its legs again. Clemenceau is quite determined to destroy it and there is no doubt as long as they have such Generals as they have got now to represent the various Nations it is not going to count much. Sackville-West is very nice but of course only a very inferior General who a year ago was Commanding a Brigade which he did admirably, but he cannot be placed on the same par with Foch, Haig etc and if Versailles is to be any use the Generals there must be absolutely in the top rank.

Notes to 6 July

1. Maurice Barrès (1862–1923). Isolated independent figure in the French Chamber. He was prominent in the 1917 campaign against Caillaux which helped bring Clemenceau to power.
2. Paul Doumer (1857–1932). Senator for Corsica, 1912–31; President of the Republic, 1931–32.
3. Léon Bourgeois (1851–1925). Twelve times a minister and once Prime Minister. Minister of State under Painlevé, September–November 1917. Early advocate of a League of Nations.
4. Marcel Sembat (1862–1922). Socialist Minister of Public Works under Viviani and Briand, August 1914–December 1916.
5. General François Anthoine (1860–1934). Commander, French First Army; Chief of Staff to Pétain.

Sunday, 7th July

PARIS

Saw Mr. Edwards who is going on Bulgarian Propaganda work to Switzerland. Has been some awful muddle about him as he got a telegram supposed to have come from me to say I wanted to see him and he was to come out immediately. I never sent such a telegram and am having matter cleared up.

Went to Church in the morning to attend the special Service to celebrate the Silver Wedding of the King and Queen. Band of the 50th Division played and I thought very indifferently.

Went to luncheon at the Café Selecte, a very pretty little café close by the Seine on the opposite side to St. Cloud. Luncheon given by the Neuflizes. Sackville-West, Cazalet,[1] Mme de Montesquieu the only other guests.

In the evening dined with M. and Mme DuPuy[2] at Versailles. A delightful house with a very nice garden. She is an American. He owns the *Petit Parisien*, probably the most read newspaper in France, a sort of *Daily Mail*. He is very friendly towards the English. The old father[3] who really started the paper was there. He has been a great man in his time. A Senator and has been a Minister. Is a tremendous Radical and looks rather askance at some of his son's friends.

Notes to 7 July

1. Victor Cazalet (1896–1943). On staff of Supreme War Council.
2. Paul DuPuy (1878–1927). Deputy and later Senator.
3. Jean DuPuy (1844–1919). Proprietor of the *Petit Parisien*.

Monday, 8th July

Very hot day. Nothing much in the morning except routine work. Lady Rodney came to luncheon.

After luncheon General Belin, the French Military Representative at Versailles came to see me. We talked over the forthcoming Conference on the Bulgarians. He of course is very keen indeed for the offensive.

Later Lytton came and we discussed the question of managing Propaganda work here. He is very sound but I foresee difficulties at G.H.Q.

where for some unearthly reason they have put in Onslow who knows nothing whatever about the work, to be the head of the whole of the Propaganda work with Alex Russell to look after him to see that he does not make any military mistake. The consequence is that if anything is required to be done it has to go through about 10 different hands. Lytton and I discussed possible ways of reconstituting the work and he is going to give me his views before I go home.

In the evening dined at the Cercle de l'Union which is the Diplomatic Club. About 40 present. Quite pleasant. The Italian Ambassador and myself were the guests of Honour. There was a storm. The first rain that I have seen for weeks.

Tuesday, 9th July

Went out early to Versailles to see Sackville-West and discussed with him our Bulgarian meeting. I cannot see that our discussion can end in anything decisive as nobody has the least idea of what they want and there is no settled Bulgarian policy. It does seem to me that after nearly 4 years of War we ought to attempt to have some idea as to what our War aims are in some part of the world. At present we have none.

Luncheon with the Biches de Castellane. A funny mixed Party. Dolly de Castellane, Mme Donnet and her daughter. Franklin Bouillon who is bitterly anti-Clemenceau, Géraud who is the chief writer of the *Echo de Paris*, and D'Aubigny[1] & Chenix. Quite an interesting luncheon. Franklin Bouillon very strong on the subject of Russia and very hot discussion with Dolly de Castellane, she of course wanting the Monarchy to be restored, but on the other hand very vague as to what he really wanted, but anything sooner than a Monarchy.

D'Aubigny is a deputy and is a man who has probably done more for aviation than most people in this country. He is madly enthusiastic about Trenchard whom he thinks and rightly too, one of the finest characters he has ever come across. Haig wants to get him back but does not like to ask for him.[2] I wish he would harden his heart and do so because there is no doubt our Air Service now is not as good as it was 6 months ago under Trenchard. He has got the extraordinary personal faculty of leading men and they would do 10 times more for him than they would do for anybody else.

Chenix is one of the principal people on the *Journal des Débats*.

Evening Pennoyers dined. Also Neville Lytton. Pennoyers may come to stay here as they cannot get a room at the Ritz with any windows in it. Impossible for the people there to repair the windows at the back owing to lack of glass.

Notes to 9 July

1. Albert D'Aubigny (1875–1945). Deputy for the Sarthe, 1905–06 and 1914–24. Member of several wartime parliamentary commissions.
2. Trenchard had resigned as Chief of the Air Staff following disagreements with the Air Secretary, Lord Rothermere.

Wednesday, 10th July

Usual meeting of the Board. Nothing very much to settle. Humphrey de Trafford[1] came to luncheon. In the afternoon saw Maclagan [with] reference to Propaganda work. He is certainly doing well here but the system is bad.

Bob Cecil and his Secretary arrived about 6 o'c.

In the evening Madame Aunay and her daughter dined. Just ourselves. Very pleasant. Girl is most attractive and knows everything that is going on in politics. The mother also who was an American and who is very much in Clemenceau's confidence also talked freely and it was rather interesting to hear her views on various politicians. Of course intense hatred of Briand and of Painlevé although perhaps in his case it is more one of contempt. They ascribe Painlevé's failure very much to his Military Chef de Cabinet, Helbrounner who they say was a most intriguing man which I can quite believe and in addition being a Jew they all hated him. I asked her opinion of the two men who I think are going to be big men in the future — Tardieu and Loucheur. This is roughly her opinion of both with the interstices filled in by the daughter who as I say knows more about politics and politicians than her mother.

Tardieu a very clever man. Probably hostile to England. Made a certain success in America but was detested by President Wilson. Is evidently only in Office to keep his mouth shut. Most conceited but quite honest and hopes to be the Prime Minister after the War. He is of the bourgeois class but in every way respectable.

Loucheur quite different. Very clever. Very rich having made his money by rather questionable means owing to his owning great factories to which as Minister of Armament he has given big orders. (Personally I believe this to be quite untrue. He happened to have big factories which have come into full employment and therefore he has made money). Quite of the lowest type but endeavouring to imagine he is a gentleman. Has bought Madame du Barry's[2] place and it is a great joke Madame Loucheur who is a most common type of woman living there and imagining she is the same type as Madame du Barry. To continue, Loucheur very crafty and scheming, buying up any number of papers and determined to be either President of the Republic or else Prime Minister. Has got an enormous popularity in the Country chiefly due to the fact that as Minister of Armament he settles the rate of wages and whenever there is a demand for more wages he not only gives them but gives more than is asked for. Altogether the impression given was of a clever and most unscrupulous man which is rather the impression I had gained of him as soon as ever I came here. In my opinion however he is a very gentlemanly fellow, very pleasant and his unscrupulousness only goes to the extent of advancing himself and not of enriching himself.

They were very amusing talking about other people. Dolly de Castellane was evidently Madame Aunay's pet aversion. She summed her up rather well. She said she would be an extremely dangerous woman if she did not talk French with a German accent. She declares she is a pure pacifist. The Poincarés of course they both hate and told many amusing stories about Madame Poincaré. They were so ashamed of her when the King and Queen were here just before the War, and when Madame Poincaré arrived at the Gala performance at the Opera without gloves and then told the Queen that of course now in Paris nobody wore gloves. I tried to draw her about Albert Thomas but I could not get a word out of her and I feel that although he and Clemenceau are bitterly opposed that the latter would like if possible to get him into the Government, but the daughter said, talking of Clemenceau's opinion of the Socialists, he did not mean to give way one inch to them. If they liked to turn him out they might but he would not buy them by concessions. Madame Aunay began to talk of Mrs. Spiers whom she had only just met and one could see that she did not like her. I am afraid therefore Spiers' days of usefulness with Clemenceau are quite numbered but I am sure the Government at home would make a great mistake if they changed him as although Clemenceau is now rather anti-Spiers he still gets most valuable information.

Altogether a most pleasant dinner and Madame Aunay is amusing and most talkative and the daughter is really very witty. Madame Aunay was bitter in the extreme against Franklin Bouillon. We had met him the previous day at luncheon, talking of him as vulgar etc. Of course he has behaved very badly about Clemenceau and attacked him in every way that he could indirectly and I agree with her that he is a vulgar sort of fellow. He is a great friend of Lloyd George's but I think simply and solely because he can talk English perfectly.

Notes to 10 July

1. Sir Humphrey de Trafford (1862–1929). Horse breeder.
2. Marie Du Barry (1743–93). Dressmaker's daughter who became the mistress of Louis XV.

Thursday, 11th July

Went out with Bob Cecil to Versailles to talk over with Sackville-West the line of action to be taken at our Conference in the afternoon. We are in entire agreement. Came back to luncheon. We had a curious mixed Party. Princesse Marie Murat, Painlevé who is being most bitterly and I think unjustly attacked at the present moment and who looks very worried. The Berthelots,[1] she quite a nice woman. I did not like him but he is a power in the land. He was Chef de Cabinet to Briand and has a position in the Foreign Office under Pichon. He is credited and I believe rightly with being very anti-English. Favre,[2] Under-Secretary to Pams at the Ministry of the Interior, a very nice fellow indeed, not particularly clever but extremely friendly in every way. Arthur Meyer the Chief man on the *Gaulois*. He is an old Jew very clever and amusing and equally most friendly, and Madame Sancay. I was rather afraid at the beginning it was going to be a frost as it was a meeting of every sort and kind of opinion but it went very well indeed but although Bob Cecil and I had to leave at 2.30 they stayed on till well after 3 o'c.

Went to Versailles to discuss what action should be taken about Bulgaria. A lot of talk. All one can say is that no harm can be done by our decision.

In the evening Moucher and Eddy dined and Simon Lovat.

Notes to 11 July

1. Philippe Berthelot (1866–1934). Enjoyed particular influence under Briand to whom he was Chef de Cabinet. When in June 1918 de Margerie collapsed from overwork, he became acting Directeur Politique at the Quai d'Orsay.
2. Albert Favre. Under-Secretary of State at the Ministry of the Interior — his only ministerial appointment.

Friday, 12th July

Bob Cecil left en route to England going to see Bobberty on the way. He is very unfavourably impressed with Versailles and with all the Military representatives. Certainly they did not come out very brilliantly yesterday but I think ours were probably the best of the lot. There is no doubt Clemenceau means to kill Versailles but he cannot do it openly so he is really letting it die of stagnation. What they ought to create there is simply a secretariat of all the different nations but unless they put better men in it is ridiculous that they should be asked to consider questions of the utmost importance. Nobody could be nicer than Sackville West but military decisions arrived at by him would carry no weight whatever in the Army. Bliss the American is by far the best of the others and is I think an extremely capable man whose opinion carries great weight with the President so that I am quite sure that the latter would not allow Versailles to go under altogether. Of course if we could really have a first class man like Maurice there as I originally suggested it might do a great deal of good especially as Maurice is the one Staff Officer that the French people always respected. Foch told me that he was by far the best Staff fellow on our side that he had come across.

Sir Charles Ellis came to see me on the subject of the new system for the payment of accounts here. The Treasury are rather stupid about it and I do not wonder at Ministers here being sometimes rather angry. Klotz proposes a scheme and they do not take the trouble to answer him, they just send a little memorandum to me to say that they think it is not feasible.

Afterwards Delmé-Radcliffe came to see me on his way to London. He gives a very glowing account of the Italians. Says they fought very well and if only they had had a few more Divisions could have made a big thing of it. As it is they got 25,000 prisoners and on the two days when they had the Austrians penned in with the river behind them and practically no bridges they killed an enormous number. He thinks the Austrians certainly lost 150,000 and probably 180,000. The Italians are perfectly secure there now unless the Germans come down and then the very idea of that makes them tremble.[1]

He said Frank was really very seedy indeed and he does not understand his not coming home and he is not likely to get fit unless he does come back for a bit. After luncheon which we had alone Sir John Pilter came to see me to explain what he was doing in the way of getting poor people out of Paris. It is almost an impossibility to move them and some of them are too old really to move but I do not know what will happen if there comes a sudden exodus. However we have done our best and if they won't go they won't, and I think all arrangements are in order.

Had an interview with the Serbian Minister as reported in the following letter which I sent to Mr. Balfour:— "Serbian Minister came to see me today to tell me certain things which he impressed upon me were quite unofficial but of course with the intention that they should be reported to you. He is not a bad fellow but of course is obsessed with hatred of Montenegro. He came to complain of the King having given honours to Montenegrin Ministers and said it would have a very bad effect on the Yugo-Slavs as they all knew that the Montenegrin King and his Government were pro-Austrian and anti-Yugo-Slav. I had expected this visit because I heard he was angry about it and there is nothing he will not do against the Montenegrins. I shut him up as quickly as I could by telling him that I noted what he said but that I thought it was not proper for the Minister of one Nation to call into question my King giving honours to anybody he pleased. Montenegro was an Ally and therefore there was no justification for his protest. He then went into a long dissertation on the subject of the past and future of Montenegro telling me that Montenegro was entirely Serbian and that whatever happened the people were quite determined to be united with Serbia and under one King. I let him have his say and said nothing. He then launched into another subject and that was at this Ceremony next Sunday when the Conseil Municipale is to change the name of the Avenue de L'Alma into Avenue George V that he knew that some of them would expect English honours to be given and he hoped I was prepared for that. That made me very angry and I told him that I thought that was no business of anybody else's, though I was sure he had meant it in a friendly spirit, that I was not prepared to receive any such suggestions from other Ministers. I was quite civil with him and we parted inviting each other to Dinner but I do not think he will try that sort of thing again. I think there is perhaps a good bit in what he says and it may be necessary to give some decoration but between ourselves I have written in the strictest confidence to Stamfordham[2] to know whether there is any chance of the King coming out here as I think it would be extraordinary good propaganda if he could just come to Paris for the day and be present at some sort of Christening Function. Then would be the moment to give the decoration. I may perhaps have to telegraph to you about it after consulting with Grahame."

The Italian Ambassador came in to see me with regard to Sunday's function. Sharp will be away but he asked whether I agreed to the Japanese Ambassador answering for all of us. I was only too delighted he should do so. I spoke to him about Honours and Decorations for the Paris Officials. He has heard nothing from his Government on the subject. He is going to consider the matter and we have agreed to work in concert together. Afterwards had a meeting with Thornton, Allen, Sir Charles Ellis and Grahame on the subject of the train service between Havre and Paris in connection with the boat. Decided to leave it to Thornton to approach Claveille. I am going to speak to Pichon this evening on the subject as the present arrangement is most unsatisfactory.

Afterwards Sir Hugh Bell[3] who is over here on Iron and Coal business came to see me though only just to pay me a formal call.

Dinner. Had practically the Versailles lot. Neuflizes, Montesquieus, etc. Played cards afterwards. First time I have played since I have been out here. A very mild game.

Notes to 12 July

1. The Italians began a counter-offensive on the Piave on 2 July.
2. Arthur Bigge (1849–1931). Baron Stamfordham, 1911. Private Secretary to George V, 1910–31.
3. Sir Hugh Bell (1844–1931). Ironmaster and colliery owner.

Saturday, 13th July

Had a long talk with Spiers who yesterday had an interview with Clemenceau. Clemenceau has treated him so badly that I have to take what he says now with a grain of salt but with that grain the interview could not have been a very pleasant one. Clemenceau is very bitter against the English. He says that everything he proposes is turned down and he summed up the situation by saying "I have always wished to treat the English as friends and Allies. I can now only treat them as Allies" adding "I am glad to think that my relations with the Americans are quite different." There is no doubt that the old man is very cross at not being allowed to have entirely his own way in everything but it is rather disquieting to know that his animosity is so bitter against Lloyd George and Milner.

Clemenceau also spoke to Spiers about our meeting at Versailles the other day and he said Pichon was much impressed by Bob Cecil's ignorance of the Balkan question which rather amuses me as the boot was on the other leg and the real cause of displeasure on the part of the French is that we declined to be led blindfold into an offensive. At the same time I do think that the Balkan question is in a very unsatisfactory condition and there seems to be no settled policy whatsoever. Until there is I do not see how we can offer any terms to Bulgaria without offending Serbia and Greece. I shall try and have a talk over this question when I get back to England.

After Spiers had gone invested Mr. Popovitch,[1] the Prime Minister of Montenegro with the G.B.E. He is a most voluble old gentleman who complains very bitterly of the way he has been treated by the French and I think he has good reason to complain as there is no doubt they insult him in every way. It is done at the instance of the Serbian Minister who is a very mean sort of fellow, married a rich American woman.

Luncheon. Pennoyers, Jack Seely[2] and his A.D.C. Prince Antoine D'Orleans, Sir Charles Ellis, Madame Sancay, Mme DuPuy, they are the people I dined with on Sunday; he is the owner of the *Petit Parisien*, and M. Boret,[3] the Food Minister here and one of the most efficient, if not the most efficient, members of the Government. Talks English well and a very nice man altogether.

Dr. Brock the new President of the Medical Board came to see me. Seems a very nice fellow. Says that so far the men coming up for examination are physically very unfit.

In the evening dined with the Italian Ambassador. Klotzs, Mme de Ludre, Comte and Comtesse Beaumont very nice people. Then a woman whose name I do not know but who is Mr. Lionel Rothschild's mother. Quite pleasant. Nearly as ugly as her daughter.

Notes to 13 July

1. M. Popovitch. Montenegrin Prime Minister since June 1917. Also acted as Foreign Secretary.
2. John E. B. Seely (1868–1947). Baron Mottistone, 1933. Liberal MP for Ilkeston, 1910–22. Secretary of State for War 1912–14. Under-Secretary of State, Ministry of Munitions, June 1918–January 1919.
3. Victor Boret. Minister of Agriculture and Food, November 1917–January 1920.

Sunday, 14th July

Review at 9 o'c in the Avenue du Bois. Began by raining heavily but cleared up as the troops went by. A very good show indeed. Needless to say our troops looked much the best. A platoon of the Grenadiers, and one of the Coldstreams, Scots Guards and Irish Guards. A Company of the Black Watch, a company of the Queen's and a composite company made up of platoons from the Australians, Canadians, New Zealanders and South Africans. The Band of the Grenadiers with them. They were quite the smartest and excellent physique and of the others the Polish and Czecho-Slavs were really a very fine lot of men. Had a few minutes talk with Clemenceau but talked of nothing of any consequence.

In the afternoon attended the formal meeting when the Conseil Municipale ratified the change of the names of the various streets. The Avenue de L'Alma is to become Avenue Georges V. The French people have absolutely no idea of how to arrange these things. We first of all had to sign our names in a book. One hundred people in a stuffy little room. Then we went into the big Hall and there standing up in the crowd with everybody pushing against one we had to listen to a lot of speeches. The only good one was Pichon's which really was first class and was most enthusiastically applauded. Sharp being away the Japanese Ambassador answered on behalf of all of us. I found myself next to Clemenceau and we had a most amusing talk. I said I was starting tomorrow for England and he began chaffing and saying "I suppose you will get back to England and talk of those damned Frenchmen. That is what many of your colleagues do" and he then went on to say "If I give you a Commission in England will you carry it out" and on my saying Yes, he said "I have got two. The first is to tell Lloyd George and Milner that they are quite mistaken in thinking that I want to interfere in their Home Affairs. I have not the least intention of doing it; nor have I the least intention of stopping what they are doing now, interfering in my own. They may do that as much as they like and the more of my work they wish to do for me the better I shall be pleased." All this was said in the most friendly and chaffing manner but like everything with Clemenceau there is something at the back of it and there is no doubt he is very resentful against Lloyd George and Milner. After he had finished I asked him what the second Commission was and of all things in the world it is to bring him back an Aberdeen Terrier. He has had one to which he was devoted and which died the day before yesterday and he says he cannot live without one. I will gladly do this for him though I cannot look forward with any great pleasure to bringing an Aberdeen Terrier out with me. I must say nothing could have been more friendly than he was to me.

Monday, 15th July

Left Paris 5.30a.m. Could distinctly hear the guns. Motored with Charlie to G.H.Q. where I just missed Haig. He was very doubtful as to whether I ought to cross to England but on the advice of Davidson[1] did so. Arrived in London that night. Dined with the Bears.

Notes to 15 July

1. John H. Davidson. Served on General Staff and as Director of Military Operations at British GHQ, 1914–18.

[NO DIARY FOR THE PERIOD OF LEAVE IN ENGLAND]

Thursday, 25th July

Left Charing Cross with Portia.[1] Victoria[2] and Mary[3] and Tortor Cadogan came to Station. Also Creedy.[4] At Folkestone met Fatty Cavan who had motored down early in the morning and just missed the early boat on the way back to Italy. Spent the crossing on the Bridge with the Captain who was very interesting having been in charge of a Seaplane Carrier in the Mediterranean and also in the North Sea, having been present at Jutland and elsewhere. Quite fine but it had been blowing hard and there were several mines loosed and had to change the course twice to avoid them.

Left Boulogne at 6 o'c in own Car. Had a splendid run and got in at 10.45 having missed the way twice.

Notes to 25 July

1. Lady Stanley, wife of Derby's son Edward. Christened Sybil, but always known as Portia.
2. Lady Victoria Stanley (1892–1927). Derby's daughter.
3. Mary Cadogan, sister of Lady Stanley.
4. Sir Herbert Creedy (1878–1973). Private Secretary to successive Secretaries of State for War, including Derby, 1913–20.

Friday, 26th July

Ordinary routine work. Grahame is making very heavy weather about Le

Roy Lewis's mistake. He has got the Embassy into rather a trouble. I do not think it will take any time however to get that straight as far as the Embassy and myself are concerned but as far as Le Roy Lewis is concerned I do not think he will ever get over it and I think I shall have to make a change. However of course I should not do that immediately.

Edward suddenly turned up having received leave a day earlier than he expected. Looking extremely well but much thinner. We three had luncheon together.

Various people came to see me and at 5 o'c I went with Mr. Roy to present Canadian Journalists to the President who was much more gracious than I have ever seen him. He said something to me about my Liverpool speech[1] which apparently has given satisfaction.

Afterwards saw Pichon on various matters. Quite satisfactory. He also alluded to the Liverpool speech and was particularly nice. The only disagreeable thing was that he told me the Government were going to ask our Government for the recall of Le Roy Lewis but that Clemenceau would speak to me on the question.

Saw Spiers, Maclagan etc in the afternoon.

Clemenceau sent for his dog in the afternoon.

Just before Dinner Johnny Du Cane came in. He had burst his last tyre and run out of petrol so he stayed and dined. Humphrey de Trafford also came in. We had a very pleasant evening and sat talking till quite late about every sort of thing.

Notes to 26 July

1. Speaking in Liverpool on 22 July at his re-election as President of the Chamber of Commerce, Derby had stressed the improvement in Anglo-French understanding and ruled out the resumption of normal trading relations with Germany once the war was over.

Saturday, 27th July

Went at 10 o'c to see Clemenceau and had the most interesting interview I have ever had with him, or with any other man. He first of all began about the dog which has already made great friends with him. It is exactly like his old dog and curiously enough has got the same name. He is awfully pleased with the dog and it jumped on his bed and played with him this morning.

He then told me that he did not for the future mean to talk to me as if I was an Ambassador but as a friend and as Clemenceau to Derby. He relied on me not to repeat any of his confidences, other than those which I might tell him at the time I thought ought to be repeated to my Government. I will not therefore put down all that passed between us. We discussed the whole Military question and I must say that I am absolutely convinced that both Clemenceau and Foch have no ulterior motives whatever. Their one idea is to win the War and they are thinking just as much of our Front as they are of the French Front. Things are going very well. More German Divisions have been used than I had any idea of and even if there is a big push made against our Front it cannot have the same force that it would have done a month ago. There is clear proof that the Germans are getting short of men as they have been forced to break up 5 Divisions and draft the men into other Divisions. One German Division attacked the other day in which the average strength of the Companies engaged was only 40. Their losses therefore must be anything between 150 and 200,000 and the amount of Stores lost is enormous and in one dump alone — Johnny Du Cane told me last night — they found a million rounds of shell. To go back to Clemenceau he told me that he had heard from their Ambassador at Washington that the latter had had a conversation with the President and the President had told him that even if the German Peace offensive, which he thinks will begin immediately, included an offer to give back Belgium and Alsace and Lorraine on condition that Germany was given a free hand in Russia he would refuse to entertain the idea of Peace at that price. This is very satisfactory because it means that gradually he will be drawn into supporting a much bigger expedition to Siberia than is at the present moment contemplated.

At the close of our conversation Clemenceau turned to me and said he must ask for the dismissal of Le Roy Lewis. I told him that I took full responsibility for what had been done. That I had myself spoken to him on the subject. That we had been in close communication with regard to our arrangements with both the present and the last Governor of Paris and that his demand meant a censure on myself even if it did not mean an application for my recall. I asked him therefore not to press the request. He was quite charming — at once withdrew it and admitted that the letter was only a pretext which they had been looking for for some time in order to get rid of Le Roy Lewis. He told me that Le Roy Lewis and Spiers were both most unpopular and unsympathetic to him and as long as they remain it would be perfectly impossible for him to give them any of the very secret information which he felt he ought to give but which he knew if given to them would be freely talked about. We had a long discussion on the subject and it was left at this that he begged me to realise that in keeping Spiers and Le Roy Lewis we were keeping two men who were repugnant to him and to the Military Authorities — I know this to be true — and therefore were of no use to us and that for my own sake and the sake of my country I should see my way to make a change. Nothing could have been nicer or kinder than he was and we parted the very best of friends. This trouble is rather serious because I know in my heart of hearts that Clemenceau is right and that with the bitter feeling there is in the Army against both Spiers and Le Roy Lewis we are being kept out of much information which we ought to have. At the same time I cannot stand the idea of being dictated to by the French as to whom we should or should not have as our representatives. They would be the first to resent it if we played the game with them. I am therefore writing to Milner to make a suggestion that there should be a clean sweep made. That the Military Attaché's Office should be made of more importance and indeed he should have both the Mission and his present work under him with good representatives to do the routine work in each place. This I think would work satisfactorily and of course if I was given my choice of a man for the post I should take Charlie Grant. Spiers and his wife came to luncheon with Edward, Portia and myself. Both of them very unhappy at Bennett-Goldney's death as he had been a sort of second father to Spiers.

In afternoon saw various people from office and did routine work.

Kermit Roosevelt[1] and his wife came to see me. They are going to dine with us tomorrow. Dinner in the evening. The Hartingtons and Humphrey de Trafford. Grahame left for London.

Notes to 27 July

1. Kermit Roosevelt (1889–1943). Son of Theodore Roosevelt. Businessman and explorer.

Sunday, 28th July

PARIS

Routine work in morning. Went to Versailles for luncheon. Neuflizes, Major and Mrs. Green, he is a leading Barrister who enlisted at the beginning of the War and is now Intelligence Officer at Versailles — very nice fellow. Agar-Robartes, Tommy Robartes'[1] brother, who is in the Grenadiers, a young French Cavalry Officer, de Vilaines, talks English perfectly and has been a good bit in London, Bullock, Portia, Edward and self.

Afterwards we all motored to St. Cloud. Not so many people there as usual. It was lovely and we set out there with the St. Aldegondes and others. They had great fun chaffing young Cazalet who is a good boy but none the worse for being rather ragged.

I forgot to mention that this morning (Sunday) General Burtchaell came to see me and we had a long talk about many things connected with the Medical Service both at home and abroad. He tells me that he is afraid that the Americans will practically absorb all credit for research in the near future. They have got any amount of money. They have got some of the best men employed upon it and they have facilities for putting results of their research before the public in a way which is infinitely superior to ours. He says they are a charming lot of men whose one idea is to do the best they can not only for their own Nation but for all others.

He tells me there is rather a feeling amongst the French that our people think that their hospitals are not well run and every effort is made to get our men out of them as soon as possible and indeed to avoid their being sent there at all with the result that many cases which ought to be dealt with immediately in French Casualty Clearing Stations are sent to more distant hospitals with often fatal results. He seems to think there is something in this and is taking steps to remedy it.

I think I ought also to mention that both before and after luncheon I had a long talk with Sackville West on the position of Le Roy Lewis and Spiers. He says that what Clemenceau told me is really common property, viz that these two officers are so much disliked that no information is given to them and their utility is gone and in his opinion there must be a change. This coincides with my opinion though I should very much regret losing either of them and it is possible I may have to go over to England to see Milner about it.

Dinner. Kermit Roosevelt and his wife came to dinner. They are both very nice. She is the daughter of the American Ambassador to Spain, and he has done extraordinarily well in Mesopotamia and has now joined up with the American Army in France. She told me that the effect of this last battle in Spain was very remarkable. That there has been gradually a change in the anti-entente feeling there and this has become very accentuated during the last fortnight. As Spain is in close contact with Germany this seems to me very significant. Other people dining were Bullock, De Vilaines and Agar Robartes.

Notes to 28 July

1. Thomas Agar-Robartes (1880–1915). Liberal MP for St. Austell, 1908–15. Died of wounds received in action.

Monday, 29th July

Nothing particular in the morning. Dubos came to luncheon with Portia, Edward and self.

Afternoon Office work till 4.30 when Billy Lambton[1] came round. Extraordinary improvement since I last saw him. He, Portia, Edward and I went for a walk. He went as far as the Rond Point. We went on and sat in the Avenue du Bois. Lovely evening.

Dinner. The Hartingtons. Charlie Grant and Billie dined. Edward and Portia left for England. They say they have enjoyed themselves so much here they want to come back and spend the last few days of Edward's leave here but I expect when they get back to England they will be like me, they will not want to come out again.

Notes to 29 July

1. Major-General Sir William Lambton (1863–1936). Commanded 4th Division, September 1915–September 1917.

Tuesday, 30th July

Murray of Elibank came round to see me with regard to his Oil Concession in Algeria. The French are stone-walling him and from his account behaving very badly to him. I telephoned to Clemenceau to ask him to see me on several matters and asked whether I might bring Murray of Elibank with me but he declined to allow the latter to come. Went to see Clemenceau who was very pleasant in every way. I spoke to him about a letter I had received from Bob Cecil detailing an interview he had with Franklin Bouillon who had apparently represented himself as coming from the French Government and had lectured Bob on certain subjects. Clemenceau was very grateful to me for coming and telling him about it. He said Franklin Bouillon had absolutely no authority to speak on behalf of the Government. Indeed he was opposing the Government in every way. He was grateful to Bob for the way he dealt with the question. I then asked him about Murray's concession. He says he won't see Murray at all. It is a matter for Klotz to decide and that the reason of their objection is that the State will receive no benefit from any oil that may be found. Clemenceau then went on to speak to me about his relationship with our Government. He told me in the strictest confidence that it was about as bad as it could be. He said he would rather not for the moment tell us what it was but that if he found I could be of any use he would at once send for me. He is evidently very much disturbed about it and says that thanks to us yesterday was one of the worst days he has ever had. It is very mysterious and I do not know what has happened. I asked him whether he was satisfied with the relationship between the Military people and he said certainly, nothing could be better. He had a most charming letter from Haig asking him to go and see our Troops. He is very much pleased at this and says he is going at the earliest possible opportunity but that he would make a great point of my going with him which of course would suit me very well indeed. It would at all events show everybody what good relations existed between us. On going out I met Klotz and spoke to him about Murray's affair. He utterly declined to see Murray. He says he has told Murray why he cannot assent to the agreement and no good would come of a further interview but if I liked he would gladly see me and explain to me all the reasons for his non-agreement. I am going to see him tomorrow at 11.30.

Saw Murray of Elibank again and explained the position to him. I think Pearsons whom he represents have been badly treated. Billy Lambton came to luncheon. After luncheon new Portuguese Minister came to pay his official visit. Not a bad sort of fellow. Later Mr. Kerney and Mr. Lewis the two heads of the American Propaganda Department came to see me. They were most friendly and their only desire is to co-operate in every way with us but they spoke perfectly frankly and deplore our propaganda work which they say is utterly useless. That we go in for nothing but leaflets and pamphlets which nobody reads and what we really require here is a man of some personality who would be able to get at all the leading journalists in Paris; influence them to write articles on our behalf and be able also to go to various big Provincial towns and get into touch by means of entertainment with all the principal newspaper people. The Americans told me that really they were very much interested in this matter because the fact of the incessant spreading of butter over them and their deeds by the French is having the effect of causing soreness amongst our troops who ask, and rightly ask, why they who have really borne the heat and burden of the day should be ignored and the Americans get all the praise. All that they said really absolutely confirms what I have already told the Ministry of Propaganda but I could get nothing done. I have however written to Arnold Bennett who is especially responsible under Beaverbrook for Propaganda Work in France.

In the evening went out to Versailles. Sackville West and I dined alone. Discussed many matters including the Propaganda work which he says must be remedied or we shall have a great deal of trouble.

Wednesday, 31st July

Went to see Klotz on the subject of the Concession to Pearsons in Algeria. Klotz most friendly and evidently anxious to do what he could and I thought justified his position entirely. It is as follows. Full permission was given to Pearsons to make any research they liked in Algeria with a view of finding oil. But no permission can be given for the exploitation of it until a law has been passed by Parliament authorising this and until this law is passed Klotz is not in a position to authorise money being raised even privately. His argument is, and I think it is a just one, that Loucheur who is the Minister responsible must draw up a definite proposal embodied in the shape of a Bill which can then be submitted to Parliament for its acceptance. Until that is done he, Klotz, is powerless to act. He told me that it would be useless to present such a law unless some portion of the profits went to the State. I pointed out to him that under the proposed agreement 26% of the profits went to the Algerian Government but in response to that he said that that was not the same thing; that the finances of the Algerian Government and of the Home Government were quite separate; that the Home Government had had to pay enormous sums to help Algerian Finances and that therefore it was essential, even if the amount did not exceed the 26%, that the law should lay down that some of the profits should go to the Home Government. I informed Murray of this and he is to see Loucheur and try and persuade the latter to bring in a Law framed on these lines.

I had received a message from Clemenceau asking me to go and see him. Again a most friendly interview and his friendliness is evinced by what he told me and which is embodied in a letter to Arthur Balfour herewith attached.

Had a meeting of the weekly Board. Nothing of any great consequence but everybody present unanimous in condemning the present Propaganda system. I have determined that if I cannot get an alteration from the Ministry of Information I will make a small Propaganda Department of my own composed of Military, Naval and Munition Representatives.

Bishop Gwynne,[1] Chaplain General of the Forces out here, came to see me in the afternoon. He is brother of the *Morning Post* Gwynne,[2] a much nicer and more dependable fellow and very popular. He talked about things generally but more especially about making Blunt the Embassy Chaplain into an Army Chaplain with which I cordially agreed. I should also like something done for Cardow who is the other Chaplain here but I am afraid from what he says they will only allow one.

After that saw Dr. Madge. He is an English Doctor, son of the man who used to be our doctor when we were children and has lived a great deal of his life in Roumania and was doctor to the King and Queen. Taking a great interest in all Roumanian matters he came to speak to me about helping the Roumanian Committee which is now being established here. He tells me there is very bitter hatred in Roumania against the Germans.

Afterwards Maclagan and Mainguy,[3] the Naval Attaché, came to see me with regard to certain Naval Propaganda work in which they both seem to be pulling opposite ways. I am absolutely in despair about Propaganda work here and until we can get a change in the personnel I am certain nothing will be done. Meanwhile the more I hear the more I feel how the bad feeling against us is again springing up, accentuated as it is by the fact that the two recent successful raids were done by Australians and Canadians, the French people having been kept in complete ignorance of the number of English Divisions there are in the present fighting. All reference to it has been kept back by the Censorship Department of the French War Office. I shall have to go and see Clemenceau about it. Something must be done but of course the whole of this could be counteracted if we had a man of any personality who could get amongst the French people and talk to them.

Afterwards went to Versailles for the night. Only man dining Ross — a very nice young fellow, a friend of Oliver's in the Rifle Brigade.

Notes to 31 July

1. Rt. Revd Llewellyn Gwynne (1863–1957). Deputy Chaplain-General in France, 1915; Bishop of Khartoum, 1908–20.
2. Howell A. Gwynne (1856–1950). Editor, *Morning Post*, 1911–37.
3. Acting-Commander Sidney Mainguy. Appointed Naval Attaché at the Paris Embassy, October 1917.

Copy of letter written to Mr. Balfour 31 July 1918

Confidential

An incident has happened today which has both disturbed and pleased me. Disturbed me because there is evidently an attempt to do something behind my back and pleased me because this attempt has been frustrated through Clemenceau's friendliness. He sent for me and showed me a letter from the P.M.'s Private Secretary Sutherland[1] to Mandel who is Chef de Cabinet, saying that the letter was being taken over by a Captain Stewart Hay who wished to speak to Clemenceau on the subject of an appeal being made by the Archbishop of Paris to Irish Catholics to serve as French soldiers. Clemenceau told me that he had seen Captain Stewart Hay though it was not a matter that really interested him very much, and he said to him that this was a subject which ought to have come through the Ambassador. Hay replied that undoubtedly that was so but that I was to know nothing whatever about it though I might be told afterwards if anything came of it. Clemenceau therefore refused to have anything to do with it and has passed it on to the President of the Republic. I cannot think that the P.M. can have known of this. If he did it is in strict contravention of the terms under which I came here which were namely that nobody was to go and see the Ministers without my knowledge. It is going behind my back and I will not stand that. I am pleased because it evidently shows Clemenceau's friendliness.

You are my master and I must have the matter cleared up because I cannot have things done which may land me and incidentally the Government in great trouble. Apart from this suggestion being a very puerile one as Clemenceau himself calls it, can you conceive anything more tactless than to ask Clemenceau to beg the Archbishop of Paris to make a Proclamation seeing what the relations between him and the Clerics are and further can you conceive anything more idiotic than sending as an emissary a man who I understand is an unfrocked priest? I admit it is only a small matter and the whole thing has been treated with absolute contempt here but it is a question of principle and I think I am justified in asking you to have the matter cleared up and an explanation sent to me.

Notes to confidential letter of 31 July

1. Sir William Sutherland (1880–1949). Journalist who was Lloyd George's Press Secretary, 1915–18 and then joint parliamentary private secretary to him, 1918–20.

August 1918

Thursday, 1st August

Frank [?Bertie] had arrived over night looking very much better than when I last saw him. He is off again tonight.

Maclagan and Mainguy again came to see me about Naval Propaganda. I think they have got it into a real muddle and I am not sure that it is not rather the latter's fault.

Hear that the French are attacking on the Soissons front and everything so far going well. I do not think they have been any too truthful in their last few communiqués. There is no doubt they have had much harder fighting than they have allowed to be the case.

Luncheon. Frank, Rendel[1] who is on the Staff of the Embassy at Madrid and who has been sent here to help us revise all the filing of papers; Henderson,[2] a very nice fellow in the Chancery, Bullock and Bridgeman.

Nothing much during the afternoon. Charlie Grant came in at tea-time. Tells me that Berthelot[3] has written a most glowing letter of praise and thanks to the Divisions under Godley[4] who were serving with him. Just the sort of thing that I want for Propaganda and yet one is never given it. I am going to get it and see if the papers will publish it but I am afraid it is a little too late. Maclagan and Mainguy came back in the evening and I hope have straightened out the question of the Propaganda tour in the South.

Notes to 1 August

1. George W. Rendel (b.1889). Posted to Madrid Embassy, October 1917.
2. Nevile Henderson (1882–1942). First Secretary at the Paris Embassy, 1918–20; Ambassador to Berlin, 1937–39.
3. General Henri-Mathias Berthelot (1861–1931). In United States, May–June 1918,

discussing transportation of American forces to France. In July assumed command of French Fifth Army.
4. General Sir Alexander Godley (1867–1957). Commanded Army Corps in France, Belgium and Germany, 1916–19.

Friday, 2nd August

Said good-bye last night to Frank who started for Italy after dinner.

Went to Versailles for the night. Birkbeck,[1] Director General of Remounts staying there; Humphrey de Trafford and his Chief, Colonel [blank]. The latter struck me as a most ordinary sort of fellow and yet he is put at Versailles as our Opposite number to the Q.M.G. to the French Army. It is not his fault but how could we expect to get our fair share in the distribution of supplies if everything was pooled as the French, and I am afraid the Americans, want it to be and we were only represented by a very junior officer.

Clemenceau sent me a copy of General Berthelot's Order to our Troops the 51st and 62nd Divisions. Nothing could be more complimentary and I am arranging to get it published. There is some advantage in being Head of the Missions as well as Ambassador as otherwise I should never have seen this and I am perfectly certain that Maclagan would never have got hold of it.

At 11 o'c I went with the Maharajah of Patiala to the President who was very gracious and made him a Grand Officier of the Légion D'Honneur, with which he was very pleased.

General Cockerill[2] and Onslow came to see me about the Propaganda work. Made it a little difficult as I wanted to talk to Cockerill about Onslow whom I look upon as one of the stumbling blocks. He is one of those Colonels who have been made for the War and he and Alex Russell[3] who is associated with him, have to make work for themselves and the consequence is the form it takes is obstruction. They are both absolutely 5th wheels to a coach.

Luncheon. The Maharajah of Patiala; Lt-Colonel Audain; Lt-Col Jogindar Singh; General Cockerill; General O'Brien; Lt-Colonel Herscher; Mr. Adam; Mr. Paul Dupuy; General Guillaumat; Colonel Le Roy Lewis; and General Sackville-West.

Patiala sat on my right and we talked racing most of the time. He is very keen about it. It was his father who bought Sprightly from Father. He told me something I did not know and that was that Sprightly won two years running and ought to have won the third only was pulled and both the trainer and jockey were, I gathered, warned off the turf for it. He wants me to find out from George Lambton if he knows of anything likely to win the Viceroy's Cup. I think the French people are very pleased at meeting him. He is the sort of man they like to see.

Guillaumat talked to me about Salonika and says we are making a mess of things with which I agree. We sent out Hereward Wake, who after all is at no times a very great soldier. He stays at Salonika 3 weeks, comes back with a report and we accept his opinion in preference to the opinion of Guillaumat who is one of the best soldiers France has got and who was out in Command there for 6 months.

Also had a talk to Dupuy afterwards. He is the owner of the *Petit Parisien*, the most widely circulated newspaper in France — on the subject of the appreciation by France of our efforts. I told him that I thought this excessive adulation of the Americans was doing a certain amount of harm in the way of alienating English people. He agreed. He told me he thought it was only a passing phase and I hope will do something to put matters straight. One thing that is borne more and more into my mind and that is that unless you can approach these journalistic people personally and as friends, you get nothing done. That if you can approach them in that way there is nothing they won't do to help you.

Sent for by Clemenceau to see him on the subject of Captain Stuart Hay's Mission.[4] For details see the two letters I wrote to Arthur Balfour and my telegram.

Went out to Versailles again. Bliss was dining. Told interminable stories at Dinner which were very tedious, but was very interesting after Dinner discussing the situation. Roughly his view is as follows. Rupprecht of Bavaria[5] and the Crown Prince[6] were each allotted a certain number of Troops with Reserves. In addition there was a General Reserve to exploit any successes either of them might gain. Each was told, on the general plan, he was to do what he could with the Troops at his disposal but was not to expect help from the General Reserve which would be under the Command of Ludendorff[7] and which would only be used where he thought fit. At the attack on the Chemin des Dames the Crown Prince succeeded better than he had ever anticipated but committed a grave fault in making so pronounced a salient. He however persuaded the Emperor to alter the plan of campaign and to allow him to make a further attempt to reach Paris as for dynastic reasons that would be most important. When this last attack was made the real big result hoped for was that south of Rheims which was anticipated would drive the French back through

Chalons. If they had done this without any further attack Verdun must have fallen. This part of the attack however was an absolute failure but in order to try and turn it into a success the Crown Prince used up all his own Reserves. The result however still was a failure. Meanwhile Foch made his counter attack and the Crown Prince had no reserves to meet it. It was so serious that Ludendorff had to put in his General Reserve and also take away some 10 Divisions from Rupprecht's Reserve and even with all this the Crown Prince had got his Army into such a narrow Salient that he was unable either to feed them or keep them supplied in ammunition. The result has been this general withdrawal which is almost a rout and the net result is that the Germans have lost much of what they gained in the May offensive; they have employed the whole of their general reserve; the whole of the Crown Prince's reserve and a portion of Rupprecht's, with the result that there is even bitterer feeling than existed before between the two Princes as Rupprecht's attack, which is bound to come off somewhere, must now lose part of its sting. Bliss' idea is that both sides have probably had equal losses and though it is difficult to get at the truth of losses generally I should say that the French had lost about 140,000 and the Americans 40,000 and you might put the German losses at about 220,000. Now as to the future. Bliss says it is quite impossible for the Germans to sit still under the present situation: that they are bound to make as big an attack as they can somewhere. He does not think it is likely now it will be in the North although I believe our people still do. He thinks that it must be somewhere in the vicinity of the present fighting and it will probably come within the next week or so. In his opinion, and Sackville-West agrees with him, it will probably come from Albert down to Noyons as they would be the only place where the Germans could really gain a success which would have great results and they would again by this means be able to threaten Paris. Bliss says that the biggest thing that has been done in the War was the withdrawal of the Germans to the Hindenburg Line.[8] That it showed great courage to make such a big retreat, especially in view of what might be felt about it in Germany and he says the German Crown Prince was not a big enough man, when he found that he had pushed his offensive to such a narrow salient at Chateau Thierry, to at once withdraw, as he ought to have done, to approximately where they are at the present moment. He is now being forced to retreat with heavy losses.

Notes to 2 August

1. Major-General Sir William Birkbeck (1863–1929). Director of Remounts at Army Headquarters, 1912–20.

2. Brigadier-General George Cockerill (1867–1957). Deputy Director of Military Operations and Military Intelligence and Director of Special Intelligence, 1915–19.
3. Colonel Alexander Russell (1856–1938). Assistant Director of Medical Services, 1914–18.
4. As Derby noted crossly on 31 July, Lloyd George wanted the Archbishop of Paris to appeal to Irish Catholics to join the French army and sent out Captain Stuart Hay to discuss this matter directly with Clemenceau.
5. Crown Prince Rupprecht of Bavaria (1869–1955). One of Germany's ablest front-line commanders. On 1 June 1918 he unsuccessfully informed the German Chancellor that Ludendorff no longer believed in victory and that peace negotiations should start at once.
6. Crown Prince Wilhelm (1882–1951). Eldest son of Kaiser Wilhelm II.
7. Erich Ludendorff (1865–1937). First Quartermaster General of the German armies, 1916–18. Fled to Sweden, November 1918.
8. Hindenburg Line. The defensive line to which the German armies on the Western Front had withdrawn in February 1917.

Copy of telegram sent to Mr. Balfour

Paris, 2nd August 1918

Private. Most Urgent.

I wrote you yesterday informing you that a letter had been sent by the Prime Minister's Secretary Sutherland to M. Mandel, Chef de Cabinet to M. Clemenceau, asking the latter to receive a certain Captain Hay. M. Clemenceau saw Captain Hay, who put forward a proposition that the Cardinal Archbishop of Paris should make an appeal through the Roman Catholic Clergy to the Irish people that they should enlist in the French Army. Captain Hay requested that I should not be informed of this but M. Clemenceau refused to agree to this and informed me of the negotiation. Captain Hay asserted that he had the authority of the War Cabinet for making this request and it was owing to bad news from Ireland and to Lord French's uneasiness with regard to the situation. M. Clemenceau sent for me today and told me that he understood that the Cardinal Archbishop was ready to write a letter, though not the one which Hay had asked him to sign. Hay has now requested that the Cardinal Archbishop should be asked to send some High Ecclesiastical Authority with the letter and with authority to make a direct appeal to the Irish people. Clemenceau is ready to do this through the President of the Republic if it is really the wish of the Government, but not otherwise. He requires an immediate answer and must have it at the latest midday tomorrow. Please telegraph what answer I am to give.

I must protest most emphatically against this method of approaching the French Government behind my back. It is entirely contrary to the conditions under which I came here and might have put me, and incidentally the Government, in a very false position had it not been saved by Clemenceau's friendship to me.

Copy of letter sent to Mr. Balfour

Confidential

2 August 1918

You will by this time have got my letter with regard to Captain Stewart Hay's Mission and a telegram sent after an interview with Clemenceau on the same subject today. Nothing could have exceeded the friendliness, and if I may say so the good faith of Clemenceau, a good faith which is not kept to me by my own Government, and I am certain if you had known anything about it you would not have allowed this incident to have arisen and will sympathise with me in my anger. If Clemenceau had not told me all about it I should have been made to look an absolute fool if an appeal had come out without my knowing a word about it. I hope you told the Prime Minister from me that either I am fit to do the work here or I am not. If he prefers to do the work through one of the anarchic embusqués of Downing Street by all means send him out to take my place but I will not have things done behind my back.

I do not know whether anything will come of this but personally I cannot conceive how such a grave mistake can be permitted and I only know that if I was at home and in Liverpool I would raise Cain. To employ the Roman Catholic hierarchy to get Irishmen to show their loyalty to England by fighting under a French Flag seems to me to be the height of folly and one which will be bitterly resented by a great number of people in England. However naturally I shall hold my tongue about it but I think I have a right to demand an explanation of this going behind my back.

I do not think Clemenceau likes the business. He won't make the appeal himself to the Cardinal Archbishop but he is ready to insist on the President doing so as he said to me "I do not like these sort of things with the clerics. It always means we have to pay for them in the end."

To show how religiously Stuart Hay tried to keep the business from me, instead of coming here to have a code telegram sent he went to Versailles. What fools people are to think they can keep these sort of things from one's knowledge.

[116]

Now to turn to other matters. Clemenceau is in a great state of excitement as today there is really excellent news and the whole line has gone forward and as he himself puts it, the Germans are retreating so fast that our people can hardly keep touch with them. I am glad this success has come because I was told privately today that the Army Commission, of which Renaudel[1] is the chief, were not up to last night at all satisfied that the gains were commensurate with the losses which are said to be equivalent to Nivelle's last spring year. My informant was told by Renaudel himself that the wounded alone are 170,000 but he was not sure whether that included ours and the Americans. Personally I should say even such a loss as that is counterbalanced by the success gained. It has always appeared to me that there are three things that we have to fight for at the moment:

(1) Defence of the Channel Ports.
(2) The prevention of our Armies being broken in two.
(3) Defence of Paris.

The latter has now to my mind been attained and incidentally it has used up so many German troops that I doubt whether either of the other two dangers are now very great. Furthermore it has given a real smack in the face to the Crown Prince and that must have a great moral effect in Germany.

I shall be very interested to see what effect this has on the Malvy[2] trial. Personally I think it will mean a verdict against him which might not otherwise have been given but I still hold to it that after the evidence of the ex-Prime Ministers he will not get any very severe sentence.

Clemenceau is in great form, very friendly to me and is taking me up on Sunday to have luncheon with Haig. I spoke to him the other day about the want of recognition of what our troops have done. He sent me this morning a copy of an Order issued by General Berthelot which is in every way satisfactory and he told me this afternoon that he is himself sending it to the French Press for publication. I think this will do a great deal of good.

Notes to confidential letter of 2 August

1. Pierre Renaudel. Leader of the main Socialist group in the Chamber.
2. Louis Malvy (1875–1949). Minister of the Interior, 1914–17. He was accused of insufficient vigilance in hunting out traitors and defeatists and was tried for this by the Senate in August 1918. He was deprived of his political rights, but resumed his career in 1924.

Saturday, 3rd August

Had luncheon with Madame de Ludre who is very much in with all the political people. Marie Murat, the Rochefoucaulds, M. Lamerie, Berry, the head of the American Chamber of Commerce, and a Deputy whose name I did not catch was there. Conversation of a general character. Nothing very interesting.

Afterwards saw Boghos Nubar[1] who is the representative of the Armenians here. A most talkative old gentleman. It was on the subject of a telegram to be sent out to the Armenians who I believe now are freely massacring the Turks and I must say I am not surprised at it.

Then saw Maclagan on the subject of Propaganda. He has settled one or two points that have been raised in a letter that I had received from Arnold Bennett.

Afterwards went to see Clemenceau on several points.

1. Owing to sinking of Justicia[2] and other big ships it is not possible to bring over as many Americans as we had anticipated. In addition to which cargo must be allotted to bring cotton for Lancashire and coal etc for Italy and France. We are going to be very badly off this winter. Rather disappointing but it cannot be helped and I somehow think we probably shall get as many Americans as they can train and assimilate.
2. Question as to whether American troops should not be trained behind our line. Clemenceau quite reasonable about it and I think we shall get it arranged as L.G. wants.
3. I had received an answer from Arthur Balfour saying Hay certainly not authorised to say what he had done. I hope my strong remonstrance may have the effect of stopping these subterranean ambassadors. Arthur Balfour himself knew nothing whatever about it and to send a man who had been got rid of from Versailles because of his unreliability on a Mission which is to be strictly unofficial and which he took in the first place to the Président du Conseil and then to the President of the Republic seems to me to be courting disaster.

Lastly we discussed the subject of Spiers and here Clemenceau is most unreasonable. I confronted him with a letter he had written on July 19th saying that he would be very happy to recognise Spiers as our representative and to give him all the information in his power. He calmly said that he had only given him that because he thought he was going and he had no intention of going back on what he had previously said to me. However it was a matter for us to decide. That Spiers did not annoy him in the slightest but he thought it would be a case of annoyance to us because he had no intention of giving him any more information than he could possibly help and he certainly was going to exclude him from his Secret Cabinet. I have written to Milner saying that I think the best thing is to let sleeping dogs lie. Leave Spiers there for the present. If we find that Clemenceau is as good as his word, and I am afraid he may be, then we may have to reconsider the whole question. I did not mention Le Roy Lewis to him because I think the latter is like a red rag to a bull to many French people over here and I expect I shall have to make a change but I do not mean to do so at once.

Dined with Spiers. Grammonts, she seemed very nice but I did not get a chance of talking to her after Dinner as the whole of my time was taken up with Tardieu. Jack Lowthers,[3] Tardieu and Charles Mendl.

Much amused to hear that the Capel-Wyndham marriage has still not come off though he telegraphed to me to say he was going to be married on Wednesday. Spiers thought they were being married that day but I shall only believe it when I know the ceremony has actually taken place.

After dinner long talk with Tardieu who was very interesting and of whom I think, as far as antagonism to England is concerned, I have perhaps formed in the first instance a wrong impression. He was most eulogistic about Reading[4] and said nobody could have any idea of what Reading had done to restore our position in America to what it was when Arthur Balfour was there.[5] It had been utterly ruined by Northcliffe and Spring Rice.[6] The former by his speeches and behaviour and the latter by his pin-pricks to the President. We then got on the subject of which I had spoken to Clemenceau in the afternoon and he was very sensible about it. He quite realises that it is not in any way our fault but that Clemenceau is inclined to think it is and holds to the opinion that it is a threat on Lloyd George's part not to bring over Americans unless his wishes that they should be trained behind our lines be at once acceded to. He therefore wants Sir Joseph Maclay to come over to France or else he will go to England. We discussed the whole question of the relationship between English, French and Americans and he tells me, and I believe it to be quite true, that he has never made a speech with regard to the Americans without pointing out that but for our assistance the Americans could never have arrived in the quantity they have. We then got on to the relationship existing between Clemenceau and Lloyd George. He is as anxious to ameliorate the position as I am but he says it is very difficult, after the way Lloyd George behaved at the last Supreme War Council. He spoke before everybody of the retreat from the Chemin des Dames as being the worst defeat the Allies had suffered since the beginning of the War which personally I think in the first place to be untrue and in the second place even if true to be very insulting.

We have agreed to work together much closer than has hitherto been the case. He finds that when I send a telegram which is connected with American affairs to Pichon that it sometimes takes a week before it gets to him and very often then he does not know what has gone on before. We are going together to see Clemenceau and ask whether it would not be advisable in such cases that I should send a copy of any telegram to him at the same time as I send it to Pichon and that we should have an understanding that if there is any matter connected with the Americans which is giving any trouble that we should meet and discuss it and prepare a joint memorandum, one to be sent to England and the other to Pichon. I am only too ready to fall in with these views and I think by doing so we probably shall obviate a lot of friction. Of course Versailles to a certain extent ought to do this but though I still adhere to Versailles as being very useful you cannot get the French people to in any way recognise them. They have put on to it a General who they openly say has orders not to give any opinion except the opinion of Foch. It therefore ceases entirely to be an independent body as far as the French are concerned.

Notes to 3 August

1. Boghos Nubar. Head of the Armenian National Delegation in Paris. Son of a finance and foreign minister of Egypt and himself once the director of the Egyptian State Railways.
2. The White Star liner *Justicia* was sunk by a German U-boat in July 1918, despite being escorted by seven destroyers.
3. Jack Lowther (1885–1977). Served with Northamptonshire Yeomanry; DSO and MC.
4. Rufus Isaacs, Marquess of Reading (1860–1935). Lord Chief Justice, 1913–21; Ambassador and High Commissioner in Washington, 1918–19.
5. Balfour had been sent on a special mission to the United States in April 1917.
6. Sir Cecil Spring Rice (1859–1918). Ambassador to the United States, 1913–18.

Sunday, 4th August

PARIS

Went to the Service at Notre Dame for the fourth anniversary of the declaration of War. The first time I had been inside Notre Dame and was rather disappointed with it as it certainly does not compare with either Westminster Abbey or St. Pauls. At the same time it was rather a fine service as it was crammed full and though I particularly dislike Roman Catholic Services it certainly lent itself to such occasions. The Cardinal Archbishop said a few words at the end, not a regular sermon but he thanked all those who were present for coming, mentioning various Ambassadors individually and thanked us for being there, so I felt that it would have been wrong if I had been away as I had intended to be. Quite a short address but really very fine language and beautifully delivered.

Godley, who has been commanding the 31st and 32nd Divisions near Rheims came to luncheon with Bobberty. Very interesting about all his time there. He says the men were perfectly magnificent as they were fighting in terrible country, all woods with the thickest possible undergrowth. They did very well indeed and were extremely well treated by the French. He says the bombing at nights was something terrible and both Chalons and Epernay were absolutely destroyed by bombs but there was not much loss of life as everybody gets down into the big wine caves.

In the afternoon I took the Jack Lowthers and Bobberty up to St. Cloud Golf Course and we walked round part of the way. Jack Lowther played with the Spiers and Guiche. Got caught in a most tremendous storm.

Dined alone.

Monday, 5th August

Bertha began again this morning.

Fabian Ware,[1] who is the head of the Graves Commission came to see me. He has done extraordinary good work but he is one of the most tiresome and long winded men I ever came across. The object of his visit was to know who he was to keep posted here with regard to his work. Up to now it has been old Henry Austin Lee. As a matter of fact there is no need to keep anybody posted. We shall see any papers that there are and that is all that is necessary.

Luncheon. Princesse Marie Murat, Mme de Sancay, Barrès, Godley, General Cockerill and Bobberty, Shute,[2] who I happened to pass in a motor in the street yesterday, and Grahame. Quite an amusing luncheon. I was glad to get Barrès to meet Godley because he is a little inclined to run down our efforts and I think a talk with Godley did good, as the latter was very unassuming but gave him a pretty accurate description of what had taken place.

The French are very excited over Berthelot's Order to our troops, as it is the first time that an Ordre du Jour has been issued by the French to allied troops, at least so Princesse Murat told me. Cockerill came straight from our Missions Office in the Avenue Marceau where a shell had fallen not 5 minutes before. It killed 3 of our men on leave and 9 civilians. There is no doubt it has been the most persistent shelling we have had at all but all shells have fallen on the other side of the river from here. Cockerill came afterwards to talk to me about propaganda work and I am glad to say we are in perfect accord. He wants to get in London exactly what I want to get here, namely some man, in his case it will have to be Beaverbrook I suppose, of influence with a small Board of really trusted representatives of Army, Navy, and Munitions. I cannot quite make up my mind who I should like here but he has suggested Sir John Simon and if Simon would take it I could not think of a better man. He would be admirable in every way and though we have differed very much in politics he has always been absolutely straight and I know from what he told me himself he is all out to make amends for what he considers the big mistake of his life — opposing conscription.[3]

Dined and slept at Versailles. Adjutant General (Macready) was there and his son. Discussed nothing in particular but Macready tells me now it is very difficult to see the S of S for War; that he only sees him about once in 5 weeks and that Macpherson is very much over-worked.

Notes to 5 August

1. Brigadier-General Fabian Ware (1869–1949). Director of Graves Registration and Enquiries since 1914.
2. Lieutenant-Colonel John Shute, commanding 5th Liverpool Regiment.
3. Simon had resigned as Home Secretary in January 1916. He remained out of government office until 1931.

Tuesday, 6th August

Saw Clemenceau. He showed me in confidence the letter which the Cardinal Archbishop of Paris was writing with regard to the enlistment of Irishmen for Labour Companies in France. A good letter but I still think it is deplorable that we should adopt this means to secure Irishmen for Service — not for fighting but for ordinary labour work. I think even if we do get them that it will have a very bad effect both at home and abroad. At home it will be looked upon as being a surrender of conscription in Ireland and abroad French people will resent men of serviceable age being engaged in what are non-combatant duties.

Clemenceau was most friendly and showed me the Order of the day which is to be issued to our Divisions that have been fighting on the left of the French Front. Most satisfactory and I hope will do some good.

Mr. Laurance Lyon[1] came to see me. I had met him before. He knows French politics pretty well having resided for many years in France. He is our Unionist candidate for Hastings and is on his way to Spain on purely private business. He sees as I do the extraordinary danger, not to ourselves, but to our Allies of having an election in England in the Autumn.[2]

Had luncheon at the Ambassadeur with Neuflizes, Tardieu and Sackville-West. Very pleasant. After luncheon had a very disagreeable interview with General Phillips who has been removed from his post here on the ground that the British Representatives in Paris think he is unsuitable for the post. I do not like the man at all. He is very blatant. At the same time I do not want to do him an injustice. I think the post is entirely unnecessary and ought to be abolished and I also think that he is unpopular with the French as he is a bounder. At the same time it is only gossip that I have heard and I do not want to ruin a man's career by having such information acted on. I am therefore seeing what I can do to save him — at all events for the time, but he ought to make somewhere else than Paris his Headquarters and only come here when it is absolutely necessary.

Frazier, who is really House's representative at the American Embassy, came to see me and told me he was very disturbed about the open way in which the French are talking to the Americans about our Army. I have known this for some time and have been trying to combat it but it is very difficult to do as I have really not got the proper staff to deal with it. Moreover I cannot help feeling that our people are just as much to blame and from Headquarters downwards, with the exception of Haig himself, there is a continual torrent of abuse of the French. All this is very bad, not only for Franco-British relationship, but also because it is undoubtedly making bad feeling between ourselves and the Americans. The Americans have the poison poured into their ear and at the same time our troops seeing the excessive adulation of the Americans are rather inclined to say to them that if they are going to get all the praise they can do all the fighting. I propose to see Clemenceau about it and at the same time to run up and see Haig as a word from him is just as necessary as a word from Clemenceau.

Mandel came to see me bringing the letter from the Cardinal Archbishop and also a reply from Foch with regard to the placing of American troops in training behind our line. As I anticipated he said it was a matter entirely for Pershing to decide. He also told me that Foch had been made Maréchal de France and Pétain had received the Médaille Militaire which is only given to Foreign Potentates, General Officers Commanding and private soldiers, no other ranks in between being allowed to have it.

Went out to Versailles. Dinner. Prince and Princesse d'Arenberg, the Neuflizes, Mrs. Gordon Bennett — the widow of the late Gordon Bennett,[3] quite a nice woman, and Macready and son. Quite an amusing dinner.

Notes to 6 August

1. Laurance Lyon (1875–1932). Conservative MP for Hastings, 1918–21.
2. It is easily forgotten that Lloyd George's plans were for a wartime election, recalling memories of the Khaki Election of 1900. In the event, the sudden collapse of the German war effort transformed the situation.
3. James Gordon Bennett (1841–1918). One of the pioneers of modern journalism, he established the reputation of the *New York Herald* as one of the world's leading newspapers.

Wednesday, 7th August

Got Victoria's telegram saying she could not come out with Portia. Dick Sutton[1] and Alastair Leveson-Gower came to see me. There are still difficulties about the latter getting a pass for Italy though I think it will be all right. They are staying here till tomorrow.

Du Bos came to see me about a matter I had written to him. The continuation of a pension to the widow of an old jockey. He told me as a friend that everybody is very bitter against Le Roy Lewis and that he is detested everywhere. I am afraid it is the truth but he is extremely useful and I think loyal to me and I do not want to get rid of him if I can possibly help it. Anyhow he will have to go on his own initiative and not by me sending him away. I must say Du Bos is a good friend to us. He is putting both Edward and Oliver up for the Jockey club which they look upon here as the greatest honour that can be done a man and he tells me also privately that I am to be elected an Honorary Member both of the French equivalent to our Jockey Club proper and National Hunt. He also told me he has seen one of the Senators who was present yesterday at the Malvy trial and he says that feeling ran very high indeed. There was a great deal of bitter recrimination but that those people who were most violent in Malvy's favour were equally violent against Caillaux and that a conviction against the latter will be perfectly certain. It just depends however by whom he is tried what his sentence will be. The High Court cannot sentence him to death but it will probably give him penal servitude for life. On the other hand if he was tried by Court Martial he would undoubtedly be shot.

Ordinary Military Meeting. Nothing of particular interest discussed with the exception of Propaganda which as usual is a burning question.

At luncheon Macready and David Henderson[2] came. General Phillips is leaving. It is rather unpleasant because I am supposed to have said that he was not fitted for the job. As a matter of fact it is fairly accurate as far as being liked by the people of Paris. I believe David Henderson is to succeed him. If so I could not have a better fellow but I am insisting that if possible the Headquarters should be outside Paris. I am sure it is a very bad thing and makes the French laugh to see Generals put in here as Commandants of Paris when the only men they have to command is 1,800 workmen in the various workshops.

Baron de Neuflizes the old banker came round to see me. He wanted me to dine — Lady Duncannon is over — but I cannot do so. He talked about the Malvy trial and tells me just what Du Bos had told me that for Malvy to be convicted means a certain conviction for Caillaux but he thinks it will be by the High Court and not by Court Martial.

Afterwards saw Maclagan on Propaganda Work and Captain Kenney, who is the liaison officer for propaganda work. Very nice fellow who sees all the shortcomings and would I think if he had his way alter them very much indeed.

Afterwards Sir Basil Zaharoff came to see me. He was really most interesting and I should think there is no man living in whom more people confide than in him — enormously rich and using his money to extremely good advantage. What he told me is contained in a letter I have written to Arthur Balfour.

Alastair Leveson-Gowers, she is not in the least pretty, and Lady Algy came round here to tea and afterwards I went to Versailles to dine and sleep. The Adjutant General was still there and General Thornton came to dinner. I had made them acquainted at luncheon but they had a good talk afterwards and A.G. has taken a great fancy to Thornton which I am very glad of as I am sure there is a reorganisation required here as General Nash is only a 5th wheel to the coach and is of far too senior a rank for the work he has to do, and if he went, Thornton with half the Staff could perfectly do, not only his own work but Nash's. Nash also has not been behaving quite straight and has been abusing the Quartermaster General to the King and trying to prejudice him. The only stranger there was DuPuy, owner of the *Petit Parisien*, who I like very much indeed. None of the other fellows would embark on talking in French with him so I had him on my own hands, not only through dinner but all the time after dinner. I must say he was most agreeable and interesting. He discussed Northclife with me. I was very careful to offer no opinion but he was open-mouthed against him and says that he thinks he is the very worst class of newspaper proprietor who has got no real patriotic feeling, whose one idea is to go for somebody and indulge in personalities rather than support any particular view. It seems to me rather a true reading of Northcliffe's character. DuPuy is much excited about "John Bull" and asked me what was the secret of Bottomley's[3] success as he could find nothing in the paper to justify any success whatever. I am bound to say it was a question I could not answer, except to say that any man who was thoroughly unscrupulous and is always hinting at scandals will invariably secure a certain number of readers.

Notes to 7 August

1. Sir Richard Sutton (1891–1918). Captain, 1st Life Guards; European War, 1914–17.
2. Lieutenant-General Sir David Henderson (1862–1921). Military Attaché, Paris, October 1918–June 1919.
3. Horatio Bottomley (1860–1933). Journalist and criminal. The sensational *John Bull*, which he created and edited, set out to expose alleged public wrongs.

Copy of letter sent to Mr. Balfour

Strictly Confidential & Personal

7 August 1918.

Sir Basil Zaharoff came to see me today and told me of conversations he had had with you, the King and Lloyd George, and in order that you may compare the story with your version I send you a short summary of what he told me.

He began by saying that he had had luncheon with you and that you had begun by asking him what his opinion of Franklin Bouillon was. That he had told you that he was a man who he, Zaharoff, had made. That he did not think very much of him but that his knowledge of English made him a useful man and therefore he had helped him with money when creating the Inter-Parliamentary Committee. That you had then told him of the talk Franklin Bouillon had had with Bob Cecil and of which the latter has written me an account. Zaharoff then told you that he was aghast at what had been said. That there was not a word of truth in the fact that Clemenceau was unpopular and that if it was not for his strict censorship of the papers there would be an outburst against him. He was then sent for to see the King and the King had told him that he looked upon Clemenceau as the pivot of the War. That he, the King, and the British people had got complete confidence in Clemenceau and he wanted Clemenceau to know that. The King then went on to speak about the question of a General Election and how in his opinion it would be a most dangerous experiment. Zaharoff entirely agreed with this and said quite apart from the uncertainty of our own Elections its influence on French politics might be fatal. Incidentally I might add here, it is exactly what I wrote to you some time ago. The King then asked Zaharoff to go and see Lloyd George which he did both on the subject of Franklin Bouillon and also on the subject of the General Election. Lloyd George told him that it was quite true that up to now Franklin Bouillon had had a great influence over him but he now saw that his confidence in him was misplaced and he carried no weight with him. On the question of the General Election he wished Zaharoff to tell his French friends that he would not have a General Election if there was any question of danger arising out of it. What he means by that I do not know and what the assurance is worth I equally do not know.

Zaharoff armed with all this information went to see Clemenceau. Clemenceau after hearing him at once said this explains everything and I see now who is the villain of the piece. He then told Zaharoff that I had already informed him of the conversation with Bob Cecil and he added that he got on very well indeed with me and was extremely pleased with the frankness with which I treated him. He told Zaharoff that he would deal with Franklin Bouillon in a way that he would not forget. He passed not much remark on the Election except to say that it was, as he had already said, fatal, but he was not going to be accused of interfering with our domestic concerns. That Lloyd George had been most insulting to him at the last Supreme War Council, insulting in a way that he could never forget and it made matters very difficult between them. Zaharoff who has I think got influence over him is going to do everything in his power, as I shall also do, to try and make peace again.

So much for the matters that were discussed with you. Now for another matter about which he spoke to me. I had received instructions to help Murray of Elibank with regard to his Algerian concessions and with that object had an interview with Klotz. Klotz is a great personal friend of Zaharoff's and in addition is his personal lawyer, therefore they are on most intimate terms and Klotz asked Zaharoff to give me a hint that it would be much better if I did not interfere in any way with the Algerian Concession. That things would probably come all right but that this particular concession having been already turned down by the Chamber of Deputies was looked upon with a very great deal of suspicion and it would be a great pity if I got in any way mixed up in it, although he quite realised that naturally I was not working on my own account but on instructions from home.

Of other things I have little to tell you. Malvy as you see got 5 years of exile and I think everybody is satisfied. It is more than some people thought he would get. On the other hand people are very pleased that Clemenceau's wishes, as they put it, have been gratified. All the people that I have seen — not many — agree, though for what reason I cannot see, that this makes the conviction of Caillaux doubly certain and it may be that the Government will harden their hearts and get Caillaux sent to be tried by Court Martial instead of by the High Court. If he is I do not think there is the least doubt either of his conviction or of the fact that he will probably be shot.

I got your telegram with regard to the next Supreme War Council being held in London and sent it round to Clemenceau. He will probably want to see me on the subject but I feel perfectly certain if possible he will try and insist on the Council being held at Versailles and I am bound to say with some reason, as if you want to have Foch, Pétain and Haig at the Conference it must be held here and not in England. I admit however that the argument that all the figures, papers, etc., with regard to transport are in England, would make it desirable that for that particular subject London was the right place. I am afraid however quite between ourselves that the desire to have the meeting in London is put down more as a desire to avoid Bertha than for the reasons that are given.

Thursday, 8th August

Tardieu came round to see me and told me that Clemenceau absolutely refused to go to England for a Supreme War Council as I thought would be the case, as he says neither he nor Foch nor Pétain could possibly leave at the present moment; nor could Douglas Haig. Clemenceau is suggesting that Pichon and Tardieu should go over to England and discuss the whole question of tonnage for American reinforcements, try and arrive at some understanding which could afterwards be ratified at a Supreme War Council to be held at Versailles. I think Lloyd George will have to agree to this. It will probably mean a Supreme War Council being held in a fortnight's time here.

Luncheon. Alastair Leveson-Gowers, Lady Algy, Dick Sutton, Alec Hardinge,[1] who has just turned up, and Brigadier General Fabian Ware who is the head of the Graves Commission.

Heaton Ellis came to see me after luncheon with a new scheme for a Propaganda Establishment here. In no way a workable scheme.

Afterwards M. Klobukowski who was the French Minister in Belgium before the War and is now their representative for propaganda in enemy countries. He is going to London for a meeting under Northcliffe's auspices next week.

Got a letter from Oliver. I hoped he might have come here on Monday from what Philip Sassoon said but he writes to say it will not be possible for him to get away before the 24th as he will be in the line till then.

Dined with the Tremouilles. Her house is a delightful one finished just a month before the War and of course now it is all anyhow as the pictures, tapestries, etc. have been sent away. It looks right down the river. Of course the crab is that it is quite close to the Eiffel Tower which rather interferes with the view from one end of the garden. He is rather a dull sort of fellow. She is most amusing and it was a delightful dinner and though I knew all the people who were there at Dinner I cannot in the least remember their names. Hugo Baring was there. He is off in a very few days to Siberia.

Notes to 8 August

1. Alexander Hardinge (1894–1960). 2nd Lieutenant, Grenadier Guards. Equerry and Assistant Private Secretary to George V, 1920–36.

Friday, 9th August

Heaton Ellis, Mendl and Allen came and discussed the plan for propaganda work that they had drawn up. I pointed out my objections with which they were in entire agreement and they have taken their plan away to rewrite. I am sure we could get a workable plan but the whole thing is, who is to work it? and as long as the Propaganda Department at home look upon Maclagan as an ideal man for the purpose so long will it be a failure. We must have a strong man who aided by an Advisory Committee will be able to go his own way and with whom there ought to be little or no interference from London. He ought to have at his disposal not only all the information which they now give but also any information for which he may telegraph, whether it be from War Office, or Admiralty, provided it is not giving information to the enemy. It is also essential that we should have lecturers with Cinemas who could go about amongst the American and French troops and these lecturers must be of the Nationality of the people to whom they lecture. To send Englishmen, however well they speak French, to lecture to French or American troops is only time and money wasted. We have also got to get out of the idea that leaflets and pamphlets are the only things that are of any use. There is also much to be done with our own troops in trying to get them to see the American and French points of view. When Beaverbrook first took up his post he told me he was going to run a weekly Illustrated Paper for our troops and I think it would have been an excellent idea but I am sorry to see announced in the House of Commons the other day that there was no intention of carrying this out.

Mrs. Bliss came to see me to ask me to forward a letter to Haig asking his attendance at a big women's meeting they are to have at which Clemenceau is to preside and Lloyd George make the principal speech. I do not myself believe it will ever come off. Lloyd George has given a conditional promise that he will attend.

General Phillips who is going and is to be replaced by General Henderson came to see me to say good-bye. We had a very long talk over things in the Balkans which he probably knows better than any man living as he was in command in Albania for some considerable time, then went to Serbia and was [there] all through the Serbian retreat and then was the English Liaison Officer with the French when Constantine was dethroned. His theory, and I admit it is the one I agree with, is that we make a great mistake in trying to break up Austria. The best thing that we can possibly do is to have a strong Austria, friendly to us which would bar the German way to the East. He tells me it is all nonsense about Bosnia and Herzegovina[1] being so bitter against Austria. Nothing of the kind. They have been extremely well governed by Austria and when the big attack on Serbia was made, which ended in the great retreat, far the bitterest fighters against the Serbians were the people from Bosnia and Herzegovina. They were absolutely brutal and shot the women right and left. He had got a profound contempt for the King of Montenegro who he says has only got a small handful of followers and he has not much respect either for the Serbians. He says it is all nonsense talking of their great patriotism for their country. As a matter of fact over 200,000 of them deserted in the retreat and are now living quite comfortably and happily in Serbia. It is evident he thinks that the Bulgarians and Roumanians are the best and that the Serbians would be far better governed by the Austrians than they ever can be by themselves. He had been with Troubridge[2] all through the war and was actually with him at the time of the Goeben and Breslau[3] incident and had to give evidence at the Court Martial that was held afterwards. He sticks up of course tremendously for Troubridge who he says is a most gallant fellow. He saw the actual telegrams, one from Milne[4] telling him to engage the Goeben and the other from Winston Churchill[5] telling him that he was on no account to engage a ship that had heavier guns than himself, which of course both the Goeben and Breslau had. He obeyed the latter order for which he was Court-Martialled but of course acquitted. Phillips says the man who ought to have been hung was Milne which I must say is what a lot of people say. He had 3 big ships and could perfectly have engaged the two Germans but as his instructions were to make safe the passage of the French Troops across the Mediterranean he steamed off west although there could have been absolutely no chance of any damage being done to the troops except by the Goeben and Breslau whom he could have engaged and would probably have sunk.

Spiers, Jack Lowthers, Bullock and Alec Hardinge dined and we went to a Cinema. Not very amusing.

Notes to 9 August

1. Bosnia and Herzegovina. Balkan provinces annexed by Austria in 1908.
2. Admiral Ernest Troubridge (1860–1926). Vice-Admiral commanding the Mediterranean Cruiser Squadron, 1912–14; Admiral commanding on the Danube, 1918.
3. On 11 August 1914 the German battlecruiser, *Goeben*, and the heavy cruiser, *Breslau*, escaped through the Dardanelles to Constantinople, where they played an

important part in hastening Turkey's entry into the war in support of the Central Powers.
4. Admiral Archibald Milne (1855–1938). Commander-in-Chief of the Mediterranean Fleet, 1912–14.
5. At the time First Lord of the Admiralty.

Saturday, 10th August

Murray of Elibank came to see me. His business is going well thanks he says to my efforts but I think it is probably much more due to Zaharoff who is one of their largest shareholders and has taken it up. Murray spoke to me again about oil on my property. He is going to let me know exactly where it is supposed to be. He says my property near Preston.[1] Thanks to the muddle however that the Government made of the Bill that they brought in for Royalties it may be difficult to work but I think perhaps we might form a private company to deal with it.

General Thornton came to see me with regard to the development of the Coal Fields in the South of France by an English Company. It appears there is a Company which already has concessions and doing well and could enormously increase the output but owing to the usual French obstruction it is impossible for them to do so.

Heaton Ellis came to see me with regard to propaganda. The scheme now is a good one but the whole thing is to find a head and that I am afraid there is considerable difficulty in doing, especially as Beaverbrook and Co. at home seem to look upon Maclagan as the right man.

Luncheon. The Lowthers, Bobby Ward, Bullock and Alec Hardinge. Edward and Portia arrived just at the end. They all missed the train but the Capels (late Diana Wyndham) motored them from Havre. Charlie declined to come and therefore will only arrive about 11 o'c tonight. It is about the first time, when special leave has been granted as in their case, that the boat arrived too late to make the connection with the early train. They came in a convoy and there was a thickish fog. Bobby Ward has now got his gun accepted and it really looks as if they might make a big thing of it. 100,000 have already been ordered and they probably will have anything up to a million ordered for ourselves and Allies and according to him they will get an average of £2 a rifle Royalty. I think this is probably an exaggerated figure both in regard to the number that will be made and the amount they will get but it probably will mean at least £200,000 of which I think Bobby gets something like 25%.

Went to see Pichon about two minor matters. Very nice and of course delighted with the news more especially as the biggish advance today was made by the French.[2] When I got back I found Charlie had arrived. From what I can make out he did not think it was comfortable coming in the motor car with all the others so he waited till they had gone, then went to the Base Commandant, said he had an important dispatch for me which must reach me by 6 o'c and got them to give him a motor car by which means he arrived in great comfort having had luncheon at Rouen on the way.

Dinner. American Ambassador and son. Mme Sincay. The Rodneys, Bullock and our own House Party which consists now of Edward, Portia, Charlie, Mrs. Lowther and Alec Hardinge. Lady Rodney has just done something which might have got both her and him into tremendous trouble. She was refused, as all English wives are, permission to go into the British War Zone, where her husband was for the moment stationed so she impersonated a French woman and went in her name. A stupid thing to do because if she had been found out by the Authorities, which so far she has not been, it would have meant her being sent back to England, which I do not think she would mind, but his leave would probably have been stopped till the end of the War.

I had a talk to Sharp after Dinner and he told me that he believed Briand had again been conferring, through the usual subterranean means, with some Austrian representatives, with a view to a separate peace. He knew nothing much about it and it is the first I have heard at all. I am going to try and make some enquiries. Personally I do not believe in these unofficial conversations but still Briand is the only man whom the Austrians would now trust as after the publication of the former letter they would naturally have nothing whatever to do with Clemenceau. I am taking what steps I can to find out if there is any truth in the rumour.

Notes to 10 August

1. Derby owned property in Preston, part of it granted to the Stanleys by Henry VII.
2. The allied Amiens offensive was launched on 8 August.

Sunday, 11th August

Portia, Mrs. Lowther, Edward and I went out to Versailles to luncheon — not a very amusing one. The Capels were there. She told me that it was her fault the marriage had been so long delayed as she could not make up her mind. I thought she seemed now extremely happy and I am sure the marriage will be a success as he is a real good fellow though a little rough but that is just what she will correct. She became a Roman Catholic either the morning of her marriage or the day before and I expect really it was making the change that made her undecided. It certainly is an extraordinary thing how whenever a Protestant marries a Catholic he or she becomes a Catholic and never the reverse. She however told me that with her the change was not so great as ever since the Lovat marriage, whenever she has been at Beaufort she has always gone with Laura Lovat to the Catholic Church and therefore made the change with her eyes open. We afterwards went on to St. Cloud and sat there for the whole afternoon, a most glorious and hot day.

In the evening Dinner consisted of the House Party plus the Italian Ambassador and his wife and the Grammonts. She is not in the least pretty but very attractive and very bright in every way and I must say I liked her very much. Grammont himself is the most delightful man. He has the most perfect manners and talks English perfectly. She also talks quite fairly well. The Italian Ambassador and his wife are also quite the nicest couple here. He is most friendly in every way and made great friends with Edward who of course knows his house, which is now a hospital — the one which Frank was in — and all the country roundabout the house, as it is just where our headquarters are.

I got a message saying the Prince of Wales[1] was coming through on Saturday and would dine here. I am getting up just a small Dinner for him.

Notes to 11 August

1. Edward, Prince of Wales (1894–1972). Known to his family as David. Edward VIII, 1936; abdicated.

Monday, 12th August

Luncheon Duc and Duchesse de Camastra, the Capels, and Rodneys.

After luncheon had interview with Radovitch[1] who was former Montenegrin Minister. He is in opposition to the present régime and wants to see the amalgamation of Serbia and Montenegro under one King. After talking to me for a long time on the various past history and future possibilities of the country he then began on the question of the Honour which was given to the present Montenegrin Prime Minister and protested against it. I pulled him up very short and told him I was not going for one minute to question the propriety of the King, in full accord with his Government, giving this Order. It in no way meant any change of the policy which the Government has laid down with regard to Yugo-Slavs, though to tell you the truth if I had been cross-questioned by him I could not have told him what that policy was and I do not know that anybody else can, but as he continued I closed the interview. He I think then saw he had made a mistake and was full of apologies. I told him that while I was very glad in any way to meet him and assist him he must clearly understand that I would neither see him nor any other representative of the Montenegrin or Serbian Government who wished to speak on this subject. That it was most unusual for an ex-Minister to question the action of another Government in such matters. We parted good friends but I do not think either he or that very slippery customer the Serbian Minister will ever refer to the subject again.

Routine work most of the afternoon.

General Shoubridge[2] came to see me. He commands the 7th Division in Italy and was previously with us as G.S.O.1 West Lancashire Territorial Division. Edward likes him very much indeed and he apparently likes Edward. He told me Edward had done very well. He is very anxious to get him back to his Division and I think probably the next Brigade will be going in that Division and Edward will therefore go back to it which he would like, although at the present moment he is very anxious to be transferred to France.

In the evening we all dined with the Spiers. The only other person there Madame de Sincay. Went to L'Abri. Rather an amusing little Theatre but they talk so fast I cannot understand all they say. There was however a very amusing song about Clemenceau.

Notes to 12 August

1. M. Radovitch. Montenegrin Prime Minister, May 1916–January 1917.
2. Major-General Herbert Shoubridge (1871–1923). Commanded East Lancashire Division, 1919–23.

Tuesday, 13th August

Jim Salisbury[1] came to see me to complain of publications in the shape of novels, etc. which he thinks are of a debasing character and which are sold by French booksellers to English Officers and men. He wanted this stopped and the booksellers ordered not to sell indecent books to Englishmen in uniform. I pointed out, and in the end made him see eye to eye with me, that this was quite impossible. That a bookseller was not the right person to say whether a book was immoral or not and that really we could not constitute ourselves censors of French morality. I said I would speak to Clemenceau but I felt certain that what he would say would be "If you can show me any books which are contrary to the spirit of morality of both nations I will stop them but you must tell me what those books are."

I afterwards went to see Clemenceau. Had a very interesting talk with him. Bob Cecil had written to me to say that Fleuriau,[2] Counsellor at the French Embassy in London, had been to see him and said that Signor Nitti[3] had pressed on him the necessity of sending American troops to Italy and had told him that the English were in perfect accord etc. Bob Cecil was perfectly frank with him and told him that he did not know anything about that and that it was not his business. In order that there should be no misunderstanding I showed Clemenceau Bob's letter. He then told me a very interesting thing. He said that although Bob Cecil undoubtedly spoke the truth, at the same time, probably without his knowledge, there had been meetings in London between Lloyd George, Milner, Henry Wilson and Nitti at which it was decided to put pressure on Foch to send American Divisions to Italy. It had all been kept very secret but that he, Clemenceau, had got a full record of what took place at the two meetings which had been held. It just shows how things get out and what a ridiculous idea exists that these intrigues can be carried on without the knowledge of the people against whom the intrigues are instituted. Clemenceau told me not to pay the slightest attention to it and thanked me for having shown him the letters and said he knew exactly now what to do. He then went on to tell me two things. First of all Nitti is a most dangerous man. That he is intriguing against Orlando[4] with a view of ousting him as he, Nitti, thinks he can come into power. Clemenceau says Orlando is a very disagreeable sort of man, still he is out for the War and it is essential that he should be kept in Office and he will not lend himself to any intrigue to oust him. Further that Nitti is really in with all the Italian Pacifists and is a most dangerous man. He told me yesterday he had seen Pershing who had spoken to him on this very subject and said that the time had now come for stopping such negotiations going on behind his back. The Americans had now formed their army and would continue to add to the Army but he was just as much an integral part of our line as Haig or Pétain. That though he would be always ready to send troops to help either, that it must be with his consent and on Foch's order. I am afraid all these sort of intrigues and bothers will not make for smooth working between Clemenceau and Lloyd George.

He then referred again I am sorry to say to Spiers and Le Roy Lewis. He said that as far as Spiers was concerned he had said all that he meant to say. That it was our business and did not affect him but that he wished again to say that he thought it was very inconvenient that we should not have as the Head of our Military Mission a man in whom both ourselves and he had complete confidence. He had no confidence in Spiers and he thought we ought to know that. He then however referred to the Le Roy Lewis incident. He has received an official letter from Pichon and there is no doubt that he wants to press for his removal. I told him that I must take the responsibility for it and he said under these circumstances of course he would not press it and he was sure we could arrange matters. But again he said he thought it was better to make a change and here I rather agree with him as apparently Le Roy Lewis has got wrong with everybody in Paris both socially and from a military point of view. I am extremely sorry because I think he is clever and a most useful man and it will be a great disadvantage for me to start with a new man. However Le Roy Lewis himself thinks that it is best for him to go and I think he will probably resign of his own accord.

I mentioned Jim Salisbury's request and he at once said he would do anything to help us that he could in this direction but said exactly what I had expected, namely that it was quite impossible to stop books at the booksellers. What he would have to do would be to have a list of the books which were thought offensive and then if they came within the code in this country he could stop their publication altogether. I have told Jim Salisbury about this.

Edward came with me and after I had finished my interview I brought him in and presented him to Clemenceau who was charming to him. Altogether I was very pleased with our interview. It showed very good feeling on Clemenceau's part towards me. He was in very good spirits and pleased with the way everything was going. He had been up yesterday to Rawlinson's[5] headquarters and seen him and Henry Wilson who happened to be there for the day.

At luncheon we had Klotz, Tardieu, Neuflizes, Bliss's, Frazier (the American Counsellor who is really House's representative) and Lady Duncannon.

After luncheon Jerrold[6] the *Daily Telegraph* representative came to see me in regard to Propaganda work. Not much of a fellow and gave no advice worth listening to.

Edward went off back to Italy.

Dinner only ourselves, that is to say Charlie, Portia, Mrs. Lowther and Alec.

Notes to 13 August

1. John Gascoyne-Cecil, 4th Marquess of Salisbury (1861–1947). Brother of Lord Robert Cecil. Lord President of the Council, 1922–24. Known as 'Jim' or 'Jem'.
2. Aimé-Joseph de Fleuriau (1870–1938). Counsellor at the French Embassy in London, 1913–20. Ambassador to London, 1924–33.
3. Francesco Nitti (1868–1953). Italian Minister of the Treasury under Orlando, October 1917–January 1919.
4. Vittorio Orlando (1860–1952). Italian Prime Minister, October 1917–June 1919.
5. General Sir Henry Rawlinson (1864–1925). Baron Rawlinson, 1919. Commander, Fourth Army, March 1918–March 1919.
6. Laurence Jerrold (1873–1918). Chief Paris Correspondent, *Daily Telegraph*, 1916–18.

Wednesday, 14th August

Had a meeting (Phipps, Bridgeman, Thornton, Capel, Addison, Sir C. Ellis) to discuss civil honours under the new arrangement by which we classify them. It is a very difficult job but I think we have got it fairly right. They all stayed to luncheon. Portia went out to have luncheon with the Bliss's.

Bridges[1] came in to see me for a minute and is going to dine tonight.

Afternoon, nothing at all.

General Bridges, General Dawes and Hugo Baring dined. The last two are off to Siberia immediately. They cannot get the French General Janin,[2] who is to command the Czech troops, to leave so they are going on ahead of him. Bridges talked a certain amount after Dinner. Not very interesting but he is the first man I have heard from America who entirely agrees with my views of the President namely that he is a very narrow minded man with no real energy, who has to be kicked by the people themselves into any action, and although I admit the enormous use the American troops are when they get here, I am certain after the War great blame will be placed on Wilson's shoulders for all the delays he has caused, especially in the Far East by his inability to make up his mind. Bridges says their efficiency in America is halved by two facts. First of all that the President is surrounded by a ring of Jews who there, like everywhere else, hamper a Nation in War. Some of these Jews are of German origin and actually have brothers still in Germany fighting for Germany. The other hindrance to efficiency is that the dividing line in politics still remains in the States and although he has made certain exceptions lately, as a general principle the President will use nobody of opposite politics to himself. They are a very long way behind in their Supply Department, not a single one of the big guns that they want for their Force is delivered. They cannot get the recoil right. When however they do the guns will come on very fast as all the component parts are ready in hundreds. But they are equally very difficult to deal with in other ways such as aeroplanes. They have got hundreds of Liberty Engines[3] but no machines to put them in. On the other hand we have got exactly the reverse, yet nothing will induce them to put their engines into our machines even though they are to be handed to the Americans to use. It is inconceivable that they should be so narrow minded about things but apparently they say they must be "all America" machines.

Notes to 14 August

1. Lieutenant-General Tom Bridges (1871–1939). Head of the British War Mission in the United States, 1918; Head of British Mission, Allied Armies of the Orient, 1918–20.
2. General Pierre Janin (1862–1946). Set out to Siberia on 30 August, arriving 16 November, as Commander-in-Chief of the Czechoslovak forces and head of the French mission in Siberia.
3. American-manufactured aero-engine designed specifically for mass production but based on a Rolls-Royce design.

Thursday, 15th August

Capel came to see me with regard to the future position of Military Attaché and Head of the Mission. He had seen Clemenceau the day before who was evidently very bitter against Lloyd George for apparently many reasons. He has still got his knife into Spiers as much as into Le Roy Lewis. Spiers came in afterwards and we discussed what would be a future arrangement and we all agreed that probably the best thing would be for Spiers to become Military Attaché and for Capel to be under him. Capel to be at French War Office and to be the intermediary who always saw Clemenceau. That this would be following very much the lines which have now been adopted in England where the Military Attaché is to be at the head of French Military Affairs. Apparently Clemenceau would accept this but rather on the condition that I become much more the head of the Missions as far as the Military ones are concerned and that Capel reported direct to me and not through Spiers. I do not myself think that that matters. What we do amongst ourselves is nothing to do with Clemenceau or anybody else. It would give me a certain amount more work to do but I think by the three of us meeting every day we could probably get the work done perfectly without the friction that at the present moment exists. It of course provides an easy way out for Le Roy Lewis whose retention is I am afraid quite impossible. The mere fact of wanting to make a Brigadier General Military Attaché over him would naturally cause him to resign. They are to draw up a paper and let me have it on my return on Saturday.

Luncheon. Very mixed party. Pichon and wife. Toulmin, head of Lloyds Bank and wife, Winston, Walter Berry, the head of the American Chamber of Commerce and the Lord Mayor of London. It all went very well. The more I see of the two Pichons the more I like them. They are a most homely couple.

Winston talked to me with regard to the difficulty there is with the French regarding the Independent Air Force. They have stuck their toes into the ground and wish to insist that it should be under Foch. He told me that Weir the Aviation Minister was over here and would like to see me. He came round and I saw him and Bonham Carter.[1] The upshot of it is that they are to put down their views on paper and then I go with Clemenceau to the front on Sunday. I am going to discuss the whole question with him on the way and try and get him to agree. I think in theory it is right that Foch should be the head and I should give way to that extent but the conditions under which he exercises his command should be so modified by regulations that practically Trenchard would have the independent command that he wants.

Motored down to Deauville in 3 hours 40 minutes. One puncture on the way. Very pretty road especially the first part after leaving Paris and very good surface. The hotel very nice and a nice room looking out on the Sea. Dined with the Neuflizes; found there Madame de Viel Castel and Captain Kirmaingand. Most amusing little fellow. Terrible people in the Royal where the Neuflizes were staying, nothing but Jews. Afterwards went to a Play.

Notes to 15 August

1. Ian Bonham Carter (1882–1953). Seconded to Royal Flying Corps, 1914; Royal Air Force, 1918.

Friday, 16th August

Met General Hickson[1] who is an extremely nice man and went up to see the Liverpool Hospital site. Met Raw and the whole of the Staff, also Miss Whitson and all the nurses. The site is one of the most lovely ones you can imagine looking right over a valley at the end of which is the Sea. I cannot imagine anything nicer. The buildings are getting on well and taking it all round have been most carefully removed by the Military Authorities.

I afterwards went round all the other Hospitals, Camps and Convalescent Homes. A year ago it was nothing but fields. Today it is a town, beautifully laid out with gardens and with vegetables growing everywhere. Also on a lovely site overlooking the valley but I must say when I see it I do not wonder at the amount of money that has been spent on it and I do not wonder at the French thinking we are going to remain there permanently. There are to be altogether 50,000 beds. The St. John's Hospital has been rebuilt there and I saw Colonel Trimble[2] our Preston friend. He had been doing magnificent work but I never saw a man more aged than he is. It was his hospital which was so badly bombed at Étaples. They lost a lot of people killed and wounded.

Walking about outside the Hotel afterwards I saw Cohn who had the cheek to come up and talk to me and I do not think that he will do it again. It really is a perfect scandal his being kept in uniform. The worst part is that Haig takes his side. I am sure some day there will be a great row about it. He only gets all these privileges because he spends the Michelham money and I now hear the Michelhams[3] won't speak to him, or at all events she won't. He therefore spread the story that she is quite mad.

Luncheon with Madame Hennessy. Met there Madame de Viel Castel, Madame de Boisgelin, a very nice woman and the Duc de Mouchi who has been with our Army in Salonika. Awfully nice looking fellow who has been most desperately ill. He was at death's door and I telegraphed to ask them to send him home which they did. He still looks very ill. Grahame also was there. Rather bored I think with his present hostess.

Strolled about during the afternoon and at 4.30 went to tea at the Golf Club and played a foursome. First game of golf for a long time. I played with Madame Hennessy against General Hickson and Madame de Viel Castel and really on the whole did not play so very badly though we were beaten by two up and one to play.

In the evening several people dined with us. The Boisgelins, the Neuflizes, Madame de Viel Castel, Madame Hennessy, Grahame and Kirmaingand. The best dinner I have had since I have been in France but frightfully expensive. I must say I should like to have stayed there a few days longer but I had to get back.

Notes to 16 August

1. Major-General Samuel Hickson (1859–1928). Royal Army Medical Corps.
2. Charles Trimble (1856–1944). Honorary Colonel, 88th Field Regiment, RA (West Lancashire).
3. Baron Michelham (1851–1919). Jewish financier; Baroness Michelham (d. 1927).

Saturday, 17th August

Left at 7.40 and got in here just before 11 o'c. Should have got here earlier but we took one wrong turning. We came along splendidly and we must have averaged 45 miles an hour to do it.

Found a message asking me to go and see Clemenceau. Went round and found him in very good humour with me but evidently spoiling for a fight with Lloyd George and Milner on the subject of our effectives at home. A great bore all this quarrelling. He based his demand for further reinforcements on a report made by Colonel Roure[1] which I believe is a tissue of falsehoods from beginning to end and has made our War Office people mad with rage.

He again referred to Le Roy Lewis and Spiers. Quite nicely as far as I was concerned and he said he was going to press nothing officially and going to leave it to me to deal with as I liked but he told me for my sake it was quite impossible to keep Le Roy Lewis.

The Prince of Wales came round. I saw him for a minute. He is coming to dine tonight.

Luncheon. The Prince of Wales could not come but Sharp and the Spiers came. Talked to Sharp again about what he told me of Briand's subterranean diplomacy and he is convinced now, as I was when he told me, that there is nothing whatever in the rumour.

Clemenceau suddenly sent for me to give me a copy of a letter received by the Cardinal Archbishop of Paris from Cardinal Logue[2] in which the latter accepts the principle of trying to secure recruits through the Irish clergy for working battalions behind the French lines. Personally I think the whole thing is a grave mistake. People at home will simply look upon it as a ruse to save the Government from the necessity of putting on Conscription and it will be bitterly resented that strong healthy young men from Ireland should be given safe jobs behind the French lines instead of going as they ought, into the ranks of our own army.

Had a talk with Spiers and Capel with regard to the rearrangement of their offices for the future. It is most difficult to get anything definite decided as Spiers quite naturally clings to the idea of being in control and with full knowledge of everything that is going on and it is impossible to make him see that Clemenceau is perfectly determined to give him nothing of a confidential nature nor to give it to anybody else who will inform Spiers of its contents. Clemenceau is a spiteful old man. He is perfectly determined if possible to get rid of Spiers altogether. I am equally determined, and I think Milner is too, to keep Spiers whose one fault has been to find out things that the French were doing diametrically opposed to our interests and having found them out communicated them to our own people.

Dinner. Italian Ambassador and his wife. Duchesse de la Tremouille, Duc and Duchesse de Gramont and his daughter in law Countess Renée de Gramont. She is about 23 and quite lovely. Mme de Polignac the American, the Capels, Bullock, the people in the House, Charlie, Portia, Alec, Lile Lowther, and myself and of course the Prince of Wales and Claude Hamilton.[3] Some of them afterwards danced to the gramophone. I never saw anybody enjoy himself more than the Prince of Wales did. He was most cheery and very frank as to not looking forward to his leave being spent at Windsor under somewhat lugubrious circumstances. I do not think he at all appreciates the rationing cum teetotal diet.[4] I must say he is a real good boy. The Spiers came in after dinner, also Edward Green and Luke White.[5]

Notes to 17 August

1. At the meeting of the Supreme War Council on 1–2 May Lloyd George agreed to allow Colonel Roure, a French military planner, to come to London to advise on manpower mobilisation. In other words he was being allowed to verify the British contention that the mobilisation of a higher proportion of their manpower would damage the country's economic war effort.
2. Cardinal Michael Logue (1840–1924). Roman Catholic Primate of All Ireland, 1887–1924.

3. Lord Claud (the text consistently has Claude) Hamilton. Captain, Grenadier Guards. ADC to Prince of Wales since January 1915.
4. In the spring of 1915 Lloyd George urged the King to set a patriotic example. Stamfordham replied on 30 March: 'If it be deemed advisable His Majesty will be prepared to set an example by giving up all alcoholic liquor himself and throughout his household'.
5. Sir Luke White (1845–1920). Liberal MP for East Riding of Yorkshire, 1910–18.

Sunday, 18th August

PARIS

I joined Clemenceau at the Ministry of War at 9 o'c and we at once started on our tour. He was most communicative and there were few things we did not discuss on the road between Paris and Amiens where we met Haig and had luncheon. I cannot remember the order in which subjects cropped up and so put them down just as I remember them, but I think it began with the well worn subject of Le Roy Lewis and Spiers and that brought us to the subject of Capel. He asked me what Mrs. Capel was like and I told him. He then turned round and said "Isn't she a niece of Mrs. Asquith's?"[1] I said yes but that no more different people existed than her mother and Mrs. Asquith, but I could see that so great is his hatred of Mrs. Asquith that the mere fact of Capel marrying her niece has rather prejudiced him. He told me that he could not conceive how any man could have risen to the position Asquith has had with such a wife. He looks upon her as having been Asquith's curse, that and, as he says, extreme laziness. He looks upon Asquith as done and he says that he sees in England just as in his own country no really promising young man of outstanding ability. From that we turned to the topic of the Election in England. He told me that he hoped it was not yet decided. He thought it was folly to have it. I asked him if it would have any effect in this country and he said No he did not think it would. That although perhaps an election here might do him good, in fact he was sure in that it would wipe out the whole of the Socialists, still he thought it was a wrong thing to do and under no circumstances would he have one. He thought ours was even a greater leap in the dark owing to the new Franchise and especially the giving of votes to women.[2] He told me he saw pressure would certainly come in this country to secure votes for women but he was absolutely determined to resist it. He thought it was only possible to give women votes in a Protestant Country and even that was a great danger but in a country like this it would simply be giving so many votes to the priests and he launched out into an attack on the clerics. From that we gradually got to discussing his own Government and I asked him about several of them. Roughly this is his opinion. Pichon a nice amiable man, perfectly straight and honest and good manners. Very weak. Unable to make up his own mind on anything and coming to him, Clemenceau, for any decision of importance or even of minor importance. Tardieu a most able man and a great organiser but at the same time with one of the worst qualities of an organiser that he is always trying to get more and more into his power and to absorb this or that office. At the same time he had a very high opinion of him. Of his other colleagues he did not think much except of two and those he told me were absolutely indispensable and he did not think he could carry on a Government without them. The first was Loucheur, the most able man he knows. Quite honest and straight. It appears that he formed a big committee of manufacturers at the beginning of the War to start certain Munition Works. They agreed between themselves they would take none of the profits for themselves but put them all by to be used for National purposes after the War and Loucheur had gone even further than that as he is much interested in many other Munition works and from all of them any profit that he gets is to be put aside for the same purpose. Clemenceau has evidently the very highest opinion of him. The other man was Claveille the Minister for the Railways and who was the Managing Director of State Railways before the War. Clemenceau spoke in the very highest terms of him and told me that the worst day he ever had since he took office was a short time ago when Claveille came and said he did not think he could go on. Curiously enough Claveille's name came up afterwards at tea and Clemenceau said publicly before everybody he did not think France realised how much she owed to Claveille.

The subject of our various Allies cropped up. First of all the question in regard to the United States Army and then with regard to Italy. The question of the command of the United States Army is evidently giving all in authority here the greatest possible anxiety. Clemenceau, Haig and Foch discussed it, so did Clemenceau and Pétain later, and they all came to the same conclusion, namely that the higher command of the American Army is practically non-existent and they all express the same fear that the Americans may be the cause this year of a set back. It appears they are absolutely lacking in officers capable of doing the Staff Work of rationing etc. The Divisions are perfectly all right when attached to the French or English Divisions because then it is all done for them but now they are on their own there is a hopeless break down. The other day in some small attack that was to be done in which an American Division was to take over a part of the line the night before, 1½ hours before they were due they sent to say they would not be able to do it as they had not been able to get up any of their food for their men. They all have the poorest opinion of Pershing who they say is a most stubborn pig-headed man and who is really the only one of the Americans who thinks that he knows everything and will not recognise that he has much to learn. Haig is particularly bitter about Pershing's treatment of him and bases his feelings on really exactly the same lines that Lloyd George takes, viz that Divisions are sent to him to help him on his front. That everything is sacrificed to make these Divisions really effective. They are given horses, guns, training, everything and as soon as they become effective they are taken away from Haig's army. Of course he says it is most disheartening and naturally his people take no interest in troops which are to be at once withdrawn before fighting with us. None of those who discussed it seemed to have any remedy whatever. Apparently they think Pershing has got the President's ear and I can see that Clemenceau's idea of the President is nearly as low a one as I have got myself.

We then turned to the Italians and here the bitter contempt of the French for the Italians came out, as Clemenceau is furious with some retirement they have in Albania. However he thinks he has steadied them by saying that if they withdraw their troops he will replace them by French troops and apparently from what I can make out he added insult to injury by saying he would replace them by black troops which he thought would be just as good as the Italians. I then asked him how matters stood with regard to the withdrawal of Italian labour which Orlando had demanded. He said that was over for the moment and when I asked him how he had done it he said that instead of sending back the 60,000 that they had asked for he demanded that they should leave them and send him 60,000 more and they were so busy now discussing the latter proposal they had quite forgotten their former demand. He summed up the Italians somewhat in this fashion. They are a Nation that has never known for centuries anything but defeat and therefore they have got the two great attributes of defeated Nations "lying and deceit" and that they practised both of them with wonderful ingenuity. He thinks Sonnino a most disagreeable man but at the same time he should be kept in office. He is the only man who really keeps Italy together and keeps Italy in the War and he deprecates very strongly any negotiations or pourparlers with Nitti who he says is a most dangerous man who he believes to be a pacifist and certainly a pro-Austrian.

With regard to Salonika I told him that I had written to Bob Cecil saying that I thought it was quite ridiculous for us to have a meeting of what is known as Political Propaganda in that region and that Bob Cecil agreed with me. He was thoroughly in accord with this. He says it is no good thinking of political propaganda until we have given them a knock and then he thinks that Political Propaganda may be of some use. I asked him whether he thought it would not be advisable to get the President of the United States to threaten war on Bulgaria. He said you had first got to get the President to find out where Bulgaria was as apparently up to a very short time ago he did not even know that and that really he did not think it made much difference whether they declared War or not but that it might be of value after we had given Bulgaria a knock. He is quite confident we should be able to do so in October and he thinks we should then be able to withdraw both English and French troops for service on the Western Front.[3]

Our conversation changed to the subject of native troops as we passed through a village full of them. He is very enthusiastic about them and very pleased with the 65,000 Senegalese and the 70,000 Moroccans which he has enlisted. He says they fight extremely well and have been of the greatest possible value and he looks forward to these extra native troops as being a great addition to his forces. He says of course it is quite impossible to use them in the winter but in the summer months they are invaluable and he seemed to think that we did not make enough of our native troops in the summer months. I pointed out to him our great difficulty, that of transport which was very different from his, and he agreed that transport did form a great difficulty for us.

On the way we stopped to see General Humbert[4] at his Headquarters. A very nice fellow indeed. Very clear headed explaining exactly what the position was with regard to his Army.

We got to the house that Haig had temporarily had given to him to entertain Clemenceau at luncheon, at about ¼ to 1 and Foch joined us there. They then discussed as I have mentioned the question of the Americans and various other matters. Clemenceau and Foch were then left to talk and I went and had a walk with Haig in the garden. I found him in good spirits but I thought tired. Very pleased however with things as they are but he told me one or two things which would make L.G. and Winston and Co. very angry. He does not believe in the Tanks to the extent at all events that some of our people at home do. He says the whippets[5] did very good work but they could not have done what they did if it had not been for the assistance given by the Cavalry and it is quite evident that the old Cavalry man comes out in him and reduction in that force he will bitterly oppose. I am bound to say his opinion was afterwards backed up by Rawlinson. Haig mentioned one or two matters that he wanted me to see about and we agreed the best thing was for him to talk privately to Clemenceau about them and then if Clemenceau said he would do what he wanted — chiefly connected with training grounds etc — I should wait for a fortnight and if it was not done, remind him.

We had a large luncheon party consisting of Haig who brought with him Lawrence, Haseltine[6] and Philip Sassoon, Clemenceau, myself, Foch, Weygand,[7] Mordacq,[8] Rawlinson and General Debeney,[9] who is the General next to Rawlinson and whom I think all our people cordially dislike; also General Lipset[10] who commanded the second Canadian Division which did the principal attack the other day. I sat next to Foch who was really most amusing and in tearing spirits, and here I must add what Clemenceau had told me about his first acquaintance with Foch. It was when he was Président du Conseil some years ago. They wanted a man for the head of the Military School and he was recommended Foch. He was told that the one thing which might be said to be against him was that he was connected with the clerical party. However the reports of him were so good that Clemenceau sent for him and he said it was a most amusing meeting. Foch came into the room in his usual abrupt way without saying good morning or anything. He began by saying "I have a brother who is a Jesuit Priest. Other members of my family are very religious and I myself occasionally go to Mass", and that was all he said. Clemenceau told me that he was so amused that he said he didn't care a rap about that and appointed him on the spot and he had never had cause to regret it.[11]

To go back to the luncheon. Clemenceau had told me he meant to confer the Médaille Militaire on Haig and at the end of luncheon he announced to all of us that he was going to do so and that it was done on the strong recommendation of Foch with which he entirely agreed. We then went into the other room when the presentation was made and the medal pinned on after two very nice little speeches by Clemenceau and Foch. Foch expressly stated how much he appreciated Haig's loyalty. Haig was really affected for the first time I have ever seen him and there is no doubt whatever that this Honour which is the greatest the French could confer has not only been richly deserved but it will be appreciated not only by our own Army but even more so by the French who have come to recognise how loyal Haig has been.

We then started off to go a sort of tour. Clemenceau with Haig and I went with Rawlinson. We went back through the main street of Amiens, where far more damage has been done than I had been led to expect, to the railway station where we saw the huge travelling gun which had been captured by the Australians in our advance. It is a train complete in itself and is the first to have been taken by the Allies. I did a good bit of propaganda work as I got Clemenceau to ask that before being sent to England, where I believe it is to be sent, it should be shown in Paris. Haig readily agreed and arrangements are to be made that it is to be put in some siding in Paris which will be easily accessible to the public. I think it will do good work. We then went and looked at captured guns etc and I have secured a captured field gun for the Embassy.

We then went on to the ground where the Canadians made their attack and Lipset described with extraordinary clearness how it was managed. It really was a wonderful performance as they only had one small bridge to cross the river by and as Lipset himself said "Once the weather really favoured us and the attack would not have been a success if it had not been for the thick fog which allowed our men to cross the Bridge in great numbers and deploy on the other side without being seen". When one sees the whole of the open ground over which they advanced it is simply marvellous they should have done what they did and with so few losses. After going all over the ground we suddenly came upon a Brigade of Canadians who had been in the fighting drawn up for Clemenceau's inspection. A remarkably fine body of men including a battalion of Highlanders from Montreal, a battalion from Nova Scotia, Princess Pat's Canadian Light Infantry which comes from Ontario and a battalion from Alberta. A really fine body of men and completely up to strength. Clemenceau went round 3 sides of a whole square and then they marched past him and I must say it was a most picturesque sight and he was evidently very much impressed.

We then motored home and stopped and had a look on the way at Montdidier where there is not a single house standing and the devastation there all round is perfectly appalling. I asked Clemenceau what he thought about rebuilding and he told me that they had decided that it would be quite impossible ever to rebuild any of these villages on their present sites and what they would do would be to remove them to some place near using the material of the old buildings as far as possible.

On the way back we stopped for tea at General Fayolle's[12] at Chantilly, a Chateau belonging to the Prince de Broglie. Full of sporting prints etc and with a most glorious view. Pétain met us there and I must say to meet him like that he is a most pleasant man and the cleanest looking Frenchman I have ever seen. He was very interesting telling us all about his various attacks and showed us exactly how one was going to begin on a somewhat large front at the very moment that we were there. Pétain was rather amusing on the subject of the leakage of information. He told us in the early part of the War he particularly wanted it to be thought that his Division was going to a certain district whereas it was going in exactly the opposite direction. He therefore motored himself through that district and having two men whom he thought talked pretty freely with him, one of whom had got a wife in one place and the other who had a friend in another place. He told them that his Division was probably going to come there but he told them in the strictest secrecy and they were not to say a word to a soul. The next day in order to again keep up the appearance that they were coming he sent his aide de camp through the district telling him to say that they were coming. When he got back the aide de camp told him there was no use in their having sent him as the whole thing was well known already, which he said proved to him how successfully false information could be spread. We had tea there and altogether most enjoyable. Pétain chaffed me about entertaining. He said that I had never asked him and he was told (I know who told him — it was Foch) that in London we gave the French people the best dinners at Derby House that they had and it was the only place where they could get good coffee, and he heard I did the same at the Embassy. I have asked him to come and dine sometime and I think he is going to do so.

Clemenceau on the road home again talked on various subjects. I asked him what he proposed to do about Caillaux and he told me that the Senate would meet in the middle of September and that then he would be sent to the High Court for trial. I asked why he had selected the High Court instead of a Court Martial. He said it was too dangerous to send him to a Court Martial. With a Court Martial there could only be either complete acquittal or complete condemnation and that Courts Martial were composed not of serving soldiers but of retired officers who might for various reasons be influenced towards an acquittal. It was therefore much safer to send him before the Senate as nobody could then say that he had not received justice and it gave an opportunity of decisions between the extreme punishments of death and acquittal. I asked him whether the High Court could condemn to death and he said most certainly they could do so but I rather gathered from him that neither did he think that they would condemn him to death nor did he wish they should do so. This is only my inference of the conversation as he did not mention anything definite.

We also talked about the Socialists. He said he was very pleased with the way he had treated them. He said when he first came in everybody expected him to be very much down on them and especially on the strikers. He said on the contrary he was most conciliatory because he knew that if he did this, especially when there was any cause for the strike, that they were perfectly certain before long to commit themselves to some act where he would be justified in taking extreme measures. The result was just what he anticipated and at the present moment he has got every dangerous socialist shut up in prison and probably nobody knows, and certainly nobody cares, what becomes of them as long as they are kept out of mischief during the War. We discussed Albert Thomas who, he says, is the most discredited politician in France and he could not resist having rather a dig at Lloyd George, alluding to Albert Thomas as "his", L.G.'s, "friend". He says he has lost a great deal of ground and he does not know now how to regain it and he mentioned in especial terms of scorn Albert Thomas having signed a declaration, which I myself missed the other day, to the effect that he was confident that the Senate had been bribed to convict Malvy. He does not think that now Thomas counts very much.

I asked him whether he did not consider Briand his most formidable opponent. He said undoubtedly but not very formidable. He is very lazy and has had his head completely turned by what he (Clemenceau) calls second class Princesses.[13] He says Briand, which is quite true, is of a very low origin[14] and he is so flattered by all the attentions that are paid to him by various ladies in Society that he really thinks only of Society at the present moment. He added however there is no doubt that Briand was extremely anxious to get back into power but he had not the slightest intention of allowing him to do so.

Another man we mentioned was Viviani and for him he has a profound contempt except as an orator and he says of course the fact of being an orator gives him great power in France. He is however entirely a man of words and not of actions and he does not think that he will ever play any very large part in politics in the future. Ribot[15] is extinct and so is Painlevé, whom he says was the worst Président du Conseil that France has ever had. He said he had absolutely nothing whatever to recommend him. That he is said to be a great mathematician but even that is doubtful as he has never found anybody except Painlevé himself to say so. Altogether he gave me the impression of looking upon all his opponents with a profound contempt and to have very little opinion of some of his own colleagues.

Of course I think his dislike of Spiers has originated from the latter's great intimacy with Painlevé and I tried to pump General Mordacq at luncheon as to what the cause of the trouble was and he says it was that Spiers interfered in things which did not concern him. I asked him "by that do you mean that he has too much intercourse with politicians" and he said Yes that was the real reason. A soldier had no business to do the work that Spiers was doing in this direction. I think I agree with him that Spiers has been doing this too much or rather too openly. All the same it has been extremely valuable work but I think it will be possible for the future to get it done in other ways. I feel that political information should be obtained by me through the Chancery and not through soldiers and I think I shall be able to put forward a scheme to Milner that would obviate vast difficulties. I am certain I could get hold of just as much information as Spiers does probably using the same agencies and nobody can complain if I do it whereas I think they have a right to do so if a soldier does.

We got back in Paris at 7.45 after one of the most enjoyable and interesting days I have ever had.

Dinner in the evening was also rather amusing. Winston came, also Lord Weir, Bonham Carter and General Tom Bridges.

We sat talking in the garden afterwards till late. Winston was really most amusing. We were chaffing him about his political career and then we got talking about various things connected with the War. He is a great admirer of the tanks and wants to make thousands of them and comb out the Army in every way to man them. His bitterness against the Admiralty and the Navy is something beyond belief. It cropped up at every turn and he said their selfishness with regard to men and material was beyond belief. I am bound to say he was supported in this by Weir and I know from painful experience how everything for the Army had to be sacrificed for the Navy. Winston's contention is that the Navy could have done all that they have done with far less in the way of men and material and that no allowance whatever was given to the fact that the American Fleet had joined ours. On the contrary even more demands were made for our Navy although with the addition of the Americans our superiority is overwhelming. He especially instanced the building of battle cruisers. I am afraid to say how many Standard Ships he said could be built for the same amount of money, and with the same amount of men and material. I think he mentioned the figure of 300. I must here mention that I had seen Weir on Saturday and he had asked me to speak to Clemenceau and Foch with regard to the Independent Air Command. I had done this but had found them both very difficult to deal with. However in the end I got them both to agree that there should be an Independent Air Force even if it was composed entirely of British Machines and personnel. I had nothing in writing and so I suggested to Weir that he should go and see Clemenceau himself which he is going to do and try and get a definite written understanding. Weir was very interesting on the subject of bombing and he told us one very curious thing, namely the amount of damage that was done at Cologne by the raid which we carried out. It was a daylight raid and all the trams were running. The amount of damage by the bombs was very great but greater damage was done by a very curious incident. As soon as ever the aeroplanes appeared over Cologne the whole of the current was switched off from the tramways which of course stopped every tram where it was. When the All Clear was given the current was switched on again with the result that all the trams started and the vast majority of them had got no drivers or conductors on them with the result that there were some heads smashed and more people were killed in that way than were actually killed in the bombardment. I hope Weir and Clemenceau will come to some understanding as Clemenceau himself is very keen about long distance bombing and showed me photographs of some new huge bombs they have got, but his contention and Foch's is that for the moment at all events all machines ought to be used for bombing behind the enemy's lines and that Foch should have complete control over this. Our contention is, and personally I think it is the right one, that we should have quite a separate force, as separate as the Navy from the Army for this long distance bombing and that it should be entirely under the command of Trenchard who would naturally consult with Foch but who would, if there was any difference of opinion, be entitled to give the deciding vote. Haig agrees with Foch but he most loyally supported the official proposal.

Notes to 18 August

1. Margot Asquith (1864–1945). Second wife of H. H. Asquith whom she married in 1894. Renowned for her indiscretions.
2. The Representation of the People Act, passed early in the year, removed almost all vestiges of property qualification, so that adult male suffrage became the norm. Women over the age of 30 were enfranchised for the first time.
3. In opposition Clemenceau had been an unrelenting opponent of the Salonika campaign. As Prime Minister, however, he was not prepared to abandon the expedition when it had already consumed so much in terms of energy and resources.
4. General Georges-Louis Humbert (1862–1921). Played key role in resisting the German offensive in 1918, especially in covering the routes to Paris.
5. Whippet tank. British light tank, officially known as the 'Medium Mark A'. It was intended as a reconnaissance and pursuit machine to fill the role of cavalry in a break-through.

6. Herbert Haseltine (1877–1962). Captain, Engineer Corps, US Army, 1918–19. Organised Camouflage Section of the American Army in France.
7. General Maxime Weygand (1867–1965). Chief of Staff to Foch in August 1914. In 1918 he became Major-General of the Allied Armies in France.
8. General J. Mordacq. Clemenceau's Chef de Cabinet for Military Affairs.
9. General Marie-Eugène Debeney (1864–1943). Commander of the French First Army. In August 1918 he took the offensive, regained Montdidier and broke through Ludendorff's front, taking 12,000 prisoners.
10. Brigadier-General Louis Lipset (1874–1918). Attached to Canadian Expeditionary Force, 1914–16; Lieutenant-Colonel Royal Irish Regiment, 1917–18.
11. For the importance of religion in promotions within the French army, see J. C. King, *Generals and Politicians* (Berkeley, 1951).
12. General Marie-Émile Fayolle (1852–1928). Commander of the group of armies of the centre. Helped to stabilise the situation after the German spring offensive, closing the routes to Amiens and Paris.
13. For Briand's affair with Princess Marie of Greece, see C. Bertin, *Marie Bonaparte: A Life* (New Haven, 1987).
14. Briand was the son of a café owner.
15. Alexandre Ribot (1842–1923). Minister of Finance, 1914–17; Prime Minister, March–September 1917; Foreign Minister, September–October 1917.

Monday, 19th August

Mr. Hall[1] came to see me in the morning. He is rather a remarkable man. An Englishman who went to America about 15 years ago. Has been Editor of the *New York World* and was Vice Chairman of Wilson's Election Committee. He has now come over here and is going to be sort of Head Press Correspondent with the Americans and at the same time to be *The Times* Correspondent with them. We had a longish talk about the relationships between England and America and he says it is no use disguising the fact that Americans do not care for Englishmen. He attributes this chiefly to the fact that in all the different schools the English History that is taught always puts England in the worst light possible. The books have chiefly been written by Germans or Irish Americans and the consequence is from the very first children are biased against England. He says that is gradually coming right and the books are being changed and he thinks that the next generation will see a very marked difference. He is however very frightened as to what our propaganda in America will do. He says if we attempt to rush the change we shall only make matters much worse than they are and he launched out against Beaverbrook's organisation. It appears the latter asked him to go on his Staff. He went there quite prepared to do so until he had gone into their organisation, or as he said where their organisation ought to be, as he found it was absolutely non-existent. He declined to have anything whatever to do with it. He says that the one thing Americans resent is any idea that they are fighting for England. They want it to be clearly understood that they are fighting for their own ideals and in a sort of sentimental way perhaps for France, but for England "No" and that all this question of entertaining etc in England is a great mistake as they say they have not come over to be entertained by England but to fight for America. On the other hand he thinks that out here a great deal of good might be done in the very way I had suggested, namely lectures by Americans to American soldiers telling them what England had done but not giving them simply rows of figures but a few figures with various stories of gallant acts. He says the worst mistake that we made in the way of Propaganda was when we removed Swinton[2] from being "eye-witness". His notes were read with the greatest possible interest in America. They were circulated all over the country and were very highly appreciated. He wishes something of the kind could be done now. He is coming to luncheon tomorrow and will give me further suggestions.

I sent for Adam the correspondent of *The Times*. I found that he had absolutely no information whatsoever with regard to Clemenceau's inspection of the Canadian Brigade. Of course there ought to have been reporters there and a Cinematograph. I gave him what particulars I could and he is going to write it up but what I feel about all these matters is that this is not my business and there ought to be somebody who is really seeing to all these things. We shall never succeed as long as we have Maclagan here as the head but I have got a letter from Arnold Bennett today saying that they think he is far and away the best man they have got; we were very lucky to get him and they will make no change. That being so I shall have to work with him as best I can but I shall also adopt other means of propaganda work.

Portia and I went to luncheon with Prince and Princesse de Lignes. She is a sister of Mouchy and Charles de Noailles, who is in London employed in our War Office. A nice boy but looked upon here as a most awful embusqué. His brother Mouchy [whom] I met the other day is a delightful fellow who has been fighting lately in Salonika where he very nearly died of Malaria.

Afternoon — nothing.

Madame de Polignac came to tea and was rather amusing giving from an American point of view her ideas and opinions on French Society. Her husband has now gone to the Front. He is one of Tardieu's young men and

I suppose will go back to America when he (Tardieu) goes. He is looked upon as a very rising fellow.

At dinner David Henderson came. He has taken over the Command from Phillips and quite rightly is not going to call himself, as the latter did, Commandant of Paris. It is a great relief to have such a man here as he is a gentleman whom everybody likes and I think will do a great deal of good. He says already that he has discovered that the Missions have got about twice as many people as they want and he is going to try and weed them out. He infuriated Portia by saying he meant to stop all people in the Missions having their wives out here. She thinks it is very hard on them. As a matter of fact I think he is perfectly right. There is no more reason why a man working in an office in Paris should have his wife out than a man working in Havre or Rouen and they are not allowed there.

Notes to 19 August

1. Henry N. Hall (1872–1949). War Correspondent with American Expeditionary Force, 1918–19.
2. Major-General Ernest Swinton (1868–1951). Assistant Secretary, Committee of Imperial Defence and War Cabinet, who journeyed through the USA, speaking about the war, 1918. The tank was very much his inspiration.

Tuesday, 20th August

Nothing in the morning.

Luncheon. Lady Edward Cecil[1] and her daughter and Mr. Hall, also Bridgeman and Luke White.

Lady Edward was quite nice and less excitable than usual. She had been to see Clemenceau in the morning. Of course she probably knows Clemenceau better than any other Englishwoman as he and her father were the greatest possible friends and used to stay together sometimes for weeks on end either in France or England.

In the afternoon Mr. Allen came to see me introduced by Lulu Harcourt.[2] He is an American Flying man who I thought came to speak to me on flying matters. As a matter of fact it was to talk about the Czecho Slovaks about whom he is a wild enthusiast and in regard to whom he was extremely interesting.

Rawly and Walter Dalkeith[3] arrived about 4 o'c. We had tea together and then Rawly, Portia and I went to the Avenue de Hois and sat there till Dinner time, a blazing hot day.

Dinner Prince and Princesse de Lignes and Marquise de Polignac. We all sat talking till 11.30 in the garden. Quite an amusing dinner. I got a message to say Clemenceau wanted to see me first thing the next morning.

Notes to 20 August

1. Lady Violet Cecil. Married Edward, youngest son of the 3rd Marquess of Salisbury. Daughter of Clemenceau's friend, Admiral Maxse.
2. Lewis Harcourt, Viscount Harcourt 1917 (1863–1922). Liberal MP 1904–17; First Commissioner of Works, 1915–16.
3. Walter Douglas-Scott, Earl of Dalkeith (1894–1973). Son and heir of Duke of Buccleuch; Captain, Grenadier Guards.

Wednesday, 21st August

Went to see Clemenceau at 9 o'c. Found him in a great state of excitement as he had just got the news in of the success of Byng's[1] Army. They had then got all their first objectives and were well on their way to the second, having effected a complete surprise. Rawly had told me the night before that the one thing they really wanted was a thick mist and they apparently had it. I have never seen Clemenceau so pleased as he was. He told me that he thought I brought him luck as he had never sent for me to come and see him about anything without having to give me good news. I only hope it will continue.

The real object though of his sending for me was to ask me to preside at this Women's Meeting tonight. Mrs. Bliss, and our own and the American Y.M.C.A. leaders were both there and it was impossible for me to refuse, especially as Pichon had undertaken to make the speech of the evening. Lloyd George has written a letter which is excellent from the point of view of England but not quite from the point of view of an International Meeting as it strongly advocates the giving of votes to women which Clemenceau is very much opposed to. After reading Lloyd George's letter he gave us a short but very interesting statement of his views on the subject. Exactly what he had said to me on Sunday, namely that in a country like England or America which on the whole were essentially Protestant, it was possible and a good thing, but where there were clergy and a confessional it was absolutely impossible and he would always oppose it.

Came back and had a long talk with Rawly who started back at once for the Front as probably now he will again be engaged in order to keep reserves from going up in front of Byng. He is always hopeful but he was really optimistic to a degree today and thinks we may have got the Bosch on the run. He says there is no doubt their morale is very much affected. They have used up practically all their reserves and even if they wanted to mount a big attack he does not think they could do it under six weeks and then only if we gave them the opportunity during those six weeks to recuperate. We discussed all our Military and Political friends and he tells me that the French, and especially Foch, who is supposed to be Henry Wilson's great friend, are now very antagonistic to him. He says Foch says that Henry Wilson cannot go straight and when he wants to get a thing he never tries to go straight for it but will go by any devious course. I think that may be true but at the same time Foch did not add that it is precisely the same attitude that the French themselves take up.

I quite forgot to mention that Eddy Hartington came to luncheon yesterday and gave me a bit of white heather which had been sent to him from Bolton[2] by, who he called "old" Wilson, who I remember so well as quite a comparatively young man when he first took over the Head Keepership at Bolton from Burch.

Afternoon. Zaharoff came to see me and the following is a copy of a letter written to Arthur Balfour on the subject.

"Zaharoff came to see me this afternoon on his return from Switzerland. I suppose he is writing to you though he did not tell me so. He rather amused me when he told me that he had written to Stamfordham for the information of the King. I do not think his visit has done very much although something may come of it. What I gather happened was that he did not see Enver[3] but saw his uncle whose name I could not catch (some name like Abdul Resid) who told him that at the last Council of War at Berlin there had been rather hot discussion and that both the Bulgarians and the Turks had for the first time asserted themselves — he says by the way that Ferdinand[4] of Bulgaria is not nearly so ill as he makes out — and that it was very obvious that the Kaiser's influence is on the wane. Hindenburg[5] and Ludendorff were very bitter against each other. It was decided to have another Council of War in about a fortnight or 3 weeks time at which not only the various heads of State and soldiers would be present but also the Foreign Ministers and the Ministers of the Interior. Zaharoff also had a talk with the Bulgarians who confirmed what the Turks had said and told him that the Turks and Bulgarians are going to try and settle their differences and think they will have no difficulty in doing so, but, as he put it, they said that they realise that their chief difficulty would be their fate as decided in France. I asked him what that meant and he said that it meant that while the Turks and Bulgarians would have no difficulty in coming to an agreement with each other they would have far more difficulty in coming to an agreement with Greece as it would mean Greece having to give up some territory and that that part of their arrangement could only stand or fall by the non-success or the reverse of the Allies in France. Both Bulgarians and Turks however seem much impressed with the way things are going in France and have told him that if he would return after the next Council of War they thought they might have something of interest to tell him. Zaharoff himself thinks that if our successes continue during that time, as I sincerely hope they will, it may be quite possible to come to terms with them, but he was very guarded as he rightly said he did not wish to give any wrong impression as to great results having been achieved by this present visit. He only came in for a very short time as he was in a hurry but I think I have given you the gist of what he told me. He is going to come up again at the end of next week to Dinner with me and if by that time he has not written to you please let me know and I will endeavour to get a more detailed account of his visit if you so wish."

I presided over the women's meeting in the evening. About 2,500 there. I had simply to do the introduction of Pichon who made a good speech but of course it was to a certain extent spoilt because — as all Frenchmen do — he read his speech, but we both agreed that we never wanted to speak to an audience composed entirely of women again. It is the most deadly thing, not a sound and they sit looking absolutely stolid. Mrs. Lyttelton, who spoke for all the women, made an extremely stupid speech in which she explained what England had done which was one thing which was not wanted and kept on talking about our invincible troops. I have always thought her one of the stupidest women I know. She also launched out into political matters as to what women would do after the War and how they would assert their rights. I must say she was justified perhaps in doing so owing to Lloyd George's message which was full of "Votes for Women". It was hardly tactful as it is the one thing Clemenceau is determined not to accede to. Got back about 10. Ended the hottest day I have ever known — at all events in Europe.

Notes to 21 August

1. General Julian Byng (1862–1935). Viscount Byng, 1926. Commander of British

3rd Army who won fame for the capture of Vimy Ridge. In the final push of the war his army captured 67,000 Germans.

2. Derby owned extensive agricultural land around Bolton which he sold between 1919 and 1925.
3. Enver Pasha (1881–1922). As War Minister he brought Turkey into the war on the side of Germany. Murdered by Soviet agents.
4. Ferdinand of Bulgaria (1861–1948). Ruler of Bulgaria, 1887–1918. He aligned Bulgaria with Germany in the war and was forced to abdicate after the defeat.
5. Paul von Hindenburg (1847–1934). German Chief of the General Staff since 1916. President of the Republic, 1925–34.

Thursday, 22nd August

Began with a morning raid about 10 o'c. I could only see one aeroplane but it will probably turn out to be a French one which got lost.

Luncheon. Monsieur and Madame Berthelot, Monsieur Favre and Commander Allen of the United States Flying Corps. Quite an amusing luncheon. Margerie is very ill and Berthelot has taken his place and is therefore the Charlie Hardinge of the Foreign Office. Both he and Favre attacked me as to the bad way in which we run our propaganda in regard to the Navy. They say it is lamentable and the people in the country know nothing whatever about what we have done. He said if only they can be made to realise that it was entirely thanks to us that the Americans were able to arrive it would be [a] very strong bond of union between our two countries. Nobody feels this more than I do but nobody feels how more impossible it is to get anything done under the present arrangements.

Favre began talking about the keeping up of our Divisions and evidently it has gone out that every means are to be taken to impress upon us that we are not doing everything we possibly can in England and that if we wished to keep up our Divisions we could do so. I told him that it was perfectly possible to keep up our Divisions to full strength on the condition that we gave them no coal. I am sure that is the line to go on. Point out to them that they can have the men if they choose to go without the coal which of course they will not do.

They then got on to a general discussion as to Peace terms and it was quite evident from the way Favre and Berthelot talked that they are in entirely different Camps, although both Ministers,[1] in regard to War Aims and especially in regard to Austria, Favre's idea being that Austria must be kept as a strong power and if possible allied with France. This Yugo Slav business is going to give us an infinity of trouble. It is so easy to promise to give them independence but to my mind it is absolutely impossible to fulfil the promise. I hate all this opportunist talk. We are made the catspaw. We always make promises which we know cannot be fulfilled and then naturally we are accused afterwards of breach of faith. It was we who turned the scale with regard to Roumania coming into the War[2] although as a matter of fact we were opposed to it and again we were made the catspaw by France.

Spiers came to see me before luncheon. He had seen Clemenceau who was extremely friendly towards him and told him to come and see him as often as he liked. Mordacq also had told him that really Clemenceau had nothing against him. It is impossible to deal with these people when they tell one man one thing and one man another but I have to take what Clemenceau says to me as being his real feeling. Capel is an invaluable connecting link with Clemenceau but I am very anxious about his health. He is very neurasthenic and I am certain he himself thinks he is going off his head which is very far from being the case. Though he talks quite freely with me they tell me when he is alone at home he sits for hours without saying a word and you cannot get him to buckle down to any work. I am sending him away for a fortnight's holiday.

After luncheon the Chargé d'affaires to the Belgian Legation came to see me in the absence of his Minister and I had to give him a rap over the knuckles. He came to ask me a series of the most indiscreet questions that his Minister would certainly not have asked me. He wanted to know what information I had had about the meeting of the two Emperors. What our objectives were yesterday and what our general objectives were and asked me the most ridiculous questions as to where I thought we should get during the next 6 weeks. I had to tell him I had no information on these subjects and if I had any I should not give them to him. His proper place to go for any such information is the Government to which he is accredited and not to me. His Minister who is a very good fellow indeed would I am certain be furious if he knew what his subordinate had done.

Johnny Du Cane came in to see me before Dinner. He had just returned from a meeting between Haig and Foch, most satisfactory in every way. I told him that I thought the bond of union in the future between the French and English would be the antagonism to Pershing who is most pig headed and he said there were signs of that already. He told me that he was afraid that the feeling caused by the last Supreme War Council was still very bad and he doubted whether it would ever be forgotten and he also told me a story I can hardly believe which was that Lloyd George saw the King before he came out here and told His Majesty to tell Clemenceau that he noticed with regret that the French were trying to get everything into their own hands and that this would not do and they must clearly understand that England would not stand that. The King is supposed to have obeyed these instructions. I can quite believe Lloyd George telling the King that, but I do not believe in his carrying it out, more especially as I know he did not see Clemenceau. He may however have said something to Poincaré. I can quite understand in some ways the irritation that is caused by the French trying to get things into their own hands and especially their patronising way of taking the Americans under their charge, but when it comes to military matters I cannot see that we have got a leg to stand on. We have placed, quite rightly I think, Foch in supreme command and Lloyd George has very publicly advertised that it was thanks to him that this was done and yet whenever Foch exercises this Command there seems to be a disposition to thwart him in every way. If only the people at home would leave Foch and Haig to carry out their work in their own way there would never be the slightest difference of opinion between them.

Du Cane told me that Foch thinks the Germans are really cracking and although some of them are fighting extremely well, others, and I gather it is the Bavarians chiefly, are quite ready to lay down their arms.

I am afraid we are going to have great trouble with the French over the man power question. They have had a most iniquitous report drawn up by one of their Colonels who went to London to study the question and he has made a report which is a tissue of falsehoods from beginning to end. I am sure if it was discussed at the Supreme War Council it can only end in a bitter row and I am trying to get the Home Authorities and then Clemenceau to agree that two independent people shall go into the figures and see whether they can arrive at some understanding which will prevent friction. In this particular report all our figures are falsified and the French refuse to give us any information about their own with which they compare ours. The consequence is the Report is worse than useless. Clemenceau unfortunately has taken it as gospel.

Dinner. Only ourselves but after Dinner Johnny Du Cane came in together with the Westmacotts[3] (who was Cissie Winn) and Charlie Winn and we sat talking. Boiling hot night.

Notes to 22 August

1. Berthelot, of course, was not a minister. But Derby's mistake is excusable. Berthelot was widely seen to have enjoyed an excessive influence over Aristide Briand

during the latter's premiership and to have exercised authority unusual in a civil servant. See J. Laroche, *Au Quai d'Orsay avec Briand et Poincaré* (Paris, 1957), pp. 30–31.
2. Romania's entry into the war in 1916 had raised spirits in the allied capitals. By mid-September, however, the advance of the Romanian army had been halted by the Central Powers.
3. Major-General Sir Richard Westmacott (1841–1925). Service in India.

Friday, 23rd August

Dr. Benes[1] the Secretary of the Czecho Slovak Committee came to see me as I had to communicate to him a telegram I had received from home begging him to get the Czecho representative at Washington to do all he could to make the President realise the extremely serious state of their troops in Siberia. It apparently is quite impossible to show President Wilson that there is any danger and he only looks upon statements to this effect, made by us, as an attempt to draw him into a big Campaign in Siberia. I am sending Benes a memorandum and he is going to send as strong a telegram as possible to his American representative.

Major Roberts[2] who is acting for Le Roy Lewis brought up Major Bodley,[3] the new Assistant Military Attaché and a son of Professor J. E. Bodley.[4] He is only two years older than Edward, is a regular serving soldier and commanded his Battalion of the Rifles (the 60th) and has been very badly gassed. It appears he has always lived in France and he, like me and incidentally Roberts who also knows Paris very well, is aghast at the want of proper propaganda that is going on. It never will improve as long as Maclagan is at the head of it though I have heard definitely from Arnold Bennett that they mean to keep him here and that he is the best man, so I am not going to go on knocking my head against a stone wall any longer. If they won't improve it they must suffer the consequences.

Luncheon. Johnny Ward came and Billy Lambton arrived about 2 o'c from Aix. Nearly 4 hours late. He is looking much better.

After luncheon General Janin, who is to command the Czechs in Siberia, came to see me before going. He is the most dilatory sort of gentleman. He does not expect to get to Siberia before the middle of October and no fighting can possibly take place after the end of October.

Later Spiers came to see me. The War Office want me if possible to try and deal with this Man Power Report so as to avoid further friction between Lloyd George and Milner on one side and Clemenceau on the other. I want to get an independent enquiry in which Colonel Georges of the French War Office and Macready (the Adjutant General's son) who is now at Versailles, should examine the Report which is a tissue of false-hoods from beginning to end and see if they cannot at all events reconcile some of the figures and explain some of the discrepancies. I do not know whether Clemenceau would agree to this but I have sent Spiers to see him and to just feel the way about it.

Dinner. General Maurice came straight from Rawly's headquarters. I was very glad to see him as we had always been great friends and person-ally I have always looked upon him as one of the ablest Staff Officers we had. I strongly advocated his going to Versailles when Henry Wilson first went there but I was over-ruled. If he had gone we should have been saved a great deal of trouble as he was strongly in favour of the unified Com-mand from the beginning and would I think [have] persuaded Robertson to agree. He had been all the way down the Front and was very interest-ing. He is not as a rule a very optimistic man and therefore one pays more attention to him than one does to most people when he says that really the German Army is to a great extent demoralised and that if we can only keep at them we may get them fairly on the run. He had come straight from Rawly who had had a great success and yesterday apparently both the 3rd and 4th Armies got their objectives comparatively easily.[5] He says that if we once get Bapaume again the Germans are almost bound to go back to the Hindenberg line and he thinks that it is their intention to do so. He thinks they have been contemplating it for some time as they will be able to save 20 Divisions by doing so, but we are forcing them back quicker than they meant to go and therefore they have not got their prepa-rations complete in the rear.

Notes to 23 August

1. Eduard Benes (1884–1948). Worked during the war to secure recognition from the Allies of Czechoslovakia's status as a nation. President, 1935–38.
2. Major Frederick Roberts. Royal Army Medical Corps.
3. Major R. V. C. Bodley. Appointed Assistant to the Military Attaché in Paris, 15 August 1918.
4. Professor J. E. Bodley (1853–1925). Historian.
5. Anglo-French forces took part in large-scale attacks in the area around Albert and Bapaume from 21 August.

Saturday, 24th August

Walked in the garden with Maurice before he left. We discussed all the disagreeable incidents which occurred before I left the War Office. He still thinks Robertson was right to go because he (Robertson) thought that the scheme of managing a Reserve by a Committee was perfectly unworkable and if he consented to stay it was equivalent to saying he thought it was workable. I do not agree with him there at all. It was perfectly possible I think — and here Maurice agreed with me — for Robertson to say that he accepted as a soldier the duty that was put upon him but at the same time stating that he did not think it was a workable scheme but that he would endeavour to make it work if it were possible.

Maurice mentioned his own case. He was very nice in talking to me about it and he said if I had been at the War Office a week longer he would still have been in the Army as he would have come to see me with his story and got me to put it forward but as he says it is no use crying over spilt milk. He is going to do in another sphere all that he possibly can to help the Army. He is bitter of course against the War Cabinet and especially against Milner. He recognises as I do that the men were there last year if the Government had only liked to pass the Bill which they did a year later when it was too late,[1] and both he and I know that the man who prevented any steps being taken to get men was always Milner.

Bridges came to see me. He had been down with the Americans. He thinks that both ourselves and the French have queered our own pitches with regard to the Americans by continually fighting over where they are to go. Pershing has now taken matters into his own hands and is going to keep an Army quite distinct as he says that the Americans are not people to be bartered about between French and English. Bridges tells me that wherever he went amongst the Americans he found great dislike of Pershing. Nobody looks upon him as being a good man. I am afraid however they won't make any change in this case until he has had a go somewhere on his own account and failed, as fail he will thanks to having no proper Staff organisation.

Luncheon. Colonel Georges who is one of Clemenceau's Military Secretaries, a most charming man. The last time he was here was on the first day of the Chemin des Dames and he said what a difference between now and then. Charlie Grant, Phipps from the Chancery, Roberts and Bodley from the Military Attaché's Office and Mr. Kerney a very full blooded Yank who is the head of the American Propaganda Department.

Oliver arrived just before Dinner.

Dinner. Lady Lovat, Spiers, Capels, Lady Rosemary Leveson Gower,[2] Bullock, Major Bodley, Humphrey de Trafford and Maurice Brett[3] together with the people in the House which included Billy Lambton.

Afterwards the Grenadiers Band played in the garden and a few people, friends of people in the Chancery, came in and listened. A lovely night and much cooler.

Notes to 24 August

1. A new Military Service Bill had been rushed through parliament in April 1918. This provided for a drastic mobilisation of available manpower, while raising the upper age limit from 42 to 50.
2. Lady Rosemary Leveson Gower. Daughter of the 4th Duke of Sutherland. In the winter of 1917–18 her name had been romantically linked with that of the Prince of Wales.
3. Captain Maurice Brett (1882–1934). Second son of 2nd Viscount Esher.

Sunday, 25th August

Luncheon. Bridges and Millie Sutherland came to luncheon.

After luncheon Sir Arthur Hardinge, our Ambassador at Madrid, came to see me. I must say he is not an imposing figure and report says that he is going to be removed. If so he has evidently got no inkling of it at the present moment. He thinks that the Spanish are going to win over their controversy with the Germans on the torpedoing of ships question. They have got the whole country behind them, even the most pro-German Spaniards, in their demand that for every Spanish Ship torpedoed they should requisition a German Ship and that they will certainly put this into execution if the Germans continue torpedoing their Ships. On the other hand he, Hardinge, thinks the Germans will stick to the principle but bow to the inevitable and order their U Boats to turn a blind eye to every Spanish Ship. He spoke somewhat bitterly of Bend Or's[1] Mission to Spain though he likes him personally and says he made himself extremely popular playing polo etc. but he doubts, and so do I, whether the information Bend Or is able to collect with regard to trade with Spain after the War is likely to be of much value. I think he resented more than Bend Or, F. E. Smith going out, as apparently the Spanish look upon him, as I am afraid the Americans did,[2] as a very second rate sort of gentleman.

Afterwards went and played golf. Oliver and I against Charlie and Portia. Had a very nice round. We won by two up.

Dinner with the Spiers. Ourselves, Madame Hennessy, Guiche and DeMun and Dick Sutton.

Billy Lambton left in the afternoon to stay for a night with Johnny Du Cane.

Notes to 25 August

1. Hugh R. A. Grosvenor, 2nd Duke of Westminster (1879–1953). Known as 'Bendor' (after his grandfather's horse, 'Ben d'Or'). Personal assistant to the Controller, Mechanical Department, Ministry of Munitions, 1917.
2. F. E. Smith had been sent on a mission to the United States in December 1917 to help encourage American recruitment.

Monday, 26th August

Mr. Hall *The Times* correspondent with the American army, who I mentioned last week, came to see me again and we had a long and very interesting talk. Without going into details it appears that the Americans are going to import lecturers for their troops in the winter months and his idea is to get these lecturers to put some of our propaganda work into their lectures. He made certain proposals which I have submitted to Arnold Bennett.

He was extremely interesting on various matters connected with America. He says that the mentality of the men coming over now is about the same as our school-boys of 14 and that for lectures, speeches, etc. you have got to employ the same language that you would use to boys of that age. The Americans are very precocious but precocious from their surroundings which they pick up very quickly. They are not in the least precocious from their education or from what they learn from books.

Hall was Editor of the *New York World*. He told me he made a rule that no word of three syllables was to be put into the paper except under very special circumstances and that the result of this innovation was to send the circulation up 30,000 copies a day. That the Americans really only understood words of one syllable and that their vocabulary is extremely limited. Probably the vocabulary in use at the outside consists of not more than 800 words. They are taught no Latin and the consequence is words with Latin derivation are very seldom used. He tells me it is very difficult to get a good feeling amongst the Americans for England owing entirely to the school books used. That I have been told by several other people but it is hoped now that there will be a re-writing of all these school books of English History.

He warned me against a man called Lippmann,[1] the Editor of the *New Republic*, who has got over here with a Commission and has gradually wormed himself into a position which gives him some authority over the Press. That he is a most dangerous man, absolutely pacifist as far as America was concerned and bitterly opposed to any giving of Alsace and Lorraine back to the French. He has already made the French Press very suspicious of him.

We then talked about Senator Lodge[2] who made a speech giving Peace terms and I asked what sort of authority he carried in America. He told me he was a strong supporter of Roosevelt's[3] or rather a bitter opponent at the last Election of Wilson and had always been for coming into the War but he had behaved extremely loyally to Wilson. He supported him when he came into the War. He supported him by backing up everything that he did and not criticising his delays. He made the best speech that was made when America came into the War and afterwards went up and shook hands with the President — the first time he had ever done so — and the President had been extremely pleased. He told me that the President probably paid more attention to Lodge's views than anybody else's outside his own Party and was more and more taking into consideration Lodge's views.

Hall tells me that Roosevelt is entirely an extinct volcano. He is losing his intellect, blind in one eye, stone deaf in one ear and missed a great opportunity when he took the action he did after the President had declared War. Hall says if then he had backed up the President and kept on hinting that it was his pressure that had made the President come into the War America would have thought that was the case, instead of which he has done nothing but abuse the President for delays and scoffed at his inefficiency. The President has turned the tables on him because Roosevelt said that a year after the War America ought to have at least 150,000 men in France and that thanks to Wilson's inefficiency they would not have half that number where as a matter of fact they had 4 times the amount that Roosevelt had suggested.

Luncheon. Cissie Westmacott, Berkheim, who is in the Ministry of Foreign Affairs and Claveille the head of the Railways. The latter is a most interesting man. He is the first French Minister I knew and we have been great friends ever since. He was head of the French State railways before the War. He took them over when they were in a very bad state and completely pulled them round. He then served under Thomas in Munitions, then Under-Secretary for Transportation and now a Minister. He is not in any way a politician. Not a Deputy. He has a thorough knowledge of his business and one of the best judges of character one could possibly meet. After luncheon he talked on every sort of subject especially of the people with whom he had been working. He puts first of all Clemenceau who he says is an extraordinarily able man and the only real man of action he has come across in France. At the same time he does not think he is a Diplomatist and says that he would be bad when negotiating terms of Peace. He thinks that when it does come to that point you must associate Briand with him. He is very enthusiastic about Briand. Says that he is a fine speaker and gets the most marvellous grasp of affairs in the shortest time of any man he knows. Whenever he had a difficult point he negotiated always up to the last fence himself. He would then have 10 minutes with Briand who in that interval would practically learn the whole subject and who was a born negotiator. He thinks that Briand is not in any way working against Clemenceau now and when it came to discussing Peace would most certainly work with him. He has no opinion of Painlevé or Ribot and not very much of Thomas. He says Thomas is a great talker but nothing much more than that and when it comes to dealing with the workmen or employers he is very cowardly and as far as the latter are concerned does not act up at all to his speeches.

In talking of the Allies he told us there was only one thing in which the Italians excelled every nation and that was as thieves and liars. He said they would steal anything and they would lie about anything and he has more difficulty with them over the subject of wagons and locomotives than all the other nations put together. They borrow wagons from him on the distinct and written understanding that they shall be returned within a certain time. They are never returned and when he asks for them he is always told the Italians cannot send them back because they have need of them.

The Americans are very boastful. In some ways they are better than any other railway people. They are quicker workers but their work is not nearly so thorough and they always start by saying they will do double as much as he knows they can do. But he has now learnt to discredit that. He says however that some of their railway methods are superior to both English and French and both nations can learn from them. At the same time from the point of view of Engine Drivers he infinitely prefers the English. He said the English learn the different signals and different ways of running a railway in a week and once having learnt it they never have an accident. The Americans learn it in 5 days and then pay no attention to any orders or advice and have an infinity of accidents. They are most prodigal of material and waste twice as much as English and French. With regard to locomotives he says that it is extraordinary how badly the Americans make them. He said if he was awarding points he would say English and French exactly the same, 20 points each, Italians 17 points and Americans 10 points, and even that he would think too high.

He told us some statistics of the Railways they have been making lately. I cannot remember them but they struck me as being extraordinary. He is evidently extremely proud of what has been done. He says by far his best workers are the German prisoners. The Chinese are good and bad according to the localities from which they come and the Italians hopeless.

He stayed with us a long time and was most interesting and it is really a compliment his coming as he never has either luncheon or dinner out. Clemenceau, as he told me last Sunday week, has the very highest opinion of him and does not know what he would do without him. Claveille told us that he would go on working his very utmost as long as Clemenceau was the head of the government but if Clemenceau went or once Peace came he meant to take a 6 months holiday but it is going to be a busman's holiday as he is going to study the Railway working in America. He is altogether a very exceptional man.

Billy Lambton came in before they went. He had just returned from seeing Foch who was more than pleased with the way things are going.

Bullock dined.

Notes to 26 August

1. Walter Lippmann (1889–1974). American editor and author. Editor of *The New Republic*, the chief organ of Progressivism.
2. Henry Cabot Lodge (1850–1924). Republican Senator (1893–1924) who became renowned for his opposition to American membership of the League of Nations.
3. Theodore Roosevelt (1858–1919). Twenty-sixth president of the USA (1901–09). Vigorous advocate of American entry into the First World War.

Tuesday, 27th August

Saw Clemenceau this morning and particulars are contained in the following copy of a letter I sent to Balfour:

"I asked to see Clemenceau this morning as I rather wanted to find out how things stood with regard to various matters. I will put down roughly for you the gist of our conversation.

I spoke to him about the Report on our Man Power. I told him that quite apart from its not being, in my opinion, an accurate statement of the situation there were certain things in it which were calculated to give trouble if it was discussed officially and (as I had received through General Spiers from the War Office a request that I should do so) I asked him whether he would allow the figures to be gone into unofficially by one of the Versailles Officers and an unbiassed officer of his own, and that they should thoroughly discuss the question, see whether it would not be possible for them to eliminate certain of the controversial points and agree to differ, as I am afraid they must do, on certain other points. The latter would have to be discussed officially between Clemenceau and Milner or the Prime Minister. I told Clemenceau that I thought this would at all events eliminate some of the dangers of controversy. He quite agreed, jumped at the proposal and is going to choose an officer, who I hope will be a certain Colonel Georges. It is absolutely unofficial. It is understood to be at my personal request and not at the request of the War Office and therefore it is perfectly possible for me to be repudiated if that becomes necessary, but I think good may come of it.

We then turned to other subjects. I reminded him of the conversation we had had last Sunday week in which both he and Foch expressed their fears that Pershing had got such influence with the President that the latter would support him against Foch. I told him, without giving my authority, that I thought this was entirely wrong and I felt perfectly certain that the President had accepted Foch as being in supreme command and they might rely on him supporting Foch even against Pershing. Clemenceau told me it was most important he should know that because it was a point on which he had great doubts in his own mind. Things were not going well between Foch and Pershing. Many of Foch's suggestions are ignored by the latter and he had not dared give him an order for the effect it might have on the President. Curiously enough however Clemenceau had told him yesterday the time had come when he must give orders and if they were not obeyed he (Clemenceau) would have to telegraph to the President on the subject. He said therefore the information I gave him was of the greatest value as it strengthened his hand.

He then told me that he wished to speak to me about the Italians. He is absolutely disgusted with them and with their inactivity (or worse). In the first place he says that they have implored the Italians to attack in Italy. He thinks Sonnino would be quite ready that there should be an attack but Diaz[1] absolutely declines to do so and that on the Albanian front they have retired very precipitately and by so doing have exposed the Flank of the French. He told me that he had sent orders for the French, if the Italians evacuated Berat, to at once seize it themselves but the Italians retreated so fast that the French were not able to get up in time. He has therefore telegraphed to his Ambassador at Rome to tell him that for the moment he (Clemenceau) looks upon the Italian Armies as a non-existent force whether in Albania or in Italy and does not propose to consult with them any further. For that reason therefore and for fear that it would create trouble he does not wish to have a Supreme War Council at the present moment. Yet at the same time he thinks that one is essential in order to decide whether the offensive is to be taken at Salonika or not. In order to get out of this difficulty of both wanting and not wanting a meeting of the Supreme War Council he wondered whether it would be possible for England and France together to agree as to what should take place in Salonika and to come before a Supreme War Council later with the decision as to what was to be done a "fait accompli" as far as England and France were concerned.

He suggests that as General Guillaumat is the man on whom he relies for advice with regard to Salonika matters he should send him *at once* to London to consult with the War Cabinet. You met him and I think you formed a high opinion of him. Certainly he is a man who has a very clear mind and puts his propositions very concisely. I think therefore this proposal might be of extreme value but if it is to be done it must be done at once because if an offensive be taken there are many requirements of the French Army in Salonika, shells, wagons, etc. which Clemenceau would send out at once. If no offensive is to be taken — of course as you know he is strongly of opinion that one should take place — he will send out none of these things.

I ought to mention here that he had had many large demands from Italy for Shells, wagons, tanks, etc. which he would have been perfectly ready to send if the Italians had consented to take the offensive but as they had refused he equally had refused to send anything to them.

He then spoke to me on the subject of where the next Supreme War Council is to be held. He told me Lloyd George wanted it to be in London and he wanted me to explain the reasons why he thought it must be at Versailles. In the first place he wanted you and the P.M. to clearly understand that it was not a question of dignity on his part, or a question of inconvenience, which made him prefer Versailles. It was that it was essential that at any meeting to consider these military matters Foch should be present and this was impossible at the present moment if the meeting were held in London. Moreover he could not leave Foch because, although, as he assured me, he interfered in no way with military matters (adding he was not such a fool as to do so) Foch did rely upon him to an inordinate extent, especially in his dealings with the Americans and that just as it was impossible for Foch to leave his Army, so it was impossible for him to leave Foch. I think therefore you may take it that if there was a Supreme War Council held in London Clemenceau himself would not go. It seems to me therefore that the only way out of the difficulty with regard to a Salonika decision is that Guillaumat should go over to London at once. If an agreement is arrived at with him well and good. If not then I suppose there would have to be a Supreme War Council and as one would be somewhat useless without Foch or Clemenceau it would be necessary to hold it at Versailles. As I have said Clemenceau is anxious to have an offensive at Salonika and is very confident of success there. He will be disappointed if England does not agree to it but at the same time I do not think that if we do not agree it will be looked upon as a great grievance or as a matter for friction.

As we were parting he just referred to the meeting which is being held in London today and he told me he was in entire accord with our people that if England put the whole of her hand on the table with regard to tonnage for bringing Americans over from the United States of America, America should equally put her hand on the table and disclose all her tonnage and the instructions to his people in London were to support this view.

Clemenceau was most friendly throughout. In high good humour as he had just received the news that the French had taken Roye.

He was rather disturbed at the "Tank" losses. He told me they started with 26 Tank Battalions and now have only got 7."

Millie Sutherland, Lord Mayor of London and Mr. Price at luncheon. The Lord Mayor very full of his Italian trip. Apparently he had been extremely well received everywhere.

Mr. Price, a very rich American who is doing all he can to improve the relationship between England and America. Interesting on American politics. He is a strong Republican and very bitter against Wilson and still more against his son in law Mr. McAdoo.[2] He says that the reason why the Americans officially do not give us the credit for having done what we have done in the way of conveying American troops over in English ships is that they are afraid it will show how lax the Government was in making the shipping arrangements. He says that the President will allow no

Republican to take any share in the administration and the feeling between the two parties is just as bitter now as it was before the War but the Republicans are behaving very patriotically and supporting Wilson although they dislike him. I asked him about Senator Lodge. He tells me that although Roosevelt is still the nominal head of the Republican Party Lodge is to all intents and purposes its leader and that anything he puts forward would be the view of the Republican Party. But the fact that it was so put forward would at once make it a bone of contention and he therefore thinks it is very dangerous that Lodge should have stated possible terms of Peace as it probably will put the President and the Democratic Party in opposition to the terms, especially those about Alsace and Lorraine. These are rather different to the views expressed to me by Hall and I think Hall has probably a better judgement in the matter than Price has.

Maklakoff, the so-called Russian Ambassador here came to see me in regard to a communication I had sent to him asking for the removal of the Russian Minister in Norway who had pro-German feelings. He stated that he wanted to know who was responsible for the statement and whether it was M. Nabokoff[3] the Russian Attaché in London and if so on what information he based his statements. The real reason however for his coming to see me was to complain bitterly that he was not allowed to correspond anywhere in cipher whereas apparently Litvinoff[4] the Bolshevist Ambassador in London was.

I saw Clemenceau again in the afternoon as he wanted to speak to me with regard to some details of our conversation in the morning. He also wanted to know what I could not tell him, namely what is going on about this appeal for Labour Battalions from Ireland.

Dinner. Ross and Humphrey de Trafford both from Versailles dined.

Notes to 27 August

1. General Armando Diaz (1861–1928). Became Italian Commander-in-Chief after the disaster at Caporetto in 1917.
2. William G. McAdoo (1863–1941). Secretary of the Treasury under Wilson, 1913–18, he married the President's daughter, Eleanor.
3. M. Nabokov. Chargé d'affaires of White Russians in London.
4. Maxim Litvinov (1876–1951). Appointed diplomatic agent to Britain after the 1917 revolution. Foreign Commissar, 1930–39.

Wednesday, 28th August

Ordinary weekly meeting. Nothing of any great importance.

Had unfortunately engaged myself to luncheon with the Berthelots. Really most amusing luncheon I have had for a long time. Pichon and the Bliss's were there but I do not know the names of anybody else. The Berthelots have rather an extraordinary history. He married his wife who is very nice and they have been together in many distant Embassies especially in China. When however the Government moved in 1914[1] people were only allowed to take their wives with them and it then turned out that the marriage was illegal. I believe there had been only the Church marriage and not the Civil marriage, or something of the kind, so they had to marry again. It did not matter as they have not got any children. The House is full of the most beautiful Chinese things you ever saw and it is most attractive.

On return to Embassy discussed propaganda questions with Maclagan's deputy.

Philip Roye came to ask me to go to luncheon to meet the new French Consul General to Canada but I am not able to do so.

Laurance Lyon the proprietor of the *Outlook* came to see me. I have known him some considerable time and he is very interesting on the subject of his visit to Spain. He says he feels perfectly certain that there will be no question of Spain coming into the War but she very likely might break off negotiations with Germany. The thing that has upset the Spanish people very much is that they feel that when there will be a Peace Conference they will not be included and they think that this will show that they are only one of the smaller nations and the result is their pride is very much offended, though why it should be, as there can be no conceivable reason why they should come in without having joined in the war, I do not know. They therefore at the present moment are thinking of breaking off relations with Germany without any Declaration of War in order to be included in the Peace Conference. He told me privately that Bend Or had really been quite a success in the way of popularising England in the sort of Upper circles where England had been anything but popular before, but all the good that he had done was undone by F. E. Smith who had offended everybody and more especially the King to whom he appears to have been very rude. Lyon tells me that he said something to him and F. E. Smith replied that the only way to treat the Spaniard was to take him by the throat and shake him and be very hard on him. I should doubt that being the case but it does seem to me a pity that F.E.S. should be allowed to go about and do so much harm as he has apparently done in Spain, and certainly he did in America.

Hartingtons and Madame de Polignac dined.

Notes to 28 August

1. With Paris thought to be under threat, the French government moved to Bordeaux in September 1914, returning to the capital in December.

Thursday, 29th August

Left about 9.45 a.m. with Oliver and went to G.H.Q. for orders. Found there Alan Fletcher and Philip Sassoon who had been attending the funeral service of poor Cox[1] who had been drowned two days before. It was the first I had heard of it. Oliver and I then went on to Advanced G.H.Q. and after tea he left for his battery. Just after he had gone Birch,[2] the head of the Artillery, came to me and told me how sorry he was to have missed Oliver as he wanted to tell him what very excellent reports had been made about him. That he was most highly spoken of not only in his own Artillery Brigade but in the Division generally and his battery was looked upon as being one of the very best in the Army. The result of that is that although they do not as a general rule take any Artillery Officer as a Brigade Major unless they have 6 to 8 years service he had been specially selected. There were difficulties in the way but Birch hoped he would be able to overcome them and that Oliver would go in a very short time as a learner. Nothing could have been more complimentary than he was and it is very satisfactory as I think Oliver rather felt that there was no chance of further promotion for him. This of course is promotion and sets him in the way of even further promotion.

Nobody dining that night. DH had been to see Foch. A long motor drive and I thought was rather tired but in very good spirits.

Notes to 29 August

1. Colonel Edgar Cox (1882–1918). DSO, 1915.
2. Major-General James Birch (b.1865). Royal Artillery, GHQ.

Friday, 30th August

All the Army Commanders came to see the Chief and I saw them before they went in to talk to him. I had not seen Plumer[1] for 2 years. He looks exactly the same as ever and as cheery as possible. They were all in very high spirits but I am glad to see none of them too optimistic.

As soon as their Conference had started I went off with Thompson on a round and had a most enjoyable day. Took our luncheon with us and motored as far as we could get over the reconquered territory. Went to Le Sars where I saw Shute who commands the Corps that has done the fighting there and David Campbell[2] who is an old friend of mine but whom I have not seen for years. He won the Grand National on Soarer. Both of them delighted at what had been done by their troops but say that their men are very tired, but not so tired as the Germans and of course as everybody says if only we had a few more fresh Divisions we could push right through. I have never seen such a scene of desolation as the whole battlefield is. I had been of course through part of it last year but it was then nothing to what it is now. The whole country looks like one vast rubbish heap and the Germans left every sort of thing behind them — Engineer Parks, Railways and, what is a blessing, most of the huts that we had put up they had failed to destroy and in addition they had made some excellent ones of their own which are all left in good repair, but nobody could believe what the Country looks like till they have seen it. The Engineers have certainly done wonders. They have repaired the Railway and the train ran into Bapaume within 24 hours of our having taken it which is a remarkable feat considering that most of the Bridges were blown up.

I went to Thiepval, Martinpuich, and as near to Bapaume as possible. Of course we could not see much of the real battle but there was a good bit of shooting going on.

Went back through Albert which is absolutely destroyed. Not a single house remaining standing and to Querrieu where I had tea with Godley and discovered that Algy[3] was living within 200 yards. Went across and saw Algy who looks extremely well.

From there motored back and arrived at G.H.Q. just in time for Dinner. All the news fairly satisfactory. We have not made as much progress as we hoped for and Mangin's[4] army had been held up on our right, but nevertheless during the day we had taken 3,500 prisoners. The only thing at all disquieting at G.H.Q. is the plague of wasps. I have never seen anything like it and I hate it.

Notes to 30 August

1. General Herbert Plumer (1857–1932). Following the Italian defeat at Caporetto in 1917, he went with a British force to help restore morale.
2. Major-General David Campbell. Commander, Infantry Battalion since 1917. Rode 'Soarer' to victory in the 1896 Grand National.
3. Algernon Francis Stanley (b.1874). Derby's brother. Colonel 2nd Life Guards, 1916.
4. General Charles Mangin (1866–1925). As Commander of the French Tenth Army in 1918 he played a leading role in the counter-offensive which drove the German army from the Aisne and the Marne. Commanded Army of the Rhine, 1919.

Saturday, 31st August

Everybody in tremendous spirits as they heard in the north we had taken Kemmel with very little fighting and in the south the Australians had taken Mount St. Quentin, a wonderful achievement. It is a commanding position which dominates the whole of the valley and will allow of the troops right and left to advance a very considerable way without much opposition for as long as we hold it the Bosche must go back. The Australians had taken 1,500 prisoners of the Prussian Guard. Nobody had thought that we could take this position except after very hard fighting and I think they would have been prepared to have had 5,000 casualties to have got it, whereas we got it with our total casualties under a hundred. It is one of the most remarkable performances that had been done.

Left G.H.Q. with a feeling that they are optimistic but not unduly so. That the Bosche has meant going back but has been driven back very much faster than he had meant to go and that that is entirely disorganising him the whole way down the line. He will try probably and hold on to the Hindenburg line but report has it that that line has been allowed to go into disrepair and will not be as effective as it was a year ago. The Bosche is still fighting well or rather he is doing what has always happened in every Army, some divisions are fighting magnificently, others badly. I think there is a great feeling amongst our people, and I believe there is amongst the French, that thanks to Pershing having insisted on creating his own Army and collecting them so as to make the Army, he has practically demobilised the whole of the American troops just at a moment when if they had been employed with our Army or the French we might almost have had a decisive result. I talked to Bacon who was the American Ambassador in Paris and is now a Liaison Officer between the Americans and Douglas Haig. He is very unhappy about it and thinks that when it gets known in America there will be a very bitter feeling against Pershing. He went down to try and persuade Pershing to change his views but all to no purpose.

I was told today that McDonough is going to succeed Cox as Head Intelligence Officer. The very best appointment that could be made from one point of view and that is from Haig's but I look with the greatest alarm on the result at home. McDonough is the one man who all through, by his wonderful power of grasping facts, has prevented these wild cat schemes in the East, or at all events limited them. He has not hit it off with Henry Wilson — that I did not know till they told me — and has been very miserable there. They are putting in a man called Thwaites[1] who everybody tells me is a good man and knows Germany from A–Z but I doubt whether he can possibly have the same influence that McDonough has.

One of the other things that I was told and which is very serious is that when Calais was bombed the other day they destroyed the sheds with all motor tyres and all the spare parts. 27,000 tyres were lost and it may cripple us enormously. Absolute folly to have stored them in a place which was within such easy bombing distance of the front.

Motored to luncheon at Rawly's at Bertangles. A most lovely old chateau from the outside but most uncomfortable looking in the inside. I had arranged to take Walter Dalkeith back with me and in the morning got a message to ask if I would also take Lady Mida Scott if she came which naturally I was only too glad to do. She came to luncheon too and to everybody's surprise a message came in to ask whether luncheon could be given to — of all people in the world — Colonel Repington.[2] Of course they knew what my position was. I told Rawly naturally I should not make any fuss and should certainly speak to him. He was very shy of me but after luncheon came up and really made me quite a handsome apology and asked leave to bury the hatchet and of course what I feel about all these things is that it is no use keeping up animosity and so the feud is over.[3] I had a talk with him afterwards and he admitted that I was right in what I did but what he said was that he knew that Lloyd George meant to have me out and had meant it for some time and that Milner meant having me out, and if I had gone with Robertson I could have gone without there being any feeling of animosity on the part of anybody against me. I do not think that this is quite the case but still I accepted what he said without comment.

Got back here soon after 6 o'c.

Dinner. House Party. Mr. & Mrs. Bliss who had just been ordered off at a moment's notice to the Hague. Raoul Hennessy and Mrs. Hyde. We had quite a pleasant dinner.

Reading arrived about 11 o'c and I sat up talking with him for some time. He tells me that not only is he to talk over with the authorities here about transport difficulties between America but he is to discuss with Clemenceau our own Man Power. This has very much upset me and I can best show what I feel about it by a copy of a letter I have written to Arthur Balfour on the subject. Reading himself realises that the whole thing is wrong but says "You know what the Prime Minister is. He always tells somebody to do somebody else's work". That is all very well but it is not a thing I am prepared to accept. Reading was very nice and as I was very tired I did not go into the question and am keeping it to talk over with him tomorrow.

Notes to 31 August

1. Major-General William Thwaites (1868–1947). Director of Military Intelligence, September 1918–April 1922.
2. Charles à Court Repington (1858–1925). Military Correspondent, *The Times*, 1904–18, and the *Daily Telegraph*, 1918–25.
3. The *Morning Post* had led the attack on Derby for his indecision at the time of Robertson's removal as CIGS.

September 1918

Copy of letter sent to Mr. Balfour 1 September 1918

Confidential & strictly personal

I had a most interesting 48 hours with Haig, Rawlinson and others at the front and was very much impressed with the total lack of unwarranted optimism. They were all very happy and pleased at the way things were going but none of them talked in the way that they did a year ago and recognised they have got many more difficulties to overcome. Still at the same time their tails are well up and anticipate further successes. There is no doubt the Germans are rattled. They are throwing in Division after Division haphazard and get their Divisions broken in retreat which is what we did in the retreat on the 21st March. There is very bitter feeling against Pershing and the Americans as they feel that if only the Divisions we had, had been left there we should have been able, with the aid of these Divisions, to follow up and completely break the German resistance and even have got a decisive decision this year. Our men however are very tired and therefore the pushing back cannot be done as far as might have been done with fresh troops.

Reading arrived here in the evening. I have only had a short talk with him but even that short talk has told me something which has considerably disturbed me. I do not wish to make a querulous complaint but I think that I am justified in laying my opinion before you. I was under the impression that Reading was coming out here to discuss American matters and especially transport of Americans and their supplies. That was perfectly all right but I now discover that he is also to deal direct with Clemenceau on the subject of our own Man Power at home and this seems to put me in an absolutely false position which I am not prepared to occupy. It is not a subject in any way connected with America and although Lloyd George I believe says it is, nobody could justify such an assertion. It is a matter which might be discussed in one of two ways. Either by the Prime Minister or Milner direct with Clemenceau, or else through me, but to send our American Ambassador as a special envoy to discuss this subject with the French Government is to make my position an intolerable one. In the first place I have to complain that papers dealing with a subject which so deeply affects the relationship between France and England have never been sent to me at all. Colonel Roure's Report was not sent from home. It was given to me by Clemenceau. Similarly the answer of the British Government to that Report is not given to me officially but through the courtesy of Reading. Here is a subject about which Clemenceau speaks to me every time that I see him and not only Clemenceau but every Minister and every prominent person in this Country (because they all know of Roure's Report) speak to me in the same strain, yet I am the one person who, having to deal with this matter almost daily, not in detail but in general argument, am the one person who gets no information and when it comes to dealing with the question officially it is not entrusted to me but to a Special Envoy. That is to me a very substantial proof that I am not trusted to deal with it and you may be perfectly certain that Clemenceau is quite quick enough to see that and my position for the future will be very [different] as far as authority is concerned to what I thought it would be and to what up to now it has been. It is simply converting me into a Post Office, a position that I think you would clearly see is not one that I could accept.

This is not quite the first instance. When it was a question of training American troops behind our line I was told to speak to Clemenceau on the subject. This I did. He sent an official answer that it was a matter for Pershing to decide and I therefore telegraphed to know whether I should see Pershing on the subject. I never even got an acknowledgement of my request. I had reason to believe then and I have still more reason to believe now that if I had seen Pershing then I might have been able to make the arrangement and I should have had the tacit support of Clemenceau. That opportunity has now gone by and I felt in that case that one had been ignored but of course I feel it ten times more now.

I am writing this early and I may have something to add after a further talk with Reading but I know the Prime Minister's little ways of always setting somebody to do somebody else's work and if he is not satisfied with the way I do my work here let him say so and put somebody else in my place. Though I should be sorry to go it would not break my heart but what I will not stand is being ignored in a very insulting way.

I write this to you unofficially and as a friend because I think probably without making any trouble you will be able to rectify the matter but unless it is put right the whole conditions under which I came here are altered in a way I could not possibly accept.

Since dictating above I have had a long talk with Reading, as a second incident has arisen. Weir has now telegraphed to ask Reading to present his case and letter on the question of an Independent Air Force to Clemenceau and discuss it with him. This Reading is refusing to do and is handing it over to me but I am certainly not going to move in the matter until I have received definite instructions. Reading thinks that this is due to a misunderstanding. I am not sure that I agree with him but it only confirms what I have written before that there is apparently an intention to alter my position here and that I cannot tolerate. Reading has been most considerate; has discussed the whole question with me and is going to tell Clemenceau tomorrow that he has so discussed it and that he is seeing him (Clemenceau) with my full knowledge; but I think you will see that although that may make it all right with Clemenceau it does not make it right for me and in order that you may realise the circumstances I would like to send you the following extract from the War Cabinet proceedings when I was appointed.

"Lord Derby would be Head of the War Missions, with the same powers as had been accorded to Lord Reading, namely, not to confine his activities to diplomatic matters but with full powers to discuss with the French Government, on behalf of the War Cabinet, matters relating to the War."

These are the conditions under which I came and if they are to be altered I must consider whether I should be justified in accepting any alteration.

Sunday, 1st September

PARIS

Talked practically the whole morning with Reading. Chiefly on the Man Power question. He is as much disturbed about it as I am and sees a considerable amount of trouble ahead.

Went up and played golf. Portia and Charlie against Madame Hennessy and myself. We were well beaten. I played abominably.

Dinner. People in the House and Madame de Janzé. She is an Irish woman of about 40. Has been very pretty. She is a widow with two children who are minors. Very interesting her discussion with Reading on the subject of the laws concerning property and I must say that many of them in France are infinitely better than ours and apparently there is every sort of obstacle in the way of a man getting rid of his fortune and ruining his family.

Monday, 2nd September

Again had a long discussion with Reading and did routine work.

Saw Mr. Richard Wilton who came on behalf of one of these numerous Russian people who are going to set the whole of Russia right if they are only given a free hand and plenty of money. He had a letter dated August 10th from Bob Cecil saying the Embassy would be instructed to give him every facility but needless to say neither the Embassy nor myself have had any communication of any sort or kind.

Luncheon. Zaharoff, Cazalet, De Robilland (the Italian Military Representative at Versailles. A very nice man with whom I had dinner during my tour in Italy) and my racing friend his A.D.C. Zgigny. Mr. Lyon whom I have mentioned before and a Mrs. Paget the French wife of an English Officer who has large property near Matlock. A very pleasant luncheon.

Several people to see me in the afternoon including a Mrs. Brodrick, sister-in-law of St. John's,[1] who wants me to make a special appeal on her behalf to break every regulation in the French Army. I am going to see what I can do for her as poor woman she has had a terrible time. Her husband died since the beginning of the War and her only son has been killed.

Then a Mr. Talbot who is here on Bulgarian Propaganda work on behalf of Northcliffe. A very level headed fellow. A great nephew of Aunt Emmy Talbot. He tells me that he very seldom sees Northcliffe who comes over about once a month and who apparently is suffering from some mysterious illness.[2] He is not impressed with the way the office is run. He says he very rarely gets a decision and when the decision is given it is never carried out. Northcliffe wants to put in a certain Sir Campbell Stuart,[3] a Canadian, whom he has taken very much under his wing and whom personally I always looked upon as half witted and I do not think that is a bad description of him — no good whatever. Incidentally I may say Reading spoke to me about Northcliffe and told me he had made an awful mess of things in America. They talk of him as such a wonderful organiser but he is absolutely useless in anything connected with organisation. He got very wrong with many people there.

General Bliss came to see Reading and we three had a long talk on the subject of American effectives. The whole question is one of transport and equipment and the American Government are unwilling to send their men over here unless they are thoroughly equipped in every respect including complete complement of guns, etc. This means inordinate delay and no possibility of concluding the War next year. Bliss is very sound on the subject. He says it is all to our advantage to get the men over here as long as they have their rifles and personal equipment and that they can perfectly fight with the number of guns we have at the present moment on the Front. That our losses in Infantry are far greater than those in other arms and therefore the proportion between guns and infantry could be maintained by putting in American troops, even if they have not got their artillery. Of course this is the right line to take and Reading is going to support it as strongly as he can.

Dinner. Only John Revelstoke[4] and Bliss, the American Secretary to the Embassy dined.

I had a long talk to Reading after dinner on the subject of his interview with Clemenceau which has been in every way satisfactory. Clemenceau of course did not go through the facts and figures at the time but the papers were left with him to consider, but he told Reading that there was only one chance that the Germans had of winning the War and that was by creating dissension amongst the Allies and that he was perfectly determined, whatever happened, should never arise. I believe him to be thoroughly genuine and I am hopeful that there will be no further trouble. Personally I advocate, and Reading agrees with me, that the only thing to do is to tell the French that we cannot have them discussing our internal arrangements and that if they will not accept our assurance that we are doing all that we can do they must accept our decision that we are doing all that we will do.

Notes to 2 September

1. William St John Brodrick (1856–1942). Secretary of State for War, 1900–03; Secretary of State for India, 1903–05. Earl of Midleton, 1920.
2. Northcliffe suffered from poor health and periods of despondency for much of his life. In his last months he became mentally unbalanced, the result of septicaemia in the valves of the heart.
3. Sir Campbell Stuart (1885–1972). Military Secretary to British War Mission to United States, 1917. Deputy Director of Propaganda in Enemy Countries, 1918.

Managing Director of *The Times* until 1922.
4. John, Baron Revelstoke (1863–1929). Director of Bank of England and partner in Baring Brothers and Co. Ltd.

Tuesday, 3rd September

Lady Mida left early and Charlie left after luncheon to stay with his friend Fels.

Went to luncheon with Loucheur. The Party consisted of himself, wife and two daughters, the Spiers, Dumesnil and wife, he is the head of the aviation, and Lamerie.

His Villa is at Louvesciennes, 20 minutes from Paris and belonged to Madame du Barry. I think it is the most lovely site I ever saw, a beautiful little Park with a view for miles. He has collected a lot of things belonging to Madame du Barry but it seems rather incongruous to see the very middle class wife of a nouveau riche in Madame du Barry's place. What strikes one so much is the sort of exaggeration that there was in the old days of the size of places. There is a picture of a Dinner given by Madame du Barry at which you would think there were at least 150 people present, whereas the Dining Room is a room in which at the outside you could only get 40 people.

I drove back with Loucheur and we talked about a good many subjects. He is one of the few people who stick up to Clemenceau and he rather regrets the latter's tiger-like attitude. He spoke about his quarrel with Spiers and thinks Clemenceau was entirely in the wrong. He tells me that both he and Tardieu are doing their very best to restore the friendship between Lloyd George and Clemenceau and he thinks it will be all right. Clemenceau would willingly go to England for a meeting of the Supreme War Council before long but Loucheur thinks Clemenceau is perfectly right when he says it is impossible for Foch to get away from here as long as operations are going on and that if a meeting is to be held at which Foch should be present that then it must be held at Versailles. I hope therefore Lloyd George will come over for the next meeting and then I am perfectly certain Clemenceau will go to London, perhaps directly afterwards, to discuss all questions of tonnage etc. Loucheur told me he tried to make up the quarrel between Albert Thomas and Clemenceau but it is quite impossible and they are irreconcilable. We talked of Briand for whom he has got the greatest respect and admiration but he says it would be fatal to try and get him back into any Cabinet as long as the War is going on but that when it comes to a question of discussing Peace Terms it is essential that Briand should be consulted as in such matters he would be infinitely Clemenceau's superior. Painlevé and Ribot he looks upon as completely done. He says that Tardieu is undoubtedly a coming man and is bound to be Président du Conseil before many years are over.[1] I have always looked upon Loucheur as a possible aspirant for this post but he certainly spoke with complete frankness when he said that he had no such ambition and that his one wish was to get out of everything and get back to his business and be comparatively quiet. There is no doubt he has been an enormous success in his office and has done marvels. He tells me he was over in England last week at the Conference presided over by Bob Cecil and he tells me that nobody could have done it better, with greater tact or with greater decision and that thanks entirely to him it was a very great success.

I talked to him on the Man Power question and he says that he thinks Clemenceau is mad on this subject but he, Loucheur, realises how essential it is that we should retain work people in England as he knows the difficulties he suffers from here under a too drastic comb out. At the same time he seems to think that there might be a certain amount of combing out but he refers more to services out here than to work people at home.

We discussed the Caillaux case. He tells me that there is not the least doubt Caillaux will be condemned by the High Court, before whom he is to be tried almost immediately, and it is quite possible that he may be shot. But even if he is not his sentence will be a very severe one and probably imprisonment in a fortress for life. He is as bitter against Caillaux as he is the reverse with regard to Malvy and he tells me that there is no real feeling in the Country about the latter's condemnation and that though there will be an interpellation on the subject he does not anticipate any difficulty. On the other hand there is to be an interpellation on the concession in Algeria to Murray of Elibank. He says the Government are going to support the concession and Clemenceau is perfectly determined to see it through but they are going to have a very difficult time and they will not be able to get all that Murray asked for. He says Murray has been stupid over it. In the first place he has asked for far too big a concession. It would have been much better to have asked for a smaller one and then afterwards asked for more which he would have been granted, and he thinks now that the amount of concession will be reduced. He also says it was a great mistake to ask for the concession in his own name and not in the name of his Company. French people are very suspicious of concessions to individuals whereas they do not object to them to Companies. I should think this is very true. I asked him whether there was not a chance of that being altered and he says Yes, that he thought the Chamber would probably only grant the concession to Murray's Company and not to himself which of course is really all that Murray asks for.

Our successes as usual have been productive of the best Propaganda. There is no doubt that Haig and his troops stand very high in the eyes of the French people at the present moment and there is a corresponding decrease in the enthusiasm for the Americans and they look upon Pershing as having practically demobilised the American Army through this movement of his, whereas if they had been employed with the French and British troops to exploit successes an almost definite conclusion might have been arrived at. The Americans talk much too freely, as our people used to, of where an offensive is going to take place and I hear on perfectly authentic authority of an American General who told the lift boy at his hotel when and where an attack would take place. Everybody knows where it is to take place but I do not think anybody knows when, for the simple reason I do not think the Americans know themselves, and you may be perfectly certain it will not be as soon as they think as they are apparently quite incapable of doing rapidly the Staff work necessary for a big offensive.

Reading is still here and very pleasant. He saw Pershing this morning. I only saw him for a minute after it. He says the meeting was most satisfactory. He has gone off now to see Foch and we are going to have a talk when he gets back this afternoon.

Quinones[2] the new Spanish Ambassador, who is a most charming fellow, very pro-Entente and a great friend of Dato's[3] the Spanish Prime Minister, made his official call on me. He has been in charge since the old Ambassador died several months ago and I got to know him quite well. We had a most interesting talk on the subject of the present Spanish position. He assures me that Spain is perfectly determined to adhere to her threat in the note to Germany.

Hall *The Times* American Correspondent came to see me and had a talk about Propaganda. It is extraordinary how much more these men who have lived in America understand that sort of work than our own people. Of course it is a much coarser kind of Propaganda but still it is infinitely more effective and I think I shall be able to get him to help me considerably in propaganda work amongst the Americans.

Smith-Dorrien[4] suddenly turned up at tea-time en route to Gibraltar. He is a most charming man and one can never be sufficiently grateful to him for all he did for Edward. He looks very old. He is very pleased indeed at his going to take up his new appointment.

Dinner. Apart from the people in the House only Sackville West dined.

Talked with Reading afterwards who seemed very satisfied with his two discussions, Pershing in the morning and Foch during the day. They are both very much alive to the necessity of sparing no effort to bring the War to a conclusion next year and they thought every sacrifice should be made to do so. From both however he seems to have gathered that there is a very bitter feeling about our effectives and he was warned that there might be a Franco-American protest on the subject. That I personally do not think is likely. Lloyd George however will put into people's mouths sentiments which they do not hold. For instance he has been saying, and so has Winston, that Foch wants everything sacrificed in order to give thousands of tanks, whereas Foch's opinion is exactly the opposite, that no infantry ought to be sacrificed for tanks. Foch also thinks we are over-doing our air programme and that the number of men that we employ and which roughly work out at 40 men for every aeroplane in the air is very excessive. Personally with all this huge number of American Flying Machines which are really coming along now, and with the personnel we can spare for them, I should have thought we might have reduced our own programme somewhat. Anyhow I feel certain we are not out of the wood with regard to our Man Power and there is more likely to be trouble over that, between ourselves, the French and the Americans than anything else I can see.

Notes to 3 September

1. Tardieu did not, in fact, become Prime Minister until November 1929.
2. J. M. Quiñones de Leon. Spanish ambassador in Paris and later Spanish delegate at the League of Nations.
3. Eduardo Dato y Iradier (1856–1930). Spanish Prime Minister, June–November 1917.
4. General Sir Horace Smith-Dorrien (1858–1930). Commander-in-Chief, East African Forces, 1915–16; Governor of Gibraltar, 1918–23.

Wednesday, 4th September

Very disturbed to get a telegram to say that the festivities for September 7th have been postponed and that I am to tell Joffre and the men who were going over for it that everything is off till October. It really is the most insulting thing to the French and I am asked to put it satisfactorily to them although the reason given in the telegram is "so many people will be away for the week end".

Luncheon. The Prince of Wales, Alastair Leveson-Gowers, and Lady Rosemary, Grahame and Bullock. At the last moment Millie Sutherland came in and later Charlie Grant and asked for luncheon.

Afternoon. Returned the official call of the Spanish Ambassador. He tells me he has no further news of how things are going between Spain and Germany.

Dinner. Stettinius,[1] of Parker Morgan & Co. who did the placing of orders for guns, munitions, etc. in America dined. Most interesting man. He is now dealing with all supply questions for Pershing.

After dinner the Prince of Wales came in and sat talking with us till quite late. I persuaded him to stay another night as I particularly want him to meet Joffre. I think that he may just help to smooth over the difficulty which has arisen owing to their countermanding at the last moment the latter's visit to England.

Notes to 4 September

1. Edward R. Stettinius (1865–1925). Businessman and Second Assistant Secretary of War under President Wilson.

Thursday, 5th September

Luncheon. Prince of Wales and Claude Hamilton. Joffre and Commandant Jouart, Tardieu, Reading, and Grimwood Mears[1] with Lady Alastair Leveson Gower, Mrs. Thomas an American and Madame Hennessy. I think everything went all right and the Prince of Wales was very nice both to Joffre and Tardieu. Joffre quite happy and looking forward to going to England in October. He wants his wife to accompany him.

Afternoon a series of interviews. First of all M. Ponsot the new French Consul General of Montreal; then Lt.-Colonel Malone[2] the new Air Attaché here who though he has got a Military title is really a Naval Officer and served with Victor in the Essex. It is very ridiculous this making an Air Attaché. He can have absolutely nothing to do and is making the Air Ministry look rather ridiculous.

Then came General Diaz. Quite a different man to what I had supposed. Very sharp and bright. Talked very frankly about things. He loves

Cavan and says that our troops get on extremely well in Italy both in fighting and with the civil population and that he cannot speak too highly of them. He then rather launched out against the French. The way the two nations hate each other is amusing, if it was not rather tragic at this moment. I must say the Italians are aggravating. There is not the slightest doubt they could do a great deal at the present moment if they would but Diaz is perfectly determined not to do any fighting and almost says in the same words what the Italian Admiral said at the Supreme War Council when he congratulated Italy on still having its fleet intact, and when asked how that came about said because he never took it out of harbour.

Then went on to see Pichon about various matters. He was most friendly. I was rather late because of Diaz and he then asked me what Diaz had told me. I told him that Diaz had expressed extreme confidence and all Pichon said was "I know, he always expresses confidence but his confidence is in the fact that French and English troops will attack but that he will not do so under any circumstances whatsoever." I must say the French have rather got reason to be bitter with the Italians about Albania where their conduct has been disgraceful. They made a big success and then deliberately threw it away and retired.

Afterwards talked with Spiers and then a long talk with Reading who has I think come to the conclusion, and I think it is by far the best solution if it can be attained, to ask Clemenceau on the subject of our Man Power to consider the discussion at an end. Roure has made his report. Milner has made his answer to it and there the matter must rest. It is perfectly impossible to allow the French to dictate to us as to how we shall distribute our man power. Reading wants Clemenceau to be brought to the frame of mind that he will say to England, "well we have put you on your mettle to do all that you possibly can. Tell us what number of Divisions you will be able to put into the field by the 1st April of next year. We leave it to your honour to put as many as possible." I hope he will succeed in getting Clemenceau to adopt this line but I do not feel quite certain about it but I am equally certain that if we get into further discussion on the subject of Roure's report and Milner's answer it will only cause very great bitterness.

At tea-time the Prince of Wales came to tea to say good-bye, evidently regretting very much having to go.

John Revelstoke and the American Ambassador dined. We really had a very pleasant evening as we talked about everything else except the War. The American Ambassador had been a lawyer and he and Reading were extremely interesting with their reminiscences.

Notes to 5 September

1. Sir Grimwood Mears (1869–1963). Accompanied Reading to Washington and was with him during his ambassadorship.
2. Lieutenant-Colonel Cecil Malone (d.1965). First British Air Attaché, British Embassy, Paris, and Air Representative, Supreme War Council, 1918.

Friday, 6th September

Several interviews in the morning, the principal one with Reading who I think has managed things most tactfully with Clemenceau. I hope we have heard the last of the Man Power question but I do not feel sure. It has been approached from what I think is the only possible line at the present moment, namely that it is not possible for one Nation to dictate to another how it shall distribute its man power but that Clemenceau should make an appeal to England's honour to do all she possibly can. I quite agree with what Reading told Clemenceau that if that line is taken we shall probably get far more men from the Government than if they assume a dictatorial attitude.

General Hallowes[1] came to see me. He is about 100 years old and tells me he is the representative of the Red Cross with the French but whom he serves under or who authorised his coming out I have not the least idea, but what I do resent is that he is wearing the four service stripes which he has no earthly right to do, as he is not serving with any Commission from the British Government or even with our own troops.

Luncheon. Just the people in the House, together with that dreadful fellow Mond[2] who came in to see Reading and whom I therefore had to ask. Johnny Du Cane and Burtchaell.

Burtchaell told me that the effect of the tanks on our men is extraordinary as it gives them much confidence. Whenever they are held up by a nest of machine guns they get a tank to come and it soon wipes it out.

Discussed the matter with Johnny Du Cane as he says that what the French feel is that we do things without proper consideration. We are now rushing into the whole question of tanks with the result that to make them and then to man them is going to wipe out a great many of the men whom we really require for the Infantry and that though Tanks do very good service they cannot win the War without infantry.

Afterwards went to see Clemenceau who was in high good humour. He told me that although he would have to write an answer to Milner's memorandum he meant not continuing but closing the discussion. He was extremely pleased with the tone of Milner's reply to Roure's report. He considered it extremely able and conciliatory and there is no doubt that the tone adopted by Milner has paved the way for Reading's good work. I then spoke to him about Weir's Independent Air Force and though I do not think he really likes it I think he will agree. He cannot do so at present as he is just going off for a tour round. He amused me enormously by saying that he was going to see the King of the Belgians[3] to find out if they had got Rifles, Munitions, Guns and Shells because he was afraid from their not using them they must have none of these 4 articles.

In the *Temps* last night appeared a paragraph to say that the American Army was now bigger than the English which is of course absolutely untrue and most mischievous and the most mischievous part of it is that it was sent out by one of the French correspondents on the Front and has been passed by their G.H.Q. and Censor's Office here. Clemenceau was very angry about it and has promised that both Censors shall be punished and a paragraph put in contradicting the statement. But the thing that of course is annoying is that it is a clear proof of want of friendliness to us on the part of Pétain's G.H.Q. and there is no doubt the tone of praising the Americans at the expense of the English is being largely set from that quarter.

There is always some tiresome incident with propaganda and now I have found that the fool in charge of propaganda here had sent a statement to the newspapers, which luckily I have been able to stop, in which he denied the truth of the *Temps* rumour and gave my name as the authority for denial.

Dinner. House Party together with Tardieu and Captain Thompson, one of Haig's A.D.C.'s who has come down to pilot Reading. Very pleasant evening. We did not discuss any business at all. I had a few words with Tardieu as he went out. He, like myself, had seen Clemenceau after his interview with Reading and he was just as satisfied as I am that although the matter of man power is not settled, still we shall have no further acute trouble with it.

Notes to 6 September

1. Major-General Henry Hallowes (1838–1926). At the time of the diary Hallowes was in fact 80 years old.
2. Sir Alfred Mond (1868–1930). Baron Melchett, 1928. First Commissioner of Works, December 1916–April 1921.
3. Albert I (1875–1934). King of the Belgians, 1909–34.

Saturday, 7th September

Reading & Co. left early. Reading wrote me a very nice letter before going. I must say he has been perfectly charming here. Most entertaining and my talks with him have been of the greatest possible interest. He has insisted on being relieved of his post within the next 6 months but as he says the great difficulty is to find anybody to go and he warned the Government when he first took it up that they must be on the look out for somebody to succeed him as it would be impossible for him to stay in Washington after the close of this year without resigning his Lord Chief Justiceship[1] which he is not ready to do. Before I had accepted Paris he begged them to ask me to go (which accounts for my having been sounded in that direction) and he even now wanted me to consider whether I would not take it. I told him that under no circumstances would I do that and so I hope that the proposal will not be put forward.

Went to see the American Ambassador about two things: (a) treatment of American Officers on way to England. They complain that they are not treated like English Officers and are subject to inspection etc. entailing inconvenience and delay. Pointed out to him that it was not our fault but that of the French. He is going to take the matter up. (b) pay of typists etc. I want to try and arrange that we shall have some sort of understanding between the different Embassies so as to pay the same and not do as we are doing now taking people from each other.

Luncheon. Simon Lovat, Harry Milner and Bullock.

Portia and I started in the afternoon for Deauville. Very hot on road and we did not have a good run as we had two punctures and then only having one more tyre had to run slow and took 4 hours. We had delightful rooms on the ground floor looking over the Sea, with a sitting room between us.

Madame de Viel Castel and the Boisgelins, Diana and Rosemary and General Hickson dined with us.

Notes to 7 September

1. Despite his appointment as Ambassador to Washington, Reading remained nominally Lord Chief Justice until 1921 when he was appointed Viceroy of India.

Sunday, 8th September

Went up to the Camp. Saw Raw and Eccles. Went over the Liverpool

Hospital buildings which are getting on very well indeed. They hope to be in and have patients by the 23rd. I have promised if that is so to go down again to see them but I do not know that I shall be able to. Sorry to hear that Miss Whitson was ill again. We then motored through all the Camps and I talked to a lot of Lancashire men. We also saw a new system of getting men fit and really it is most extraordinary. There were two fields with about 2,500 men in each just by the seaside. They play every sort of game and dancing with a band, also singing and the men are as cheery as they can be. The last successes have had a most wonderful effect on the morale of the men and instead of trying to stay as long as they can there they try and stay as short a time as possible. Many men who have come down one day for a rest begged to go back within 48 hours as they are afraid unless they do they will not go back to their old Battalions.

Luncheon. The Boisgelins came to luncheon and brought his daughter and her step daughter, Princesse de Chimay. Very nice little woman. Ralph Lambton and a friend of his Captain Thompson of the Ayrshire Yeomanry came and John Ponsonby[1] also had luncheon with us.

In the afternoon played golf. Portia and I being well beaten by General Hickson and Madame Viel Castel.

Evening. Our two selves, the General, Madame Viel Castel, the Bates (she was Miss Vera Arkwright) dined together.

Notes to 8 September

1. Major-General John Ponsonby (1866–1952). Commander, 40th Division, 1917–18.

Monday, 9th September

Nothing in the morning.

In the afternoon played a return match of golf. This time Portia and I won easily. A very rough day blowing a gale.

In the evening Madame Hennessy, General Hickson, Henry Wilson, Duncannon and Dick Molyneux dined.

Tuesday, 10th September

Morning. Very heavy showers but Henry Wilson and I went out and had a long walk and talk discussing various matters. I gather they are having a rather difficult time in the War Office and things are not going any too smoothly. He told me of the circumstances under which Macready went as Head of the Police. He made his own terms and the Government had to agree to them. People seem to have an idea that Macready was ungummed but apparently that was very far from the case and it is a very decided promotion for him. He was specially promoted and is allowed to remain on in the army. Great difficulty about filling his place and it was decided to appoint Macdonogh, a most excellent appointment, but one I should never myself have dreamt of as he is such an expert in the Intelligence work that I should have doubted the wisdom of transferring him. It is not quite certain yet whether he will take it. Apparently Lloyd George has butted in, instigated Henry Wilson thinks by Winston and Geddes, and when everything was practically settled that the post should be offered to Macdonogh he suddenly blew in and said that such appointment must not be made until he had considered a complete reorganisation of the office. I believe this made Milner furious and I do not wonder at it and I think he is beginning to find out now what it is to have outside interference with the running of your office.

We then got on to the subject of the Military Attaché and I am glad to say that they all like my proposal that David Henderson should be Military Attaché, Head of the Mission over Spiers and at the same time command the troops in Paris. It will give him a good position and really something to do whereas his present post is a sinecure. We agreed to telegraph to David Henderson to meet us in Paris the next day and talk everything over.

After our walk we again went to see the men exercising and Portia and I then went to see Miss Whitson. Personally I think she is completely broken down. She has such bad asthma that she cannot sleep at all and they are sending her home for a rest. Personally I doubt her coming out again. Raw rather pooh poohs the matter and says it is not much but I think that is because he dislikes Miss Wild the Assistant Matron and says that he could not stand her in Miss Whitson's place. Raw himself is very much altered and has become an old man, but he is still as energetic as ever.

I had a final big luncheon and I must say the food at the Hotel is the best food I think I have ever had. My Party consisted of Henry Wilson, Duncannon, General Hickson, Diana and Rosemary, Madame Hennessy and Madame Viel Castel.

Afterwards Portia and I started. Had an extraordinary fine run back to

Paris doing it in 3 hours and a quarter although we stopped on the way to talk to Henry Wilson who left half an hour before us but had a puncture.

I found Charlie had arranged a Dinner in the evening consisting of Mrs. Hyde, Duc de Deaudeauville [*sic*: Deauville], Comte de Gramont, Henri de Mun, Grahame and Bullock. The 2nd Life Guards Band played afterwards.

Wednesday, 11th September

Dick Cavendish[1] came in the afternoon to stay.

Dinner. There were us 5 in the House, Harry Milner, Humphrey de Trafford, Henry Wilson and Duncannon, Sackville-West and David Henderson.

Henry Wilson, David Henderson, Sackville-West and myself discussed afterwards the question of the Military Attaché's office. Glad to say they all entirely fell in with my proposal that David Henderson should be the head of both offices, details to be worked out afterwards.

Notes to 11 September

1. Lord Richard Cavendish (1871–1946). Brother of the Duke of Devonshire. Liberal Unionist MP for North Lonsdale, 1895–1906. European War, 1914–15.

Thursday, 12th September

Mr. McFadden from the American Embassy came to see me. He seemed very nice. Told me that like so many of his people they came over here with no details as to what they are or who they are under but he apparently corresponds to our representative of the Ministry of Blockade. He wants to have a Control Board of Blockade for Switzerland and Spain and to have a Central Board for dealing with it here. Seems quite friendly. He is very alarmed at the position of supplies as he says it is no use talking of millions of Americans coming over here as at the present moment it would be perfectly impossible to keep them.

Bridges came to see me. General conversation. He is going back to America.

Luncheon at the Palais D'Orsay to journalists from Australia, New Zealand, South Africa and Newfoundland. Not a bad lot of fellows. Very pleased at what they had seen at the front but very disgruntled at the arrangements made for them to visit the French front. I think however I was able to show them that really the whole difficulty arose from military reasons. Several speeches. I got through all right.

After luncheon took the journalists first of all to Poincaré, afterwards to see Clemenceau who made them a delightful little speech. They were enchanted with him.

When I came back Colonel Sutherland[1] came to see me on behalf of Simon Lovat, really on practically the same question, as far as timber was concerned, as McFadden in the morning. He says that the Americans and French are pulling in together to our exclusion but on examination I think I see that the real truth is that we had practically the monopoly and now we have to share with the Americans and this really is right.

Winston Churchill came in. We had a long talk. He tells me that Lloyd George is really quite determined about the Election and thinks he will have an enormous majority. I told him that I thought that the last thing Lloyd George ought to have was a new House of Commons which would be full of new brooms wanting to sweep very clean, giving him an infinity of trouble. All would have made pledges chiefly in the direction of giving advances of pay to soldiers and sailors and wages to munition workers etc., which pledges would either have to be redeemed by the Government or else repudiated which would put all the members in a very false position. I do not think it ever quite struck him in that light and he told me he was going to speak to Lloyd George about it.

He told me the Police Strike[2] was the nastiest thing he had ever known. They had really struck right at the heart of good order in England. The Police were extremely nasty. They went round pulling out all the constables who were ready to go on duty and they cut all the telephone wires to the police stations. Of course as he says it was inevitable something like this should happen if their demands were not met as some of them were getting less wages than women conductors on omnibuses. Personally I think it is an excellent example of what will happen if we have a General Election, namely that all these demands will be put forward. Members will pledge themselves to support them in Parliament and the Bill will be too large a one for even this Government to put up.

In the evening John Ponsonby and his 2 A.D.C.'s dined, also Harry Milner and Humphrey de Trafford. I must say Dick Molyneux and Harry Milner are great fun together.

Notes to 12 September

1. Colonel John Sutherland (1865–1952). Assistant Director of Forestry in France, 1917-19.
2. Strikes intensified throughout the summer and autumn of 1918. The most spectacular was one staged by the Metropolitan Police who demanded recognition of their union.

Friday, 13th September

Went to see Clemenceau 9.30. Quite pleased with the American advance. He says prisoners taken say that they had been told to hang on at all cost but they were unable to do so and the Americans swept them clean off their legs. I expect the latter's losses have been heavy but they have taken over 8,000 prisoners and 60 guns and apparently have got the Germans thoroughly disorganised. It really looks as if we might be going to make a very big advance all along the line.[1]

Neville Lytton came to see me about various Propaganda questions. Nothing new but the same old story, absolute lack of knowledge at home of what is required out here, especially with regard to films. Films are looked at simply from the point of view whether they will be popular and bring in money in England and not from the value that they would be in this country for propaganda purposes.

Afterwards Father Logan came to see me. He is the Roman Catholic chaplain working here in Paris and had been all over Ireland. He tells me that he found in Ireland that they all recognise that they are doing themselves an infinity of harm by not fighting but they will not join the English Forces until they have got Home Rule. He thinks however that the number of Sinn Feiners are very much decreasing and that they are now limited to a very small minority of extremists.[2] He did not offer any valuable suggestions but I think his visit over there may have done good in two ways. First of all he has seen a lot of the clergy and told them with what contempt they are looked upon by the Roman Catholic clergy out here and then coming back and being able to say that he sees no inclination on the part of the Irish to fight will put Americans as well as French people against them.

Prince Philippe de Chimay came to see me with reference to a Mission to England to get more aeroplanes for the Belgians. He is hardly the sort of fellow I should have sent myself but I gave him a letter to Lord Weir.

Afterwards Comte Fels came to see me. They are very anxious to give a

Fête in honour of English victories but I had rather to pour cold water on the scheme as they want Haig and other Generals to be present but naturally it is quite impossible for them to make any promise to be so and I advised its being abandoned for the year as quite apart from the weather it is not possible to make it a success.

David Henderson came afterwards to see me to discuss the question of his relationship with Spiers. I think all will be well but Spiers is a little suffering from swollen head and he will have to recognise he is very lucky to have got where he has.

Fatty Cavan in great form with Clamwilliam[3] arrived. They had luncheon as also did the Italian Ambassador and Harry Milner.

Kerney the Head of the American Propaganda came to see me with Major Roberts on the everlasting theme of English propaganda. He is taking up my proposal very favourably and is going to run our English propaganda in connection with theirs amongst the American troops. Afterwards Sir William Bull[4] came to see me and talked to me about politics generally at home of which he gives rather a gloomy account and then he told me that the subject of his business over here was that Michelham had given him full power of Attorney to deal with his affairs. He had taken everything over and that they had eliminated Cohn altogether from any participation in the arrangements. He proposes to put the Cap Martin Hospital at my disposal. I gather there may be further developments but I am bound to say I am glad to think that Michelham at last will get full credit for all he is doing and Cohn will be eliminated. He has got far too great a hold on some of the people in high places at G.H.Q.

Guillaumat came to see me to thank for his Reception in England. He said everybody had been most kind and sympathetic to him and he was delighted to have his views upheld. He is extremely confident of success and of course if there is a success it might have very far reaching results.

Dinner. The Heaton-Ellis's and Rosslyn Wemyss[5] together with people in the House. Not a very amusing dinner. Wemyss very enthusiastic about Geddes but I hear from other people that Geddes who is very much a rolling-stone is very anxious to leave the Admiralty and to take on other work and I believe what he suggests is that he should be a sort of General Manager out here which I do not think would work at all. In that way he would practically supersede the Quartermaster General and to a certain extent the Adjutant General and I am sure the Army would resent that. On the other hand if we could get somebody out here to deal with all accounts and try and cut down the enormous expense it would be of great value.

Notes to 13 September

1. American forces began an assault on the Saint-Mihiel salient on 12 September. Pershing's troops took over 13,000 prisoners. See D. Woodward, *Trial by Friendship: Anglo-American Relations 1917–1918* (Lexington, 1993), pp. 201–02.
2. In fact 73 Sinn Fein MPs would be elected in December — and only seven of the more moderate Irish Nationalists.
3. Earl of Clamwilliam (1873–1953). Served in South African War.
4. Sir William Bull (1863–1931). Conservative MP for Hammersmith South, 1918–29.
5. Vice-Admiral Rosslyn Wemyss (1864–1933). Baron Wemyss, 1919. First Sea Lord, 1917–19.

Saturday, 14th September

Mr. Raymond Recouly[1] came to see me this morning. He is the writer of the very eulogistic article on England in the *Figaro*, very nice fellow indeed. Was for two years London correspondent of the *Temps* and therefore knows England well. He is at the present moment serving on the staff of Jonnart the Governor of Algeria who he tells me is coming over here on leave in about a month's time. I hear privately that there is a chance of him being appointed to succeed Cambon in London.

Went to luncheon at Versailles with General de Robiland the Italian Representative there and he had got his nice racing A.D.C. and another A.D.C. who married his daughter. The only other people there were Marie Murat and the Curator at Versailles who is very anxious to show me over the place again. I should like to go there and spend the whole day. You do not see it all as you only go through it hurriedly as we did last time.

In the afternoon M. Grosclaude[2] came to see me. He is Mrs. Lionel de Rothschild's father. Very nice but a very talkative man. Very anxious to go over to England and I am glad to say they have invited him to do so. Afterwards Henderson and Spiers came to further discuss the question of the new organisation. Spiers was bent on being made Military Attaché but I have put my foot down about that. There is absolutely no reason why because Henderson is put over him he should be put over others. It is much better that the two offices should be kept quite separate but be under one head. I am afraid I am going to have trouble with Spiers which is stupid of him if he does give it to me because it can only end in his being beaten and he has got so high and so quickly that he would make a great mistake if he chucked it as he says he is going to do. He would simply go back to be a Junior Captain in a Cavalry Regiment.

Major and Mrs. Ward, she was Muriel Wilson, came to tea. Also Charlie Grant who says that the Americans have really done quite a big thing and that their Supply arrangements contrary to all expectation were quite good. Their losses are comparatively small but apparently at one time they were right on top of the Germans and shot at them at point blank range and they probably killed a great many of them. There were wild statements as to the number of prisoners and guns, some people going as high as 60,000 but from what I hear there are about 20,000 of which 5,000 were Austrians. That brings up the total of prisoners since the 15th July, just two months, to about 180,000, a really wonderful performance and much to the credit of Foch. Lloyd George certainly did not pay him any too high a tribute but what I do regret in the latter's speech is that he said nothing about Haig's successes and Haig's extraordinary loyalty to Foch.

Notes to 14 September

1. Raymond Recouly. Journalist and writer. Author of *The Third Republic* (London, 1928).
2. Etienne Grosclaude (1858–1932). Journalist and writer.

Sunday, 15th September

PARIS

Went to luncheon at Versailles. Only people besides ourselves there were Madame de Neuflizes and Mr. Tobin, the American Naval Censor, a man most unlike George's dear colleague.

We all paid a visit to Mrs. Wolff's to see her garden which was perfectly lovely as it was a glorious day. Then went and played golf at St. Cloud, Charlie and Humphrey de Trafford easily beating Portia and me. It is a horrible course and if you get a yard off the course you are in dense underwood and not only cannot play but generally cannot find your ball, in addition to which most of the holes are on the slope of a hill. All the same it is a lovely place and very nice to go there.

Got back to find Milner here with Colonel Bowley his Secretary.

Had a short time with Milner before dinner. He seems low about things and is certainly not as enthusiastic about our successes on this Front as the French are.

Dinner. Lady Edward Cecil and her daughter, Major and Mrs. Ward.

He is really a very nice fellow. Only general conversation after Dinner.
Very heavy raid at night.

Monday, 16th September

Orpen[1] came to see me. He wants to paint Clemenceau. I am going to try
and arrange it for him.

Had a long talk with Milner. Very satisfactory. I think he is very much
worried with Lloyd George's interference. He feels now what I always felt
that Lloyd George always wants to give somebody else your business to
do. He had a great deal of trouble about the Adjutant General's post but
stuck to his guns and got his way. He thinks Geddes and Winston have
both very bad influence over the Prime Minister. Geddes is a rolling
stone, is tired to death of the Admiralty and wants to start on something
new and that new seems to be taking control of everything connected with
the War Office. He is however going to America for a time and that will
keep him quiet.

Luncheon. People in the house, David Henderson, the Spiers, Mr.
Kerney the head of the American Propaganda Department who is helping me very much and a Mr. Blythe the proprietor of the *New York Sun*
which has an enormous circulation and great influence. He is very pro-
English.

In the afternoon Roberts,[2] Minister of Labour, came to see me. He is a
very nice little man and a strong man too. He has had the courage to break
with the Labour Party and the result is has far more influence than he
would have if he had remained with them. He wanted 8 or 10 of the others
to do the same as he did but they all funked with the exception of himself
and Barnes. He talked to me about the Police strike. He said what was
even more disastrous than the strike itself was Lloyd George's method of
settling it. It has been a rule from which the Labour Department has
never departed that they will not consider anything with regard to
increase of wages whilst the men are out on strike. If they go back then it
shall be considered, not otherwise, but Lloyd George having taken this
line of dealing with the men whilst actually on strike has upset the whole
applecart with the result they have had two serious strikes, one in Liverpool with the coal heavers and with the greatest difficulty they got the
men back without considering their cases until they were back. He anticipates great difficulty in the cotton trade in Lancashire and is very much
afraid of Lloyd George's visit to Lancashire as he was afraid he might

interfere. He therefore looks upon his illness[3] rather as a Godsend. It will come he thinks to a very big fight but it is perfectly certain that if the Government are firm as he means them to be if possible that it will be satisfactorily settled.

Had a visit from Captain Pitt Rivers,[4] son in law of Harry Forster, whose wife has just come over here for his 10 days leave and has I believe unfortunately been taken ill. Seems a very nice boy.

Robert Jones[5] and Sir Herbert Styles came to see me. Poor Jones looks very much knocked out by his wife's death. He and other consultant surgeons and physicians are paying visits all along the front and are just off to Italy. He is going to see me when he comes back. He is much impressed by the way everything in the Medical Services is being done.

In the evening just House Party with Sackville-West, Grahame and Humphrey de Trafford to Dinner, Dick Molyneux having left in the morning. Milner afterwards had a talk with Sackville-West and then with Spiers, having seen Henderson in the afternoon and everything is now definitely settled. Spiers I am afraid is giving a lot of trouble backed up by Winston who cannot resist having his finger in every pie. It has got nothing whatever to do with him and I have telephoned round to ask him to come and see me and I mean to tell him so.

Of course the whole difficulty is that Spiers will not realise that the French will have nothing whatever to do with him. He says that they are perfectly civil to him and asserts that they tell him everything. I know of course that they do not trust him and from the mere fact that Clemenceau has told me several secret things of a military nature which he has not communicated to Spiers. However it is all definitely settled now and Milner was very firm and told him it is not a question of what he wants to do, it is what he has got to do and that if he does not carry it out loyally he will have to go. I can see that Milner himself thinks the arrangement is a very good one but that the flaw in it is keeping Spiers and he would be perfectly willing to find some other job for him and remove him. This I should be extremely sorry for as I think Spiers has really done us very well.

Notes to 16 September

1. Major Sir William Orpen (1878–1931). Artist. Exhibition of war pictures, 1918, many of which he presented to the nation.
2. George Henry Roberts (1868–1928). Minister of Labour, August 1917–January 1919.

3. Lloyd George was one of the victims of the influenza epidemic. Hankey heard that at one point his condition was 'touch and go'.
4. George H. L. F. Pitt-Rivers (1890–1966). European War, 1914–18; severely wounded.
5. Robert Jones (1888–1933). Orthopaedic surgeon. Treasurer, Liverpool Medical Institution.

Tuesday, 17th September

Nash came to see me. He is very perturbed as I am myself over the coal question. The demands are going up every day, especially from the Americans and the output is decreasing. I do not know what the outcome of it will be. I am afraid we shall have a great deal of trouble both at home and abroad if we have a hard winter.

Luncheon — see copy of enclosed letter to Arthur Balfour.

After luncheon Winston Churchill came to have a talk with me. He was under the impression I wanted to put his Mission under David Henderson. I entirely disabused his mind of any such intention and I begged him to get Spiers, who is a great personal friend of his, to view the matter in a proper light. I also asked him and he consented to give me an officer here to do Munitions Cipher Work.

Heaton Ellis came to see me with regard to *Evénement*, Cohn's newspaper. He tells me that although it was undoubtedly bought with Michelham's money, Michelham's name does not appear, such is Cohn's astuteness, and the 4 registered owners are two Frenchmen, Cohn and Mendl who is Cohn's partner and a very able man and I think quite straight. Michelham therefore cannot stop the *Evénement* but can cut off supplies, but apparently they have got a rich Frenchman who will be ready to put money into it. My impression is the rich Frenchman will turn out to be Loucheur.

Saw Lord Burnham[1] who had been with Hughes on the Australian Front. Interesting if he was not the whole time impressing me with the grave dangers he had run. He gave a very gloomy account of things at home. He is especially disturbed that the A.S.E. gave £1,000 to the Police during their strike and as the A.S.E. is frankly revolutionary it is rather a bad sign.

Saw Spiers who is very sore and has gone off on 10 days leave, the best thing he could do. I am afraid he does not mean to work the scheme in which case he will have to go.

Dinner. Italian Ambassador and his wife and Signor Orlando dined.

Also Lady Edward Cecil and her daughter. Orlando and Milner had a long talk after dinner. Apparently the Italians are annoyed at our reducing our 12 battalion divisions to 9 but as they do not fight and do not mean to fight I think it is perfectly right to reduce the force there and I hope the Government at home will stick to it.

Notes to 17 September

1. Harry Lawson, Baron Burnham (1862–1933). Unionist MP, Mile End, 1910–16.

Copy of letter sent to Rt. Hon. A. J. Balfour, M.P. 17 September 1918

Confidential & Personal

I had a small luncheon Party here today which was rather amusing. Quinones, the new Spanish Ambassador, Klotz, Zaharoff, Roberts our Labour Minister, and the Princesse Marie Murat whom you know. Conversation was of course general at luncheon though universal approval was expressed of your speech[1] and indeed I congratulate you on it most sincerely. It is just the line everybody here wants to see adopted. After luncheon I walked about in the garden with Quinones and in course of conversation he told me certain things which I have telegraphed to you. I must tell you that he is a great personal friend of the King's and of Dato's and only arrived last night from Spain where he had seen them both. He tells me that Dato is quite determined to adhere to their note to Germany and he is strongly supported by the King and Maura,[2] but many of the Cabinet are wavering and there is no doubt that it may mean trouble in Spain as the rupture of negotiations will lead to War. Before however committing his Government to this Dato is very anxious to know what amount of support he can receive for the protection of the Spanish Coasts. They are evidently afraid of bombardment by submarines and I should think were totally unprepared. They also wish for some financial arrangement as otherwise they are afraid of a crisis. He tells me that the Germans were prepared to come to some arrangement if the Spanish would consent to refuse to sell to England or to provide any munitions of War, but as they realise to do this would be to close down their mines and ruin their people the Government refused to consider this suggestion. After telling me of this he got on to the subject which I am perfectly certain is uppermost in their mind, namely the arrival at some better understanding from their point of view, with the French with regard to Tangier.[3] I know so little of this subject that I did not encourage him to go into details but roughly it came to this that while they were prepared to let everything that is French go on in the French Administration, that the whole thing should be done under the Spanish Flag. I was convinced from what he told me that the question whether they declare War or not on Germany will depend, not so much on what assistance we can give them, although that is an important factor, but what France is ready to do for them in the matter of Tangier. In other words they want to use this occasion to put pressure on the French. He wanted me to see Clemenceau on the subject and if possible before he himself saw Clemenceau tomorrow morning. Naturally such a visit would be quite unofficial. I shall consult with Milner but my present intention is to see Clemenceau and mention the matter to him not saying I have got the information through Quinones but quite unofficially from some other source. Of course I do not quite know whether you at home want Spain to come in or not. My impression is when it was discussed earlier in the year both Army and Naval Authorities were decidedly in favour of her remaining neutral. The only danger perhaps of snubbing Spain in the present instance is that you might turn an anti-German into an anti-Entente Government.

I afterwards had a talk with Zaharoff. First of all on the subject of the Chair of French Literature. I asked him point blank what he meant to do. He told me at once that he meant to endow such a Chair but not for the University which had already had a meeting at the Mansion House to get funds. He was not however sure which the University was. I told him I gathered from a letter I have received it was Cambridge. He said "Then the Chair which I will endow will be at Oxford."[4] Apparently he had thought that some resolution to the effect that the occupant of the Chair should be English was narrow minded. He therefore in his endowment of £25,000 is making a proviso that the occupant should be approved by the Paris University. He is writing to me officially on the subject and I will forward the letter to you in the course of a day or so.

He then started talking about his visit to Switzerland forgetting I think that I had already seen him since his return and you have a letter from me on the subject. The only thing new he told me was this. He was off again to Switzerland tonight to see Turkish representatives but that they had put him off telling him not to come for the moment as they had great hopes of persuading Austria to accept their views — whatever these may be I do not know — and coming to some arrangement. I do not quite understand what this meant but probably you will know. He tells me that feeling between Turks and Bulgars is very acute and at a big meeting the other day between them one of the Turkish Generals spat in the face of Ferdinand. I give you all this for what it is worth and you will be able to see if it is of any value.

By the way what are you going to do about calling him "Sir Basil"?[5] I of course call him nothing but M. Zaharoff but he always has himself announced as Sir Basil, and I think that it will hurt his feeling very much indeed if he is told that he is not to call himself by that title.

Another thing which may be of interest to you. A man came to see me today whom I can implicitly trust — an Englishman, who has been in close communication with Kurbatof and something he told me shows how great is the leakage from the French Foreign Office. You may remember that you sent me a Secret telegram warning the French to be careful of their dealings with Kurbatof as since you had first brought him to their notice you had heard things which were not entirely in his favour. I told that most confidentially to Pichon but Kurbatof knows of it. What is of interest about him is this. That his (K's) views are known to the President and are very sympathetically received by him. That they accord very much with his own wishes namely that the regeneration of Russia should be performed by Russians and it is probable that Kurbatof will go to America at the request of the American Government. My informant who has apparently seen a good bit of Kurbatof lately is very much impressed with his honesty.

Other news I have none for you. Orlando is arriving here today and is dining with me tonight in order to have a talk with Milner. I gather that Clemenceau is again rather on the War path with regard to our effectives. Milner will probably however see him on the subject and I hope he will be able to avoid any further trouble.

Notes to confidential letter of 17 September

1. At the Savoy Hotel on 16 September Balfour dismissed recent Austrian proposals for informal peace talks as a cynical attempt to divide the allied nations.
2. Antonio Maura y Montaner (1853–1925). Spanish Prime Minister, March–November 1918.
3. In October 1914, Britain, France and Spain agreed to place Tangier under an international municipal administration. The Spanish government, however, wary of compromising their neutrality, refused to ratify the agreement. See K. Hamilton, 'The Poor Relation: Spain in Anglo-French Relations, 1898–1914' in A. Sharp and G. Stone (eds), *Anglo-French Relations in the Twentieth Century* (London, 2000), pp. 50–70.
4. The Marshal Foch Chair of French Studies was duly established at Oxford.
5. Zaharoff had been created a GBE in March 1918. Derby's misgivings may relate

to Zaharoff's non-British origins or to his dubious past — which included a bigamous marriage.

Wednesday, 18th September

Saw M. Gouin a big and very rich manufacturer. It was rather amusing, a Mr. Walter Behrens[1] who is a most pushing Jew asked whether he might bring M. Gouin whom I knew to see me. I said that as I knew M. Gouin there was no need for him to accompany him. He simply wished to show his importance. When M. Gouin came I found, as I expected, he had really nothing to talk to me about except to ask me what my opinion was about the Channel Tunnel.[2] I told him I knew nothing and cared less and at the present moment the Government had got other things to do than to consider this subject which was one which should very rightly be considered when we obtained Peace. He was quite nice and thoroughly understood the position.

Usual meeting of Heads of Missions. Nothing particular to discuss.

Milner had luncheon with us afterwards.

After luncheon a Mr. Lavanchy Clarke a most extraordinary individual came to see me, a Swiss and a friend of Lord Leverhulme's.[3] He wandered over every sort of subject and went away without my having the least idea of what he wanted.

Milner and I dined alone and had a long talk. He strikes me as being very tired and to be far more worried by his office than he thought he would be. He tells me that Lloyd George is at times a great thorn in his side and that on two occasions he has had to put his foot down and say that if Lloyd George persisted in certain suggestions he would look upon it as being a question of want of confidence. This was particularly the case with regard to the appointment of Macdonogh as AG and he attributes the Prime Minister's attitude to Geddes and Winston Churchill, both of whom seem to have the ear of the Prime Minister on every subject.

Milner like everybody else I have seen or who has written to me is opposed to the General Election. He sees no good in it but thinks that Lloyd George is determined to have a certain number of men pledged to support him and in that way to make a Party not only for the War but after the War. He, Milner, thinks that as a matter of fact Lloyd George will be the leader of our Party and is the only possible anti-Bolshevist leader and whether we like it or not we shall have to support him. We discussed other colleagues. He is very frank about them. Arthur Balfour he looks upon as a past number. Says that we in England appreciate him and his great ability but that foreign representatives, especially at the Supreme War Council do not appreciate his dialectic skill and only see in him a great amount of indecision. Bonar Law[4] can be dismissed as useless. Smuts he thinks a clever man but far too much use has been made of him in matters which have been entirely outside his province.

Milner was very pleased with his meeting with Clemenceau and said he was in high good humour and therefore in a very good temper. He thinks that he will insist on putting in an answer to the memorandum on Man Power. He only hopes that it won't be of a pugnacious kind as if so it will be like a red rag to a bull to Lloyd George. He is afraid of these two meeting. He says they are both naturally so combative that even though they promise to restrain themselves they cannot help going for each other. He is therefore doing all he can to put the Supreme War Council off as long as he possibly can.

It was a very pleasant conversation and the general sense of it showed that he is doing his best for the Army but that he does not really know the army well and he has got no affection for it. He looks upon all the old Army as being a very narrow Trades Union body. I think he resents interference but at the same time feels himself powerless to withstand it.

I discussed with him what the position of Haig and the Prime Minister was and he tells me that he thinks that it is just the same as it was when I went away, namely that the P.M. does not like Haig. Would like to get rid of him if he could but does not see anybody to take his place. Milner himself has a high opinion of Haig. Does not look upon him as a very brilliant leader and considers he has narrow views but at the same time he cannot honestly say that he sees anybody in the Army who would either be equal to or as good as he is. I told him that I thought the French people would be aghast now at any change because they realise how very loyal Haig has been to Foch and a change now would be looked upon as an attack on Foch and the Supreme Command.

Notes to 18 September

1. Walter Behrens (1856–1922). Official agent of the Commercial Committee of the House of Lords in Paris.
2. See K. Wilson, *Channel Tunnel Visions, 1850–1945: Dreams and Nightmares* (London, 1995).
3. William Hesketh Lever, 1st Baron Leverhulme (1851–1925). Viscount Leverhulme, 1922. Manufacturer and philanthropist.

4. Andrew Bonar Law (1858–1923). Conservative leader, 1911–21 and 1922–23;
    Chancellor of the Exchequer, December 1916–January 1919; Prime Minister,
    1922–23.

Thursday, 19th September

Sykes came to see me with reference to the Independent Air Force. I told
him that I had just received a message from Clemenceau to say that he was
not prepared yet to give an answer. He would try to do so within the next
3 days. I am afraid when the answer does come it will be unfavourable as
I hear that the Americans are as opposed as the French are to this Force.

Rennell Rodd[1] afterwards came to see me on his way through. He has
also been appointed, as I am, High Commissioner to deal with the various
Missions. He asked me what sort of methods I adopted and I have told
him all that I can do to help him. I think his task will be probably a little
more difficult than mine as most of his people are not quite on their own
as mine are. They are subordinate to the people here. For instance the
Munitions man is Sir Charles Ellis's representative, not the direct representative of the Munitions Department in England.

Luncheon. Comte and Comtesse S. de Castellane, M. and Madame du
Puy, Henri Robert the head of the Paris Bar, a most charming man, and
Rennell Rodd. Very interesting. All of us pleased with the latest War
news. Last night we had been rather afraid that our attack had not been a
complete success but apparently it has been.

Afternoon Sir Campbell Stuart came to see me partly to ask whether I
would give a luncheon to the Mayor of Rome and Marconi who were passing through on Saturday and partly to discuss with me propaganda. It is
rather amusing the rivalry between the two, Northcliffe and Beaverbrook.
Northcliffe absolutely declines to allow himself to be considered under
Beaverbrook. He has therefore made Beaverbrook give up to him Propaganda work not only in enemy countries but in Italy and he proposes to
set up yet another Mission here. Campbell Stuart who evidently knows
what he is talking about, a very sensible level headed fellow, is anxious if
possible we should hit on a man who would do for both Beaverbrook and
Northcliffe and luckily a letter has come in from Beaverbrook to say he
has appointed Lytton,[2] not Neville, but his brother Lord Lytton who I
think will be in every way a suitable person. Campbell Stuart agreed with
me Maclagan was worse than useless and apparently he has done [*sic*
?gone].

[211]

Afterwards Lady Algy, Charlie Grant came in to tea and stayed talking till quite late.

Dinner. Portia and Charlie dined out with the Italian Ambassador and I went in there afterwards. Cynthia,[3] Humphrey and Bullock dined with me.

Notes to 19 September

1. James Rennell Rodd (1858–1941). British Ambassador to Rome, 1908–19.
2. Victor Bulwer Lytton, 2nd earl of Lytton (1876–1947). British Commissioner for Propaganda in France, 1918.
3. Cynthia Cadogan, sister of Sybil (Portia) Cadogan. She married Humphrey de Trafford.

Friday, 20th September

Nothing in the morning.

Luncheon. Klotz, Madame de Polignac and the Comte and Comtesse Carrabbio. He is the A.D.C. and she is the daughter of General de Robi-land, the Italian representative at Versailles. Also Archie Myer who is in extremely good spirits considering that his wife, who is young and very pretty, has just run away from him.

After luncheon David Henderson came to see me. He is going away for a week and then will come back to take over from Le Roy Lewis who equally has gone away for a week's holiday in France.

Then came a Mr. Lingeman, a British subject here who had been introduced to me by Sir William Forwood.[1] Does not seem at all a bad sort of fellow. In the evening dined with the Wedl's. She was Mme Vanandree. He is now the Swedish Minister, a very jolly old fellow. They have got a delightful house which they bought and had done up since the beginning of the War with some very good pictures etc. I suppose most of them belonged to Vanandree though I believe he was very well off too.

There was a big farewell dinner to Cazalet who left at 10.15 to go straight through as fast as he could to Vladivostock, there to be A.D.C. to Knox.[2] He is a good boy. Everybody liked him and he will be very much missed here.

Cynthia, Humphrey and Portia also dined and there were several other fellows from Versailles, also a young Norwegian who is an extraordinary boy. He is only just 21. His father was a shipowner on a very small scale.

He sent his son to learn the business in New York and afterwards in Liverpool. The boy did so well that he has made his father's ships into quite a big tramp line of steamers and is now very well off indeed. He lived for 6 months in Bootle which he says he did not find very lively. Talks English perfectly and plays the piano beautifully.

Notes to 20 September

1. Sir William Forwood (1840–1928). Member of the Liverpool City Council for 58 years.
2. Major-General Alfred Knox (1870–1964). Commander of British Military Mission to Siberia, 1918–20. See R. R. James, *Victor Cazalet* (London, 1976), pp. 44ff.

Saturday, 21st September

Jefferson Cohn came to see me in regard to his position. I must say he was perfectly straightforward. He told me that he had not the least fear, and I can quite believe this, of his books being looked into. He has received nothing for himself from Michelham. I expect however the way he made his money was by buying and selling for Michelham and taking a Commission as his broker. He consulted me about *L'Evénement* and told me of the conditions under which it was run. He believes it to be thoroughly in favour of Clemenceau but as a matter of fact I received a private hint only yesterday that Clemenceau viewed it with a great deal of suspicion and would like to have it stopped. I advised Cohn to see Mandel and I shall tell Mandel that he had better say perfectly frankly what Clemenceau wishes as Cohn would apparently be quite ready to stop the newspaper if Clemenceau so wished. Of course it was created to support Briand and there is no doubt Briand sees the people connected with it a great deal. Clemenceau gets to hear of this and perhaps imagines it is more against him than it really is. Cohn tells me he is applying for further work but I do not know what that work would be. I told him that he must look upon his Honorary Commission as ceasing as it was only given to him for the purpose of running the Michelham Hospitals and was an "ad hoc" Honorary Commission. He does not wish to take off his uniform at once as he says that would be looked upon as if he was disgraced. I told him I did not think that would be necessary but it ought to be done soon and I am writing home on the subject.

When I said to Cohn that of course I knew the paper was being run at a loss which loss was being made good by Michelham, he told me there was no trouble about that as both Loucheur and Klotz were anxious to put up money for it. I cannot make up my mind whether I will tell Clemenceau that or not.

Luncheon. The Mayor of Rome, Prince di Sonnino, who is a second brother in the Collonna family, very nice fellow. Marconi, the Italian ambassador and his wife, Melville Stone the big American journalist, Humphrey, Cynthia and Dick Molyneux who arrived back last night. One of the pleasantest luncheons we have had.

Colonel Sutherland came to see me. For particulars see letter to Arthur Balfour.

Dined Franco-American club. Tardieu, Sharp and myself had to speak. Quite a pleasant evening though the room was appallingly hot — about 180 people there.

Copy of letter to Mr. Balfour 21 September 1918

Confidential & Personal

Colonel Sutherland came to see me again today on the subject about which I wrote to you before namely the question of a new Convention with Switzerland for the provision of timber. He had seen Mr. McFadden American representative and things I am afraid have progressed further than they had then and not at all in the direction we could wish. According to Colonel Sutherland's statement Mr. McFadden informed him that it was no use England trying to make arrangements for timber from Switzerland because he had already made one which I gathered would give him the monopoly of timber and he said that he was able to do this because America was able to give Switzerland things which she wanted and England was not. I understand that having purchased this timber he intends to distribute it amongst the Allies but taking the lion's share, more than half for America, the rest being divided between France and ourselves but whether in equal proportions or not Colonel Sutherland was not sure. Mr. McFadden told Colonel Sutherland that it was quite impossible for him to do business with the English in the same way that he did with the French. That he had the most intimate relations with the latter going to the Ministry of Foreign Affairs for an hour or so every day whereas he never knew whom he had to deal with in reference to English requirements. I am afraid what he says is true and the result is we shall be terribly short of timber unless something is done and done immediately to give us more than would otherwise be allotted to us and it seems to me that while it may be perfectly true that America can give Switzerland what she wants England is practically the only country that can do the transportation and that ought to be considered in the bargain.

I write this to you as though Colonel Sutherland represents the Forestry Department under Lovat and therefore under W.O. it seems to me that this may be a case in which diplomatic intervention may have to be made. Will you therefore very kindly either deal with it yourself or in conjunction with Milner to whom perhaps you will send a copy of this letter.

There is no news here at the present moment but I expect to hear some tonight at a Dinner I am going to in which case I will write to you again tomorrow.

Sunday, 22nd September

PARIS

Luncheon with Thornton and large party at the Racing Club in the Bois de Boulogne. Not particularly amusing and a bad luncheon. It was held there because the Flying Corps Sports were on at the same place.

Saw a lot of people I knew there including Jellicoe[1] who tells me his wife is very much better and will be quite all right in about a month's time. He tells me he heard from the Ministry of Marine that our successes in Palestine[2] are simply gigantic and we have taken from 25,000 to 30,000 prisoners. I have not myself seen any confirmation of that. If it is confirmed I must say it gives a legitimate right to Lloyd George to crow as whenever Repington and Co. attack him in the Press for these side shows something always comes off which shows we are hitting the Turk hard. I do not quite like the Salonika news.[3] I do not think it is a big enough success to really knock the Bulgar out but I really have seen nobody. I hope to see Clemenceau tomorrow morning.

We afterwards went on to golf but after playing 3 holes it came down in such torrents we came back to the Embassy.

Dinner. House Party together with Lord Jellicoe, Mainguy (Naval Attaché), Bullock and Humphrey de Trafford. After Dinner Portia, Cynthia, Jellicoe, Mainguy and Dick Molyneux left for England. Very sorry to part with both Portia and Cynthia as they have been quite delightful during their stay here.

Notes to 22 September

1. John Jellicoe, 1st Earl Jellicoe (1859–1935). First Sea Lord, 1916–17. Led the Royal Navy at the Battle of Jutland, 1916. Lady Jellicoe had been seriously ill following the birth of a son in April.
2. The British campaign against the Turks in the Levant culminated in the brilliantly executed battle of Megiddo and the capture of Jerusalem and Damascus, thus freeing Palestine and Syria from Ottoman rule.
3. Franchet d'Espérey took the offensive on 15 September. This led to an immediate débâcle in the now disintegrating Bulgarian army.

Monday, 23rd September

Saw Clemenceau. The result of interview best shown by copies of letters attached to Arthur Balfour and Milner.

I also spoke to him about *L'Evénement* and told him Cohn was going to see Mandel on the subject. He told me that he did not like that idea. That nothing was going to induce him to say that they wished the paper stopped as it was not their business to do so, but at the same time he told me privately that if I could get it stopped he would be much obliged. He told me that although it is supposed to be a paper written in his favour, as a matter of fact all the people who write in it are people, who whatever they may say in the paper, are violently opposed to him and doing all they can against him. I shall have therefore to do what I can to get it stopped but it is a little difficult.

Copy of letter sent to Viscount Milner

Strictly confidential

23 September 1918.

I hope you got back all right and had a good time. It was very pleasant having you here and I am extremely glad to have seen you and talked over the various matters. I am not going to bother you again on the Military Attaché question. I have written to Henry Wilson on that subject.

I saw Clemenceau this morning and was rather amused to find, quite between ourselves, that he showed no enthusiasm about Palestine though I cracked up our success as indeed it ought to be cracked up. Of course he will not believe for one minute in there being any chance of detaching any of Germany's allies, whether it be Austria, Turkey or Bulgaria. For my own part it seems to me that we are more likely to detach Turkey than any other Nation and if Turkey once went then I think Bulgaria would have to go, but that is only the opinion of an outsider.

He then referred to Salonika. Very pleased with the result of the Franco-Serbian advance and saying he quite understood our having a check as we had far the most difficult task. He then turned to something which you had said to him and which he was not quite sure whether he had rightly understood. As I understand it from him you told him that when this offensive in Salonika was over and if it attained a general success which it was hoped it might, you were prepared to relieve English troops by Indian Regiments and bring these English troops to the Western Front but that you also added that if France wished to bring any of her white troops away you would be prepared to equally replace them with Indian troops. He hoped that he had understood you right as it would be an enormous assistance to him if this could be done as it might enable him to bring 50 or 60,000 white troops to this front. Of course he said both English and French would have to leave some troops there but if the majority could be relieved by Indian troops it might have a very marked effect on this front. I told him that you had not mentioned the matter to me and therefore I could not give him any information on the subject but that I would write to you, and I should be obliged if you could send me some note on the subject which I could show to him.

Copy of letter sent to Rt. Hon. A. J. Balfour 23 September 1918

Confidential

I have sent you a telegram with regard to the question of Spanish intervention in the War. I had a talk with Clemenceau this morning for about half an hour and for the first time in my life thought him tired but it is hardly to be wondered at when I tell you that yesterday he was 14 hours in his motor and that at the age of 77!

Quinones had had apparently precisely the same instructions as the Spanish Ambassador in London and had put them forward to Clemenceau but as Clemenceau told me the requests made were of a more definite character than those made in London. I could not quite make out what that meant. Possibly it may be they gave more detail with regard to the amount of financial assistance required. Clemenceau told him as I have telegraphed to you that he was perfectly ready on behalf of France to help financially and against submarines so long as England was in agreement but he emphasised to the Ambassador the fact that under no circumstances would he take any action or utter any words which could be construed into asking Spain to go into the War. If she went in well and good but she must go in entirely of her own accord and because she thought it right to do so and if she did then he would give financial and other assistance asked for.

He told me that after this part of the conversation was finished the Ambassador broached the subject of Morocco and said that it was very desirable an understanding should be arrived at. Clemenceau agreed and told him that he himself was strongly in favour of some arrangement being arrived at but he told me, as he told the Ambassador, that this was not the time for it and that he would have nothing to do with any such question until after the War. To do so now would appear to be bribing Spain to enter the War and that was a suggestion he would not countenance for a minute. He told me that the Ambassador seemed satisfied and expressed himself so.

My own belief is that Quinones who has just been appointed Ambassador was trying to make a coup and to get Clemenceau to come to some agreement now in order to enhance his own position. He probably was told unofficially to do what he could but I doubt there being any instruction to him to bring this matter officially before the French Government. Spain is evidently hovering on the brink of going into the War but does not like plunging into the cold water and though the Ambassador here informs me that they are quite determined to carry out the threat contained in their note to Germany, and which would undoubtedly provoke war, I think they will try and find some way of avoiding it.

I also spoke to Clemenceau on the subject of our English Company in the South of France Coal Mines and told him what difficulty I had had in getting any answer to repeated requests I had made for some assistance being given to this Company to obtain a greater increase of coal. I left a copy of the letter I had sent to Pichon with him. He tells me that the real man to deal with this question is Loucheur. That he will see him privately on the subject and he quite realises the importance of doing everything to get more coal but without knowing all the details he was unable to give me an answer. The despatch from Foreign Office seemed rather to hint that I had been negligent in not pushing this matter but such is not the case. I have done everything I possibly can both by memorandum and by private conversation to endeavour to arrive at some settlement but there is no doubt whatever that exploitation of French industries by English, and I think even by Americans, is very much resented at the present moment.

Monday, 23rd September [continued]

Had luncheon at the Inter-Allié Club with Vesnitch, the Serbian Minister to meet their Prime Minister. A tremendous gathering of swells including Klotz, Pichon, Barthou and Painlevé. Quite an amazing luncheon.

Sammy Scott[1] arrived here directly after luncheon.

In the evening Charlie, Sammy and I dined at Paillards and then went on to the Théâtre Michel, a most amusing Revue.

Notes to 23 September

1. Samuel Scott (1873–1943). Conservative MP for Marylebone, 1918–22.

Tuesday, 24th September

M. Pachitch[1] the Serbian Prime Minister came to see me. He is rather a fine old boy, talks the most abominable French and as he has no teeth it is extremely difficult to understand him. He stayed with me a considerable time meandering on about various things. He is going to London and I gather has several woes he wants to pour out there but it is always the same thing. They all hate each other like poison and all want to get something out of the scramble and of course if Serbia can do any harm to Montenegro it will.

Du Bos our only guest at luncheon. No news of any kind.

Paid return calls on the Swedish and Chinese Ministers. Did not stay long at the latter. Had a long talk with the first. He tells me his Government is very much upset at the condition of affairs in Finland and looks forward with the greatest apprehension to the new state of affairs. The King is to be selected in a few days. He says there is no doubt that it will be the Duke of Hesse and that in order to make his election safe they have imprisoned the whole of the Socialist members of Parliament. There ought to be 240 voting altogether but there will not be more than 90 and even those won't be unanimous. It is therefore obvious that the new King will have to be kept on his throne by force of German arms and it practically will become a German Colony. He told me that the one thing they were all hoping there was that England and France would declare that they would not accept him as King and would insist on his deposition in the terms of Peace. The thing that perhaps frightens them the most is that the Aland Islands will pass into German hands. The population is entirely composed of Swedes. It is only 75 kilometres from Stockholm and as he says with justice with Berthas mounted on the island Germany will have Stockholm and therefore Sweden at her mercy. He tells me the state of Finland is appalling. That Germany cannot supply her with anything in the way of food nor can Sweden who has barely enough for itself and naturally as he says we are not going to send anything. He thinks the population will die by the thousands of starvation.

He led me on to the subject of Bulgaria and kept on insisting that it might be possible to get Bulgaria out of the War. That Bulgaria was on extremely bad terms with Turkey and now that they saw Turkey was being beaten it was just the sort of role that Ferdinand would like to play to come over to our side and attack his old ally. He was very insistent on this. Whether he knows anything or not I could not make out. He is supposed here to be frankly pro-Ally but I cannot vouch for this. He said we had stated that Turkey must be driven out of Europe and if so who were we going to give her territory to? Would it not be possible to give it, with the exception of Constantinople, to Bulgaria and by that means buy out that country. I did not argue the question with him but told him I thought that it would be very repugnant to the Allies to let Ferdinand in any way profit by his treachery. He said he quite understood that but surely to shorten the War, as it would by many months, it was worth the sacrifice.

Saw Clemenceau who handed me his answer to Weir. I had not time to read it before it went off and I am not sure whether it is quite satisfactory to our people.

Clemenceau was in great spirits. Of course the French rather ignore our successes in Palestine as it is putting their nose out of joint with regard to influence in Syria where they have always wished to be predominant and thought they were. Macedonia going extremely well. Far exceeding any of our most favourable hopes and the question is now not how far we shall get on but how far we can allow our troops to go on. Clemenceau tells me that Guillaumat will go out at once to take over command for 6 weeks but not to really command in the battle but in view of our great successes to see how far they ought to be pushed. Clemenceau seems to anticipate a great effect from this victory and he again asked me to find out from Lord Milner whether he would be prepared to substitute Indian troops for French troops if they were withdrawn.

He was most friendly but he then turned on me and said that I was not a good friend in allowing one of my friends at luncheon here to abuse him to one of his colleagues. I asked him who the friend was and he said Lord

Durham.[2] I was delighted to be able to catch him out and to tell him in the first place that if it was Lord Durham neither I nor anybody else connected with the Government would ever be responsible for what he said or did and then to be able to tell him that Durham had never been to Paris since I had been there. He also told me that Austen Chamberlain[3] had done the same thing. It is quite obvious the reports come from London and I told him so. He is going to make further enquiries and let me know but I again repeated that it was not worth paying the slightest attention to what Durham said. I thought I would be quite frank with him and asked him if he had made a mistake and meant Lambton who had been here but to my knowledge had made no remark whatever about the Man Power Report. He said "No" he was quite sure it was Durham and not his brother so at all events my conscience is clear.

I also spoke to him about the questions of the formation and equipping of Russian troops in Siberia. He is looking into the matter but I am afraid there is a great deal of friction between the English and French Missions in Siberia. The French as usual are trying to get everything into their own hands and Knox our man out there is not one who suffers fools gladly. I shall have to see Clemenceau again on the subject in a day or two.

In the evening Charlie, Sammy and I dined at L'Ecrivisse, a small restaurant in Montmartre. Excellent dinner and then went to the Marigny to see an American Revue which was quite the rottenest show I have ever seen in my life.

Notes to 24 September

1. Nickola Pašić (1846–1926). Serbian Prime Minister, 1912–18 (in exile from 1915).
2. John George Lambton, 3rd Earl of Durham (1855–1928).
3. Austen Chamberlain (1863–1937). Minister without Portfolio in the War Cabinet, April 1918–January 1919.

Wednesday, 25th September

I did not have the usual Military Meeting today as there was nothing definite for us to consider but I told anybody of our Party who liked to come to luncheon to do so. Sackville West, Nash, Thornton, Elsworthy, representing Spiers, and Heaton Ellis turned up. I had a talk with Sackville West afterwards. He tells me that G.H.Q. is rather difficult at the present moment and is very much afraid of anything passing out of its hands into anybody else's and they are kicking against a certain supply Committee which it is proposed to form and it may be that this is the reason why Douglas Haig is objecting to Henderson. Sackville West is not too happy about the success in Macedonia as he does not quite see what real advantage we shall get out of it, his idea being that unless Bulgaria asks for Peace the only result of our advance will be to regain Serbian territory which the Bulgarians do not mind giving up as they have destroyed everything and the length of our line is considerably increased which will mean more troops. He says our English losses have been very heavy and that the Indian troops that are supposed to replace British troops are only newly raised levées and very much untrained. Of course I take what he says with a grain of salt as Versailles was very much opposed to any operations whatsoever saying we could not possibly get through. My own opinion is that the loss of material and guns is much more important than the taking of prisoners as replacement can only come from Germany. He equally was very doubtful as to any result accruing from our Palestine success for exactly the same cause. He did not think it would bring any definite conclusion in the way of eliminating Turkey from the War. He pointed out with a certain amount of force Bulgaria and Turkey are both at each other's throats and that the effect of our defeating both of them leaves them in relatively the same position whereas if we had only defeated Turkey it might have been possible to come to some arrangement with Turkey owing to her fear of what Bulgaria might do. I think all this is a little far fetched and I do not see how any country can but suffer from the defeats that Bulgaria and Turkey have had.

Nash and Thornton are both very alarmed about the coal position. America has asked for 8 million tons a year and after going into their figures, which they say are admirably produced and in the minutest detail, they have come to the conclusion that America's demands are if anything under-estimated. This coming on the news in the papers this morning of the strike in South Wales makes one feel that the gains we have in the War itself are nullified by the want of patriotism of our people at home.

Major Roberts acting for Le Roy Lewis came to see me. He had been approached by two Russian Officers who had been sent to him by DMI in London though they had lost their credentials, asking for his help to get Russian Officers now serving with the French away from the French in order to send them to Siberia to help in raising Russian troops under an English command. They want him to go to the Russian Embassy tomorrow. I warned him to be extremely careful as it is a subject on which the French are very touchy. They have demanded that they shall organise and command Russian troops and they are dependent on these officers to help them. Anything he did must be strictly unofficial and he must keep me thoroughly well informed. One of the main difficulties is that almost all these officers are Monarchists and their idea of getting back to Russia is to organise a force which will reestablish the Monarchy. Personally I think that is a Utopian idea although a Monarchy is the only thing that could bring about a united Russia, but with France and America both opposed to any restoration of a Monarchy one has to be very careful in dealing with such a subject and not give any opportunity for them to say the English Embassy has supported the idea.

Count Zamoyski[1] came to see me on behalf of the Polish Committee. The avowed intention of the visit was to ask me to send a telegram of congratulations to Allenby which I agreed should be forwarded.[2] He then got on to general matters regarding Poland and told me that the situation in that country is perfectly appalling at the present moment and even the richest people are starving. That a suit of clothes costs 1,800 kronen and that the whole situation is deplorable. His information also is that things are very bad in Austria and there is a continuous stream of deserters from the Austrian Army. He says there are already over a million deserters and that everywhere the country is ripe for a revolution. At the same time he is not very hopeful about the end of the War which he thinks will certainly last another 18 months. He then got on to the subject of a Generalissimo of Polish Forces. He wants a General Joseph Haller[3] appointed. The reason he gives for this now is that the Polish Army in France has acquired certain dimensions. They already have one Division ready to go into the line and others to follow and although they like their French General they are naturally anxious that the Poles should be under a Pole. I asked however how that would work with regard to the Polish Forces in Murman and Siberia as I thought it would hamper matters if everything had to be referred to a Generalissimo who would be in France. He told me he did not mean it to be a Generalissimo in the ordinary sense of the word and it really would be Chief of the Staff more who could be referred to on matters connected with Poland. In reply to my question as to the attitude of the French he told me he had approached them. An answer was to be given within the course of the next 48 hours and he understood that that answer would be favourable. If it was favourable he hoped that England and Italy would agree. He is to come and see me again when the answer has been received and will then put forward a formal request. He spoke in the highest terms of Captain Leveson Gower who he said had spared no pains to thoroughly understand the position and to whom they felt they could always go to as a friend. I must say I endorse this opinion. Leveson Gower has done everything he possibly can to put himself in complete touch with the Polish Committee and I am certain they treat him with the utmost confidence.

Simon Lovat arrived before Dinner.

Charlie and I dined with Thornton. There were also Sir Charles Ellis and Thornton's A.D.C. Mayer who is a writer and producer of plays as was his father before him. His father produced Sarah Bernhardt[4] for the first time in England. Most agreeable and interesting fellow. We dined at the most extraordinary little Café. They have four private rooms which each hold 5 people and that is the maximum they can do. It is called I believe the Maierbau. A most excellent dinner and the Patron who was most amusing came in with every dish and explained exactly how it was cooked, etc and produced the most marvellous white wine. Quite a simple dinner but excellent. We then went to the Casino de Paris for a Revue which was extremely good. Altogether a very pleasant evening.

Thornton is one of the most amusing men and the best host I have ever seen. He is an American who was brought over to manage the Great Eastern Railway and I should think was probably the best Railway General Manager that we have got. He is most popular and especially amongst his men.

Notes to 25 September

1. Count Maurycy Zamoyski. Leading member of the Polish National Committee which was formed in Lausanne in August 1917, but which moved to Paris to champion the Polish cause in the Allied camp.
2. General Edmund Allenby (1861–1936). Commanded expeditionary force based in Egypt to fight the Turks. His great cavalry campaign led to the annihilation of the Turkish armies, with Damascus falling on 1 October.
3. The 2nd Corps of the Polish army, surrounded by German troops, was forced to surrender on 13 May 1918 near Kanev on the Dnieper. A small contingent under Haller escaped. He travelled to France and took command of the Polish army.
4. Sarah Bernhardt (1844–1923). Celebrated French actress. She continued to act after the loss of a leg in 1915.

Thursday, 26th September

Mr. Gompers[1] with Mr. Wallace, and another man whose name I did not catch, came to see me. Gompers was just the sort of man I imagined him to be with very decided opinions with regard to our Labour Party at home. His expression was "They have entirely forgotten labour and think only of 'politics'". They have lost complete touch with the workers and that is the cause of all the trouble at the present moment. They are only thinking of political matters. They were all very much impressed with their meeting with the King and Queen and he tells me perhaps the most impressed men of all were two Irish Americans, sons of Fenians, who subsequently went to Ireland and came back saying they would have nothing more to do with Ireland and very bitter against the Irish. He tells me from what he hears there is even more abuse of America amongst the Irish than there is of England and the feeling generally in America is to wash their hands of Ireland and Irish affairs. He was very pleasant and I liked my talk with him very much. He is going to come and see me again and have luncheon with me on their way back from Italy.

Luncheon. Apart from House Party, self, Charlie, Lovat and Sammy Scott the following lunched. M. Nail,[2] Minister of Justice, M. Roux, Préfet de la Police, M. Wedels, and M. and Mme Jacquemare. He is Clemenceau's grandson. They have been married about a year and half. He is a very nice boy who has been badly wounded. She is extraordinarily nice and pretty and they both talk English quite well, but I find that everybody now tries to make me talk French instead of talking English to me. I suppose it is good practice.

Dined with Murats. He however had to be away so his son who is on the Staff of Salonika took his place. Very nice boy. There was also the second son who was an aviateur who lost his leg and who dined with me before. One of the nicest boys I have come across. Also Madame Castéja, the American who married the second son. She was a Miss Garrison. Du Bos and Madame de Sevignie who I believe was a friend of Her Grace's. Also Reinach (Polybe). They were all very excited about the American news[3] but apparently not much was to be said about it as the French had not got on, the Germans having tried the same trick on them as succeeded when Gouraud[4] tried it on the Germans on the 18th, namely evacuating all the front line trenches. Gouraud however did not fall into the trap but naturally it delayed the advance.

Notes to 26 September

1. Samuel Gompers (1850–1924). President of the American Federation of Labour.
2. Buis Nail (1864–1920). Minister of Justice, November 1917–January 1920.
3. French and American forces launched the Battle of Meuse-Argonne on a front of

40 miles in the early hours of 26 September.
4. General Henri Gouraud (1867–1946). Commander, French 4th Army. Rose to prominence after victory over Ludendorff on 15 July 1918.

Friday, 27th September

Prof. Djoukitch came here and I presented him on behalf of the Government with a Silver Inkstand in appreciation of his work for our Hospitals attached to the Serbian Army during the Serbian retreat.

Afterwards Dr. Weizmann[1] came to see me. He is the head of the Zionist Commission. He was interesting about his time in Palestine. He said that in order to try and deceive the enemy he gave it out that he was very disappointed that England had decided not to make any further advance and got this well circulated amongst the Turks. He waited till he found that the rumour had been well circulated and then left Palestine before the attack began again saying that the reason for his going was that he was so disgusted he would not stay. He anticipates many difficulties with the French Government. They insisted on sending a M. Picot[2] who was an intolerable nuisance and who called himself High Commissioner for Palestine. They also included what they called a French contingent of troops. As a matter of fact they were all Armenians with a few officers and the total strength was only 5,000. But the French Government are now opening their mouths very wide as they look upon Syria as being their particular sphere of influence and apparently owing to an extremely stupid agreement drawn up by Mark Sykes,[3] who I always thought would get us into trouble, and Picot, they have some reason for taking this view as to Syria being under their influence. The papers are already beginning to talk about it. It appears that both Jews and Arabs hate the idea of the French coming in and Weizmann, who saw Sonnino on his way through, says that although the Italians have really no desire for possessions in this part of the world, if the French insist on having certain rights they must equally insist and one demand is that if the French have Beyrout [Beirut] the Italians must have Alexandria [sic: Alexandretta]. Weizmann thinks there is only one way of settling the matter and that is of getting the President of the U.S. to act as arbitrator. There are a large number of Jews of all nationalities in America and he therefore could bring to it an unbiased mind and as America has no territorial desires there probably all Nations would accept willingly any decision they arrived at.

Weizmann is going to see Pichon and then going to London and after that he hopes to go to America. He seems a most intelligent man. He had seen Jimmy Rothschild[4] who is not as I thought commanding a Jewish Battalion but is liaison officer between the Jews in the north of Palestine and Allenby.

Luncheon with Guillaumat at the Inter-Allié Club. Everybody very excited about the news and naturally Guillaumat much pleased as this attack was his plan and it is entirely due to his energy and persuasive powers that it was authorised — our Government having been very much against it for a long time. I sat between Admiral Fournier and the Préfet de la Seine, a very nice fellow indeed.

Afternoon played golf with Charlie and Simon Lovat. Came back to find a great deal to do.

Evening dined with Madame de Polignac. Quite a small dinner. Tardieu, Roux, Préfet de Police and a lady whose name I did not quite catch, but I think it was Madame de Jarres. Very attractive and very talkative. Quite amusing. Tardieu is a most amusing man. He goes to England on Saturday, back here on Thursday and then to America the next week. He says only for 3 weeks but I have bet him a dinner that [he] won't be back by December 1st. I am sure when he gets there he will find he will have a great deal more to do than he thinks. He apparently is having plenty of difficulties with the Americans and he confirms everything I have heard about Baker,[5] the American Secretary for War, namely that he is a man who knows very little of what is going on and has absolutely no authority. He has got himself into a tremendous hole by promising to pool the whole of American shipping, which of course is the right thing to do, but this promise has exasperated the American Shipping Controller.

Notes to 27 September

1. Chaim Weizmann (1874–1952). President of the World Zionist Organisation. He worked in the British Admiralty during the war, pressing Zionist issues on the British government.
2. François Georges-Picot. French diplomat. Became French Consul-General in Beirut in March 1914.
3. Sir Mark Sykes (1879–1919). Unionist MP, 1911–19. His agreement with Picot, signed in May 1916, allowed for the division of the Ottoman Empire into British, French, Italian and Russian spheres of influence.
4. James A. de Rothschild (d.1957). Major, Royal Fusiliers, 1918.
5. Newton D. Baker (1871–1937). American Secretary of War, 1916–21.

Saturday, 28th September

Went to see Clemenceau 9.30 to ask him about the future plan in Salonika. He thinks that the Bulgarian offer is perfectly genuine and he has received intelligence that when Franchet D'Espérey's answer went back it was unanimously determined by both Government and opposition that negotiations should at once take place for what I take to be a complete surrender. In other words that we shall occupy Bulgaria with its railways etc. and a total disarmament of the country. If this is only carried out it can only be a question almost of days before Turkey equally asks for an armistice. Clemenceau very anxious that White troops should be replaced as far as possible by Indian troops and begged me to again impress upon Milner how grateful he would be if we could send more Indian Battalions and thereby release French Battalions for the Western Front. Of course if this can be done it will probably mean the putting of something like 250,000 more men on the Western Front.

Motored with Charlie to Fontainebleau to have luncheon with Klotz. Took us an hour and a half including one puncture. At luncheon M. and Mme Gouin, Mme Edouard Gouin a sister-in-law, and Mme de Billy,[1] the wife of the French Minister at Athens. Afterwards went to see the Palace at Fontainebleau. I must say except for its historic interest there is nothing in it that appeals to me very much and as apparently Louis Philippe[2] with Victorian ideas redecorated most of it some of the ceilings etc are awful.

We then motored on to tea at the Chateau de Vaux which I think is the most lovely and perfect thing I have ever seen. It belonged to Fouquet,[3] Louis XIV's Finance Minister. It was all built in 5 years and when completed the King was to go there for a night. He arrived, was so angry at seeing this huge chateau which he said must have been built out of robberies from him that he left without staying for the night and confiscated the place afterwards. It then passed into the Villars family. There was one family in between and then it was bought by M. Sommier the father of the present owner. He is a very rich sugar refiner and he has spent a million francs for 10 successive years in restoring the place to what it was before and most beautifully he has done it and also in buying things which originally belonged to it. The couple who now own it — he was not there as he is at the front. She is a most charming woman whom everybody apparently adores as she has had a hospital there from the beginning of the War and works the whole thing herself. It is difficult to give a description of the place. Roughly it is this. There is a huge courtyard the front of which is a big iron fencing of very pretty design, flanked on each side by square blocks of red brick building, each of them about the size of the stables at Knowsley. One side is the stables, the other was the Orangerie which is now used as the Hospital. The house itself is a great big stone building with two short wings and approached by a flight of stairs the breadth of the whole house. Going into the house there is an entrance hall and then you go into a big saloon which goes up two stories and the front of which is circular shaped. It has old marble flooring with a most curious sundial. A disc is arranged in the window on which the sunlight can fall and that shows the hour cut in figures on the floor. The furniture etc is all of the same period and the ceilings were painted by Le Brun. The one in the saloon is painted like the sky with a great eagle hovering in the centre, also painted, and it really makes you feel as if you were in the open air. There are various beautiful rooms off it, each of them done entirely in the period. Altogether it is well worth a visit and I hope to go there again. There was one Englishman in the Hospital who had been very badly wounded. He had been there 4 months. I went and had a talk with him and he said people were kindness itself. He came from the north of London, joined up under my scheme and was evidently a widower and an oldish man, but as keen as mustard.

After luncheon I had a little walk before going to Fontainebleau with Klotz and we talked over Wilson's speech.[4] Of course the report so far has been condensed but we both agreed it was mischievous in the extreme and might give rise to endless trouble. In the first place his saying that we will not treat with Germany seems to shut the door completely to any Peace offers from that country and I do not see how we are going to have Peace except by treating with Germany. Then when he goes on to say there must be no distinction made after the War between the various Nations he has said something which will irritate people here and in England. It is all very well for America who has not suffered in any way comparable either in loss of men or money to what England and France have done and who has had none of their towns bombed or shelled or destroyed, to talk like that but I am perfectly certain that our people will never stand any system by which Germany in the future shall be put in a position to oust us from our commerce.

In the evening Sir Henry Norman and Furse dined with Sammy, Charlie and myself. It was rather amusing because of course Furse and Henry Norman hate each other, a hatred which is shared as far as Norman is concerned by both Sammy Scott and myself, but I wanted to see him and try and find out what job he is over here on, as he is one of L.G.'s spies. He is one of the most shifty men I have ever come across and I am certain he really is, or his father was, a German Jew. He was mixed up in the Marconi scandal[5] and also was one of the people who agitated for the Masden Gun.[6] In fact he always takes the part of anybody who is doing something mean or dishonest.

Notes to 28 September

1. Robert de Billy. Appointed French representative to the Greek Provisional government at Salonika in 1917.
2. Louis Philippe (1773–1850). King of France, 1830–48.
3. Nicolas Fouquet, Marquis de Belle-Isle (1615–1680). The story goes that Louis XIV visited Vaux and was so impressed by the wealth it exhibited that he promptly sacked his finance minister.
4. Wilson's speech was delivered at the Metropolitan Opera House, New York, on 27 September. Of it the President said: 'there are many things in it which will displease the Imperialists of Great Britain, France and Italy. The world must be convinced that ... America has her own plan for a world settlement, a plan which does not contain the germs of another war.'
5. Share-dealing controversy of 1912 in which several members of the Liberal government, including Lloyd George, were involved.
6. Light, portable machine gun of Danish design.

Sunday, 29th September

Went to Versailles. Saw Sackville-West. Had a talk with him about various matters. He, like me, thinks that it is very dangerous not having a Supreme War Council to discuss matters but he thinks they are bound to have one at the end of this week either here or in London.

Then went on to luncheon with Miss de Wolff. The American Ambassador, Madame de Polignac, and a few rather interesting people there.

Madame de Polignac reminded me of something which I had forgotten to put down at the Dinner I had with her the other night. Tardieu told us that Mr. Kerney the head of the American Propaganda had got into most frightful trouble. It appears he had been writing home and in his letters complaining bitterly that England and France had only one object and that was to try and make money out of Americans. He apparently said many other things most uncomplimentary to France, quite forgetting that his letters were liable to be opened and opened they were. The result is a row and he has got to go home. I am sorry because whatever he may have said about England he was undoubtedly helping us a good bit with regard to our propaganda.

Had a long talk with the American Ambassador afterwards. All his information is that Spain is going to come into the War.

Dinner in the evening, Le Roy Lewis and Marie Louise. We had a very amusing discussion on Paris Society afterwards.

Monday, 30th September

Sammy Scott left.

Saw the Bolivian Minister. He put a lot of questions to me with regard to our domestic affairs at home none of which I answered.

Received a telephone message from Lloyd George to say that he had received a telegram from Milne to say an Armistice had been agreed on but that they had no idea as to what the terms were.[1] Went off at once to see Clemenceau who told me that owing to his absence at the Front all yesterday he had been unable to telegraph to Lloyd George till this morning but a telegram had now been sent telling him all details.

There is no doubt that Bulgaria has capitulated entirely and as far as War in the East is concerned it is the beginning of the end. Clemenceau very excited over the whole thing. We talked a little about general subjects. He told me that he thought Peace would not come before the winter and chiefly because the American organisation was so extraordinarily bad. He said until you saw it you could not have any idea of the confusion due to bad staff work that their troops were in. The men fight brilliantly but everything else is missing. I think he sees more than he even did before how impossible it is for the Americans to form an Army and how much better it is for them to fight in Divisions either with us or the French.

Had luncheon with Count Fels at the Crillion. It was ostensibly to meet Mandel but as on every other previous occasion Mandel chucked at the last moment. He always declines to have either luncheon or dinner out. I did not catch the names of all present but roughly there were Favre, General Ferrier, who is the Military critic of *L'Humanité*, Sellac and another man whose name I did not catch. The conversation after luncheon was most interesting. Favre who was one of the deputies of the Commission de L'Armée at the time of the Nivelle attack told us some of the incidents previous to that attack. I put them down as far as I remember them. When Nivelle's great attack was arranged the chief element of success was that of surprise and it was to take the form of two attacks by the English and then a tremendous attack by the French. Between the middle of December, when this was settled, and the time that the attack was to be launched, much had happened. The Germans had given up all the ground to Bapaume and had retired on the Hindenburg line. It was obvious therefore that on that front we were unprepared to attack and could not be prepared for some months; that no attack could be made there and therefore the Germans knew that an attack must be made by us in the North and by the French between Soissons and Rheims, and they naturally knew the latter would be the big attack. When Favre as Deputy had seen General Michelin[2] in the middle of February he was full of success of the plan but after the retirement he saw him again on March 25th and Michelin then told him that while before the odds were strongly in favour of success they were now just as strongly against it. He so impressed Favre that the latter came back to see Painlevé who was then Minister of War and Ribot who was Président du Conseil and told them what had happened. Painlevé said that it was absolutely necessary to hold a small meeting and this meeting was held, as far as I remember, on April 6th. There were present Ribot, Painlevé, Favre, Michelin, Nivelle, Franchet D'Espérey, Mangin and Castelnau. Painlevé placed before the meeting what Michelin had told him. Nivelle then spoke. He was very vehement in support of his plan and said it was bound to be a success. The other Generals all disagreed with him but in the presence of a senior officer they apparently were more lukewarm than they had been when talking privately with Favre, but it was sufficient to show Nivelle that the balance of opinion was dead against him. He therefore addressed Ribot by saying that the reason why the attack was being made was to keep engagements with the English. Favre interjected that the English were not so foolish as not to see that there had been a great change in the circumstances and that the plan should be altered to meet these changed circumstances. Nivelle said "No" that it was a direct agreement and that the attack must go on but that as he saw that not only was Painlevé against him but that he had lost the confidence of his subordinates he wished to hand in his resignation as it was obvious confidence was no longer placed in him. Ribot refused to accept this saying they all had full confidence in him and of course if it was a question of keeping a bargain with the English the attack must go on. Nivelle said very well but he wished to resign. They were going then to déjeuner: the attack went on although it had been condemned by everybody except Nivelle himself and the result is only too well known.[3] As far as my own recollection goes not one word of this was ever conveyed to the

British Government. There is no doubt we attacked so as to keep our faith with the French Government and apparently every man that we put into the attacks then was sacrificed because Ribot and Painlevé could not make up their minds to do what evidently they thought right, namely to alter the whole plan of campaign and to stop Nivelle's great offensive. Favre told me he could swear to the whole of this and if necessary bring documentary evidence. If any information of this was conveyed to England it must have been conveyed to Lloyd George and Robertson and withheld from me but my implicit belief is that nothing whatever of this meeting was allowed to transpire.

In afternoon saw David Henderson who accepts the Military Attaché-ship I am glad to say even if Haig will not agree to his doing his work as well.

I also saw Spiers and I am afraid I am going to have a great deal of trouble with him. Not in open rebellion but as a passive resister. He wants me to do certain things over David Henderson's head which I certainly shall not do.

In the evening Charlie and I dined at a little restaurant, the Becasse. Extraordinarily good and most reasonable in price as prices go at the present moment.

Notes to 30 September

1. On 27 September a Bulgarian delegation arrived in Salonika to sue for peace and an armistice was signed two days later.
2. Presumably General Alfred Micheler (1861–1931) who led the Group of Armies of Reserve during Nivelle's offensive. His initial enthusiasm for Nivelle's tactics won him the command of the attacking forces.
3. Cf. R. M. Watt, *Dare Call it Treason* (London, 1963), pp. 142ff.

October 1918

Tuesday, 1st October

Saw Baron d'Erlanger.[1] It was only just to make his acquaintance. He is an enthusiast about the Channel Tunnel and seemed to want my assistance in putting the matter forward. I told him that however sympathetic I might personally be towards the scheme it was a matter in which I could only express an opinion if so instructed by my Government and whatever opinion they had would be the one that I should have to support. He is not at all well looked on here and is supposed to have been very pro-Bosch but he has been very good to the Leave Club. He owns a big hotel here which he has given them free of all expense and contributes very largely to it so from our point of view we have every reason to be grateful to him.

Afterwards M. Maklakoff the so called Russian Ambassador came to see me. For what passed see attached letter to Mr. Balfour.

Luncheon. Mr. Henry Burton,[2] Minister of Railways and Harbours, South African Representative at the Imperial conference; Mr. G. W. Pilkington, Private Secretary, Mr. C. du P. Chiappini, Mr. E. Oppenheimer, 3 people with him. Reinach, Sevastopoulo, and Mr. Gifford a well known American who is a great friend of Baker the Secretary of State for War.

Very amusing luncheon. The principal topic of discussion was the point of view that Europe as a whole looked upon the Black races as compared with the point of view of those in America and South Africa who have to live with these races.

Chiappini is the most talkative man. He has been the Commercial Agent of South Africa in England. He was a Boer who fought against us and lost an arm but he is more British than the British and his hatred of Germany was more intense than anybody's I have ever met. Burton and his party have really had a remarkable time. Coming to England they ran into one of their own destroyer escorts with the result that the depth charges exploded and blew the fore part of the vessel up. Going back they were on the Galway Castle, were torpedoed and were 8 or 10 hours in an open boat before being picked up. They are now making a third attempt to get home. They were not very pleased at the arrangements that were made for them at Boulogne and elsewhere but I think we have got everything settled all right here and they were apparently quite pleased to come.

Dined early with Charlie and went to the Comédie Française to see Marionette. Beautifully acted.

Notes to 1 October

1. Baron d'Erlanger (1866–1939). Chairman, Erlangers Ltd.
2. Henry Burton (1866–1935). South African Minister of Railways and Harbours, 1912–20; member of the Imperial War Cabinet.

Copy of letter sent to Rt. Hon. A. J. Balfour 1 October 1918

Confidential

Maklakoff the so-called Russian Ambassador came to see me this morning with two requests. First that I should receive a deputation from Russians here who will present an Address expressing horror of the murder of our Naval Attaché[1] at Petrograd. I have said yes as though it does not do any good it can do no harm.

He then went on to speak of a despatch handed by the Russian Ambassador in Rome to the Italian Foreign Office with which he associated himself, begging that all refuge should be prohibited after the War and now to those who were guilty of the Bolshevist crimes in Russia. He told me that the Bolshevists evidently saw that their end was coming and they were feathering their nests in neutral countries. He says he knew of 33 millions in gold which had been sent in the names of Bolshevists to Switzerland and he hoped that every step would be taken both now and when it came to discussing Peace to bring these men to justice and to secure for Russia the sums which they had stolen and which might still be recoverable from neutral and enemy countries. He told me that he did not think we could have any idea of the reign of terror that is going on in Russia. He says nobody knows who has or who has not been murdered and he himself is still doubtful as to whether the Empress and her daughters have been murdered. He told me it was reported that his brother a former Minister had been shot. He asked the Swedish Minister to make enquiries about it and the answer he had just got was to this effect, that it was quite impossible to say whether it was true or not. That men and women all through the country were being shot by the hundred, hastily buried or thrown into rivers and that nobody knew even the names of some of those who were so being shot. It was an absolute reign of terror such as the world had never seen.

He referred somewhat bitterly to our having kept a Bolshevist Ambassador in England even though we did not recognise him and there is no doubt that Russians here do think that we showed extraordinary leniency to Lenin[2] and Co. and that by showing such leniency we gave a strength to the Bolshevist movement which they would otherwise never have had.

I hope that the telegrams I have sent you with regard to the Bulgarian Armistice have been sufficiently explicit. I have just got a telegram off from the Foreign Office at 5.50 last night saying that you were still unaware of the exact terms of the armistice. As I had telegraphed them very fully before 1.30 yesterday I am doubtful as to whether my telegram was explicit enough or whether you had not yet received it. If the latter it does show that something must be done to expedite the transmission of messages from me to you. I had written about a direct telephone wire but apparently that is not able to be arranged though I think that it is very essential at such a moment as this that something of the kind should be established.

I am afraid like many of my letters lately this does not give you much information but really there is very little to give at the present moment. Things political are very quiet. I cannot find out anything as to when the Caillaux trial is likely to take place but the putting forward of a more serious charge against Humbert[3] looks to me as if they were getting more and more information inculpating Caillaux.

There are various small strikes in progress here but nothing of any consequence and though the socialists are to a certain extent raising their head the whole feeling of the country is really so dead against them, and Clemenceau is so much a dictator at the present moment, that I think very little attention need be paid to academic resolutions that they pass. What I am looking for and expect to see every day is an agitation that would try to compel Clemenceau to bring Briand into his counsels with regard to Peace. There is no doubt however great is the country's faith in Clemenceau in time of actual warfare when the time for making Peace comes they will want to have somebody associated with him who is not quite so much the bull in the china shop.

I am afraid I have very little news for you and this letter is of very little interest but I hope you like getting just one's ideas of what is going on.

Notes to confidential letter of 1 October

1. On 31 August Bolshevik troops had forced their way into the British Embassy in Petrograd. The British Naval Attaché, Captain Francis Cromie (1882–1918) managed to kill three Bolshevik soldiers, but was then shot dead.
2. Vladimir Ilyich Lenin (1870–1924). Creator and first leader of the Soviet State.
3. The leading Senator and publisher, Charles Humbert, had become involved with Bolo Pasha and had hopelessly compromised himself with German money.

Wednesday, 2nd October

Received telegram from Lloyd George telling me to see Clemenceau at once and say that he (L.G.) was coming over Friday or Saturday to talk over matters and urge that Orlando should be sent for in order that they might together insist on the Italians taking the offensive. Went off to Clemenceau at once. Found him in entire agreement with Lloyd George. He is mad with the Italians who will do absolutely nothing and yet pretend in their Press and elsewhere that their inactivity is in entire accord with Foch's plans.

I mentioned about [Henry] Wilson coming over and I then found out for the first time with what profound contempt apparently both Clemenceau and Foch regarded him. Clemenceau says he is no good whatever. He has never commanded troops and his advice is not worth having, but whenever he is asked an opinion all he does, as Clemenceau described it, is to grin from ear to ear, to put his left leg over his right shoulder and to say "Truly I don't know". He says therefore to discuss military matters with him is useless. He swore me to secrecy over this. I am rather disturbed about it as I am very divided in my opinion as to whether I ought not under the circumstances to tell Arthur Balfour but I feel I cannot do so without permission from Clemenceau.

He then told me about the American Army. He says we can have no idea of the confusion in which it is in. The absolute lack of higher control and happy-go-lucky way in which things are done. He says until he had seen it himself he could not have believed it. The other day the two Divisions acting with us went right forward regardless of communication with their flanks and at one time were completely surrounded by Germans and if it had not been for two English Divisions they must have been lost. Their traffic arrangements are beneath contempt. If a man driving a lorry wants to have his luncheon he just stops and has it regardless of the fact that he may be delaying 200 other cars behind his. He says that is no exaggeration and has actually occurred. He was on the point of telegraphing to Wilson to say that unless a change was made there would be a disaster but he found Foch had anticipated him and had broken the American Army up into two and that he hoped now things would go better but the American Army was nothing like pulling its weight.

I asked him whether the fighting was very hard and he said No, not really so hard as it appeared but what they were anxious to do was to advance with as little loss of life as possible. They were in a country where tanks could not operate and therefore they were held up a great deal by machine guns. A German Officer who was taken prisoner two days ago, when asked why it was they were not fighting as well as they did some time ago replied, "You see for yourself I have fought all right because I am wounded but the men will not fight because we have no artillery to support us." Clemenceau thinks that it is not only the loss of their guns which now amount to over 3,000 but to the absence of ammunition and that they are obliged now to save the latter in every way that they possibly can.

He tells me there are rumours of a large number of German and Austrian troops going down to the Balkans but there is no real confirmation of that and he does not know, if they are sending the troops, from where they are getting them. He is very confident that Germany has cracked but at the same time I can see that he is very anxious over the position and the anxiety chiefly comes from the fact of Italy practically being non-fighting. Both he and Lloyd George consider it essential that the Italians should attack if simply to hold the Austrian troops on that front.

As I say Clemenceau was very confident but for the first time I have seen him really rather worried.

Ordinary Military Meeting with luncheon afterwards. Sackville-West had a private talk with me in which he told me he did not think Spiers was playing the game. As he said the other day when there was a question of the terms of the Bulgarian armistice I kept him fully informed and he had the copy of my telegrams and letters whereas on the other hand Spiers was sending telegrams which he did not give to him. He also noticed what I had noticed, namely how unnecessary it was for Spiers to have gone to have seen Clemenceau. He only got information in the afternoon which I had telegraphed in the morning and even then he did not get as full information as Clemenceau had given me. As Henderson is definitely to be appointed I hope I shall be able to remedy these things but I am afraid Spiers is not going to work in, in which case he will have to go.

After luncheon Murray of Elibank came to see me. Very much dis-

turbed with regard to the debate the other day on the Algerian Concession. He talked very much about the French Government having treated
their agreement with him as a scrap of paper and he looks upon them as
having been guilty of a grave breach of faith. As a matter of fact he had no
real engagement and there was his great mistake and moreover he had to
admit to me that if they gave him what they have now promised — of
course it is much less than he asked for — it would still be a paying proposition to him. He thinks there were reflections made on him and on his
firm but that I am bound to say I cannot read into the utterances of the
ministers although undoubtedly one or two uncontrollable deputies did
make remarks about them and their work in Mexico. I told him and I
must say he entirely agreed with me, that it was impossible for me now to
approach the French Government on the question unless I received
instructions from the Foreign Office who would have to tell me exactly
what points they wanted me to urge on the French Government. He
thinks he will get Balfour to do that but I very much doubt it.

Went to see Pichon in the afternoon to try and get answers to various
outstanding matters, also to see what the French Government proposed
with regard to Diplomatic and Consular Agents in Bulgaria. Pichon
wants to talk it over with Lloyd George but I told him I thought that
would be impossible as Lloyd George would know nothing about it. They
had better let me have their views in order that I may submit them to the
Government at home.

In the evening Charlie and I dined with the Bates. She was Vera Arkwright. They have got a very tiny flat in an old historic building just at the
back of Notre Dame. It was a real picnic as they did a good bit of their own
cooking and Dinner was perfectly excellent and it was really a most amusing evening. We meant to go away early as they both have to go off at 7 o'c
to a Hospital. We ended by staying till 11.30. The Bretts were there and a
certain Colonel Hutchinson who is the head of the big American Hospital, a very nice and interesting man who has been out with an American
Hospital unit since the beginning of 1915. He was very guarded in what
he said but he practically confirmed all that I am hearing elsewhere and
that is that the American Medical arrangements have absolutely and
entirely broken down. He has got a Hospital which at the outside is supposed to have 1,000 beds and he has got 1,700 in it. Men lying in the cor-
ridors etc. I do not think it is so much want of personnel as want of proper
accommodation. He has been trying to get Convalescent Camps like we
have got but his representations have no effect. It is all the same story. The
Staff work from Pershing downwards in the American Army is very raw

and though they are the most willing lot of men and ready to learn they are really being made to run before they can walk.

Thursday, 3rd October

M. de Sillac came to see me on behalf of the Inter-Allié Club. They want to have a sort of afternoon festivity to celebrate England's victories. It is very nice of them but I think myself it is a great mistake. They expect Wemyss, Haig, Prince of Wales, Prime Minister and every sort of person to be present, which of course they cannot be and I absolutely refused to allow them to send out invitations, which they would do, saying that these people would be present. It is very nice of them but nothing will choke them off having this celebration. It means a speech from me which I particularly dislike.

The Prince of Wales came to see me on his way back to England. The idea of a course at Cambridge has been abandoned and he is coming out next Tuesday to go first to the Canadians, then to the Australians,[1] then I believe he will come here for a short time, but during his visits to the Canadians and the Australians he will come down here occasionally so as to have luncheon and dinner to meet a few political and other people. Just as he was leaving before luncheon a message came in to say Oliver was wounded and at first I could not find out where he was. It was a very anxious time. I had a small luncheon party but at the last moment 4 Generals proposed themselves so it very much increased in size. The following came to luncheon. Madame de Sancay, Madame de Cartessac a great friend of hers, Madame Hennessy and her brother Henri de Mun, David Henderson, Henry Wilson, Sackville-West, Johnny Du Cane and Duncannon.

By 3 o'c they had found out for me that Oliver was only very slightly wounded and where he was and at 3.30 I started to go to Montreuil. Had a first class run there and got in by 10 minutes past 7. Found Fowke the A.G. waiting for me at the cross roads and he very kindly took me back to his house, gave me dinner and put me up and made every arrangement for me. I dined with him and his Staff which consists entirely of Generals. Burnett Stuart,[2] Livingston Learmouth,[3] Howard the Provost Marshal who I think an awful fellow but who Macready is taking to assist him as Commissioner of Police, and Wroughton[4] who is a great friend of Cohn's and a very nice little A.D.C., Sacre. They had found out all about Oliver and that there was no cause for anxiety and made arrangements for me to go out and see him the next day. After Dinner we were talking over various matters and they told me that nobody could exaggerate the hopeless confusion in which the American Troops were. That they have absolutely no idea of fighting except from the purely courageous point of view. Two Divisions were sent in the other day. They were to go to a certain point and then the Australians were to leap-frog with them. The Americans got to this point but instead of stopping they went right on with the result that the Germans came in between them and cut them completely off. The Australians fought desperately hard and after 48 hours managed to get most of them out but they came back in driblets in twos and threes and the Australians set up recruiting booths advertising for men to join the Australians "where at all events you will be fed" and telling them there were not many vacancies and if they did not come soon there would be no room for them. The amusing part is that the Americans did what the Australians asked with the result that every Australian battalion the next day instead of being down to 700 was about 1200 strong. In other parts of the line the Americans were three days without anything to eat or drink and had to evacuate the positions simply because their transport arrangements had collapsed. The same thing happened for a different reason with the Belgians. After the rain it was perfectly impossible to get over all the old fighting ground of Passchendaele and they had to be rationed by our aeroplanes coming down to within 300 feet and dropping rations of bread and meat. It was a wonderful performance on the part of the aeroplanes and pulled the whole thing through.

Notes to 3 October

1. It had been planned that the prince should spend three months taking a staff course at Cambridge, but Haig pleaded that he should instead visit the Dominion and American Troops in France.
2. Colonel John Burnett Stuart (1875–1958). Director of Military Operations and Intelligence, 1922–26.
3. Brigadier-General John Livingston Learmouth (1876–1936). DSO, 1915.
4. Brigadier-General John Wroughton (1874–1940). Adjutant-General's staff, GHQ.

Friday, 4th October

Started off early to No. 17 Casualty Clearing Station about 5 or 6 miles the other side of Hazebroucke which meant a run of about 55 miles. Most comfortable as Fowke lent me his own car. He telegraphed to say that if

Oliver was sufficiently well to leave the Hospital he was to be allowed to come away with me. Was met on arrival by the Commandant of the Hospital who took me straight to Oliver who I found very cheerful. His wound not bad but awfully knocked about in other ways. He had a most lucky escape. The shell fell on the Mess Hut and killed or wounded everybody in it. It fell on the Kitchen side and so they got the worst of it. Oliver was just opening the door to go into the Kitchen when it happened. He told me poor Middleton was very bad and I went to see him. I have never met a pluckier fellow in my life. He never said anything whatever about his own wounds. The first thing he wanted to know was how Oliver was. His voice was extraordinarily strong and he looked a very good colour and even with all the amount of pluck there was amongst the other fellows, the doctors were surprised at his courage. They had taken 12 hours getting them down as they had to be carried a great portion of the way as the ground was perfectly impossible and the result was that in his right arm gas gangrene set in and they had to take it off just above the elbow. The left was very badly wounded in the elbow and they fear there is some damage to the bone and he is also wounded in the leg. He stood his operation very well and although they would not say he was out of danger they thought it was practically certain he would pull through. He will be there for 4 days and then goes to Boulogne for evacuation home. I want to find out where he is as soon as possible because the only thing you can do for him is to have his left arm seen to. Otherwise he may lose power in it and I shall get Robert Jones to take him specially in hand.

Oliver and I motored back to Fowke's house where we had luncheon about 3 miles out of Montreuil, then back to Montreuil where Oliver had his Board and they gave him 3 weeks leave to be spent with me till he is fit to travel and then to go to England for the rest of the time, but of course at the end of that he will have to have another Board as he certainly won't be fit to come out. He thinks himself he will be able to get Slater Booth at Shoeburyness to take him on.

I am very bitter about the way they have delayed in giving him a Brigade Majorship. He does not want me to make a row and so I must not but I am going to say what I think about the conduct of one particular individual who simply out of jealousy kept him from going. If Orders had been carried out both he and Middleton would have been at the School a week before this happened.

We then motored to Paris getting in just at 7 o'c. Very good run but naturally Oliver was very beat when he got here and I confess I was done to a turn.

Found on arrival that Cavan had been telegraphed for to go back to Italy at once. Charlie had very wisely sent Bullock to meet him at the Station and found out under the altered circumstances whether Edward would get leave and as Cavan said he would not, I telephoned at once to London to tell Portia not to come out. It was no use her hanging about here. I do not suppose leave will be opened for another 6 weeks or so.

Doctor came to see Oliver. Says his wound is quite healthy but that he is bruised all over and very much knocked about. He thinks however he will be fit to travel on Wednesday night and Charlie has arranged to stop and go with him.

Misfortunes never come singly and found that Grahame is very ill with the flu and threatened with pneumonia. They hope the danger is past but one is naturally anxious as he is very delicate especially in his lungs.

Saturday, 5th October

Got a message from the Prime Minister to say that he wanted to come to luncheon and he was bringing the Serbian Minister with him.

Oliver had had a very good night but was still very uncomfortable and his wound hurt him a bit but he was very stiff and sore all over. Think a good bit of that is due to the motor drive as I feel rather the same.

Ian Malcolm came to see me. Arthur Balfour is apparently rather seedy. He wanted to know what I thought about the question of a Diplomatic Versailles. I told him I was absolutely opposed to it. That it is what makes so much trouble. People are put in to do the work like I am and then somebody else is put in without any responsibility to do the same work. If they want somebody else to do this work let them say so but to create a Diplomatic Versailles would I think make us a laughing stock besides committing ourselves into the hands of some under-strapper who would agree in counsel with others to something which might have to be repudiated.

Frazier from the United States Embassy came to see me afterwards, rather bitterly complaining that a hole-in-the-corner Supreme War Council is being held, consisting of Lloyd George, Clemenceau and Orlando, from which apparently the Americans are excluded. He tells me that the Italians at Versailles are so ashamed of their country not fighting that they have practically left the place.

Major Ian Hay Beith[1] ("Ian Hay" of the First Hundred Thousand) came to see me to talk to me about Propaganda. He seems a very nice fellow.

Imperiali[2] the Italian Ambassador in London came in just before luncheon to say that Orlando was there and particularly wanted to have a private conversation with Lloyd George. I asked them both to luncheon so our luncheon party consisted of Lloyd George, Orlando, Imperiali, Henry Wilson, Maurice Hankey, Sackville-West, and Admiral Hope. While we were waiting for Orlando and Imperiali I had a few minutes with Lloyd George who I found in a somewhat excitable state. He complained that he had not had all the information with regard to Bulgaria that he ought to have had. I asked him whether that meant that I did not give it to him. He accused Clemenceau of having withheld it. I tried to get him down to exactly what had been withheld and the only thing he could say was that they had not known of the terms of the armistice before they were agreed on. I pointed out to him that I did not think in the first place that Clemenceau knew them and that I was sure the actual terms of the armistice were Franchet D'Espérey's own, although perhaps he may have talked them over with Clemenceau before he went out there in case the situation arose, and I pointed out further that surely it was the duty of the Government and the Military Authorities to have discussed the question before it arose and not to wait until it was actually upon them. He was very excited and said that the French were trying to get everything in their own hands and concealing everything from us. However he was in quite a good humour with me generally.

After luncheon I left him to talk with Orlando and Imperiali and I walked about the garden with Hankey. Hankey tells me that Lloyd George is the only one of the Government who thinks that he was not given the proper information and that it was kept back etc. and everybody else is quite satisfied. Apparently the meeting in the morning had not been very satisfactory but more of that later.

After Lloyd George's conversation with Orlando was finished he saw Frazier from the American Embassy who wanted to know what was going on and I do not think he got much satisfaction.

Lloyd George then said he wanted to go for a drive and I took him up to St. Cloud Golf Course and during the drive there and during our walk, and afterwards going back to Villa Romaine, he talked very frankly about every sort of thing. It appears the reason Orlando wanted to see him was because he said he was being treated like dirt by the French. They insulted him in every way. In regard to the question of an attack by the Italians, they were quite ready to attack if Foch authorised them to do so. Foch said he could not authorise them to attack unless he had been down there himself. Their answer was "Why don't you come down" to which

Foch's reply was "I am too busy to get away". Orlando therefore is perfectly furious and says it is not fair for Foch to say that they won't attack when he won't himself take the responsibility of ordering the attack.[3]

The meeting had been adjourned and they were to meet again at 5 o'c with Foch present.

Lloyd George also talked to me about the General Election and I am convinced he means to have it and to have it almost immediately. He says the difficulties in the way of having an election now would be even greater in the Spring if it came to terms of Peace with Germany and he means to be master in his own house and be quite certain of his position. He says that as far as the Country is concerned the worst that could happen would be that Asquith would be in a majority instead of him but he evidently does not think that in the least likely.

I again tackled him as to what he meant by saying he had not got the full information but I could really get nothing out of him except that he evidently thinks that Clemenceau is out to swindle us all and there I am certain he is wrong, though the way the French are grasping commands does make matters difficult.

At the Villa Romaine I had a talk with Henry Wilson and I see who has been putting these ideas into Lloyd George's head. It is Esher who has written a letter to Henry Wilson to say that he knows that the French knew all along that the Bulgarians were going to give way and deliberately concealed it. It is the most mischievous thing to say and absolutely untrue as I told Henry Wilson. Guillaumat has all along said what would happen. He has always predicted that Bulgaria, if we got in a good blow, would crack up and there would be a debacle, and that it was very different — a man saying "If you do something I know that something else will happen" which does happen, from saying that that man deliberately concealed from you some secret information which would make him sanguine that his plan would succeed. Henry Wilson I think quite agreed and said he thought probably that was the right solution. He then told me of the various discussions in the morning as to what was to happen in Bulgaria and Serbia and it seems to me they have absolutely no plan of any sort or kind thought out. Everybody is giving different advice and there is nothing but confusion. It seems to me from what Lloyd George says that we are being rather petty complaining that the French do not give us enough credit for Palestine and for the part we have played at Salonika. I really do not see that that matters in the least. If they like to think France is doing everything let them do so. It cannot for one minute alter the fact that we have done all the fighting in Palestine; that the War with Turkey is ours and nobody else's. I asked him "suppose Turkey now asks for an armistice have you settled what the terms are to be?" His answer was that the soldiers knew what they wanted but as far as he knew the various Foreign Offices had never discussed the matter and he is determined to try and get it settled at the afternoon Conference.

Various proposals which I won't put on paper were discussed but they all seem to me to be dangerous with the exception of Henry Wilson's which I look upon as being the right solution which I hope he will carry through, but I do not think the afternoon meeting is likely to be a very harmonious affair. Lloyd George told me "What I like is having a thing out. I do not bear any grudge afterwards." As I tried to point out to him other people are different, especially the French and Italians. They do not understand having a thing out when every sort of insulting thing is said on both sides and they do bear resentment.

The only thing that affects me is the question whether I have given them the right amount of information and I am perfectly certain that Clemenceau has kept nothing back from me over all this and that I have given them everything that he said. There is one paragraph in the armistice, connected with the employment of Greeks, which is open to two constructions. They take a different one to what Clemenceau does. That is all that I can see that is wrong.

Charlie and I dined together. About midnight I was awakened by Monson[4] to tell me the news that the Central Powers had asked for an armistice.

Notes to 5 October

1. Major-General John Hay Beith (1876–1952). Novelist and playwright. *The First Hundred Thousand* was published in 1915.
2. Marquis Guglielmo Imperiali (1858–1944). Italian ambassador to London, 1910–20.
3. See G. H. Cassar, *The Forgotten Front: The British Campaign in Italy 1917–1918* (London, 1998), chapters 8–9.
4. Edmund St J. D. J. Monson (1883–1969). Second Secretary at the Paris Embassy since April 1914.

Sunday, 6th October

Victoria and B. Pembroke[1] arrived. Both very flourishing but they had had a shocking bad crossing and Victoria had succumbed. They said they were treated royally on the way. The only result is that Lady B. has lost all her luggage and has nothing but what she stands up in.

The news keeps on coming in with regard to the Peace Offer but it is all very confused and as far as I know there is nothing really official.

Joffre's doctor came in to see me to say that Joffre had got the influenza and could not go to England which is an awful nuisance. He wants it postponed for a week but I do not know if that will be possible.

At luncheon P.M., Henry Wilson, Sackville-West, Duncannon, Admiral Hope, Hankey, four from the House and the Serbian Minister.

Great amount of telegraphing going on and everything rather at six's and sevens but nothing for me to record.

Had seen Pichon in the morning. He had given me a satisfactory answer about the exchange of Letminoff only to send me a telephone message when I got back making certain reservations which when I got them I found did exactly the opposite to what he has said. It is going to be rather an awkward business. The French have behaved very badly about it but I am not quite certain that our own Foreign Office have not let us down.

Went out and played 9 holes at St. Cloud. Self and Madame Hennessy against Guiche and Victoria. All square.

Came back to find the whole Party back at tea. I think they have made considerable progress but it is most inconvenient their living out at Versailles as you cannot get hold of them and it is not safe to telephone. Bonar Law had arrived having flown over. Very plucky as the weather was very bad.

Evening. Capels, Polignacs and Bullock dined.

Notes to 6 October

1. Lady Beatrice Pembroke, wife of 15th Earl of Pembroke, whom she married in 1904.

Monday, 7th October

A Russian Deputation came to see me to say that they regretted the Bolshevik's action. I should think a thoroughly unrepresentative Committee but I received their address and have forwarded it on to the Government at home.

Luncheon only Henry Wilson, Sackville-West, Bullock and Charlie

Winn came.

I gather the interview with Foch in the morning was entirely satisfactory and things were going well but at the present moment there is nothing from President Wilson and really it is almost a scandal that at a time like this everything should have to wait for the decision of an autocrat 3,000 miles away who does not really understand what the position in Europe is and won't delegate his authority to anybody. The more I see of his actions the more I feel that when the history of the War comes to be written his will be a part that will be very difficult to justify.

Johnny Du Cane came in after luncheon. We had a talk. The Prime Minister had been very rude to him on the subject of man power. Personally I think Johnny Du Cane has got all the facts on his side but one must make some allowance for a man who is as worried and as hard worked as the Prime Minister, and at the big Conference later he seems to have been most amenable.

Tea time Henry Wilson and Bob Cecil came back from the Conference which had gone extremely well and everything apparently quite harmonious, or at all events the settlement was.

Henry Wilson came with Charlie, Lady B, Victoria and myself to Dinner at the Becasse. He went back to Versailles and Lady B, not being well having a chill, came home. We three went on to the Michel. More amusing each time I see it.

Tuesday, 8th October

This morning saw Burtchaell who just came in to report himself and we discussed various matters. I see a great attempt is being made to keep Cohn in some capacity but it will never do and I know Henry Wilson means to stop it.

Simon Lovat came in passing through.

Saw Bob Cecil. Nothing of any importance to note.

Hall, *The Times* correspondent with the Americans came to see me. Gave me a most deplorable account of the fearful mess-up the Americans have got into. They are absolutely incapable of fighting unless the Staff work is done for them. The men fought extremely well but they have committed all the faults that our troops committed at the battle of the Somme rushing on and leaving Germans behind them who attack them from the rear etc. but their Staff work as regards supplies is something appalling. They got one road so blocked that not a single wheel was turned on it for 20 hours and many of the men in the front line were 36 hours without food and water. Their horse arrangements are appalling and whenever a horse is hurt at all or ill they do not make any attempt to keep him as they have got no veterinary surgeons and they simply shoot him. Altogether a most deplorable account.

Luncheon. Princesse Marie Murat, Princesse D'Arenberg, M. and Madame Berthelot (deputy Minister for Foreign Affairs)[1] the Prime Minister, Bonar Law, Henry Wilson, Sackville-West and Johnny Du Cane. A very amusing luncheon.

Good news came in of our attack which is apparently succeeding extraordinarily well and the Cavalry are through. It is reported that thousands of prisoners have been taken. It is only a rumour and no real details.[2]

Oliver came down but it tired him very much and he had to go back to bed again afterwards.

Various conferences and talks here afterwards but of course nothing much can be done until Wilson's opinions have been received and I do not think they can get them till this evening.

General Moinier[3] the new Governor General of Paris in Guillaumat's place came to see me. A very different sort of man and nothing like as attractive as the latter who has gone to take over the command of Berthelot's Army, who in turn has been sent to Roumania.[4]

Saw M. Paléologue[5] who used to be the French Minister in Roumania and afterwards in Russia, who got at loggerheads with Clemenceau and was dismissed. He told me one thing that was interesting but I really do not believe it and that is that Ferdinand of Bulgaria is absolutely penniless. He speculated with all the money that he had and he really has got at the present moment nothing but debts and is entirely dependent for any money on his brother-in-law Prince Philip of Coburg.

In the evening House Party, Hall, *Times* correspondent with the American Army whom I have mentioned before, Major Beith (Ian Hay of the First Hundred Thousand). Henry Wilson, Sackville-West and Hankey dined. Nothing particular talked about.

Notes to 8 October

1. Not for the first time Derby was exaggerating Philippe Berthelot's position at the Quai d'Orsay.
2. British forces launched the second battle of Le Cateau on 6 October as part of the general allied advance and achieved rapid success.
3. General Charles-Emile Moinier (1855–1919). Served in Morocco from 1908 until July 1918, when he succeeded Guillaumat as Military Governor of Paris.

4. General Henri Berthelot, who had commanded an army in Champagne, was now sent to Romania as head of the French Military Mission.
5. Maurice Paléologue (1859–1944). Entered Quai d'Orsay, 1880. French ambassador in St Petersburg, 1914–18. Close friend of President Poincaré.

Lord Robert Cecil's conversation with M. Berthelot (October 8th, 1918)

I had a conversation with M. Berthelot today about Briand.[1] He told me that Briand was the son of an orange-seller at St. Nazaire. One of the Masters at his school was in the habit of picking out two or three of the brightest of the boys and talking to them and giving them verbal instruction. This man advised Briand never to read a book as reading destroyed originality. This advice Berthelot assured me Briand had rigidly followed. He never reads anything, but picks up his information by conversation. He has a feminine quickness in acquiring knowledge in this way, and a gift for putting himself en rapport with anyone who happens to be there. In many ways he was an attractive Chief, but there were some disadvantages. He never gave any instructions to his subordinates. He would not even tell them what had passed at Cabinet Councils. Berthelot therefore had to draft his telegrams by guess-work, and whatever he drafted Briand signed as a matter of course. The result was that Berthelot was constantly accused of flouting the decisions of the Cabinet when, in point of fact, he knew nothing about them. Briand never prepares any of his speeches. He assured Berthelot that he didn't even prepare two or three points in them or the opening sentence or anything. When he was a young man he was an extreme Socialist, almost an Anarchist, and he had learnt his speaking in that school, with the result that he regarded speaking in the Senate or Chamber as child's play. His method was to get up into the Tribune, look around his audience, and improvise the speech which he thought would be the most persuasive. I asked whether on that system he didn't make a good many blunders, and Berthelot admitted that he did make blunders, but he uttered them so persuasively that no-one minded. He may be described as an artist in speaking and an artist of genius. His whole interest lies in the game of facing a hostile audience and persuading them to believe him. For office he cares nothing. He leaves it without a regret, though he is still a very poor man. He lives on the sixth storey practically without servants, and dines at a restaurant for twenty-five sous; but his charm of voice and manner are unequalled.

Notes to Cecil's conversation

1. Cf. D. Dutton, '"A Nation of Shopkeepers in Search of a Suitable Frenchman": Britain and Briand, 1915–1930', *Modern and Contemporary France*, 6/4 (1998), pp. 463–78.

Wednesday, 9th October

Went to see Clemenceau about the Independent Air Force. He is very much upset by his son-in-law's death.[1] He had only been married 4 months and died in 48 hours from the Spanish Flue. He promises to give me an answer within 48 hours but practically the whole thing is settled.

I asked him what he thought of President Wilson's answer.[2] He said he approved of it very highly and that it was a very good move. I told him that I thought the last paragraph which practically says that nobody could deal with the present Government is going a little too far. He did not seem to think there was any harm in that.

Luncheon. Bonar Law and Lloyd George had promised to come but chucked at the last moment and not only did that but kept Bob Cecil with them. They really are the rudest lot of people I know and it was more particularly aggravating because I had made a special point of Bonar Law being there as Klotz wanted to see him and therefore I had asked him to luncheon. To make matters worse Bonar Law telephoned to say that he would come directly after luncheon to see Klotz and at the last moment telephoned again to say he was not coming. At luncheon Italian Ambassador and wife, Klotz's, Madame Hennessy, Henry Wilson and Sackville-West.

Had a short talk with Klotz afterwards. He approves generally of the President's answer and he thinks that it may put Germany in as much a hole as the offer of an armistice put us. He says that President Wilson is very vague in his statements and he does not in the least know what "Freedom of the Seas" means or whether evacuation of territory means the evacuation of Alsace and Lorraine.

I think he agreed with Henry Wilson that it is really impertinent of the President answering direct to a note addressed to him as one of several Allies, without ever consulting those Allies or what is even worse communicating his answer to the Press before it had even been communicated to the French and English Governments. We did get it early this morning but the Italian Ambassador had not even seen it. We are going to have a great deal of trouble with Wilson and apparently he thinks he can ride rough-shod over everybody because he has got all these troops in this country. If he only knew what a mess they have made of things, though the men fight splendidly, he might sing another tune.

Bob Cecil had a long talk yesterday with Berthelot at luncheon, who gave him a description of Briand. Bob dictated it and I add a copy to my Diary. Berthelot probably knows him better than any other man.

We had to stay in the whole afternoon as various people were coming in. Saw Lloyd George and Bonar Law, who were very satisfied with their day's work. Lloyd George persuaded Clemenceau that President Wilson's answer was most unsatisfactory. That it may commit us to something which will allow the Bosche to take away all his guns and men and take up a shorter line of defence which he could not possibly do under the present circumstances.

It appears that at the meeting this afternoon Foch said he wanted to preface the meeting by saying how much was due to Sir Douglas Haig and his British troops. He said it was perfectly magnificent and that it might be the decisive battle of the War. It certainly has gone extraordinarily well and there is really nothing in front of Rawlinson's Army. Montgomery,[3] his Chief of the Staff, when asked today what they were doing, said they hoped to be at Le Cateau tonight and then they proposed to march by Mons and Liège to Cologne and I really believe they could do it. I have seen very little of Bonar Law. I wish I had been able to see him, as I wanted to talk over political matters with him. Mark Sykes came in for tea and very amusing on the subject of George Curzon. Reggie Pembroke[4] arrived. Very seedy having had the flue.

Evening. Henry Wilson, Bridgeman and Guy Colebrook[5] dined. Only general conversation. We got very good news from the Front and apparently the Germans are really on the run throwing away arms and equipment etc.

Notes to 9 October

1. Clemenceau's daughter, Thérèse, had married Jules-René Jung.
2. The German government had asked Wilson 'to take steps for the restoration of peace, to notify all belligerents of this request, and to invite them to delegate plenipotentiaries for the purpose of taking up negotiations'. In his reply Wilson asked whether the German government 'accepts the terms laid down by the President in his address to the Congress of the United States on 8 January last and in subsequent addresses and that its object in entering into discussions would be only to agree upon the practical details of their application'. He also called for the evacuation of occupied allied territory.

3. Archibald Montgomery-Massingberd (1871–1947). Chief of Staff to Rawlinson with IV Corps and 4th Army, 1916–18; CIGS, 1931–36.
4. Reginald, 15th Earl of Pembroke (1880–1960). Royal Horse Guards. European War, 1914–18.
5. Guy Colebrooke. Appointed temporary secretary to British Ambassador in Rome, November 1918.

Thursday, 10th October

Bob Cecil, Charlie and Oliver left 8.20 by Special Train for England. Telegram came in from the United States which I think is the greatest cheek I ever heard. They complain of our making a settlement with Bulgaria without consulting them and saying any terms ought to be considered as part and parcel of the whole settlement and apparently this would equally refer to Turkey. Considering what the President has done in answering without consultation the German Note and equally considering that America is not at War with either Bulgaria or Turkey and has not contributed therefore in any way to our success in these countries, it is nothing but the grossest piece of impertinence on the part of the President to dictate to us. The more I see of his action the more convinced I feel he is going to give us an infinity of trouble before we have done with him.

Deputation came to me from the Volny Club, which is an American French Artists' Club at which I spoke the other day, asking me to become an Honorary Member. They are going to admit English people into it which they have not hitherto done. I agreed.

Luncheon. Only Bullock came and in the afternoon nothing but routine work. Very calm after the last few days rush.

Dined with Madame de Sévigné. A most amusing dinner. Sat between her and the Duchesse de la Tremouille. Victoria came and amused herself very much. Others there were Madame Francis de Croisset, Monsieur Huerta, and Comte de Gabriac.

Friday, 11th October

M. Jean Guillemin came to see me. He has been appointed on a special Mission from France to Spain and I had a most interesting talk with him.

First of all who he is. He was the French Minister at Athens and quarrelled with Briand and was removed.[1] He gave me a short account of it. He said that he knew all through that King Constantine was practically an Ally of Germany and that to deal with him instead of Venizelos was futile. That he warned Briand of this but the latter, who was very much in with the Greek Royal Family, refused to believe him and in the end removed him. As he says everything he told his Government then has since been justified.

He gave me a curious confirmation of what Berthelot had told Bob Cecil. Talking of Briand he said he is a most charming man. Very able but never reads anything and only gathers his information from personal conversations and he used this particular phrase. He says "He deals with Foreign politics just as he deals with an audience. He improvises and seems to have a wonderful intuition as to what will please and what will give him a majority", which is almost word for word what Berthelot told Bob.

I then asked him if he was succeeding M. Thierry the French Ambassador to Spain who had just died. He said No he was not and that he did not know who the successor was going to be. It should be M. Martin the head of the Protocol here but at the present moment everything of that kind was being given either to Senators or Deputies and he thought a Senator (I think he said his name was Seves, but I could not quite catch it) had the best chance of being appointed.

M. Guillemin is going nominally to inspect the Consular Agents etc but he let out that really what his Mission is, is to do Propaganda Work and especially with regard to Trade after the War. He says that the trade between France and Spain could be enormously developed and he is going to try and lay the foundations for such development.

He told me that he has reports that the German agents are very busy in Spain at the present moment and one point of attack is with regard to the Banks which are now to a great extent English and French. That Germans are saying to the Spaniards "Why don't you have your own Banks and do your own work" and are attempting to set up Spanish Banks but really with German money. He thinks this could easily be checked at the present moment, but if it gains headway it may mean the gradual exclusion of French and English Bankers. One of his objects is to endeavour to strengthen the position of French Banks in Spain.

We then got on to general politics and he began talking about Wilson's answer. He is very angry about it and I think his view really reflects the view of the man in the Street although a different view is given in the newspapers. He says Wilson is suffering from a swollen head. That he thinks he is "God inspired" and that he has not only got to dictate terms of peace to Germany but also to his Allies as well. He dislikes Wilson's answer as he says that if the Germans accept it we might be put in a very difficult position. He told me that he had been asked to dine and speak at an American Club two nights ago and he had then asked those present to go through the 14 articles of Wilson's speech[2] and say exactly what they thought each article meant. He said there was complete disagreement on every single point and he mentioned two in particular "Freedom of the Seas"[3] and "Poland".[4] Freedom of the Seas nobody understood in the least what it meant but the majority thought the maintenance of the present state of affairs. Poland — nobody had the least idea of what Territory should be included in Poland. He therefore sees the greatest possible difficulties ahead of us if the Germans do accept the 14 conditions because he says if individuals can differ so much on what these points really mean it is certain Nations will differ even more acutely and the Germans may succeed in doing what they have always wanted to do, drive wedges in between the Allies. He talks English perfectly and struck me as a most intelligent and interesting man.

Motored with Victoria and Lady B to Breau, Johnny Du Cane's Headquarters. Had luncheon with him, Charlie Grant and Staff.

Johnny Du Cane very bitter at the way Lloyd George had insulted him and especially as he was entirely in the right.

Had a talk to him afterwards. He says that the talk of this armistice is having a bad effect on the French and Belgian Armies and although they are still fighting all right certainly we are bearing the brunt of the attack. I think the real explanation of the people in this country being inclined if possible to accept an armistice, even on terms which we should hardly think acceptable, is that they are genuinely frightened by the burning of all these big towns which they see no chance of being able to rebuild, at all events for many years, and if therefore they can get an armistice which would mean the retirement of the Germans without this wanton destruction I think they would be very much inclined to accept it.

I then went on to see Foch and had an half hour's talk with him. Found him as usual in tearing spirits. I congratulated him on his success but he said on the contrary why he had made the appointment with me was that he might congratulate me on the splendid work of the English Army. He said the last 15 days battle by our troops was probably one of the finest things that had ever been done in military history. He showed me his map and it is apparent that the Germans are going back everywhere and he thinks they are evacuating the coastline also as quickly as they can. I asked him if he had any idea as to where the next stand would be and he said that he did not think they would go back any further than they were pushed, in other words that unless we could keep at them they would remain in their present situation.

We then started talking about general topics and he was enthusiastic about Haig. He said that he did not think that the Government, and by that I think he means Lloyd George, quite realises what a really fine soldier he is and how much superior to any of our other Generals and he said to me that he was always frightened because if anything happened to Haig he did not know whom we could get to replace him. I said I hoped nothing like that would occur because I had always been of the same opinion as he was, but of course if anything did happen and you had to look about for a second string to your bow, what about Plumer or Allenby. He made his usual gestureism of contempt with regard to Allenby; and Plumer he said "Well, if you could not get anybody better he would have to do". Rawlinson he has no very high opinion of. He said that he had always had extraordinary luck but he agreed with me when I said that the General who always has luck is generally the man who has done well and who has deserved that luck. He likes Horne[5] and he likes Byng. I think his feeling with regard to Rawlinson is probably somewhat tainted by Debeney who is fighting next to Rawly and who does not get on with him. I think personally that Debeney is a most detestable character.

He then began talking about other theatres of War and he told me that he is a little anxious about our particular branch of the Salonika expedition. I said by that did he mean to say that it was wrong tactics, but he said "No, certainly not" but he said it would have to be very carefully thought out as it would never do to have a check out there now. I could see there was something at the back of his mind and I asked him therefore what reason he had to think that it would not be well thought out, and after some hesitation I found that it was that he has nothing like the confidence in Henry Wilson in thinking out these details as he had in Robertson and that it makes him anxious. We then drifted into a discussion on the subject of Robertson and Maurice being forgiven. He said the latter had committed a "bêtise" but that in none of our countries had we such a number of good Generals that we could afford to dispense with them and that he looked upon Maurice as being one of the very best Staff Officers that we had. With regard to Robertson he said there is no doubt he was a far sounder man than Wilson and he had the utmost confidence in him. He said of course his great mistake was that he did not realise that in War the opinion of the Country behind the soldiers had to be taken into account and that you must give some thought to what the Government of the Country, who represented the people, wished, even if you did not always entirely agree with it. It was in this respect that Robertson had failed. He however held the highest possible opinion of him.

Conversation drifted on to the subject of the armistice and President Wilson's possible action. He is afraid of Wilson. He said if Wilson only knew the truth about the American Army he would not think of having an armistice at the present moment. That if he did, when History came to be related, he would find it would clearly prove that the American Army as a fighting force did not really exist. It was nothing more or less than a rabble as there was absolutely no Staff of any sort or kind, and that although the men fought well they were very badly trained and nobody could fight well under such an organisation. I asked him whether with his great powers it would not be possible for him to get Pershing superseded if he was no good. He said "Yes" and he would take such action if the Americans had got anybody to put in his place but that the only man who could replace him (I believe he said his name was Marsh)[6] was in the United States and his information was that if anything he was a slightly less good soldier than Pershing. That really there was nobody in the American Force capable of commanding it.

He does not think the Germans will accept Wilson's terms and that there will be further correspondence during which time he hopes to get them still more demoralised than they are at the present moment. Anyhow he says it would never do to make a Peace or even an Armistice until we have got them really thoroughly and finally beaten. He said if we did it now we should only have what he called a "bon marché" Peace.

He was most interesting all through and I think I have put down roughly everything that we talked about.

It appears that they offered Pétain's Chief of the Staff — I cannot remember his name now, but they say he is a first class man — to Pershing to be his Chief Staff Officer but Pershing declined and said he could not have any acceptance from the French of an officer above the rank of Major. Foch did not tell me that, it was Johnny Du Cane.

When I got back I went to see Clemenceau to ask him whether he would give me the terms of the letter of remonstrance that he sent to Jusserand[7] with regard to the American Minister in Bulgaria, and his interference in the Bulgarian armistice. He looked at me and said "Do you know if a man came to me and said 'Do £6 and £5 make £11' I should say to him, I won't tell you until you tell me what you want to know for, because I should be thinking he was going to borrow the money from me". He said therefore "Tell me what you want it for". I told him right out "To give to my Government. The Prime Minister is in entire accord with you in this matter and if it is necessary to make any further remonstrance it would be as well that we should know exactly in what terms you made the original protest." He told me he was just off to see the President and then going to the Front for two days, but if I would come and see him on Tuesday he would let me have it. He told me he was very much annoyed at the President having protested against the terms of any possible armistice having been submitted to Versailles and thought that it was very unnecessary and impertinent on his part.

Evening. Went to see Dress Rehearsal of "Zig-Zag" with Lady B, Victoria, Bullock and the Bates. It was most amusing and I was very glad to see my old friend Mr. Allen there. I also saw De Courville who is producing the piece and who is Shirley Kellog's husband. He told me that she was very grateful to Alice for her kindness to her and was very anxious to see her again. I told him that Alice was not here but Victoria is going to ask her to tea.

Notes to 11 October

1. See D. Dutton, *The Politics of Diplomacy* (London, 1998), pp. 107–08.
2. In a speech to Congress on 8 January 1918, Wilson had set out his Fourteen Points as the basis of a future peace. As Clemenceau famously commented: 'the good Lord Himself required only ten points'.
3. In the second of his Fourteen Points Wilson proclaimed the 'freedom of the seas', a concept which, whatever its precise meaning, was bound to have serious implications for Britain as the world's leading maritime power.
4. The thirteenth of Wilson's Fourteen Points called for the creation of an independent Poland. Poland had disappeared from the map of Europe following the third partition of 1795.
5. General Henry Horne (1861–1929), Baron Horne, 1919. Commander First Army in France; GOC in Chief, Eastern Command, 1919–23.
6. Major-General Peyton C. March (1864–1955). Appointed US Chief of Staff and thus the top-ranking American soldier in March 1918.
7. Jules Jusserand (1855–1932). French Ambassador in Washington, 1902–24.

Saturday, 12th October

Tardieu came to see me this morning and we have had a long talk and I must say I like him more and more each time I see him. Of course he is playing all out for France. At the same time I think he is quite loyal to us. He is off to America on Tuesday.

We discussed the Americans very thoroughly. He thinks that Wilson's answer is good but he agrees with me that it would be a calamity if it was taken as a precedent that Wilson was to answer any enemy proposals without consultation with his Allies.

I told him that I thought Wilson was mixing up too much terms for an armistice and terms of Peace. He said he thought not although there was some appearance of that and he told me that he did not think Wilson meant by evacuation of invaded territory that the Germans should evacuate it on whatever terms they pleased. He told me that in a telegram to Jusserand the latter had been instructed to impress this upon President Wilson and to point out that to allow the Germans to evacuate, without such military conditions as might be imposed by the Allied Military Authorities, would be to play into Germany's hands. Just the one thing she wanted was to get her troops and stores back, perhaps even to the Rhine and then resist on the Western Front while still pursuing her plans of amalgamation on the Eastern Front.

We discussed the personalities in America. He told me that he had no very high opinion of Jusserand and he could describe him best as a second Spring-Rice with less intelligence but more sympathetic to the Americans. He himself is only out there for a short time and as he says must confine his attentions entirely to questions of supply and not to politics. He however told me that he felt whenever Reading was over there, from a political point of view, not only England but the whole Allied cause was quite safe. He has a tremendously high opinion of him. He tells me he does not think however they will make any change in Jusserand. It seems to me therefore that from the Allied political standpoint Reading will be supreme.

He, like me, and everybody else I have talked to, is extremely disturbed at the chaos in the American Army and what affects him even more is Pershing's attitude towards it. He told me what I did not know that British and French instructors in America were being withdrawn. It is evident this was done entirely at Pershing's instigation and he told me that he had had a private letter from him in which this extraordinary phrase occurred. "It is necessary to make this change because both British and French instructors, having seen nothing for the last 4 years but defensive warfare are quite incapable of instructing our troops when it comes to an offensive." He was up with Pershing the other day and gave me an example of what the congestion is. It was 6 days after Montfaucon had been taken and he wanted to go up and see it and he asked a Staff Officer if he might do so. Under ordinary circumstances on a French or British Front he could have gone up there and seen what he wanted to see and have been back in 4 hours, but the Staff Officer, whom he asked to arrange it, told him that such was the congestion on the roads that he must allow at least 24. I asked him whether it would not be possible to make a change. He told me that it was a thing that it was perfectly impossible for any civilian to propose and that the initiative, if a change was to be made, must come from Foch. That if Foch said that a change ought to be made it would be made at once. I asked him if he knew of any man who could succeed Pershing if a change were made and he said No, and he said once you got past the rank of Captain there is not a single man in the American Army who stands out as fit for higher command and the only thing to do is either to allow Pershing to remain and insist on his having a French or British Staff, or else for Foch to leave Pershing with a few Divisions and do what we had always wanted, put American Divisions with British and French. He told me that the feeling in the American Army amongst all the junior ranks is very strong against Pershing and indeed against all the various Staffs and of course that will soon filter back to America.

He has a great belief in the American President. He says he is very clear-headed and is perfectly determined to see the thing through and he considers that this telegram objecting to our having made the armistice with Bulgaria and having considered possible terms of an armistice with Turkey is entirely due to Wilson's fear that we may be thinking of concluding a Peace which he would not think a lasting one.

He tells me that he thinks Wilson has got very clear ideas as to all these terms of Peace. That he has been thinking over them most carefully and that he has very definite views as to what constitutes "Freedom of the Seas", the Status of Poland etc. etc. I asked him what he meant by Poland, and he said it certainly included the 4 Prussian provinces and that he was convinced that the President also meant that. The President was quite determined not to break Germany but to completely break Prussia as being the evil genius of Germany.[1]

I asked him whether he thought it was possible for the President either to come over or to send somebody to represent him. He said he did not think he could come over but he might send House, but even House would have a limited sphere of action. House was much more intent on what he called the American political situation and how far terms of Peace would be acceptable to America, than to a broad view which would accept European opinion. He says it is no use thinking that the President will devolve any of his powers on a subordinate and he instanced Baker. He said Baker was over here and is trusted by the President, but as regards the question of Inter-Allied Policy, all he did was to see Clemenceau for 5 minutes, Tardieu for 10 and Foch for 15, and the rest of the time he was over here he entirely confined his attention to visiting American troops and camps.

Sherif Pasha came to see me. He is a very voluble and long-winded gentleman as a rule but luckily I had received a telephone message to say Pichon could see me at one so I was able to cut our conversation short. He had no information to impart and said he had only come just to make my acquaintance. He tells me that the Sultan of Turkey is very Anglophile but is in an extremely difficult position. Although he may have changed his Prime Minister and put Tewfik[2] in, the latter is an old and weak man and Enver and Talart[3] will still be pulling the strings. I asked him whether he did not think the Sultan had sufficient power to arrest these two and to really form an anglophile Government. He said he thought not. The Germans had still got such a hold that if he made such an attempt he would probably be assassinated. As he said if you live surrounded by brigands it is very difficult to be an honest man. He thought Turkey would certainly have to appeal for an armistice but he is afraid it would not come just yet.

I went to see Pichon. Found him very elated with the latest communiqués which showed considerable advance both by English and French. I gathered that the French had been able to make their advance with very little fighting. I showed him a message I had got from the F.O. asking whether the French Government would agree to the proposed terms of armistice with Turkey being communicated to the President of the United States if asked for by him. He told me it was quite impossible for him to give an answer without consulting Clemenceau who was away for two days or more at the Front. He promised to get on to him by telephone and give me the answer by this afternoon.

On return here met Captain Arthur Lynch, M.P.[4] on the doorstep. I had not time to talk to him then so asked him to come to luncheon to meet Hughes tomorrow.

I then had a visit from Count Sobansky who simply came to pay his respects. He seems very hopeful with regard to the future of Poland but says for the moment nothing whatever can be done as it is so entirely in the grip of the German, but once they could find substantial assistance being given to them by Allied Troops, he has no doubt that a revolution could perfectly be brought about.

Venizelos and the Greek Minister came to luncheon, also Bridgeman and Leveson Gore [?Gower] who had both been in Greece, the former at Athens and the latter at Salonika and who knew him. He does not strike one, when you first meet him as being a very big man and his French is about as bad as mine. Luncheon was therefore rather a frost. After I had a talk with him and then he was very interesting. Personally I think it is a great mistake Lloyd George having sent for him but it is so like L.G. He says it is most important to have so and so here and he at once sends a telegram for him to come. This wretched man has travelled straight through from Salonika and goes on to London tonight. He was nearly dead when he got here. What he will be when he gets to London I do not know. I told Clemenceau he was coming through and then he told me that Lloyd George had telegraphed for him and he added "a very stupid thing to do because he will come full of many requests which L.G. will have to refuse and it is so much easier to refuse a thing to a man many hundreds of miles off than it is when he comes to see you". I feel that many requests will be made because he began telling me of some of the numerous things that are required. I do not think the Greek troops got on quite well with the French, at all events Venizelos seemed very anxious that they should be brigaded with ours.

Victoria, Lady B and I went to the performance at the Alhambra by the New Zealand Divisional Troupe "The Kiwis". Really extraordinarily good and amusing. I had only meant to stay for an hour but ended by staying for two. It was very full and I hope they have made a considerable amount of money as it was in aid of the British Army & Navy League Club.

Dined at the Harvard Club of Paris. A big meeting about 320 people there including the American Ambassador. I had a short talk with him before the Dinner actually began. He is evidently very much disturbed at the way Wilson's answer has been received in England and asked me whether I thought the feeling was bitter against Wilson. I told him No but it was a case of "You have done this once but you had better not do it again and you must consult with your Allies". He told me that he thought there was no fear but that he would. We had heard rumours that the Germans had accepted Wilson's proposals but it had not been actually confirmed. I said to him I hoped there was no doubt but that Wilson understood that the terms of the Armistice could not be supplied by him or even by the politicians. It was a soldier's job, though naturally subject to the assent of the various Governments. He told me he thought there was no question but that this was so and Wilson would not attempt to interfere with the conditions which Foch might lay down. I told him I wish I felt as certain as he did on that point.

The Dinner was a great success. I had to speak. It went off all right, but a reference I made to the fact that I hoped in America they would recognise and do justice to the effort England had made in the War was received in a most extraordinary fashion. They all got up and cheered again and again which was very satisfactory.

Victoria, Lady B, Reggie and Bullock dined here and went to the Play.

Notes to 12 October

1. An interesting illustration of the contemporary idea that the problem of Germany lay in 'Prussian militarism'. In a speech at the Guildhall as early as November 1914 Prime Minister Asquith had demanded the destruction of Prussian militarism as an essential British war aim.
2. Ahmed Tewfik Pasha (1843–1936). Prime Minister of Turkey, November 1918–March 1919.
3. Mehmed Talart Pasha (1872–1921). Prime Minister of Turkey, February 1917–October 1918.
4. Captain Arthur Lynch (1861–1934). Irish Nationalist MP for Clare West, 1910–18.

Sunday, 13th October

PARIS

The German answer is in the papers.[1] My first impression is that they have scored and in two ways. First of all they are assuming that a mixed Commission shall sit to determine the conditions under which evacuation is to take place. If such a Commission sits it is bound to take a considerable time arriving at a settlement and the Germans will fight every proposal the soldiers put forward and meanwhile they will be able to complete their retirement unmolested and withdraw all their guns etc. The second is that they assume, as I think they have almost a right to do, that all the Allied Nations are in thorough agreement with Wilson's 19 [sic] proposals and it seems to me that over this there is going to be endless difficulty as we cannot possibly consent to any definition of the "Freedom of the Seas" except our own definition and it will be very difficult also to agree to any conditions with regard to the retention of the German Colonies we have conquered.[2]

I ought to mention that last night I sat next to a very nice Frenchman who had been an officer, who had been badly wounded and who for a year had been a lecturer at the Harvard University. He anticipates one great danger and that is that Germany will retire having smashed up all the manufacturing towns. That it will take France several years to rebuild her factories and get to work again and meanwhile the Germans would be capturing the trade. He put forward an extraordinary proposal which I told him I did not think was a feasible one, namely that the French should take over certain manufacturing towns in Germany, turn the Germans out and putting in refugees, using their machinery and of course making what profit there was out of manufactures by this means until such time as France has been reconstructed. I think he voiced to a very large extent the frightened feeling there is in France with regard to her industries which have been destroyed. The possibility of the Germans being able to start work at once and so capture the markets before the French can really get going again.

Ian Malcolm came to see me for a minute. He looks very seedy indeed. I asked him to press upon A.J.B. the necessity of keeping me more fully informed than I am of the Government's wishes and ideas. I want to have the telegrams that pass between Wilson and the Supreme War Council or the Government sent to me and I also want letters written to me to tell me what line they want me to take on any particular point. At the present moment I get no instructions whatsoever of that kind.

Maclagan afterwards came in to see me. He is going back to take Arnold Bennett's place in the Ministry of Information.[3] He knows all our requirements very well and therefore should be able to assist us very much indeed. I must say he did his level best here but he was not the man for the post. He had not got personality enough but I think in his new post he ought to do extremely well.

Luncheon. Victoria had a bit of a chill so did not come down. Hughes, Sir Newton Moore,[4] new M.P. for St. George's, Hanover Square. Mr. Deane his Secretary, Lytton and Colonel Arthur Lynch M.P.

Hughes as usual very outspoken and thoroughly indiscreet. He objects most strongly to Wilson's action and thinks that Germany made a clever move in assuming the Allies' agreement with his articles, whereas as a matter of fact we probably should agree about none. He says that as far as Australia is concerned he would consent to no handing over of the conquered Colonies to any Nation. We also discussed politics at home. He says that although he is a Labour man he is frightened at the extraordinary leap in the dark we have made by this enlarged franchise. It must in the long run mean a Labour Government though it will not come at the present moment as there is nobody big enough to lead them, but such a man will undoubtedly come. It is no use with the Labour Party trying to obstruct them. You must try to guide them. He instanced the fact by his young days when he was with cattle. In a stampede to get in front of them meant certain death whereas you could gradually edge them off into any particular direction. He and Lynch discussed the Irish question and there was intense bitterness on the part of both of them to the Roman Catholics, perhaps even more bitter on the part of Lynch than on the part of Hughes. Lynch said that given a free hand he believed he could settle the question and he would do it by cutting off supplies from the Pope. He says that unless we do crush for ever the Papal power it will always be a source of mischief in the world. He mentioned that he had spoken to a very prominent Roman Catholic who had had an interview with the Pope and he came away perfectly horrified with the latter's Bosch sentiments.[5]

He talked about recruiting in Ireland and said that he did not believe that we should get the men and he regretted that this Note should have come just as it did because it will prevent Conscription in Ireland and he said the fact that Peace may be made without Ireland having contributed her share to the War will undoubtedly militate against Home Rule.

Hughes agreed with him and said he had been a Home Ruler all his life but he could not say that he would support it for the future. The mere fact of Ireland having kept out of this struggle prevented her being considered as a Nation.

After Luncheon he asked me to have a private talk with him. He then told me, though I knew, that he was going to have déjeuner with Pichon tomorrow and he supposed that he would have to make a speech. I told him that I thought it was likely though I know nothing definite. He then said that he wanted to make a speech and he told me what he would say. After hearing him I begged him to say absolutely nothing that could be construed as being an attack on the President and his Note or on Americans generally, but that one line he intended to take would I thought be very acceptable here and that was that in the reconstruction schemes something should be done, probably by withholding of raw material, which would prevent Germany with her factories untouched taking advantage in the markets of the world, of France who had so much of her manufacturing districts destroyed, and I added I thought he might also put in a good word for England by saying that Germany's mercantile fleet should be confiscated to make good the losses that our mercantile fleet had suffered.

If he would only adopt a moderate line I do not think any harm would be done. He told me however that it did not matter what settlement was arrived at, in Australia they did not intend to sell any of their raw material to Germany. I begged him not to say that at this moment as that would appear to run entirely contrary to one of Wilson's conditions. He said that he had no intention whatever of saying it at the present moment but that he meant to do it and neither Wilson nor anybody else would prevent him doing so.

He is going to see Clemenceau tomorrow morning and I am going to try and arrange to see the latter beforehand so as to warn him what the position is. I think that, if warned, Clemenceau will give him good advice which he will take, as I impressed upon Hughes, not only that Clemenceau was practically the Government in himself, but what I think appealed to him more, that if he said anything contrary to Clemenceau's advice it would not be allowed to go into the Press.

Dinner. Madame de Polignac, General Barnes who commands the 57th (2nd West Lancashire) Division, and his A.D.C. Percy Thellusson.

Notes to 13 October

1. The German reply, as the British had feared, interpreted Wilson's message as meaning that evacuation of occupied territories was the sole prerequisite of an armistice.
2. In his fifth point the President had advocated 'a free, open-minded and absolutely impartial adjustment of all colonial claims' — an indication that Britain, the British Dominions and France could not necessarily expect to hold on to those German colonies which they had captured during the War.
3. After serving as Controller for France at the Ministry of Information in 1918, Maclagan was attached to the Press Section of the British Peace Delegation the following year.
4. Sir Newton Moore (1870–1936). Premier, Western Australia, 1906–11. Conservative MP for St George's, Hanover Square, 1918, and for Islington North, 1918–23.
5. While protesting against inhuman methods of warfare, Benedict XV maintained strict neutrality, leading both sides to accuse him of favouring the other.

Monday, 14th October

Went to see Clemenceau to ask him to warn Hughes to be careful what he said at Pichon's luncheon. He told me that he did not mean to see Hughes. He saw no reason for doing so and therefore declined.

We then discussed the question of the German answer to President Wilson. He was anxious to know what the Government at home thought about it. I had luckily received copies of telegrams that had been sent to Washington and taking them as my text told him what the Government's views were and found him in entire accord. I wired this to Balfour and also asked that I might be allowed to give him a paraphrase of the telegrams. I think doing so would most certainly prevent any misunderstanding.

Clemenceau told me everything was going very well indeed and he evidently himself thinks that the Germans, although they will not at the present moment accept our terms, will undoubtedly do so in the long run. He had been for 48 hours at the front. Yesterday he was with Haig all day and went into Cambrai. He tells me the whole of the Centre of the town is burnt out and in every single pillar of the big Church there had been a hole bored for a mine, but luckily they had not exploded, but the intention was evident.

Afterwards saw Howard and Collis and settled details of body for new Car.

Luncheon. Ourselves. The American Ambassador and his wife. Zaharoff, General Barnes and Thellusson.

Had a few minutes conversation with the American Ambassador before luncheon. He is very much disturbed at the tone of the French papers and says that for the first time since he has been Ambassador he sees a disposition to criticise the President and some of the articles, especially that of the *Temps* of last night, he much resents. I told him I thought he was thin-skinned about it. If he had had to go through what I had to a few months ago he would have recognised that the criticism was of the mildest character. On the other hand I do not think it is at all a bad thing that both he and the President should recognise that there is a certain amount of criticism at their action.

After luncheon talked with Zaharoff who is just off to England. He tells me that after having luncheon with me the other day he went home to find a telegram from Venizelos telling him to go out to Salonika at once and he started with 10 million francs and that had just done the trick with the Bulgarians. He again repeated to me a conversation he had told me about the other day of his meeting with Enver in Switzerland. He said it is all working up to a conclusion and there is no doubt whatever in his mind that whatever happens to Germany, Austria and Turkey will make separate Peaces with us. That Enver from having been very pro-German is now bitterly anti-German and considers he has been absolutely sold by them. That they gave him a definite promise to send men to help in Palestine and 50,000 men had actually got as far as Constantinople, when 40,000 were ordered back. The other 10,000 went on and most of them have been captured. Venizelos had told him that he did not mind how many Austrian Divisions were sent against him as the first thing they did was either to run away or to surrender.

He looks upon the whole thing as over as far as the East is concerned. I asked him about Boris[1] the new King of Bulgaria and he gave a very lurid description of him. Said he is very pro-German but he really will have no power of any sort or kind now. He anticipates no trouble from him. He has promised to come and see me on his return from London. He thinks that we ought to begin to tell Italy that we are not going to give her all that we had promised for two reasons. One, that Russia having been a party to the agreement[2] and having fallen out, the whole Treaty comes to the ground, and also as she has not played her part and struggled for herself she cannot expect to get all she would have done if she had made a genuine effort.

Visited the ASC Workshops at St. Denis. Colonel Hawkins in charge — very interesting. It is a gigantic business employing over 1,000 men. The motors come in a fearful state and they practically turn out 20 lorries as good as new each week. He told me a curious incident of his appointing a Sergeant to act as storekeeper to an officer in one branch and then discovered that the latter had been the former's fag at Eton. It rather amused me also when one officer said he wanted to ask me a private question. I saw him and the question was whether I could give him a good double for the Cesarewitch and Cambridgeshire.

When I got back, heard from Spiers who tells me that there is a rumour in London that Prince Max[3] had resigned the Chancellorship. If it is true I cannot conceive what it means unless it is that the Military Party have again got the upper hand.

Evening. Dined with Madame Hennessy. Very pleasant evening. Pembrokes, Victoria, self, Madame de Polignac, the Capels, M. Regnier, Paléologue, who was French Ambassador at Sofia, and Duc de Guiche.

Notes to 14 October

1. Boris III (b.1894). Became King of Bulgaria upon the abdication of his father, 3 October 1918.
2. The Treaty of London, April 1915. Under this Italy was to receive Trentino, Trieste, Istria and large areas of Dalmatia.
3. Prince Maximilian of Baden (1867–1929). The last Chancellor of Imperial Germany, he took office on 3 October 1918 and negotiated the armistice before resigning in favour of Friedrich Ebert, the leader of the Social Democrats.

Tuesday, 15th October

10.30 Started with Lady B and Victoria. Motored through Senlis and Compiègne, to Montdidier and back through Beauvais. Took our luncheon with us. Very amusing expedition. Got back about 5.

Dinner. Philip Sassoon came. He was rather amusing about Clemenceau's entry into Cambrai. Guards of Honour, Bands, etc. He told us one very interesting thing. They found there a man in the 11th Hussars who had been there since the first days of the War. He had been kept with a French family and lived in a cellar the whole time. I think everybody is very annoyed at Lloyd George's telegram to Haig in which he said he had been informed by Marshal Foch of English victories. I explained to him that even if it was badly worded I knew that it was meant well because the Premier and Henry Wilson were here at the time.

Wednesday, 16th October

Collard[1] came to see me. He told me several very disturbing things about the Liverpool Hospital and I am afraid that Raw had behaved very badly and has got a reputation for not being any too brave. It appears the Hospital at Etaples was closed, not by authority of the Military Authorities but on his own responsibility as he says he could not stand the bombing any longer. Altogether I fear there is considerable trouble there which will have to be gone into.

Sir Alfred Butt[2] came to see me with reference to Joffre's visit to London. We decided on the whole it would be better to abandon the whole proposal. It would have been extremely difficult to have got up enthusiasm again, in addition to which the change of Lord Mayor makes it difficult.

Usual military Mission meeting and luncheon afterwards.

McFadden the representative of the American War Trade Board came to see me. Mr. Cahil[3] the new Commercial Attaché here was present and we discussed the whole question of Swiss and Spanish purchases. He seemed to me very moderate in his demands and very clear in his conception of the form in which purchases from these two countries should be made. He is going to give Mr. Cahil further information and to go with him through a despatch which I am sending home in order that we may be quite clear as to what his proposals are. Of course there is no doubt whatever that we have made advantageous agreements for ourselves before America came in and now that America has come in and we have got to share with her, we may not get quite all that we asked for, but I am sure that anything that can be done to save tonnage is worth doing.

Dinner. Duff Cooper[4] dined. I never saw such a change in a boy in my life. He is in the Grenadiers and has done extraordinarily well and after being out only three months got the D.S.O. Johnny Baird[5] suddenly turned up before Dinner having come from Trenchard. He came in to Dinner. He stayed behind with me when the others went to the Play and we had a long talk chiefly about things political at home. He tells me that negotiations are going on between our Party and L.G. and that there has been an inter-change of papers as to future policy. Sir George Younger[6] put up ours and Lloyd George had made an answer which was to be considered by our Shadow Cabinet the day he came away. He tells me he sees in Lloyd George's paper nothing that we could not agree to. It is practically the same as our proposals only rather more detailed. He foresees a great deal of trouble with a certain wing of our Party, Salisbury, Bob Cecil, Banbury,[7] Selborne,[8] Halsbury[9] & Co, but he thinks the bulk would accept such arrangement. He had talked to Bonar Law, whose Private Secretary he had been, on the subject and asked the latter whether he realised that that put him permanently in a second place. He said "Yes" he had accepted that when he came into the Coalition Government and therefore he did not mind continuing in the same position. Bonar Law told him that he thought if we could get hold of Lloyd George he would know that he would only remain in power by being supported by the bulk of our Party and the best Labour people. Otherwise he would probably go in with the extreme socialists and be very dangerous.

We then discussed the question of a General Election. He told me he had been very much opposed to an immediate Election but he was gradually coming round to it. I told him I had been exactly the same but I thought the events of the last week had considerably altered the position and if we could come to an arrangement with Lloyd George satisfactory to our Party, when an armistice was signed I think an immediate Election would probably be the best thing that could happen. Lloyd George and the Party would be able to go to the country and say "We are the people who brought you a victorious armistice" — because that is what it would be —"now we want authority from you to settle the terms of Peace so as to prevent the fruits of your victory being robbed from you by the pacifist element". We discussed whether it would not be very inconvenient having an election actually while the armistice was on. I told him I did not think so because the instant it comes to a question of settling the terms of the armistice everything passes out of the hands of the politicians into the hands of the soldiers.

I understand the Circus is coming out here almost immediately so I probably shall hear further details.

Notes to 16 October

1. Major Alfred Collard (1865–1941). Liverpool shipowner. Commander, Stretcher Bearers, British Red Cross.
2. Sir Alfred Butt (1878–1962). Bloodstock breeder. Director of Rationing, Ministry of Food, 1917–18. MP for Balham and Tooting, 1922–36.
3. (Joseph) Robert Cahil (1879–1953). Acting Commercial Attaché, British Embassy, Paris, 1918–19.
4. Alfred Duff Cooper (1890–1954). Grenadier Guards. Cabinet minister, 1935–38 and 1940–43; British ambassador in Paris, 1944–47. For his meeting with Derby see J. Charmley, *Duff Cooper* (London, 1986), p. 27.
5. John Lawrence Baird (1874–1941). Viscount Stonehaven, 1925. Unionist MP, 1910–25; Parliamentary Under-Secretary for the RAF, 1918.
6. Sir George Younger (1851–1929). Viscount Younger, 1923. Conservative MP for Ayr Burghs, 1906–22. Chairman of Conservative Party Organisation, 1916–23.
7. Frederick G. Banbury (1850–1936). Baron Banbury, 1924. Conservative MP, 1892–1924.
8. William Waldegrave Palmer, 2nd Earl of Selborne (1859–1942). President of the Board of Agriculture, May 1915–July 1916.
9. H. S. Giffard, Earl of Halsbury (1823–1921). Lord Chancellor, 1885–86, 1886–92 and 1895–1905.

Thursday, 17th October

Miss Fells, daughter of old Mr. Fells of Ulverston, a great political opponent of my father's, came to see me. She and a friend have been in America lecturing and appealing for Funds for "The Fatherless Children of France" and she had had very great success having collected nearly 20 million francs. She is now going back to America and feels that she would be able to do — quite unostentatiously — a certain amount of English Propaganda work and she wishes to be put in touch with the people who are in charge of such work in America. I have written to Lord Beaverbrook on the matter as I think she might be of great use.

Luncheon as usual grew from a quite small one to be one of 12. Benes, who is the Czecho Slovak representative. Bingham[1] and his wife, David

Henderson, Thwaites the new D.M.I. and his Chief Staff Officer Cornwall, General Bridges, Leveson-Gower, with the House Party.

Had a talk to Benes afterwards. A most interesting man and the recognised head of the Czecho-Slovaks. He tells me that the Germans are doing everything they possibly can to detach the Czecho-Slovaks, not only from the Entente but also from Austria and are trying exactly the same game as they did in Poland. He says they will have no success of any sort or kind. That the Czecho-Slovaks in Prague and elsewhere are taking all their orders from here. That he is quite convinced that they are getting these orders because he sees what he writes to them to do done within a fortnight after the despatch of the letters. He has just returned from Italy where he is very pleased at the success of his Mission.

He had a long talk with Bridges who is on his way to be Chief of our Mission with Franchet D'Espérey and they are to meet again this afternoon.

Before luncheon I had a long talk with Bridges who is very keen about his new job. He is taking Alastair Leveson-Gower as his A.D.C. He knows Franchet D'Espérey well and does not like him. He thinks that at first his berth will be an unpleasant one and uphill work.

After luncheon Thwaites, Henderson and I discussed the conditions under which the various Missions, including Spiers', are to work. Very satisfactory. Thwaites was very strongly of opinion that Spiers must be definitely under Henderson. He evidently is not so much impressed with Spiers' work. He says it is pure routine except for his private letters which he writes to everybody in the War Office and which he thinks ought to be stopped. He sees much more clearly than his predecessor how dangerous it is for the members of the Military Mission to engage in political work. He is going to see Henry Wilson when he gets home and I hope the whole thing will be settled within the next 10 days.

In afternoon received the news that Lille had been taken. Arranged with Bridgeman, on Grahame's suggestion, to do a bit of Propaganda by having a big Laurel Wreath put up in my name on the Statue to Lille in the Place de la Concorde.

Heaton-Ellis came to see me. We discussed the question of an Admiralissimo in the Mediterranean which personally I think is of the greatest importance but which he tells me has now been dropped.

In the evening Duff Cooper dined and the four of them played Bridge. I personally have resolutely refused to play cards out here. I played once at mild baccarat. It bored me so intensely that I am not going to do it again.

Notes to 17 October

1. Charles Clive Bingham, Viscount Mersey (1872–1956). General Staff Officer, commanding military mission to French War Office, 1916–19.

Friday, 18th October

Bridgeman reported he had put up the wreath and it had been a great success.

Curiously enough I have received a letter from Lloyd George asking me to see Clemenceau and press the question of an Admiralissimo.

Went off at once to see Clemenceau but only caught him in the Hall just as he was going to see Foch and Pétain. He did not receive the proposal very amiably but naturally he could not discuss it at that moment and as he won't be back till Monday night I shall not get an answer till Tuesday. These visits of his to the Front, though doubtless very useful in the way of strengthening the morale of the French Troops, are very inconvenient when one has to discuss business with him.

Luncheon. Madame de Polignac, Mrs. Capel, the Spanish Ambassador, Baron Berkheim, who is a delightful little man employed in the Ministry of Foreign Affairs and Colonel Georges, who has often been here before and who is in Clemenceau's Military Cabinet, and Charlie Grant. Nothing of particular interest in the conversation except that Berkheim told me in the strictest confidence he knew the Vatican had strongly advised its adherents in the Austrian and German Parliaments to accept Wilson's conditions.

Charlie Grant stayed on afterwards. He was very insistent that the Supreme War Council should meet as soon as possible as otherwise if the Germans did accept the armistice it would find us totally unprepared as to the exact conditions. Personally I am not quite sure that he is right as I think that at the last meeting these terms were more or less discussed and arranged. Anyhow it will be the soldiers who will have to dictate them. At the same time the P.M. will probably have something to say on the terms and it is much better to say them before they assume a cut and dried aspect than after they have been agreed to between Clemenceau and Foch.

There is no doubt the feeling between the Americans and the French is very intense and the other day some American Patrol Posts shot some French Lorry Drivers who did not stop when they were told. Pershing has had to hang one or two of them over it. Still the bitter feeling remains. He says there is absolutely no discipline, especially amongst the semi-civilians who are employed behind the lines. The Americans are employing Managing Directors of different American railways and no one Director will take orders from another. Consequently there is hideous confusion. They are gradually getting sorted out but there is no doubt that the Americans have had very large and very unnecessary losses. They refuse to accept any assistance from either British or French Staff Officers. On the other hand the two Divisions fighting with us willingly accept help and the result is their losses have not been very great, except in one case through going on when they were told not to — and everything has worked perfectly smoothly.

Everybody extremely pleased that the King of the Belgians has had such a success though I hear he is very much impressed about his losses especially as naturally it is impossible for him to make them good.

Lille has been surrounded but not actually taken. There are no Germans in it but I understand there is not going to be any sort of entry of troops for a time, which is probably correct, although as Clemenceau is going up there himself they may have some sort of Military show for him.

Pichon came to thank me on behalf of the Government for the laurel wreath which I had had placed on the Lille Statue in the Place de la Concorde. We walked together in the garden and I asked him what he thought would be the German answer. He told me he thought they would undoubtedly accept practically any terms we liked to impose and then he told me that he and the Government here were very much disturbed by certain information that they had got from Germany as to that Country being on the eve of a revolution. He says that they are as full of Bolshevism as Russia itself was before the Revolution, and it may break out at any time. They have got a Provisional Committee which he says is practically a Provisional Government actually established with its Headquarters in the Russian Embassy at Berlin. In fact he says the position is exactly the same there as it was before Kerensky brought off the Russian Revolution. What frightens him is the fact, as he says, that Bolshevism is very contagious and he is evidently considerably alarmed as to what may happen in this country. I told him that I thought there was the essential difference between the two countries that whereas Germany was under a very autocratic Government and the reason of a revolution was complete defeat, on the other hand France was under a Democratic Government with victory to its credit. He agreed but still said that he was gravely anxious. I asked him if there were any signs of trouble here and he told me "none" but whether he was concealing anything from me or not I cannot tell. My impression is that he was not.

De Courville and his wife (Miss Shirley Kellog) came to tea. He is one of the most amusing men I think I have ever listened to describing the difficulties of producing his Revue here. We had been extremely amused at the actual Dress Rehearsal with the Scotchman who was carrying the big banner, and was evidently quite unaccustomed to it. It turns out that he was a Frenchman enlisted for the occasion who hated having to wear a kilt. There are two pipers too and about them he was extremely amusing. He says they do nothing but fight with each other. They speak an absolutely unintelligible language to each other and his whole time is taken up in reconciling them. Each says that the other cannot really play the pipes. He told us other incidents connected with the production which are extremely amusing. Mainguy and Bullock came to tea.

Dined with Madame de Sancis. A large dinner party given for little Willie de Grünne. Four of us, Bullock, Duchesse D'Uzes, Comte and Comtesse de Cartissac, Princesse Souzlou, a Roumanian, another woman whose name I did not make out, Berenson the Art Critic and Count Zamoyski the uncrowned King of Poland, and the American Military Attaché.

The evening would have been quite amusing if it had not been that the rooms were in a fearful state of heat. I sat next to Duchesse D'Uzes whom I had long wanted to know. She is a most determined woman, has been mixed up in every sort of political intrigue but her one topic is her hatred of democracy which she gives vent to on every possible occasion and which has therefore not endeared her to the French Officials. She is of course an out-and-out Royalist and Legitimist[1] and asserted to me that if only they had anybody who was fit to put on the throne they could put him there tomorrow. A very great stretch of imagination. She of course like others is an admirer of Clemenceau but is very much afraid of his Chef de Cabinet, Mandel, whose real name she told me is Rothschild but as he wanted to get on in political life he changed it as people told him with such a name as Rothschild he could never succeed unless he had their wealth which he has not.[2]

Mrs Capel at luncheon had asked me whether we could put up Joan Poynder. She was going to take her in but the whole of her household is down with flue. She came in just after we got home in the evening. It seems an extraordinary thing to let a girl like that off entirely on her own to drive a motor for the French. She was supposed to be only here for one night but from what she says no arrangements have been made for her and her 5 friends to go to the French and I should think she would be here for some days. Seems a very nice sort of girl.

Notes to 18 October

1. Supporter of the claim to the French throne of the senior branch of the Bourbon family represented by the Comte de Chambord (d.1883), grandson of Charles X.
2. Mandel's original name was Louis Rothschild. When he began writing articles for left-wing journals he decided that Rothschild gave an unfortunate impression of affluence and chose to adopt his mother's maiden name. He changed his first name to Georges in order to avoid being confused with his uncle.

Saturday, 19th October

Sir Albert Scallon[1] and three officers with him of which one was Dick Norton, came to see me. They are here in connection with the Cadet Parade tomorrow. Nothing I can do for them and as they go away I cannot give them Dinner or anything.

Afterwards Arthur Balfour[2] who served with me on a Railway Commission and who is the head of a big steel works in Sheffield, came to see me. He is very much disturbed about the future of Sheffield trade in this country and also in America after the War. Of course I did not discuss with him the American situation but here he tells me that the French were encouraged at the beginning of the War, and by ourselves, to increase in every way their output of high-speed steel with the result that the Sheffield people had to teach them their methods. The French have now learnt them and can really turn out the steel, not quite as good as the Sheffield Steel, but still very nearly. The result is that now Sheffield wants to begin to export loom steel, etc. the French say they won't give them import licences because they say they can make them themselves, in addition to which Tungsten is now so largely produced that whereas we had ⅔ of the world's production dealt with in England, the reverse is now the case. Altogether he looks on things as very serious. He is going to see the various officials here and hopes to be able to get some concessions. From what I know of the French it will be extremely difficult to do and I am perfectly certain that if they take that line the only way of obtaining redress is to shut off their supply of coal. Coal is really the only weapon England has got left to enforce other countries to take our goods.

Luncheon. Joffre and his wife. She is quite a nice woman and talks English. Princesse Philippe de Chimay, he [Prince Philippe] is a Belgian attached to the Flying Corps in Belgium. Not a bad sort of fellow but he was away and could not come. Comte and Comtesse Etienne de Beaumont, both very nice. He is very delicate but doing good work with the Red Cross. In the seventh heaven at our advance in the north because he gets all his money from the mines near Lens. He hopes that they will be in full working order again in about 2 or 3 years. Personally I think they will probably get to work before that if they will only use what is called the Freeze and Block system instead of Pumping. Lieut. Kermaingant, a very nice little fellow. Most amusing. Talks English well. I met him at Deauville. He is a great Orleanist[3] and is frequently over in England shooting. Commandant Jonart rather a dull dog, who is Joffre's A.D.C. and Comte de Salis. General conversation after luncheon but B talked to Joffre whom she said was extremely nice and generous about the present successes. He does not much like Haig and we all know he did not like French, although they keep up a semblance of friendship. He said far and away our cleverest soldier was Robertson. He used not to think so and so I suppose it is both of them having been displaced makes him have a sympathetic feeling.

In the evening Sir Horace Rumbold,[4] our Minister at Berne came to see me. I have read with intense amusement for the last two years the telegrams he has sent from Berne. The most extravagant rumours have been detailed at length in his various communications and if they were put together now they would show even greater flights of imagination than H. G. Wells'[5] books. All interest in the telegrams has gone since I have seen him as I recognise now that it was not a spirit of imagination that prompted him to send them. It was sheer stupidity. I never came across a more stupid man in my life, both in appearance and in conversation. The only thing of interest he told me, and I should think it was untrue, was that he knows that this question of an armistice is being forced on by the Military Party in Germany as Bolshevism is getting so rife amongst the troops that they feel the only way to stop it is by making Peace and disbanding the Army. That whilst men are together they can organise Revolution which they would not be able to do if they were separated all over the country.

In the evening we had a thoroughly English Party and went to Zig Zag. Our own House Party, 5, Victor Paget,[6] B's brother who turned up in the afternoon on leave. Bullock, Mainguy and Alastair Leveson Gower who is leaving today as A.D.C. to Tom Bridges and the new head of the Mission with Franchet D'Espérey.

Notes to 19 October

1. Probably Sir Robert Scallon (1857–1939). Staff-Lieutenant, Headquarters, War Office, 1918–20.
2. Arthur Balfour (b.1873). Master Cutler of Sheffield; head of steel works.
3. Supporter of the claim to the French monarchy of the descendants of Louis Philippe.
4. Sir Horace Rumbold (1869–1941). British minister at Berne, 1916–19. Though Derby writes of Rumbold's stupidity, the latter is best remembered for his prescient comments on the early Nazi regime. He was ambassador in Berlin, 1928–33.
5. Herbert George Wells (1866–1946). Novelist.
6. Lord Victor Paget (1889–1952). Heir presumptive to the Marquess of Anglesey; European War, 1914–18.

Sunday, 20th October

Pouring wet day. Went to luncheon at Versailles. The Capels, Lady Johnstone (Alan Johnstone's[1] wife) and her son who is now Sackville West's A.D.C. Studd,[2] Ross and Green. Came away early so as to go to what had been intended to be a Review of the 1920 Class but it had degenerated through influenza into a very scratch show of Boy Scouts, etc with a few representatives of the 1920 Class. The President got a very poor reception but Clemenceau, who had come back specially for it, an extraordinary good one.

Found myself standing next to him so asked him what he thought of the American President's answer. We could not discuss it as there were so many people there but he told me he was very much annoyed about it and he said to me "We have got to take some means to stop these American ways of doing business". He told me I was to telephone him on Tuesday morning and he would then see me.

Later on Frazier from the American Embassy came to see me. Very nice of him as it was simply to tell me how much praise he had heard given by French people to the placing of the wreath on the Lille Statue. We then got gradually into general discussion and he warned me against Berthelot of the Foreign Office who he says is bitterly anti-English. He says the safeguard with him is that Clemenceau hates him so. I thanked him for his warning and said I was very careful with Berthelot as I had been warned against him, but I felt he was the man who was the hidden hand behind Pichon and therefore it was necessary to be on good terms with him. He agreed with me that he certainly was the moving spirit in the Foreign Office at the present moment thanks to Margerie's continued illness.

He is pleased with the American President's answer to Austria as he thinks it is extremely clever in saying that things have changed so much since the latter's 14 proposals were put forward. I asked him what he thought the President meant by it because I could not really understand. He says that it means that the President is not satisfied with an idea of a Federated Austria and that he is determined to break Austria up by making Czecho-Slovaks and Yugo-Slavs into separate Nations. He says that the President at one time was strongly in favour of detaching Austria but he had found it no good and therefore was determined to break Austria-Hungary up. We then got on to the subject of the President's two notes to the German Government and I said what seemed to me illogical in the Notes was that he has always said that each Country must have the Government which it thinks best and yet when he comes to Germany he declines to treat apparently with the recognised Government of that Country. I said what did he want and he said of course what the President is really perhaps thinking of is that it would be best to treat with Germany after it had become a Republic.

Frazier then spoke about Gompers who he said left for home yesterday. I told him I was disappointed in not having seen him again because he had told me he would call before he went. Frazier said that the reason why he left so hurriedly was that he got news that his daughter, to whom he was devoted, had died suddenly. He told me that Gompers had been to see him and had said that he was perfectly certain that he had done good and had put some backbone into [Arthur] Henderson in our country, into Albert Thomas in this and into the Italians. He does not think the Italian industrial situation is as bad as it has been made out. He is quite certain that the present moment would be a very inopportune moment to make Peace with Germany. That they are not sufficiently beaten and a Peace now would only mean a recrudescence of the War and he said that is what he is going to preach as soon as he gets back to America.

Dinner. People in the House. Johnny Du Cane and his wife, Spiers and his wife, and Mainguy.

Notes to 20 October

1. Sir Alan Johnstone (1858–1932). British Minister at The Hague, 1910–17.
2. Colonel Herbert W. Studd (1870–1947). Chief Officer, British Section, Supreme War Council, 1917–19.

Monday, 21st October

Charlie arrived from London. Tells me that there is some new arrangement with regard to the boats crossing, by which the Channel Boat is kept two hours in the outer harbour before coming alongside. I cannot conceive any reason for that and of course it is going to make it very difficult for people coming over here as apparently if he had not been specially met he would have missed the train. Some Admiralty Order. I am bound to say from what I see of the Admiralty they never consult anybody's convenience.

Attended funeral service of Captain Loxley, the Adjutant of the Flying Corps here who died suddenly two days ago.

Luncheon. General Haller, Count Maurice Zamoyski, Captain Leveson-Gower, M. Dumesnil, Lt-Colonel Peal[1] and General Moinier.

Moinier is the new Governor of Paris, in Guillaumat's place. Rather a dry old stick. Nothing like as interesting as the latter. Dumesnil very nice — Minister for Aviation. Haller is the Commander in Chief of the Polish Armies throughout the world. A most interesting man whose one idea is Poland. At the beginning of the War he looked upon the Czar as being the chief enemy of Poland. He therefore fought with the Austrians against the Russians. When the Revolution took place he transferred himself with his Polish legions to the Russian side and fought the Germans. He fought them, I think it was 10 days, with overwhelming forces against him and then began to talk of an armistice. During the armistice which he delayed as long as he could he managed gradually to disperse the whole of his army and the consequence was that when the Germans took over they found nobody there. A good object lesson of what we might expect if we are not careful about our armistice on the Western Front. The men disappeared in all directions and gradually formed forces in Siberia, in [blank] and some even down in the Ukraine, and he escaped himself with the greatest possible difficulty. After luncheon he was most interesting telling us about the tremendous national sentiment there is for Poland and how men are pouring in from America, Canada and indeed everywhere in the world to fight for Poland, although many of them have been settled in their new homes for 15 to 20 years. He is most optimistic as to the future. At the same time he sees the great danger of Bolshevism. They are getting quite satisfactory reports from Poland and they have no doubt if once he could get there — and he hopes to do so via Roumania — he would soon have an army of many hundred thousands. He said that Austria had the chance of her life in trying to make terms with the Poles but she has insulted them in every conceivable way and now there can be no reconciliation whatever between the Polish Nation and the Austrians. He says that even in the Polish provinces of Germany Polish sentiment is still as strong as ever. That Germany had a census made a few years ago of children whose parents still considered themselves Poles instead of Germans and he said when you see this census you see what the limits of Poland are and to use his own words "the children of Poland have given us our boundary lines".

Spiers sent me a copy of a very interesting letter he got from his Commanding Officer with regard to the man Fowler, whom our troops found in Cambrai after being there 4 years. Charlie says it has appeared in the papers in London but for interest's sake I attach it to my Diary.

Raikes[2] senior King's Messenger came to see me, as he said to pay his respects. He reminded me that he came to see me some time ago and then I remembered him as in my opinion he was blind to the world on that occasion. He sent for me when I was in the middle of Dinner to say he had something important to tell me and that was that he was a bosom friend of dear old Charlie, but when I asked Charlie about him he had never even heard of him.

The Italian Ambassadress always has her "Day" on Monday and I have always promised to go and have never been so I went today with Victoria and B. A most formal and frightening performance but luckily Mme Castéja came in so I had one friend, also a man whose name I can't remember who married the Speaker's sister.

Hearn the Consul General came to see me in the evening very much disturbed by a letter which tells him that after the War his services will no longer be required. It seems rather hard on him as he has been doing very good work. He succeeded a man whom I am told behaved very badly in 1914 and certainly during the trying times of May and June nobody could have given me more assistance and been thoroughly calm and practical than Hearn was. I am writing therefore to Eric Drummond to see whether there cannot be a reconsideration of the decision.

Victor Paget dined. They all played Bridge. Got a rumour in that Germany had capitulated unconditionally but no confirmation till later when found it was very far from an unconditional surrender.[3]

Received a letter from Clemenceau on the subject of the Admiralissimo in the Mediterranean. A very lengthy well argued document with a nasty tone running through it ending by a blank refusal. I foresee considerable trouble over this.

Notes to 21 October

1. Lieutenant-Colonel Edward Peel (1884–1967). European War, 1914–19.
2. Francis Edward Raikes (1870–1922). King's Foreign Service Messenger.
3. According to Maurice Hankey, the German reply to President Wilson's note 'again side-tracked the discussion of terms of [an] armistice' (Roskill, *Hankey*, vol. I, p.619).

Communicated by the O.C. 11th Hussars

Private Fowler formed one of a Party of the 11th Hussars which was cut off after the battle of Le Cateau on August 26th 1914.

He lived behind the German lines for over 4 years, and was found by British troops on their arrival on October 9th 1918.

Extract from my Diary of October 12th:—

"Motored over to Bertry to see the people who had looked after Fowler. On August 26th '14 he was cut off with a party of "A" squadron near Busigny Station. On Jan 15th 1915 he was discovered, ill and dying of starvation, in the Bois de Catigny.

The man who found him, named Louis Basquin, brought him back by night to the village and asked his mother-in-law, Madame Belment-Gobert, to look after him. She at once agreed.

The house they lived in was very small, consisting of two rooms and a loft. The latter, for the greater part of the time, was occupied by 15 Germans.

For two months Fowler was concealed in a cupboard, where he could just sit hunched up. He could only get out during the short periods between one party marching out and the next coming in. He then exercised himself by skipping and jumping in the loft. For days together he lay under a mattress, the centre part of which had been hollowed out. At other times he stood in a small, deep hole under the stairs, with a basket of potatoes over his head. During the night the Germans used to come down and steal the potatoes.

All this time his protectors stuck to him. They were practically starving, but never failed to share with him such food as they had.

A Corporal of the Regiment, whose name we do not yet know was discovered. He was taken out, made to dig his own grave and shot. The woman who looked after him had her hair cut off and was sent to Germany. She has never been heard of since. Her three small children were literally left to starve, but were looked after by the people of the village.

This life continued for four years. With no wish for or prospect of reward, with the prospect of instant death, or at the best deportation and imprisonment if they were discovered these devoted people never relaxed their care for the soldier they had promised to protect.

When I saw Louis Basquin today he was lying in bed dying of consumption. I tried to thank him. His answer showed a flash of the pure and beautiful patriotism of the French people. 'Monsieur, you have nothing to thank me for. I was too ill to fight for my Country and I wished to do my duty. I could do no less.'"

Tuesday, 22nd October

Mr. Balfour, Mr. McGregor, Mr. Everett and Mr. Cahil the new acting Commercial Attaché came at 12.30 to tell me how they had got on with regard to their representations in respect of import trade. They seemed very satisfied that they had made an impression and indeed they have already had concessions. Afterwards had luncheon with me. Very interesting, all of them being able men, thoroughly knowing their work and able to explain very clearly what they want. A very different body of men to one I saw after luncheon, which consisted of Lord Blyth,[1] Sir Dennis Bayley,[2] with the Duc de Clermont-Tonnerre to act as their interpreter. They represent two very different Societies. One the Royal Agricultural Society's Relief of Allies Committee and the other the British Ambulance Committee. We did not have any talk about the latter. I think that is going on all right. With regard to the Relief Committee I must congratulate the Royal on having discovered one who is to my mind the stupidest man in England to represent them. You can get nothing into his head and he talks the most awful rot and thinks that with the money at his disposal, which is only a few thousand pounds, he is going to restore the whole of the agricultural population of Northern France. He also thinks that he can go anywhere and do exactly what he likes. The other two I must say did understand when one told them how impossible it was for them to get about and how difficult it was to do what they wanted, except perhaps to concentrate their attention on some small area and to begin as far back as possible and gradually work up to the fighting area. It does seem a pity to me that when a big Society like the Royal is to be represented out here they should choose such a man to represent them who can only give a very bad impression.

Went to tea with Madame Hennessy. Several people there including

Paléologue. Madame Hennessy herself has never been very pro-American but everybody one has ever met there has been and therefore it is extremely amusing and interesting to watch the change of tone of what I may call Society and semi-Political people as regards the Americans. They are getting very bitter against them and resent bitterly the way Wilson is taking charge. They all seem to think that the Germans will be much too clever for Wilson and will get round him and I am much amused to find myself championing Wilson against them.

In the evening 16 to Dinner. People in the House together with Madame de Neuflizes, Sackville-West, Studd, Capels, Bates, Bullock and Major Rogan.[3]

Afterwards the Coldstream Band played and about 50 or 60 people turned up belonging to the various Missions whom I had asked to come in if they wished to do so.

I did not get a chance of talking to anybody for any length of time. I only know what happened at two conversations. First of all Boni de Castellane, who came with one of the Mission people, had a long talk with Lady B. He was extremely bitter against Clemenceau and abused him roundly saying that he was nothing but a clown. His bitterness is apparently due principally to the fact that he thinks Clemenceau wishes to crush Austria even more than he wishes to crush Germany. That he does this simply and solely because of his hatred of the Catholic Party. He has no faith in Clemenceau's powers and says if the world is to be saved it must be saved by England though he did not specify in what manner this was to be done. He told Lady B that he was certain that Clemenceau was not acting straightly by us and was in private communication with Wilson though he did not know what the subject of the letters were. I had heard something of this before and that the subject of their private discussion is "what is meant by the Freedom of the Seas". I have been able to get no definite information on this point but I feel pretty certain that some negotiations have been going on.

The other conversation was one that David Henderson had with Baron Gunsberg.[4] The latter is a prominent Jew here who was a great friend of Bertie's. Gunsberg told Henderson he knew the terms that Foch was going to ask for an armistice. Personally I think that they are inaccurate. The conditions are:

1. German troops to clear out of France, Belgium and Alsace and Lorraine within 15 days. Any material they are unable to remove in that time to be confiscated by the Allies.

2. Metz and Strasbourg to be garrisoned by Allied troops.
3. Bridgeheads to be created and held by Allied troops across the Rhine.

Notes to 22 October

1. James Blyth, Baron Blyth (1841–1925). Farmer.
2. Sir Dennis Readett-Bayley (1878–1940). Coal owner and iron-master; founder of the Dennis Bayley Fund for the transportation of the wounded.
3. Major John Mackenzie-Rogan (1855–1932). Bandmaster, Coldstream Guards.
4. Baron Jacques de Gunzburg. A banker of Russian origin. Esher once wrote of the 'notorious intimacy' between Bertie and de Gunzburg and of the suspicion which de Gunzburg's 'paramount' influence over the ambassador raised among Frenchmen (P. Fraser, *Lord Esher: A Political Biography* [London, 1973], p. 347).

Wednesday, 23rd October

Victor Fisher[1] came to see me. I must say I think it would surprise the French people to see one of our leading Socialists with a top hat. He is one of the smartest dressed men I have seen for a long time. He was very interesting about affairs at home. We discussed Bolshevism. He told me he did not think it was making any real headway in England, but that the Labour Leaders generally were so weak and so ready to be driven in any direction that one never knew what might happen. He said that his information was there would be a General Election the first week in December and that the pacifists would be swept out except in Glasgow and in the West Riding of Yorkshire, where he said things were rotten. He confirms the view I had gathered of Gompers' opinion of our Labour Leaders, namely that they were no good and put politics above the real interests of Labour. He has gone to Italy and is coming to see me on his return. He also discussed the President of the United States. He was very upset at the way in which the latter is taking charge and said he had no knowledge whatever of European politics and he described him as a sort of American John Morley,[2] but living even more apart from the world than the latter did.

Luncheon. Captain Graham[3] and Lady Evelyn Graham. He is a son of Lady Askwith[4] by her first marriage. He is now Adjutant of the 2nd Life Guards and he brought me down a letter from Algy. She is a very nice little thing and he is having his 6 days leave in Paris. Tweedmouth also came. Pembrokes had luncheon out. Prince Albert[5] was expected having telephoned to say he was flying over. As a matter of fact he did not turn up till 6 o'c staying here for the night.

In the afternoon a Reception in honour of England at the Inter-Allié Club. The place was crowded and the President came to it. Deschanel[6] spoke and Jean Richepin delivered a very fine poem written for the occasion and I had to acknowledge. Spoke in English and I think got through all right though nothing very wonderful. However everybody seemed pleased and it is nice to think that England's efforts are at last being recognised in this Country but these constant speeches are rather a trial.

Prince Albert and Major Greig[7] arrived at 6 o'c.

Only Thornton dined.

Notes to 23 October

1. Victor Fisher (1870–1954). Resigned from Labour Party in 1914 because of its pacifist policy. Founder and Hon. Secretary of the British Workers' League, 1915–18.
2. John Morley, 1st Viscount Morley (1838–1923). Resigned from government over Britain's entry into the War in 1914. Biographer of Gladstone.
3. Captain Henry Graham (1892–1970). Grenadier Guards.
4. Lady Ellen Askwith, widow of Major Henry Graham; married Baron Askwith, 1908.
5. Prince Albert (1895–1952). Second son of George V, he reigned as George VI, 1936–52.
6. Paul Deschanel (1855–1922). President of the French Chamber. Elected President of the Republic in 1920, he was obliged to resign because of mental illness after only nine months.
7. Major Louis Greig (1880–1953). Equerry to Prince Albert.

Thursday, 24th October

Mr. Macalister came on the part of the Wagon Company of Canada. I had heard that he had been going about saying that I was not doing my best to help him, so I spoke to him very sharply. He assured me there was not a word of truth in it and in the presence of Mr. Cahil he told me he recognised that I had done everything that was possible to be done for the Company. I had taken care to have a witness in the room.

Mr Horodyski came to see me. For an account of my interview with him refer to copy of letter I have sent to Arthur Balfour attached.

After luncheon we all motored up to the Racing Club where Thornton, Victoria, Greig and Prince Albert played lawn tennis.[1] Charlie, B and I walked back.

At 4.30 went to see Clemenceau. Found him in tearing good spirits and best of humour with me but in great excitement over President Wilson's answer which I had not seen.[2] He was very bitter against Wilson whom he will describe as an idiot. He told me that he had sent for Foch to talk over terms of armistice but that he meant to make them very severe. We never even touched on the question of the Turks and he asked me to come back at 6.30 when he would have finished with Foch. I went back and found Foch and Pétain still there. Foch most complimentary about our troops. Said they were perfectly wonderful what they were doing and the day before they had captured over 8,000 prisoners and 200 guns. In his usual jerky fashion he emphasised how grateful he was for what the English troops had done.

I then went in to see Clemenceau and he told me that what he had arranged was that at the earliest possible moment, and he hoped the next day, Foch, Pétain, Pershing and Haig would meet to draw up the terms of the armistice. I asked him if there were any general principles and he said "Yes, two very obvious ones". First that [there should be] every possible safeguard and guarantee for our troops during the armistice, and second that Germany should be in a no better position than she is now if she decided to go on with the War. That was a little eye-wash because he then went on to tell me what he really meant. He said that he was determined that if we had an armistice it should be quite impossible for Germany to begin fighting again and I understood, though he would not be very definite about it, that roughly the terms are: Giving up so many men; giving up so many guns; retiring to the Rhine; we to hold Bridgeheads across the Rhine; also to occupy chief German towns. The Naval question of armistice he did not deal with but looked upon that as a matter to be dictated by us. I told him that my prophecy had been that there would be an armistice by the 1st of January and Peace by the 1st of June and I had made a bet on that. He said he thought that I should win the second part and lose the first as he did not think the armistice would come before the end or the middle of January. He felt perfectly certain Germany would not accept the terms of the armistice at the present moment. I gather what the French official people think is that Germany has no intention of accepting the terms of Armistice whether they be mild or whether they be harsh. That whatever they be the Emperor will go to the German Nation and say, "what is evident is not that the Allies want to make Peace but that they want to crush Germany". He will retire to his own frontier and then call upon all Germany to defend the Fatherland, and they think he will succeed in making this a popular battle cry.

Reading through the President's Note I do not find much fault in it except that part in which he lectures them about the form of Government that they are to have and that I think is not only gross impertinence on his part, but it is an undue assumption of authority. He practically says to them they are to have a Republic. I do not think that is the view of any of his Allies, least of all is it the view of the French. Of course they won't say so publicly but privately they do not hesitate to state that they dread a Republic in Germany as they think it will undoubtedly afford ground for Bolshevik seed and Bolshevism they look upon as very dangerous at the present moment. I have never seen Clemenceau in such form though he admitted to me that he was rather tired. There is one thing that galvanises him into life at any moment and that is the mention of Lloyd George's name. I foresee terrible friction between these two in the coming months.

We dined early and Victoria, Prince Albert, Greig, Charlie and I went to the "Michel" which I had already seen twice but it amused our two guests very much.

Notes to 24 October

1. In 1926 Greig and Prince Albert (by then the Duke of York) competed in the men's doubles at the Wimbledon Championships.
2. Wilson's latest message indicated a readiness to take up the question of an armisitice but only with 'veritable representatives of the German people who have been assured of a genuine constitutional standing as the real rulers of Germany'.

Letter to A. J. Balfour 24 October 1918

Confidential

Horodyski came to see me this morning. He is off to London tonight and therefore will probably see you, perhaps even before you get this letter, but I just note down what he told me for your information and for my own reference.

As you know when I wrote to you before I did not look upon him as a very trustworthy man and I am bound to say that interesting as he was, I still have the same opinion of him.

The account I give is rather disjointed as I am going to put it down just as it occurs to me. He stayed talking with me on every subject for nearly an hour.

In the first place he says that he is perfectly certain that Germany is not in as bad a position as she tries to make out and as we believe. The reason for the armistice proposal is that the people generally have been reading during the last few months of Wilson's declaration with these 14 articles of faith, and that having read them they see very little that they do not agree with. Pressure therefore to accept them has become very great and much against their will the Emperor and the Military Party have had to bow to this pressure. At the same time they feel that they will be able to show when it comes actually to dealing with the Allies, that the conditions are not at all what they appear to be in the 14 articles and that the terms really offered to Germany will be very drastic and severe. They are beginning to prove that through the armistice and they are hoping to get such hard terms proposed for this suspension of hostilities as will enable the Military Party to go both to the Army and the Country and prove that the terms are so degrading to Germany that she must resist them at all costs and have really a "levée en masse". They would probably go right back to their own frontier and then make an appeal to the German Nation to defend its own soil. Meanwhile he says they are gradually getting more and more powerful in the East and that though opinions differ as to the strength of the Bolshevist Army, whether it be 300,000 or 500,000 does not matter and is of small account compared to the fact that thanks to German officers it is becoming a very real and a very powerful army.

He then began to describe the position in the Balkans. He does not believe in Turkey wanting to make a separate Peace or asking for an armistice. In fact he felt certain that Turkey would not do so. This rather amused me knowing what I do. I asked him what his reason for thinking this was. He said that the Turks know they are beaten but they have a sort of Kismet feeling and there seems to be nobody who can take any decision. I told him what General Shea[1] had related to me the other day of the hatred of the Turkish prisoners in Palestine towards the Germans and how they murdered them on the slightest provocation. He said he knew all that but that did not alter his opinion that the Turk was always a man of such weakness of decision and could not make up his mind to take any strong steps with regard to ousting the German from Constantinople. He said that the way the Bulgarian affair would be settled, would not be by any question of Turkey coming out of the War but rather by the re-entry of Roumania into the War. That Mr. Maghlimon[2] was now very much pro-Entente and was only waiting for the opportunity to again fight the German. Horodyski then went on to say that the only way this could be brought about would be by bringing Poles, whom they had in various parts of Russia and in Asia Minor to Roumania, making an army of some 60,000 men and then advancing from Bucharest, Mr. Maghlimon having expressed his willingness to co-operate with the Poles for the release of Poland. He said in order to secure this concentration of Polish troops it was essential that we should get the passage through the Dardanelles and get complete command of the Black Sea. I pointed out to him that in view of his opinion that Turkey would not come out of the War this was easier said than done. What makes me distrust his judgement is that he is quite willing to put forward proposals which when they are really examined are almost incapable of being carried out.

Austria then he discussed. He says there is no doubt whatever that Austria is in a bad way. Not from the point of view of food — he believes the shortage is greatly exaggerated — but there is no doubt that the Austrians are sick of the War. That the Austrian Army only wants one blow to make it fall to pieces and if Italy would only make an effort he is certain it would be successful. He was very bitter against Italy. He says their cowardice is something beyond belief. That they will find every lying excuse they can to avoid making an attack. First they declare that there are scores of German Divisions coming down. When that has been proved to them to be a lie they take some other lie as an excuse and the one that they are adopting at the present moment is that they are dying to fight but that Foch won't let them do so. He told me that he had seen Mr. Marcus Stone, the American Journalist, a day or so ago, and the latter had seen the King of Italy[3] who had himself told him that he meant to get rid of Diaz who was an old woman and put Giordini in his place. I asked him if he saw any signs of the Italians attacking and he said "None".

We gradually drifted from that into a discussion with regard to America and this arose from our discussing the intervention of America in Siberia. He thinks we made a great mistake in always poking at the President and telling him he must go on. This irritated him and coupled with reports from his own people who feared Japanese intervention it has made him very stubborn in the matter. He thinks the President will eventually realise that he has made a mistake but for the present he certainly is unconvinced. He told me that House was arriving via England tomorrow or the next day. I had understood that House was coming direct to Brest but I suppose that has been circulated here so as to make his journey more secret than it might otherwise have been. He apparently has no very high opinion of House and thinks we are making a great mistake in attributing to him the powers of the Almighty as far as his influence on Wilson is concerned. He says that House, though a great personal friend, is afraid of the President and the President knows this, and though House by his advice may prevent the President doing something by showing him that it is wrong, he can never persuade the President to take any action by proving to him it would be right to do so. He says House has got no real position in America and is not a well known man. On the other hand there is an extremely powerful man over there in Hoover.[4] Hoover is a man who he says has got by far the biggest position in America after the President. That he is the best known man. He has got public opinion behind him and the President is afraid of him. Although his task is only one of provisioning the Allies, as a matter of fact he sees the President 2 or 3 times a week and the President discusses with him general policy and is very much influenced by his advice. He considers therefore that when we want to influence the President, Hoover is the man whom we should try and get hold of.

That brought us to the subject of French politicians and Tardieu in particular. He says that Tardieu is a tremendous intriguer. That he is not really friendly to England. In this I am bound to say I disagree with him. Tardieu is out to create a position for himself that will make him one of the big men in France when the War is over and that he is continually pressing the President to do this or that with a view of being able to say that it was his influence that got the President to move. This was especially the case with regard to intervention in Siberia where Tardieu was playing a hand in the game on his own account and in the hopes of his own glorification. He tells me that Tardieu and Berthelot are as thick as thieves and that I do know to be true. That Berthelot is anti-English — that I believe. That he is an intriguer — certainly true. A most ambitious man equally correct. That Tardieu is relying on Berthelot to assist him in his upward rise. That Berthelot is ready to do this as he thinks it will carry him along at the same time and he knows as far as he is concerned his personality is not one which would put him really at the top of the tree although he might be the influence behind the scenes. Curiously enough it confirmed what Frazier had said to me the other day, that Pichon is an old man and very lazy and depends entirely on Berthelot and takes his advice in everything. Berthelot unfortunately has had this great opportunity given to him owing to the illness of Margerie who though nothing like as clever is not an intriguer. During his absence through illness Berthelot has been able to supplant him.[5]

He then told me of a third person working with those two and more especially with Berthelot and that is the French Minister at Berne, M. Du Tasta[6] who is a natural son of Clemenceau. A very able man who has Clemenceau's support and at the same time the friendship of Berthelot notwithstanding the fact that Clemenceau and Berthelot hate each other.

Horodyski says when he talks to Du Tasta after he has been to France he always finds him much more difficult to deal with in regard to the English side of the question than he was before he had paid a visit to Paris and seen Berthelot.

Notes to confidential letter of 24 October

1. Major-General John Shea (1869–1966). European War, 1914–18.
2. Alexandru Marghiloman (1854–1925). Roumanian Prime Minister, March–November 1918.
3. Victor Emmanuel III (1869–1947). King of Italy, 1900–46.
4. Herbert Hoover (1874–1964). Became well known for his organisation of famine relief in Belgium and elsewhere, eventually becoming US food administrator. Thirty-first President of the United States, 1929–33.
5. For Berthelot's influence at the Quai d'Orsay, see R. D. Challener, 'The French Foreign Office: The Era of Philippe Berthelot', in G. A. Craig and F. Gilbert (eds), *The Diplomats 1919–1939* (Princeton, 1953), pp. 49–85.
6. Paul Dutasta. Appointed Secretary-General of the Paris Peace Conference, 1919. Harold Nicolson found him 'a weak, flustered, surprised but not unamiable man' (H. Nicolson, *Peacemaking 1919* [London, 1933], p. 119).

Friday, 25th October

Motored out at 8.20 to Versailles to see Milner, who had arrived over night, before his interview with Clemenceau to put him in touch with everything as far as I knew it.

I forgot to say in my note of yesterday that Clemenceau was very much upset by Milner's interview with the *Evening Standard*[1] and said it had had a very profound effect here. I told him that I thought he ought to read the whole speech before he condemned it. But there is no doubt that Northcliffe's speech, and again today I see Hughes's speech, on this particular interview has done a great deal of harm out here. The result is that Milner is looked upon as somewhat of a défaitist and Clemenceau was evidently fearful yesterday that in dealing with Milner he would be dealing with somebody who wanted to be more conciliatory to the Germans than he Clemenceau has any intention of being.

I ought also to add with regard to yesterday's interview that Clemenceau said he meant to brush aside Wilson's Notes as if they had never occurred and simply treat this question of an armistice "de novo" and as if the Germans had sent in a White Flag to Foch. I think he is right but I am not sure that he won't get into difficulties with Wilson over it.

Milner was very nice. We drove in together and I dropped him at the Ministry of War. Came back to the Embassy just in time to see Prince Albert and Greig go off to Trenchard to whose Staff they are attached.

Reggie Pembroke also left about the same time for England, to be attached to a Japanese Prince who is coming over.

Captain van Baerle who has been doing the Recruiting Tribunal work here came to see me to say good-bye. His work has been well done and he has been extremely tactful over it.

Afterwards Onslow came to see me. He has been appointed North-cliffe's representative here for Propaganda in Enemy Countries and Italy. He tells me that Victor [Stanley] is coming out on his Staff. I cannot conceive why Victor accepted. It simply means his being absolutely side-tracked and will surely be the end of his Naval career.

Admiral Hope came in directly after Onslow had gone and I mentioned the fact of Victor coming out and he said exactly the same thing, that he was making a big mistake. Hope only came to wait for Milner. We discussed the various questions including that of the armistice with Turkey, in which I do not think we have got at all a strong position. It appears to be simply a question of "amour propre" with the Navy.

Before luncheon Milner, Admiral Hope and Johnny Du Cane came to my room. I am sorry to say there has been trouble between Foch and Haig. They had a meeting yesterday and there was a regular flare up.[2] Haig is not a quarrelsome man and I cannot make out who it is who is always encouraging him to fight the French. He had both right and wrong on his side. He protests against the 2nd Army remaining under the Command of the King of the Belgians. There I think he is perfectly right. It was sent there for a particular purpose which is achieved and it ought now to return to Haig's command, just in the same way as Debeney's army will return to Pétain's Command as soon as the particular work they had in hand with Rawlinson is finished. On the other hand Haig refuses to carry out certain orders of Foch with regard to an attack. In that I think he is right because he is perfectly justified, under the terms of the agreement, in appealing to his own Government, but I cannot help thinking his refusal was due more to his wanting to have a quarrel with Foch than to anything else. There is no doubt there is one thing which our people feel very much indeed and rightly feel, and that is that we are doing all the fighting and the French are doing none and until Foch can get his people to fight I do not see why we should be called upon to do the whole of the work. It simply means at the end of the War we shall be left with a vastly reduced army while the French will — at all events for the last couple of months and probably for the future — have suffered very little. They also quarrelled about the terms of the armistice and here I think Foch is right, as Haig wants to make the terms much easier than personally I should make them, and much easier than I think the people at home would accept. These quarrels are a great bore. They get known throughout the army and you get a feeling between the two armies which no amount of propaganda work will be able to eliminate.

Milner was quite pleased with his talk to Clemenceau who he said was most friendly, but he kept Pichon in the room the whole time and therefore had to rather show off before him. Milner is going to see him privately this afternoon and thinks he will make better progress in settling things than he had had up to date.

Luncheon developed into a big one — 15. Our own party Victoria, B, Charlie, Joan Poynder and myself. Pichon and wife; the Belgian Minister and wife; Baron Greeffier; M. and Madame Dupuy and Huerta a member of the Spanish Embassy; Milner and Admiral Hope.

Did not get a chance of talking to many of them. Got a few words with Dupuy who has really been splendid in the *Petit Parisien* and *L'Illustration,* his picture paper, in maintaining the Entente between France and England. There is nothing he has not done in the way of propaganda work and I told him how grateful I was to him.

Apparently my speech at the Club the other day went very well and the curious part is they say I spoke so distinctly that most of the French people who knew a little English understood every word I had said. Madame Pichon told me there was only one sentence which she had not quite understood.

Dined with Spiers to meet Miss Bordon Harriman who is one of the ten thousand people who know President Wilson better than anybody else. She is head of part of the Red Cross here and seems a most masterful sort of woman, though talking to her I could not ascertain that she had any more knowledge of the President than any of the other ten thousand people I have mentioned.

Other people there Princesse Ghicka, Mrs. Hyde, Guiche, Henri du Mun, Dr. Benes and Colonel Georges. Quite a pleasant dinner.

Notes to 25 October

1. In an interview in the *Evening Standard* on 17 October Milner had argued for reasonably 'generous peace terms' for Germany.
2. See R. Blake (ed.), *The Private Papers of Douglas Haig 1914–1919* (London, 1952), pp. 335–36.

Saturday, 26th October

Early this morning telegram from home Government telling me to make certain representations to Clemenceau with regard to the general principles on which armistice was to be framed. I could not see any difference between Clemenceau's principles and President Wilson's. The Government at home seemed to. Clemenceau equally could not see the difference nor could Milner. However I saw Clemenceau. After seeing him I sent what I hope will be a soothing telegram.

Went to see Haig at the Crillon. Found him I thought tired and rather irritable. He for very excellent reasons is not desirous of imposing too strict terms for the armistice. Milner came in and we had a short talk together and I came back to the Embassy.

Milner came in later. We together drafted a telegram with regard to Turkish proposals for an armistice. Milner afterwards put me in possession of all the points on which he had discussion with Clemenceau, Pichon and Haig.

Luncheon, only Amery[1] came.

Dinner. Jonnart, Governor General of Algeria who is also head of the Suez Canal and is the man who was specially deputed to turn Tino[2] off his throne. A most charming man. He told me the first time he met me was at the opening of the big Gladstone Dock at Liverpool. He was a great friend of John Hughes.[3] Haig, Lawrence, Alan Fletcher and Philip Sassoon, the Phipps and Du Cane.

After Dinner Haig said he wanted to have a talk with me so we went away and he told me of his row with Foch which I am sorry to say is very serious. To put the story briefly it is this. When it was decided that the Belgians were to attack, which they were induced to do with the greatest difficulty, they said they would only do so if there were two English Divisions attached to help them and placed under the Command of the King who has as his Chief of the Staff a French General De Goutte. Haig not only met them half way but went further and said that he would put the whole of the 2nd Army commanded by Plumer under the King of the Belgians, but on the distinct understanding that it was only for one particular operation. This operation was over and Haig then asked Foch to hand back the 2nd Army. Foch declined to do so. Haig then declined to allow the 2nd Army, which as he says and I think rightly, has been called upon to do the whole of the work, to operate any further and told Foch if he wished to keep it he must put it in writing. This he has now done and given a direct order to

Haig that the 2nd Army has to remain under the King of the Belgians till he thinks fit to send it back. Haig is going to appeal to our Government which he has the right to do and if our Government do not support him he means to be asked to be relieved of his Command, but what he wanted me to do was as a friend of his and as a friend of Clemenceau's, to see the latter unofficially. Tell him all the circumstances of the case and beg him to try and arrange this matter without making it an affair between the two Governments. I told him I would certainly do this but I felt it would not be right for me to act without informing Milner of what I was going to do. He told me he hoped even if Milner disapproved I would still do it as if not he would have to speak to Clemenceau himself and that would be less easy than my doing so. I said I would do all I could and would see Milner in the morning. There is no doubt Foch is entirely in the wrong but after all these months of loyal work it is most unfortunate that there should be this trouble. I hope I may be able to put it right but I know that the relationships between Clemenceau and Foch are not quite what they were and he may have difficulties with Foch.[4] Curiously enough the latter has got slightly swollen headed lately.

I afterwards had a short talk with Jonnart on the subject of Murray of Elibank's Oil Concessions. He says the Government is behaving atrociously to Pearsons, that Loucheur's speech was infamous and he has told Clemenceau so and he says if necessary he means to say so publicly.

Notes to 26 October

1. Leopold C. M. S. Amery (1873–1955). Political Secretary to the War Cabinet, 1916; secretariat of Supreme War Council, 1918.
2. King Constantine I of Greece.
3. John Hughes (1830–95). Mayor of Liverpool, 1881–82.
4. See J. C. King, *Foch versus Clemenceau: France and German Dismemberment 1918–1919* (Cambridge, Mass., 1960).

Sunday, 27th October

Went out at 8.15 to have breakfast at Versailles and talk to Milner and Henry Wilson. They are all in favour of my seeing Clemenceau and seeing if I can arrange matters. Milner thinks I may be successful. I don't think Henry Wilson does, but they have both told me that the Cabinet has considered the whole of this question and have decided to thoroughly support Haig and I am to use that weapon if I think right with Clemenceau.

I had a short talk with Henry Wilson on the subject of terms of armistice. He is for very stern terms which of course differs from Haig's views. Haig's view is that we ought to get good enough terms to suit us now without going to extreme measures and that our position next year will not be at all good. I must say he takes rather a gloomy view of the position next year. He says the French are not fighting now at all. That we shall be down to something like 40 Divisions. I think he forgets that if Turkey comes in we may have some more. The American Army is absolutely useless, which is only too true, and if the Germans go back to the line even of the Meuse they are able to reduce their front from 220 to 140 miles which will give them 80 Divisions in Reserve. They have got the whole of their 1920 class and they might easily protract the War for a year or even longer. I cannot help thinking that there is a middle course between the two and to ask what Foch & Co. want, namely the absolute surrender of Germany is something that they could not possibly accede to. Henry Wilson's idea is that they should go back to the Rhine, that the Rhine provinces should be occupied by American Troops temporarily during the armistice with the Germans who should deliver all guns and submarines. It may be that Germany is in such a bad state and she may accept. Personally though these terms look to me the same as asking for an unconditional surrender.

12.15 went to see Clemenceau and asked him to let me speak to him as a friend to a friend and about a friend — namely Haig. I told him the whole story. He expressed himself very strongly in favour of Haig. Said he was a most extraordinary loyal man and he thought he had absolute right on his side. I asked him therefore whether he would speak to Foch. He then told me something in the strictest confidence. He said he and Foch unfortunately were not on the best of terms. That Foch had got a very swollen head, that he would not carry out his orders and altogether made himself extremely unpleasant. He (Clemenceau) had told him 4 times he was to order Pershing to send American Divisions up to the English and each time Foch had refused to carry out his order. He said that he used always to go and see Foch every day but that things were so unpleasant now that he never went. He was going to see Foch in the afternoon and he suggested it might be a good thing for me to see Foch. I told him I should be perfectly willing to as long as it was understood that I did so quite unofficially and simply as a friend. He said he would "tâter le terrain" with Foch and let me know and if I would go again at 6.30 he would tell me what the result was. He impressed upon me how reasonable Haig had always been and how right he thought he was in making this demand.

Then went on to luncheon at Versailles. Huge luncheon party. Italian Ambassador and his wife, Mme Castéja, the wife of the younger brother, 3 of ourselves, Milner, Frazier, Amery, Henry Wilson and the Staff.

After luncheon went to play golf. David Henderson and I played Victoria and Guiche. We could only play 14 holes and we were all square then. Quite a good game.

Came back and then went to see Clemenceau. He had talked to Foch who was in a very amiable frame of mind but absolutely immovable. He gave a lot of arguments as to why he should keep the Army under the King of the Belgians and it was evident that Clemenceau had weakened on the subject as he seemed to a little stick up for Foch. He ended by saying that he had done my commission and that Foch would see me at Senlis tomorrow morning at 9 o'c. I told him I must very carefully consider the question before I went as it seemed to me that unless it was a question of friendly arrangement amongst friends it would be wrong for me to mix myself up in it especially if Foch was going to argue that it was for purely military reasons that the 2nd Army was retained under the King of the Belgians.

Went to the Crillon to see Haig and talked the matter over with him and by agreement Henry Wilson came there too. I told them what I thought and that on the whole it would be advisable for me not to go. At first Haig was inclined to think that I could do good by going. At the end both of them came to the conclusion it would be better that I should not go but that Henry Wilson should. I also advised, and they took my advice, that Haig should write a private and conciliatory letter to Foch giving his reasons for making the change. I ought to mention here that Foch told Clemenceau that Haig had never given him any reasons for making the change. That he had simply written him a short letter asking that the 2nd Army should be returned to him and then left for England, and so he had not been able to discuss the question with him, but of course if Haig could give him any reasons he would be only too glad to consider them favourably. Haig said of course he had given him reasons but what Foch seemed to forget was that he had discussed the question personally with him for nearly an hour. I argued however that perhaps Foch was looking for a loophole and that it was best to write a letter. It was agreed therefore Haig would write it tonight and Henry Wilson would take it on tomorrow to Foch. Henry Wilson has got a trump card in his hand as our Government have decided that the Army is to go back whatever Foch may say but naturally it is as well not to put your foot down if you can get what you want by other means.[1]

Victoria, Joan Poynder and myself dined with the Bates. The same delightful picnic Dinner as before. Stayed talking till very late.

Notes to 27 October

1. See Blake, *Haig Papers*, pp. 337–38.

Monday, 28th October

Went to see Pichon to make representations in regard to a very stupid action of the French Admiral in the Mediterranean in sending a Ship to celebrate the victory of Navarino[1] after it had been agreed between the English and French that one should not be sent. While I was there a telegram came in from Austria completely surrendering.[2] It is the death warrant of the Austrian Empire as it practically agrees to the independence of the Czecho-Slovaks and Yugo-Slavs and there is nothing left of Austria. Pichon was almost frightened at the speed at which things are going as he says, so rightly, we are not at all agreed amongst ourselves on the 14 articles of President Wilson and further with a complete break up of Austria there is the grave danger — which the papers have been instructed for the last few days to point out — of the German part of Austria attaching itself to Germany and thereby compensating Germany for the loss of Alsace and Lorraine and making her just as powerful for mischief as she is now. It is a grave danger which for the moment I do not see how we are going to combat as we certainly cannot prevent a whole unit from attaching itself to Germany instead of Austria if it so wishes.[3]

Then went on to see Reading. Had a short talk with him. Rather disturbed at the Conference being put off till Wednesday as he had to catch his Boat on Friday or Saturday. He is coming to stay here, though the House will be very full.

Luncheon. Duchesse de Sermonetta; Colonel Griscom[4] now liaison officer between London and Pershing and formerly Ambassador at Rome; Haig, Davidson, Fletcher and Henry Wilson.

Henry Wilson had been to see Foch who was apparently rather annoyed at my butting in. Clemenceau had not properly explained to him that I did so purely unofficially and only as a friend of Haig's. He thinks however he is more annoyed with Clemenceau than he is with me. Haig went off to see him in the afternoon. I see endless difficulties ahead which are complicated in a minor degree but still a very irritating one, by the fact that Lloyd George will live at Versailles and demands that everybody shall go out to see him instead of living in Paris as he ought to do, where people are within beck and call. There was good reason for going out there when Paris was bombed and shelled but there is absolutely none now.

The Prime Minister and Arthur Balfour arrived at 7 o'c. I went to meet them at the Station. Brought Arthur back. We then had a discussion with Milner and Reading but Arthur and I soon left leaving the other two to discuss things, Milner I think being rather annoyed at having been interrupted. A.J.B. made a most amusing remark about Reading. Said that he thoroughly appreciated and admired him. Still he had discovered one thing when working with him and that was his extraordinary loquacity and that he took 20 minutes to say what anybody else could say in 5; and ended up by saying it had always been a marvel to him how a man with that failing could have made such a success at the Bar.[5]

16 to Dinner. Our own party of 8 in the House as Eric Drummond is staying here as well as Reading and Arthur. Madame Hennessy, Madame Castéja, M. Laborder and M. De Gheest. Haig, Davidson, Philip and Alan Fletcher. Quite an amusing Dinner and I think Haig, although always very shy of coming to a Dinner Party, liked it as for the first time for many months he has been taken out of his immediate surroundings. I had a word with him and he told me he had been down to see Foch and everything had been most satisfactory. The conciliatory letter he had written had given a loophole for Foch and had been quite successful. Foch had taken the loophole and now everything was all well.

Nobody seems in the least to know what the next move is to be. Whether the Governments — having decided on the terms of the Armistice — which by the way they have not done yet — should then communicate them to the German Government through the Swiss Government and to Austria through the Swedish Government, or whether they both have to go to Wilson for him to submit. Of course the more Austria's note is looked into the more it looks like the death knell of the Austrian Empire and it seems to me that it is going to give rise to endless future quarrels as we shall only be creating in Austria a second Balkans. Arthur and Reading discussed a very curious legal point in which they are both in agreement, though I understand Clemenceau, Lloyd George and Co. won't accept it, and that is that if we make an armistice under present conditions we "ipso facto" accept the whole of Wilson's 14 articles of faith, together with his subsequent declarations; but what is still more important is that not only do we accept them but we accept a state of affairs by which we cannot add to these articles. They are so to speak in a ring fence and we have to stand or fall by them without diminution and without addition. It seems to me an almost impossible position. Reading said that he had had a talk with House, who is not very well, on the subject of the Freedom of the Seas Clause and he believes everything would be quite satisfactory with the President. I must say for a man who is supposed to be perfectly honest and straightforward, the President is able to do more hairsplitting than any man I have ever heard or read of.

Notes to 28 October

1. British victory over Turkish and Egyptian fleet in Greek War of Independence, 20 October 1827.
2. The Austrian request for an armistice was granted on 4 November.
3. In the event Germany and Austria were obliged to remove any reference to a union from their constitutions. The French insisted that any such union could only take place with the approval of the Council of the League of Nations.
4. Colonel Lloyd C. Griscom. Pershing's personal representative to Lord Milner in the British War Office.
5. As Sir Rufus Isaacs, Reading was one of the most celebrated and highly paid barristers of the age. He was successively Solicitor-General and Attorney-General in the years 1910–13.

Tuesday, 29th October

Capel came to see me before luncheon. I want him to try and find out for me what French political opinion is with reference to Command of the Seas and disposition of the German Colonies. It is a hard job but I think he will be able to discover more than most people.

Luncheon Duc D'Alb, Capels, Milner, Haig and Davidson; Bliss, Henry Wilson, Sackville West and Hankey; and ourselves. 16.

Short talks with various people after luncheon. Hankey told me that he had strange confirmation from the other side of the Atlantic of what I had told him about there being some indirect communications going on between Clemenceau and the President on the question of the Freedom of the Seas.

Haig impressed upon Henry Wilson that the thing to go for was mild military and severe naval terms in the armistice. I was very glad to see the relationship between Henry Wilson and Haig is so good. Haig said quite openly that Robertson always fussed him and then went off to see the French and was continually making unnecessary mischief and he was very grateful to Henry Wilson for having left him so much alone and for having supported him.

Reading came in afterwards from his luncheon with House. I think he is rather depressed at the way things are going. He says whenever they get to a difficulty and there is a fence to be jumped, everybody refuses and goes off to find some other place to get through. The result is that there is a lot of misunderstanding which must be cleared up. He was very alarmed last night at the attitude which I told him I thought Clemenceau had taken up, that he (C) wiped out all that had happened in the way of negotiation between Wilson and the Germans and Austrians and was going to start "de novo" as if the White Flag had come in asking for terms of surrender, an attitude which Milner also said he found Clemenceau in. Reading says that that would at once bring House and Clemenceau to loggerheads. What he says we have got to do, and I must say it seems right, is to say to the Germans that we accept President Wilson's 14 articles in principle, though the details will be told to them more definitely when we come to talk terms of Peace, but that we must add to the 14 articles some general phrase of reparation for all damage done by land or sea, which would include burning of villages, bombing of towns and sinking of ships. This is a slightly different attitude to the one I thought last night he was taking up. Apparently there is some discussion going on as to where the Peace Conference should sit but most people are for Paris. Lloyd George is for Geneva and Henry Wilson thinks that is simply because if the meeting was in Paris Clemenceau would have to be in the Chair. I told him I was perfectly certain that if as is stated, though very confidentially, the President himself is coming over, Clemenceau would at once move that he be in the Chair whether it be in Paris or in Geneva and that if they went to Geneva they would be met with endless difficulties which would not exist in Paris. Henry Wilson entirely agrees as he said he felt if it was held in Paris it would be possible for Lloyd George, as one of our representatives at the Peace Conference, to equally remain Prime Minister of England, as with an accelerated train service, which of course could be arranged, he could always get over to England for 48 hours, whereas from Geneva that would be impossible.

A purely British dinner. House Party 7 (Eric Drummond dining out). Geddes, Wemyss and Steele (Geddes's Secretary). Haig, Davidson, Ian Malcolm, Lytton and Henderson from the Chancery.

Balfour dictated a memorandum afterwards and discussed questions privately with Reading.

Wednesday, 30th October

Luncheon. Usual House Party together with Prime Minister, Capels, Sir William Wiseman[1] and Hankey. Bonar Law was expected, flying over from England but did not turn up. The Prime Minister in great form and very pleased with his talk in the morning with Clemenceau and House. From what A.J.B. tells me they made real progress and things seem to be gradually shaping out.

A telegram came in, which had been intercepted, sent by the Emperor of Austria to Diaz offering, if an immediate armistice was granted, to retire from all the invaded territory without further fighting. There is no doubt Austria is completely out of the War and their one desire is to get out as quickly as possible so as to preserve in some way the vestige of Empire.

After luncheon various people came in, including Wemyss. Murray of Elibank then came to see me about the Algerian concession. Pearsons have been atrociously treated and I am glad to say the Home Government is taking it up very strongly and have sent a very hot dispatch which they want me to hand in to Pichon. I discussed it previously with A.J.B. and made a suggestion to him, of which he approved, and which Murray of Elibank thought the best way of dealing with the matter, and that was that I should see Loucheur privately, show him a copy of the Dispatch and tell him unless he settled matters, that would be handed in and there would be a great deal of trouble, far more than he anticipated.

Bonar Law came in at tea-time. He had come over very fast but as he did not get in till ¼ to 2 thought he was too late to come in to luncheon. I had a few words conversation with him and he says he wants to talk to me about things political at home. Apparently they are in considerable trouble. The House of Commons people are all right for a Coalition Government Election but apparently a lot of people in the House of Lords are kicking and will have nothing to do with it. There is to be a private meeting of Members of the House of Lords and he is anxious that I should go over for it. He does not think that it would in any way be wrong in my present position to do so. I do not feel so certain myself and I shall talk to A.J.B. about it. He tells me that there has been rather a row and that Lloyd George has dismissed Hayes Fisher from the Local Government Board, or rather was dismissing him in a most brutal fashion but Bonar Law got it hung up till he had talked to Lloyd George again. He wants to push him into the Chancellor of the Duchy Office which is vacant owing to Beaverbrook's resignation. He tells me that Hayes Fisher is absolutely useless where he is and they mean to replace him by Auckland Geddes. The National Service Department is now practically at an end of its work and Geddes can perfectly run the two. Beaverbrook he says is very bad. It is a growth in his throat but they say it is not cancer.[2] He has got a fair chance of recovery.

Met John Campbell[3] the Coldstream V.C. in the street. He tells me it is extraordinary the difference between German Divisions. He has had some very stout-hearted fellows in front of him who fought really to the last man. The next day he would attack a Division which would practically hold up their hands at once.

Dinner. Victoria and Charlie dined out. Lloyd George, Bonar Law and Briand dined.

Briand was extremely interesting and amusing. At dinner we got on the subject of Caillaux and he told us some remarkable stories about him. He said that when Caillaux came into office he proceeded to denounce every Treaty he could, Briand adding "it was an additional pleasure for him to do so as I was the man who had been principally concerned in making them". Of course this got him into difficulties, especially at the time of the Agadir incident and he had to get out of them as best he could.[4] Meanwhile he was endeavouring to have Briand assassinated — of that Briand had no doubt whatever as he had been warned, also because as he said Caillaux really deals with politics as they were dealt with in the days of Borgia.[5]

As an instance of his unscrupulous and ruthless methods Briand told of an occasion on which Caillaux was having difficulties with Spain. He sent for the Spanish Ambassador who endeavoured to get his own way adding that his King was urging him to carry that particular point. Caillaux cut short the Ambassador with the following. "You can tell your King that I have several tame anarchists residing on the Spanish Frontier and if there is any more trouble I will release them into Spain!"

After a time however Caillaux found he would have to get Briand's help so he went to see Briand. Briand at the end of the conversation said it was rather an extraordinary thing for him to come and see him considering that he was trying to have him assassinated. All Caillaux replied was "Dans la politique on fait souvent des bêtises". He ended up by asking Briand to come out shooting with him. Briand thought nothing of it but could not go that time. Caillaux then wrote a second time and asked him to go but Caillaux's wife (his first wife) came to Briand and said unless he was extremely keen to go out shooting she advised him not to go as her husband was a little erratic in his shooting. Briand did not go. After a further interval Caillaux again pressed Briand to go and shoot with him. Briand demurred upon which Caillaux turned to him and said "Ah! I know the reason for your refusal. You are afraid I may shoot you. My wife has warned you."

He said Caillaux's one overwhelming thought was International Finance and he thought of nothing else and that outweighed any feelings of patriotism. He added "You have got the same in every country. You have got your Cassel[6] in England."

He said Caillaux had been to him after his downfall, but of course before his present arrest, and had said how bitterly he felt the fact that the only thing that could ever return him to Power would be the downfall of his own Country. He was an extremely able man, a pleasant man to talk to with such inordinate conceit that he was unbalanced in mind, or as Briand described him "C'est un détraqué".

Briand did not think that the High Court would condemn him to death as he certainly would have been had he gone before a Court Martial.

After Dinner Lloyd George proceeded to put to him some extremely searching questions to which Briand gave the most amusing and elusive answers. As Lloyd George himself said his answers reminded him irresistibly of his old Chief.[7] One direct question was "What would you do if you were in power with regard to an armistice?" to which he gave the very obvious answer that then he would have the full information, which he had not now, as to the circumstances of Germany which would enable him to come to a decision.

In the course of conversation he mentioned the fact that he had been 6 times "Président du Conseil". On being asked by Bonar Law how many times he expected again to fill that office he wittily replied. "Ah! I do not expect that illness will attack me again. I have been well inoculated."[8]

He told us that he had seen Mangin who had told him that the retreat was a very orderly one, that the Germans were getting all their stores away although they were losing guns and ammunition, that they were still fighting well and there was no doubt that their power of military resistance was still very great.

As to the terms of armistice Briand said that he hoped that the Powers would not be led away by the clap-trap of the newspapers and people who did not know the circumstances of the case. As long as you have got the real power which would prevent Germany making War again and would keep her permanently from ever becoming a Military Power again, that was what you wanted and these demands for absolutely crushing her seemed to him very much exaggerated. He said "It is worth months of war to secure the building but it is not worth a day's war to put a facade on to that building". From what he said it is obvious his view of the situation is very much what Haig's is.

After he and L.G. had gone A.J.B. amused us very much indeed by saying that except they spoke a different language he never could tell the difference between them. They were exactly alike.

Notes to 30 October

1. Sir William Wiseman (1885–1962). Businessman and Head of British Intelligence in the USA during the war, he acted as an intermediary between Colonel House and the British government.
2. After resigning as Minister of Information on 21 October, Beaverbrook had an operation for a glandular swelling in his neck. He quickly recovered.
3. Lieutenant-Colonel John Vaughan Campbell (1876–1944). Coldstream Guards. Awarded the VC on 15 September 1916.
4. As Prime Minister June 1911 to January 1912, Caillaux set out to resolve the Agadir crisis on the basis of agreement with Germany, thereby incurring the lasting animosity of, among others, Clemenceau.
5. Lucrezia Borgia (1480–1519). Italian noblewoman, often accused of complicity in her family's crimes and moral excesses.
6. Sir Ernest Cassel (1852–1921). Financier and philanthropist. Gave away £2 million to charities during his lifetime.
7. Presumably a reference to H. H. Asquith.
8. In fact Briand would hold the premiership on five further occasions.

Thursday, 31st October

Capel came in to tell me that he had been trying to find out Jonnart's views on the question of the retention of our Colonies. Jonnart is popularly supposed to be one of the three Peace Delegates that France will send to the Peace Conference. A.J.B. came in just after he arrived and Capel then told me, in the first place Jonnart was extraordinarily pro-English and with regard to the Colonies he was strongly of opinion that France should keep those which by agreement have been allotted to her and that England should keep those which she had conquered, but that the value of the Colonies would have to be taken into consideration when assessing the Indemnity to be paid by the Central Powers and that the value of any Colony kept by either England or France would have to be set against their share of the Indemnity. I told him to try and find out what Jules

Cambon's opinion was as he is another who is mentioned as a Peace Delegate, though I had heard privately that he was more likely to be nominated as the Governor of Alsace and perhaps of Alsace and Lorraine together.[1]

Arthur Balfour then told me about yesterday's meeting which seems to have been a very stormy one. It turned entirely on the question as to who should sign any terms of Armistice with Turkey and it got very hot indeed between Clemenceau and Lloyd George, the latter being in his best platform style, quoting fabulous figures as to the number of troops we had in Mesopotamia, Palestine and Salonika and twitting Clemenceau with the fact that most of his troops were what he, L.G., called "nigger policemen" quite forgetting that the mass of our troops in the three places named are equally coloured troops. However in the end L.G. won but the feeling between the two was very marked.[2] I asked Arthur whether he did not think that what really would have to happen would be first of all that the armistice should be agreed to now and should be kept as far apart from the terms of Peace as the stupid utterances in the letters of President Wilson will allow. Secondly, that there should be an inter-Allied Conference held in Paris to discuss the terms of Peace to be offered to Germany and 3rdly a Conference which presumably would have to be held in some neutral place where the terms of Peace would be presented to Germany. He said he thought probably that would be the order of events but we ought to settle the terms of the armistice within the next 48 hours. That the allies would then have to meet in about a month's time to discuss the terms of Peace, which would probably take another month or 6 weeks and that then the third Conference would be held. He did not think that would take very long as if Germany accepted the terms of armistice she would not be in a position to renew the War and would practically therefore have to accept any terms that we chose to dictate to her. He seemed to think that Peace might be signed by about March. Lloyd George on the other hand told me last night he thought it would be signed by the 1st of January.

I then went to see Loucheur with reference to Cowdray's[3] Oil Concession. I showed him a copy of the very hot Despatch that the Foreign Office have sent me. He seemed somewhat impressed by it as also by the fact that I told him there was a very strong feeling in industrial circles on the subject and I was quite sure unless he met Cowdray that the French would find there was retaliation both in Great Britain and the Colonies which would prevent the French participating in industrial works which they might be anxious to do. He assured me he had no wish whatever to treat Murray harshly but he said Murray had behaved stupidly all through. He would not take his (Loucheur's) advice 6 months ago and that he relied instead on lobbying against Loucheur. He asked for 75,000 hectares concession whereas the biggest concession the French Government had ever given was 1,000 hectares, but he (Loucheur) had given his word that Cowdray should not lose over it; that they had never pledged themselves to the extent that Murray stated and that Murray could produce no documentary evidence to justify his statements. That certain Deputies had asked that no concessions should be made but he had definitely informed the Chamber that he would make them and he proposed to give about 25,000 hectares and that he genuinely meant to behave honestly by Cowdray. I am afraid I do not think he does. On the other hand, I do not think Murray has been very over-wise in the way that he has lobbied. Loucheur then promised to give me a note to give to Murray. All this was done quite unofficially and I told him that I entirely reserved my right to present a note to Pichon. He quite understood this and apparently was meeting me in a most friendly spirit.

He then started talking about yesterday's meeting. He told me that Clemenceau was very angry with Lloyd George who he thought had behaved very badly to him. I told him that I thought Lloyd George was entirely in his right. We had done the whole of the fighting against the Turk and when it came to receiving the White Flag of armistice why should not the English have the honour of receiving it. He said Lloyd George had demanded it as a right of England. I told him that I thought there was no right in this question except from a moral point of view and we were morally entitled to this. Moreover, the offer had been made to us and there was no reason why under the circumstances we should hand over the honour to the French. There really is no answer to our argument but the French "amour propre", and their extraordinary greed in these sort of matters, are very difficult to combat. The only thing I regret about the whole matter is that it undoubtedly has left a bad feeling on the part of Clemenceau towards Lloyd George, which will make things difficult in further negotiations. The extraordinary thing is one cannot persuade Lloyd George of the effect his remarks may have. I spoke to him about it the other day and he told me that he never resented in the least what anybody said to him and he could not see why they should resent what he said in reply. Against such a statement there is no arguing. He won't see that the difference of race is one that must be taken into account.

I ought to add that Loucheur told me that he thought the terms of Armistice to Germany would be signed by the 15th of November, that she would accept every term that was offered to her, providing our Naval terms, which I think everybody agrees are too drastic, are somewhat diminished, and that Peace would be signed by the 15th of January. I told him that I had not seen the full Naval terms, but he must remember this, that if the French desired very drastic terms for military reasons we had just as much reason for demanding drastic terms in Naval matters. I believe however as a matter of fact that both A.J.B. and Lloyd George think that the terms are more severe than they need be to secure immunity from the recrudescence of the War.

Charlie and Victoria went off to racing so we only had a small luncheon party. B, Arthur Balfour, Reading, Ian Malcolm and Eric Drummond. General conversation on every sort of point, Arthur Balfour being very amusing in the extraordinary detached view he takes of everything.

Mark Sykes came in after luncheon and I then had a talk with him. He is off on a Mission to Allenby to act as a go-between with Allenby and the Arabs and also with the French. He has got a very difficult part to play but he is most anxious to keep friendly with the French. He had seen Pichon and Goût⁴ this morning. Both of them are very sore about the Turkish armistice procedure and evidently Clemenceau's anger is reflected through the whole of the French Ministry.

Turkey's full surrender was known this morning and Austria has made really a most grovelling "ad misericordiam" appeal to stop fighting at once. The more one thinks of it the more amazed one is at the sudden collapse of the whole enemy coalition. One has always been told to expect that once the break up came it would mean an entire collapse but I do not think anybody ever thought it would come so quickly and so dramatically as it has.

Afternoon. A Deputation came from the Chamber of Commerce to see me to protest against what they call the unfavourable attitude of French officials towards English Trade. Introduced by Mr. Fletcher, and Mr. Cahil and Ian Malcolm (representing Mr. Balfour) were present to hear what they said. I am afraid there is no doubt that there is opposition to English Trade but I was not very much impressed by the way they put their case forward with the exception of one man who represented Lever Brothers. They could only make vague accusations and the complaints of one of the four representatives were entirely confined to our own government. The real truth is the French are adopting the attitude of "France for the French" and it is very difficult to combat that, especially when in England the one cry that is really popular is "England for the English". However, I shall see if anything can be done. Ian Malcolm is going to take it up with the Foreign Office because in making any representations to the French Government I must be supported by the Foreign Office.

Evening. Rawlinson arrived. We had a short talk before Dinner. He is just a little anxious as to what the effect on the men will be of the present situation, as the Germans are showering leaflets on our troops telling them that an armistice has been signed, etc. He said that at the present moment they look upon it as a Bosche lie but naturally not only the men are reluctant to fight if there really is going to be Peace immediately, but Generals and Commanding Officers are equally reluctant to have to ask them to do so. Rawly staying in the House.

Dinner. House Party plus Henry Wilson, Murray of Elibank and a Mr. Cobb.[5] The latter is the Editor of the *New York World*. A great personal friend of House and over here with him. A great lover of England much more than he is of France. We only had a sort of general conversation but it was very interesting on many subjects. The one thing which impressed me the most was how completely the Middle West in America, which was at one time against the War, is now pro-War. They are subscribing better than anybody else to the Liberty Loan[6] and they are really War mad. He says that Bryan,[7] who of course was anti-war, made a speech when America came in and said that now America was in, he was going to do all that he possibly could to assist and behaved splendidly. His influence is very great and he has used it in every way that he could to support the President. Apparently the President's appeal to his Party has created a tremendous ferment in America and I should think was really the first false move he has made. It is worth while looking at *The Times* of Tuesday and seeing the counter-Address that has been put forward by the Republicans. The hit at House is really most amusing.

Apparently at the Meeting today there was complete harmony. The terms of the Armistice with Austria were settled and have been sent off to Diaz to communicate as in that particular case the White Flag has actually come into the Italian Lines. But a curious thing has happened. It has suddenly been discovered that the White Flag did not come from the Commander-in-Chief of the Austrian Armies but from the Commanders of one of the separate armies. I do not think this amounts to much but it does seem to show in what an extraordinary state of disintegration the Austrians are.

Notes to 31 October

1. In fact Cambon was one of Clemenceau's choice of plenipotentiaries; Jonnart was not.
2. See Roskill, *Hankey*, vol. 1, pp. 623–24.

3. 1st Viscount Cowdray (1856–1927). Liberal MP for Colchester, 1895–1910; head of the firm of S. Pearson and Son Ltd.

4. Jean Goût. Sous-directeur d'Asie at the Quai d'Orsay and member of the Comité de l'Asie Française.

5. Frank Cobb (1869–1923). Editor, *New York World*, 1911–23. Contemporaries credited his editorials with securing the Democratic presidential nomination for Woodrow Wilson in 1912.

6. Liberty Loan. Long-term financing of the American war effort came through a series of five small-denomination bonds, the first four of which were called Liberty Loans.

7. William J. Bryan (1860–1925). US Secretary of State, 1913–15. Resigned after the sinking of the *Lusitania*, fearing Wilson's protest would lead to war.

November 1918

Friday, 1st November

Luncheon. Reading had luncheon out. Rawly and his A.D.C. [blank] whose father had been at Wellington with me and who is a great friend of Arty's, had luncheon, also Henry Wilson. He would talk of nothing else but the news which apparently is official that the Kaiser has abdicated, and as far as they know in favour of nobody, so it may mean a Republic; that the Yugo-Slavs had revolted and seized the whole of the Austrian Fleet and also the mercantile fleet. Hideous complications are likely to come from this as they have sent official notice that if any Italian lands on the soil they claim he will be shot and that they will hand over the Fleet to nobody except the Americans. Meanwhile the Italians having got nobody to fight have announced their intention of advancing right through Austria. There is a further complication that apparently Austria is now just as Russia was after the Revolution and there is practically nobody to make Peace with. Altogether things are in a very disagreeable state.

I forgot to say that Bonar Law came to see me this morning and we had a walk in the garden. There is a tremendous row going on about Hayes Fisher. Roughly the story is this. It has now been discovered that, owing to the Registrars of the various electoral districts not having sent in their returns in sufficient time to the War Office Record Office, if they have an Election in December only about one third of the soldiers will be able to vote. They are keeping this very secret for the moment but of course it will create a tremendous row. The Registrars are under the Local Government Board and Lloyd George blames Hayes Fisher for this contretemps, but he goes rather further and does not blame him for having made the mistake but thinks he has done it deliberately working with Walter Long because he is opposed to an immediate Election. He therefore wrote a letter dismissing Hayes Fisher and sent it up to London the day before he left for Paris. The letter was sent to the Treasury to be copied and was brought to Bonar Law who as soon as he saw it stopped its being sent and telegraphed to Lloyd George telling him that he would not be a Party to such a letter going and that he begged him to hold his hand until they had been able to discuss the matter. They discussed it here and apparently there was a great deal of feeling shown. Lloyd George abused B.L. for stopping it and said that he prevented him getting rid of any inefficient man when that man happened to be a Unionist. B.L. then asked Lloyd George whether he realised that if the letter had gone in, he B.L. would have been obliged to resign. L.G. said yes he had and he was prepared to have accepted it and faced the consequences. Bonar said very well why did you telegraph to me to come over if you were not going to discuss the matter amicably. There the matter dropped for the moment but it has not been settled and it is further complicated by the Unionist Members of the Government at home taking a strong line and saying they will not have one of their colleagues treated in this way and also the fact that it has already got into the papers and especially into the *Daily News*. Bonar agrees that Hayes Fisher ought to go but thinks he ought to be sent away in a different fashion namely by making him Chancellor of the Duchy.[1] How it will end I do not know.

We then discussed the question of a programme and B.L. tells me that he has drawn up a letter for L.G. to write to him and which if it is written Bonar thinks will be accepted by our Party.

Ireland is dealt with by a statement to the effect that now is not the moment to give Home Rule to Ireland but that the Prime Minister reserves to himself the right to give some form of self-Government but with a distinct understanding that there shall be no coercion of Ulster.

Welsh Church by a declaration that the Bill must stand[2] but by a promise to deal with the Disendowment part of the scheme.

Fiscal Policy by a general statement that the Prime Minister will approach the subject with a perfectly open mind and without bias either to Free Trade or Protection, stating at the same time that it was desirable in every way that the production of England shall be assisted and to secure that he is prepared to take any steps to prevent goods from abroad being dumped in England.

A further statement that the Corn Bill having dealt with the question of rates for cereals for several years to come, it is not necessary at the present moment to deal with the subject of taxation in that direction, but under no circumstances would a tax be put upon food.

This document will be signed also by Barnes and if it were issued signed by Lloyd George, Bonar Law and Barnes, Bonar thinks that they would sweep the country.

There was some talk of a compromise with Asquith but it has come to nothing[3] and apparently there will be an open rupture at the Election and we shall run candidates against the Asquith people. At the present moment it is contemplated having an Election about the 10th or so of December but as B.L. says quite rightly, the object of having an election now which was to prevent there being an election directly after Peace was declared is to a great extent vitiated by the fact that two thirds of our soldiers will not be able to vote, and Asquith and Co. will undoubtedly have right on their side when they say that the result does not truly represent the views of the whole country, when perhaps two million of the men who have been fighting have never had a chance of registering their vote.

There is to be a small Party Meeting in London next Friday, which Bonar is very anxious for me to attend but I do not think I shall do so. In the first place I do not want to leave France next week when I think I may have a great deal to do and secondly I think it would be a pity to mix up in politics at the present moment. If ever I want to go back to them, and I very much doubt it, it will be much better to do so when matters have settled down.

Went for walk in the afternoon.

Dinner. Northcliffe and Sir Campbell Stuart dined. [With] Northcliffe after Dinner there was rather a disagreeable incident. Arthur Balfour was sitting on the sofa reading a very confidential letter to me and Reading. He was reading it too loud and we were trying to stop him reading it, and he happened to say "Am I reading it so that anybody else could hear". Northcliffe who was at the other end of the room was listening for every word. When that was said and Arthur Balfour dropped his voice, he came over to us and began talking to Arthur Balfour and entering into violent abuse of Milner. He said that the Country was furious with Milner and that they thought that the Country was being sold at Versailles. I must say Arthur Balfour behaved extraordinarily well. He perhaps gave rather more information to Northcliffe than was altogether advisable but he argued with him and put him on his back time after time and I think Northcliffe saw that many of the things that he thought were being done out here — one of which was that he was under the impression that Milner attended all the Conferences whereas he has attended none — were inaccurate.

Geddes and Wemyss came in after and every sort of Conference went on till about 12.30.

Victoria was laid up with a bad throat and temperature.

Notes to 1 November

1. Hayes Fisher became Chancellor of the Duchy of Lancaster in November 1918.
2. As in the case of Irish Home Rule, a bill to disestablish the Welsh Church had been passed under the terms of the Parliament Act in 1914, although its operation was suspended for the duration of hostilities.
3. Asquith turned down a suggestion that he should take on a senior position, perhaps the Lord Chancellorship, in Lloyd George's government.

Saturday, 2nd November

Victoria better but still in bed. They say it is not the flu but I think it is something very like it. Her temperature last night went up to 103 but this morning it is only just above normal. The doctor says there is no cause for anxiety.

Various people came in, David Henderson, Henry Wilson. None of them on matters of any importance.

Went to luncheon today with the Dupuys. Very nice. The Biche de Castellanes, Duchesse de Clermont-Tonnerre, Lytton, Neville Lytton and another man whose name I did not know, a Roumanian.

Stayed there till about ¼ to 3 and then went up to the Villa Romaine. I saw the P.M., B.L., etc.

Things are all in a most unsettled state. Austria has completely broken up and it does not look as if there would be a responsible Government with whom we could make Peace. The Yugo-Slavs and the Italians ready to fly at each other's throats even if they have not already done so as there is a report that last night the Italians torpedoed and sank two of the Battleships handed over to the Yugo-Slavs. Altogether a nice kettle of fish; and with the President very stuffy on two things that are vital to us, namely Freedom of the Seas and Economic Barriers, I foresee plenty of difficulties before we get out of the wood. At the same time I think there is a better feeling prevailing all round than there was and I should hope that as the Soldiers and the Sailors have now been able to arrange their terms for an Armistice it won't take long for the Politicians to come to a similar understanding. The whole difficulty is Wilson's 14 articles and if the Armistice is to be based on them they cannot be accepted without qualifications.[1]

Evening. Only people in the House to Dinner but afterwards continuous stream of people coming in and meetings in every room. Things have not gone very well thanks to a great extent to L.G. and House having fallen out.

Notes to 2 November

1. See Roskill, *Hankey*, vol. 1, p. 626.

Sunday, 3rd November

PARIS

Attended a service, Memorial to the Dead, in the Embassy Church. Church packed. Band of the Blues played.

Early luncheon and then went out to play golf. Charlie and Eric Drummond played together and I played my usual foursome with Guiche, Madame Hennessy, but as Victoria could not come Capel took her place. Pouring with rain and could only play 12 holes but quite a good match.

Tea time. Prime Minister came and a letter was drafted with regard to the Freedom of the Seas which Reading showed to House and with which he entirely agreed, so I hope that trouble is over — at all events for the moment, though I am afraid the President is still very sticky.

Lloyd George in great form. Came to my room afterwards and we discussed the political situation. He told me that what had happened was this. He and B.L. had practically come to an understanding as to the terms on which a Coalition could be formed. As I have mentioned before B.L. had told me the terms and said they were quite fair and Arthur Balfour told me that he did not think any reasonable member of our Party could refuse to accept them. Lloyd George then said that the Liberal Party had been trying to get him very hard to go back to them. They told him that they quite understood if he went back he would be the Prime Minister and they would get rid of Asquith, but he told them "No", that that would not be playing the game by our Party. That for a whole year the Liberal Party had been kicking him and doing everything they could against him while our Party had loyally supported him and if it had not been for them he would not be in his present position now and he was not going back on them if they would have him as their Leader.

I afterwards spoke to Arthur Balfour and he told me there was no doubt L.G. was playing the game like a gentleman and he hoped our Party would not be so foolish as not to accept the conditions, though he quite expected there would be a certain amount of resentment, especially on the part of men like Walter Long and as he said "my own family"[1] and there is to be a Party Meeting this week and I hope there will be unanimity. I shall not myself be able to go back for it though I should rather like to have been there.

In the evening I dined with the Comte and Comtesse de Beaumont. Very nice couple. They were both rather old. Lovely house and a very amusing Party. The Grammonts. I sat next to her and she is delightful. Princesse de Pois, Princesse Chimay, Princesse Marie Murat and a Mrs. Garrett wife of the American Minister at the Hague who has been sent here on a Special Mission. The men were Bontout, Daudet,[2] a brother of the writer,[3] Biche de Castellane and two other men whose names I did not catch. I left early as I wanted to get back to hear what had gone on. I found them all in very good humour. Only the House Party dined together with Cowans[4] and Evelyn Fitzgerald.[5] Arthur Balfour and Reading most amusing talking about every sort of subject. I think the more one sees of Arthur Balfour the more delightful he becomes.

Notes to 3 November

1. Leading Conservatives, Lord Selborne, Lord Salisbury, Lord Robert Cecil and Lord Hugh Cecil were all cousins of Balfour. His brother, Gerald, had also been a cabinet minister.
2. Ernest Daudet (1837–1921). Writer and journalist.
3. Alphonse Daudet (1840–97). Writer.
4. Major-General John Cowans (1862–1921). Quartermaster General, 1912–19.
5. Evelyn Fitzgerald (d.1946). Private Secretary to the Quartermaster General, December 1914–March 1919.

Monday, 4th November

Lloyd George suddenly rushed in to say that he had determined to go home today. There was nothing more to settle here and he wanted to get home for obvious Home reasons. He wanted Arthur Balfour to go with him in a couple of hours time. Arthur declined to do that, and as it turned out afterwards, quite rightly as he was wanted to represent the Prime Minister at a meeting of the Supreme War Council in the afternoon. He went off to play Lawn Tennis. Lloyd George left expecting to come back probably next Monday or Tuesday. Apparently what has been decided is this. The terms of the armistice have now been settled and the President of the United States of course knows about them. The President will simply telegraph to the Swiss Government to say that if the Germans send in a White Flag to Foch they will be told the terms of the armistice. They will then have to consider them and, if they accept, then there will be an Inter-Allied Conference held here at once to discuss the terms of Peace that are to be put forward. Lloyd George thinks that will only take a short time but judging from what has been going on lately I am certain it will take at least a couple of months, especially as the President is coming over for it. The terms will then be handed to Germany and I suppose a Conference held, though I think that that Conference will be more or less of a farce as the terms will have been considered beforehand. The Allies won't weaken on them and Germany will be impotent to restart the War. I expect therefore myself that Peace will probably be signed somewhere about the middle of February. Of course this is all supposing that the Germans accept the terms of armistice which personally I do not feel that they will do. They are very stringent and it looks as if there was still a good deal of fight left in them. They are blowing up bridges, railways and roads more systematically during the last few days than they have done any time during the Retreat. On the other hand I do not see what they have got to look forward to — a bad winter, a starving and discontented population and the certainty that not only will our Army be stronger on the Western Front for an offensive in the Spring but that they will have to deal with a big army on their Bavarian Frontier. They may however keep on up to the Spring in the hopes that something may turn up which will sow dissension amongst the Allies. Of course I am laughed at when I suggest that they will be able during the winter months to organise a very considerable Russian Force and that they will enter into an Alliance with the Bolshevik Government — though they will be rather frightened about doing so — and we shall have to fight Russia as well as Germany in the Spring. I admit this is rather a pessimistic view to take but I still think there is a possibility of it. Meanwhile, I suppose we shall push forward our forces through the Tyrol right on to the Bavarian Frontier.

Evening House Party plus Cowans, Evelyn Fitzgerald and Bullock.

A.J.B. told me of a grievance of Geddes's. It is a long story but it is worth putting down as there may be future reference to it. I think I referred previously to a very confidential letter which Arthur Balfour read out to us and which he had sent to Bonar Law and which we were unable to discuss owing to Northcliffe coming over and joining us. The subject of the letter was the difference of opinion between A.J.B. and the Supreme War Council with regard to those terms of armistice connected with the internment of Ships, A.J.B. arguing that the internment of German Ships was not adequate as it might mean their internment in some neutral country who, in the event of the armistice being broken, would restore them to Germany. He told us at the time that his view was taken by Geddes. He had also written another letter to Bonar Law telling him of his letter to Lloyd George and asking him to see it and see whether he agreed with it. That was on Friday night. This morning (Monday) Lloyd George talking to Arthur Balfour and me said it was all perfectly right and that the question of the internment of ships was exactly the same as if they had been handed over, as they would be interned in either the Maas or the Schelde; they would only have caretakers on board and we should have troops within 10 miles of them so that within a few hours of any breaking of the armistice we should be able to seize them; and that Geddes agreed to this. Both Arthur and I said that that entirely differed from what Geddes had told us previously and A.J.B. said he was very surprised that Geddes should have changed his opinions and taken one so diametrically opposed to what he had held only 2 days before, but there for the moment the matter dropped. Geddes, however, telephoned to say that he would like to come to luncheon as he had something very important to talk over with A.J.B. After luncheon they had a talk and Geddes motored out to Versailles with A.J.B. and back with him and the following is the story as far as I make out. There is not a word of truth in L.G.'s statement that Geddes had agreed to the change. On the contrary, he held very strongly to his late opinion and what was more extraordinary than anything was that at the meeting of the Prime Minister when this was discussed Geddes was not even in attendance but Admiral Hope was sent for and attended to give what Lloyd George said was some technical information. When Geddes tackled him with it L.G. said that he deliberately excluded Geddes because he had been lobbying with Arthur Balfour and Bonar Law to get them to back his (Geddes') contention. This has made Geddes furious and as A.J.B. said himself it is an impossible position for a Prime Minister to take up that two or three of his colleagues should not discuss things together and if they agree in their views to make a joint representation to the Prime Minister. I do not know what the outcome of it will be but apparently Geddes deeply resents his position. He told A.J.B. that he could not help thinking that Lloyd George was deliberately putting into his Government men who, as he phrased it, had no political roots. In other words, men who had no political following of any sort or kind. He instanced himself, his brother, Stanley[1] and Fisher.[2] As he said, if any of them were thrown over by Lloyd George it was one individual who went and he carried nobody with him which from L.G.'s point of view was a great advantage. On the other hand if he put men in who had a political following, however small, it might mean not only losing the individual but also losing the support of other members of Parliament.

Notes to 4 November

1. Albert Stanley (1874–1948). Baron Ashfield, 1920. President of the Board of Trade, December 1916–May 1919.
2. Herbert A. L. Fisher (1865–1940). President of the Board of Education, December 1916–October 1922.

Tuesday, 5th November

Arthur Balfour and Eric Drummond left at 9 o'clock. A.J.B. not at all happy as it has been blowing a gale during the night.

Got a telegram from George Curzon asking whether I could put him and Lady Curzon up at the end of the week. I have written to say that I could put them up from Saturday to Monday but not after that as if A.J.B. returns I should want the room that I should otherwise give to Lady Curzon.

Luncheon. Ourselves, Johnny Du Cane, Henry Wilson and Milner. I spoke to the latter again about Military Allowances in Paris and he has promised to take the matter up as soon as he gets to London. We also discussed the Cohn question of which the Military Secretary in London (Joey Davies)[1] has made a real mess. He gazetted him out and used the wrong initials with the result they had to cancel the Gazette and now Haig has begged them to take no further action until they receive a letter from him. Henry Wilson is apparently determined to have Cohn out and I hope Milner will be firm. For my own part I do not care in the least what his private character may be. What I do feel is that it is entirely wrong that a man wearing a British uniform should be the proprietor of a French newspaper. I also think it is scandalous that Sidney Clive, who is our Director of Military Intelligence, should be in such close touch with him as naturally it may give rise to serious misunderstandings if anything appears in his paper which has been denied to other papers.

Foch told Henry Wilson he did not think that the Boche would accept the terms now but he hoped to have him completely beaten by Christmas time when he would be compelled to accept any terms that we offered. It might be an advantage in some ways for the War to go on a short time as if he rejects the armistice now we shall be able to throw overboard, or at all events discuss from an entirely different point of view, the fourteen articles of Wilson which are such a bugbear at the present moment.

General Townshend[2] came to see me and the bad impression I had of him before the War was intensified when I met him again. Of all the conceited bounders I have ever met I think he is the worst. He began by saying to me "Here you see the man who by making Peace with Turkey[3] has saved tens of thousands of lives and millions of pounds" and all through he was only thinking of himself and how his Military career had been sacrificed out of loyalty to his Country. I am sure he is going to give a great deal of trouble when he gets back to England as he will pose as a martyr unless they give him some Command, and I am perfectly certain any Command he is given would mean the destruction of the troops under him.

He told me that he had been very well treated on the whole by the Turks and what struck me about him was his practical unconcern with regard to all those poor devils who served under him and so many of whom died like flies. I feel perfectly certain he could have done a great deal for them but he apparently did very little as when I asked him what he had been able to do for those who had been prisoners in Turkey, all he could say was that he had had parcels packed up for them in Constantinople.

He was rather interesting in a way about the method in which the proposal for an armistice was conveyed by the Turks. It appears he had two Turkish (A.D.C.'s he called them) attached to him. I suppose they were really men seeing that he did not escape. He talked to one of them after they heard of the fall of Damascus and told him that Germany was evidently at the end, that England was not resentful and why didn't they try and make Peace. The A.D.C. asked whether he might repeat the conversation to Izett Pasha and he consented. The next day Izett Pasha asked him whether he would be prepared to go and interview the English Admiral. He said Yes provided he was at once given his liberty — again nothing about the poor fellows who had served under him. This was granted. The next day he went in a Turkish Destroyer with the White Flag taking a Turkish Officer with him. On Admiral Calthorpe[4] saying he would be willing to receive envoys this man flew back and the envoys arrived the next day.

To go back to his story, he says that the Turks are dying like flies of hunger. They say it is typhus but it is not, it is pure famine and men, women and children are dying in the streets from it. He himself got everything he wanted to eat but at a fearful price. His monthly bill for himself, his A.D.C. and two English servants was £300. I took him in to tea with Victoria and he then began going over his stories. He told us one thing which shows the sort of value that he puts upon himself. He got a Turkish flying man to desert and to take a letter with him saying that if a seaplane could be sent to a certain place on a certain day, and he gave 3 dates, they would find him there and he would be able to get away. The man demanded £30,000 for doing it and Townshend agreed to give it to him, though he said it was an exorbitant price, but perhaps not more than his escape was worth. The man went off but was shot down by one of their own Turkish gunners. He fell into the sea and was drowned but they found Townshend's letter on him. Townshend of course did not know of this and went to the appointed place 3 times, rowing 8 miles there and 8 miles back. Of course on none of the occasions finding the seaplane he expected. It never seemed to occur to him that apparently the Turks did not much mind whether he escaped or not, as he certainly could not have got to this place after the Turks knowing he was going to attempt to do it if they had really wanted to stop him and they made no difference in their treatment afterwards of him. He was apparently allowed to write whatever he liked home and to receive any letters he liked back through the Dutch Legation, none of his letters having been censored.

I am bound to again repeat that I do not think I have ever come across a man to whom I took a more intense dislike but what I feel is he is the sort of man the British public will probably go mad about and allow him to pose as a hero and a martyr. I am told his A.D.C. loathes the sight of him and if he, Townshend, writes a report, which he says he is going to do, the A.D.C. is going to write one which will give a very different aspect not only of the time in Turkey but also of his behaviour during the siege at Kut.[5] He is going to demand that he should at once be given a Command in France in order to show, as he himself put it, that he is one of the best soldiers the Empire has got.

Attended Dinner given by the Directorate of Ship Repairs, Paris. Sat between M. Leygues and M. Cley. I came away directly after Dinner before the speeches began as I wanted to talk to Henry Wilson. Dinner quite pleasant. Talked to Leygues about many things. He was very bitter against Malvy who he said was a real bad lot. As for Caillaux he evidently hopes that he will be shot. He says the High Court has perfect power to do it and he hoped they would. He said of course the verdict is a foregone conclusion but the punishment is something that nobody can even anticipate at the present moment.

He said Clemenceau's effort in the Chamber in the afternoon was magnificent. The old man had a tremendous reception and was evidently very much moved.[6]

Notes to 5 November

1. Sir Joseph Davies (1866–1954). Lloyd George's secretariat, 1916–20.
2. Major-General Sir Charles Townshend (1861–1924). British Commander at the battles of Kut-el-Amara and Ctesiphon in Mesopotamia, and the subsequent disastrous defence of Kut and surrender to the Turks.
3. Townshend had been released from captivity in October to convey peace overtures from the Turks.
4. Admiral Somerset A. G. Calthorpe (1864–1937). Commander-in-Chief in the Mediterranean, 1917–19.
5. See R. Miller, *Kut: The Death of an Army* (London, 1969).
6. Clemenceau recalled that he was the last survivor of those who had signed a formal protest against the surrender of Alsace and Lorraine in 1871. He warned that the problems of peace would be as great as those of the war.

Wednesday, 6th November

Admiral Hope came in in the morning and told me in the strictest confidence that they had intercepted a wireless from which it was obvious a mutiny had broken out in the German Fleet.[1] The wireless summoned all men in the Fleet, who still supported the Kaiser and the Government, to rendezvous at a certain ship. Hope's reading of the position is that the Germans wanted to play one last card and send out their Fleet but the men feeling they were going to certain death and destruction refused. I think that is probably the proper reading but I cannot help feeling there may be some trick behind it.

Although there is a general retreat along the whole of the German Front there is no doubt they are still putting up a very fine fight. The general opinion here is that they will not accept the armistice at once but that they will have to do so before Christmas. I am beginning to doubt that view myself. I think if this is really true about the Fleet they have tried to play a last card and failed and they have no alternative but to accept the armistice.

Just for amusement's sake I make a prophecy of what I think will happen.

They will accept the armistice about the 14th.

An Inter-Allied Conference will assemble here to discuss the terms of Peace and begin their work by December 1st, although there may be preliminary meetings before that.

The discussion of terms of Peace will probably take until the middle or end of January. They will then be transmitted to Germany and certain pourparlers will take place, the Germans asking for modifications. If we, as I hope, remain perfectly firm and refuse to modify our terms and if the armistice is, as I hope, perfectly water-tight and they are unable to recommence the War, I think that the final meeting for the signing of the terms will probably be held and the Treaty of Peace signed by the end of March at the latest.[2]

The Inter-Allied Conference I think will be held here and Clemenceau will certainly make a great push to have the final one held at Versailles. Lloyd George will oppose this but I expect it will be supported by the Americans and the Italians.

Ordinary Military Meeting. Nothing of any consequence.

Major General Price Davies, V.C.,[3] brother-in-law to Henry Wilson, came in just before luncheon and stayed for luncheon. He is back from Italy. He says the 48th Division, in which Edward's Brigade is, did a marvellous bit of work. They captured 30,000 prisoners and I think he said 400 guns and their total casualties were under 200. I asked him what he thought of the Italians. He said it was a very anxious moment. The Italian attacks failed and the only one that succeeded was ours. We got across the river and made a Bridgehead. We were able then to pass the Italian Corps, which were under Fatty Cavan, behind us and aided by our barrage they attacked. He said they were magnificently brave and did splendidly. He said the Austrian prisoners are very insulting to the Italians and tell them they never would have surrendered if it had only been the Italians they were fighting but with the British they knew they were up against something different and they had surrendered to the British and not to them.

Hearn, the Consul General, came in afterwards to ask me again to intercede in his favour as he has got to retire after the War. I have told him I will do what I can for him. It is extremely hard on him. At the same time I told him that I could hold out no hope that the Foreign Office would change the decision. He is writing me a letter and I am sending in a covering letter with it to the F.O.

Afterwards Walter Berry and Bennet came to see me to ask me to get Lloyd George to be their principal guest on November 28th at the American Thanksgiving Day Banquet they wish to give in his honour.

David Henderson came in to tell me that he had had telegrams and telephone messages from London to tell him to go and see Townshend and severely reprimand him for giving interviews to newspaper people. So the fun is beginning already. I was certain it would.

Charlie went to tea with Mrs. Leeds who said she wanted to consult him on a most important matter. He has just told me what it was. Such an extraordinary story I think it is worth recording. It appears that Prince Christopher of Greece[4] was approached by the Lithuanians some months ago, before Germany's defeat, and asked to become King of their Country, the people who approached him being the Lithuanian Committee which like all these intriguing Committees is now settled in Switzerland. They have returned to the charge and a few days ago a man called Whitehouse, attached to the American Embassy here, brought Mrs. Leeds a letter sent by the American Minister at Berne, from this same Committee, in which they begged her to return to Switzerland to marry Prince Christopher and at the same time persuade him to take the Crown which they again were prepared to offer him. They told her that the proposition had the consent and full approbation of all the Allies and would be especially welcome in America. They gave various reasons why it would be popular, the most amusing of which was that if she married him there would not be the same necessity, which might otherwise exist, for the Lithuanian people to find a big Civil List. She told Charlie the whole thing was done most officially, Whitehouse coming in uniform to see her. She asked Charlie's advice and he very wisely said before she made any move she had better find out whether there was any truth in the statement that the Allies approved of the suggestion and he is going to consult Arthur Balfour on her behalf the next time he comes out. I am perfectly certain that the whole thing is a fraud from beginning to end.

Dinner only Victoria, B., Reggie and self.

After Dinner Charlie Grant came in. He had been sent up to meet Wemyss who goes with Foch to receive the Parlementaire. They had intercepted [a] wireless saying that the Peace Delegates had left Berlin for the Front and they thought they might come over at any time.

Charlie afterwards came in, having dined with the Edmond Rothschilds. Edouard Rothschild had telephoned there to say that the envoys had crossed the line and had already been received by Foch at 6 o'c. As Charlie Grant had only left Foch at 6.30 there was a very easy proof that the Jews do not know everything as they think they do.

Notes to 6 November

1. Three thousand German sailors and workers raised the red flag at Kiel. Efforts by the Governor of Kiel to bring the situation under control were unsuccessful.
2. In fact the Treaty of Versailles was not signed until 28 June 1919.
3. Major-General Llewelyn Price-Davies (1878–1965). VC, 1901; Brigade commander, 1915–18.
4. Brother of the deposed King Constantine.

Thursday, 7th November

Charlie Grant came in first thing to say that a wireless had been received in the night from the Germans to ask for their plenipotentiaries to be received and asking by what route they should come in.

I then went to the President to introduce David Henderson. The President much more talkative than I have ever known him. Pleased to receive David Henderson, very nice to him and then turned round and began talking about general politics. He showed me the actual communication from Germany in which they asked to be received and had the cheek to say that even before the signing of the armistice they hoped fighting should stop temporarily. Foch's answer was very curt and to the point. Said he would receive them and gave them the route by which they were to come in. If I had had a bet with Charlie last night I should have won it as he bet me that I would not know what route they would come in by until after they had come and gone, but Foch's telegram of course gave that away. The route is from Chimay to Guise.

Received a telegram from Home Government telling me to see Clemenceau and House with reference to an alteration they wished made in terms of armistice. Went off at once to see Clemenceau. He entirely agreed with proposed alterations and added that if Lloyd George had not been in such a hurry to go away it would have been settled before he went. He asked me to get House's consent and also inform the Italian Ambassador. Meanwhile he sent a special message to Foch to have the requisite words inserted. I thought him a little tired and rattled. Went on to see House who also entirely agreed with the proposed alteration and we then had a very interesting talk. He told me that his great anxiety was that friendship should exist after the War between England and America and he begged me to do all I could to help him in this direction. I naturally gave him that assurance. I wanted to find out why he had suddenly said this and it gradually leaked out he was very anxious as to the attitude, not only of Lloyd George, but also of Clemenceau to the President. He said that everybody was trying to make mischief. He himself had heard Clemenceau had said certain things about him (House) namely that the French did not want him over but he insisted on coming, and he had gone straight off to see Clemenceau and told him what had been said. Naturally of course Clemenceau pointed out to him it was quite untrue and he ought to know that from the fact that the invitation to come was given in the name of all the Allies by the French Ambassador. We then talked about the President coming over here and he told me that there was no doubt whatever that he would come but he did not think he would attend the actual Conference. He would come for preliminary discussions and to see the Troops, and as he put it to get the atmosphere. That he was so far away he did not seem to realise some of the difficulties and that he hoped he would be able to persuade him to come, though not as he said to stay for the Conference itself. He again reverted to difficulties that might arise between individuals, as he put it, and the President. He told me that if it was a question of A.J.B. and the President discussing matters together there would be no difficulty as they thoroughly understood each other and could work in perfect harmony and it was quite evident that he wanted me to give a hint to A.J.B. that it was essential, as far as possible, negotiations should go on between him and the President rather than with L.G. He did not say so in so many words but I am perfectly certain I am right in my impression as to his meaning.

I then went on to see the Italian Ambassador and told him what Clemenceau's decision was and begged him to inform his Government. I told him of course there was no question of waiting to hear what his Government's view on the point was as it had to be dealt with at once, but he quite agreed that the condition was essential and he anticipated no difficulty whatsoever.

Afterwards went to a luncheon given at the Elysées by the President for Colonel and Mrs. House. Sat between Mrs. Sharp and Madame Pichon. Took in the latter. We had a long talk over the past 5 months and what a change there had been and she told me that there were moments when they almost despaired and that up to the 15th July the situation had been one constant worry and anxiety to her husband. She was good enough to say she appreciated what a very difficult position I had been in and apparently thought I had got through all right.

After luncheon talked first of all to Admiral Le Bon.[1] He is rather disturbed at the Naval terms of the armistice, and does not think they are severe enough. Of course he says a certain amount will turn on how they are carried out but he thinks we could easily have imposed far severer conditions. He believes that the mutiny at Wilhelmshaven is much worse than they first thought and apparently they have got snatches of wireless in which the loyal ships are exhorted to fire on those which have hoisted the Red Flag. He thinks there has actually been a fight between them but none of the information seemed to be very definite or very accurate.

I then had a talk with Loucheur who I am a little suspicious of. He told me his one idea was to help in every way the friendship between English and French and especially in Commercial Matters. I told him that I thought he was going the wrong way about it at the present moment and he would have to change his ways very much before I could really believe that was his view. I do not think he quite liked it but he knows perfectly well what I meant. I think the speaking plainly just a little scared him. I talked pretty openly of our being able to give blow for blow unless they mended their ways.

He then told me an interesting thing and that was that the day before the Cabinet had discussed the question of the Freedom of the Seas and Clemenceau had made a very animated appeal to them to support the English in their reading of what the Freedom of the Seas should be. He said it was to our Fleet we owed to a great extent the Victory. That they had been with us from the very beginning and there had been one thing we could always rely on and it was the duty of France to support England if necessary against America. He said that there was absolute unanimity in the Cabinet on this subject and that I might reckon on France's support, but that the President might be troublesome. He was quite certain England and France sticking together would certainly win the day.

When I got back home I found yet another telegram from the Home Government asking me to make certain representations about the prisoners. It really is very annoying they could not think of all these things before instead of waiting till absolutely the 11th hour to bring them forward.

I went off to see Clemenceau again, showed him the telegram which he at once had telephoned out to Foch telling him that he was to carry out the instruction given. He showed me various telegrams which he said he was communicating direct to England. Nothing of any very great importance except the names of those who were coming as delegates from Germany. When I was there a telegram came in giving the wireless account of an appeal addressed to the German people. From this he deduced, and I think rightly, that the Germans coming are rather more than delegates. They are Plenipotentiaries and have the power to accept or reject the terms of armistice. They would probably be with Foch by 7 o'c and it was possible that the matter might be decided tonight. He however thought probably it would not be till tomorrow morning.

He then gave me a great blow as I had decided to go up to Rawlinson tomorrow with Victoria and B and Charlie. He said on no account must I leave so after I had seen him I had to arrange with Captain Barker that passes should be made out for these three to go without me. Clemenceau was in a much better humour than he had been in the morning and he always has some sort of chaff for me and as I was going out of the room he put his hand on my shoulder and said "I want to give you if I may as an older man a bit of advice". I asked him what it was and he said "If I were you I should not at the present moment invest anything in German stock. It is not likely to go up in the next few months."

I forgot to say that the Belgian Minister told me at the Elysées Déjeuner that he was furious at Clemenceau having omitted any reference to Belgium in his speech and he left the Ambassador's Box as a protest. He says he thought that Clemenceau had made the omission intentionally.

One other omission in his speech was also commented on but I am sure was not deliberate and that was any reference to the work of our Fleet.

Dinner. Bullock and Bridgeman dined. Got a message after Dinner to say that Haig was not able to sanction the two ladies visiting Rawly's Headquarters. There has been a nice mess made over the whole thing as Rawly telegraphed to say that he had fixed it all up with the Chief.

Notes to 7 November

1. Vice-Admiral Ferdinand Le Bon (1861–1923), Chief of the French Naval General Staff, 1916–19.

Friday, 8th November

Clemenceau sent for me. I went to see him and he gave me the latest report from the Armistice negotiations which I telegraphed off to London. He then turned to me and said as I was going out "Now, remember, is the time when we have got to remain firmer friends than ever". I told him he need have no fear about me and he said he knew that. He thought I knew as well as he did what he referred to. Of course it was Lloyd George's attitude to him and I again assured him I would do everything in my power to help him and the old man was really quite affected and he took me by both hands and said he knew he could rely upon me as being a true friend and then said "Isn't it nice to think that we who have been through such bad days together should now be seeing these happy days". I said that he had every reason to be happy. He was really affected and the tears were streaming down his face. He said he never thought he could be as happy as he was at that moment.

I must say I did not think it possible at one time that I should ever be on the friendly terms that I am with him but I see with him great dangers ahead and it will require all the tact at one's disposal if we are to avoid trouble. Personally I think that more trouble is to be expected from the extraordinary grasping nature of the French in money matters than from anything else.

Luncheon. Only Victoria, B, Dolly and myself.

Two things I ought to have put in the Diary which I have suddenly remembered. First of all at the Dinner on Tuesday night Leygues the Minister of Marine told me that he thought that their lawyers had an overwhelming case for our reading of Freedom of the Seas. It was gone into most carefully at the time of the Blockade and he was certain that by their arguments Wilson would be entirely persuaded that our view was right and that the French were entirely with us in it.

The other thing I heard was that Clemenceau was very angry at Bob Cecil having said that the Peace Conference ought to be held at Brussels. He is supposed to have said this either in the House of Commons or in some speech. I certainly did not see it myself.

Went round to see Alan Fletcher who has been very ill with flu. He is stupidly going about now instead of being in bed which is the proper place for him. He tells me D.H.'s chauffeur got the flu the same day as he did and died that morning. All the hotels here are full of this beastly illness.

Mr Wicksted Steed[1] came to see me. He told me that nobody could believe how badly the Italians have behaved with reference to the Yugo-Slavs. It appears that the Yugo-Slavs really practically got possession of the Austrian Fleet a month before the coup actually came off. They sent over to Italy to tell the Italian Government. The Italian Government put the envoys in Prison and kept them there without telling a soul. They then sent over another emissary to see M. Trumbic[2] who was in Rome trying to get in communication with them. The Italians again imprisoned the man, kept him for 5 days while Trumbic was in Rome without telling the latter a word. I asked Wicksted Steed to come to Dinner and talk again.

David Henderson came to see me and told me he had taken the Annexe to the Majestic for Lloyd George and Party.

Evening Lady Curzon and Wicksted Steed dined. The latter was very interesting but I should think rather a wild visionary. I won't attempt to describe all he told us about the Czecho-Slovaks and Yugo-Slavs. He reeled off facts and figures at an alarming rate and one's head was in a whirl. There are two things worth recording and both rather outside this particular question. He talked about Northcliffe. Of course he is the Foreign Editor of *The Times* and a great supporter of Northcliffe. Said Northcliffe had done an enormous amount of good. I said I thought it was a great pity that whenever he wanted to advocate or oppose anything he did not support or oppose the proposal itself but attacked some individual connected with it in a most bitter personal way. He said that was his great mistake and I mentioned his attack on Milner. He then launched out about Milner and said it was not Milner so much as his entourage and especially Amery. That they were rather fed up in *The Times* with Milner as Geoffrey Dawson[3] is an absolute slave of his and everything Milner said was right. I asked him why he attacked Amery and he said because Amery was Milner's evil genius with regard to things in Eastern Europe. That he had put in a long Memorandum to the Cabinet in March in which he advocated Peace then with Germany, some concessions to be made with regard to Alsace and Lorraine, we to keep all our Colonies we had captured, and Germany to be given a free hand in Russia; and he said there was no doubt that Milner endorsed that idea. He then began to describe Amery.[4] I cannot remember the whole of the story but roughly it is this. Amery's father was a Buda Pesth Jew who married a Jewess from some part of Germany. His father was taken into the Indian Forestry Department and something happened of a disagreeable character with the result that he disappeared from the scenes altogether. Amery's education was undertaken by his uncle, his mother's brother, another Jew whose name I think he said was Lembach. This man was a rolling stone and turned up in Demarara where he made money and from there sent Amery to school at Harrow. Amery then, after leaving Harrow and before he became Press Correspondent in South Africa, roamed about Austria and the Balkans and had got a smattering of knowledge with regard to those places. After the South African War he was Lord Milner's Private Secretary and exercised a great influence over him but he had not a drop of English blood in his veins and was most untrustworthy. It was no use attacking in the papers a man of Amery's standing. They had to attack the man of standing who Amery influenced.

The second anecdote was in connection with Lord Lansdowne.[5] It appears that Northcliffe got information to the effect that when the Deputation consisting of Cave, Newton[6] and Belfield[7] went over to Holland in connection with the exchange of prisoners the Germans had let it be understood that they were going to try and talk Peace. Lansdowne hearing of this called together his supporters. Told them what was happening and prepared a letter to be issued to the Press the first day that the meeting was to be held urging that the opportunity should be taken of seeing if Peace terms could not be arranged. Northcliffe heard of this and at once had a violent letter in the *Daily Mail* protesting against there being any Peace talk at this particular Conference. The result was Lansdowne was afraid of issuing the letter and the whole thing collapsed. Steed was very positive in his mind as to the Frontier Lines for the various States. He says there is great difficulty with regard to Serbia who wants to absorb Bosnia and Herzegovina into a greater Serbia while these States are determined not to be absorbed. They would be agreeable to being Federated States possibly under a King common to all. Prince Alexander of Serbia[8] was mentioned as he has done very well in the War and would be popular. He says that the Italians are already taking possession of places on the Dalmatian Coast to which they are not entitled and which will certain [*sic*] bring them into conflict with the Yugo-Slavs. He says that the Convention of London will have to be denounced and Italy will have to make up her mind to take less than they had asked for but that there is sure to be a great deal of trouble over this. Steed talked without stopping for an hour and a half, but as I said I really cannot remember all that he told us.

Notes to 8 November

1. Derby means Wickham Steed.
2. Ante Trumbitch (1864–1938). Fled Austrian Empire before 1914, setting up the Yugo-Slav Committee in London.
3. Geoffrey Dawson (1874–1944). Changed name from Robinson, 1917. Editor of *The Times*, 1912–19 and 1923–41.
4. See W. D. Rubinstein, 'The Secret of Leopold Amery', *History Today*, 49/2, February 1999, pp. 17–23.
5. Henry C. K. Petty-Fitzmaurice, 5th Marquess of Lansdowne (1845–1927). Minister without Portfolio, May 1915–December 1916. His 1917 letter, published in the *Daily Telegraph*, advocating a negotiated peace with Germany as an alternative to the complete destruction of civilisation, caused a sensation.
6. Thomas Woodhouse Legh, 2nd Baron Newton (1857–1942). Controller of Prisoners of War Department, 1916–19. For Hague Prisoners of War Conference, see Lord Newton, *Retrospection* (London, 1941), pp. 236–41.

7. Lieutenant-General Sir Herbert Belfield (1857–1934). Director of Prisoners of War, 1914–20.
8. Alexander of Serbia (1888–1934). King of Serbs, Croats and Slovenes, 1921–29 and of Yugoslavia, 1929–34. Assassinated.

Saturday, 9th November

Went to see Clemenceau to find out if there was any news. He says that after allowing their Deputation to come through they blew up the Bridges behind them with the result that the Courier will take some time to get back to Spa and is not likely to arrive there before tonight. The armistice therefore cannot be accepted or rejected before tomorrow night or possibly there may be an extension till Monday night. Clemenceau still thinks that they will accept.

I then spoke to him about the great desirability of helping us to get proper buildings for a Conference and I told him I thought if we could not it would have to be considered whether the Conference should not be held elsewhere. He blazed up at once and said if it was held anywhere else except Paris it would be held without him. I told him I thought he ought to make things easy for us by requisitioning any buildings that we wanted. He was very much surprised when I told him that the Staff to be brought over from London would be 370 people. He said "are you bringing over the whole British Army?". He was chaffing but I think he was surprised at the number. He will be still more surprised when he hears that the Americans are bringing even a bigger number. However he promised to do what he could to help and has sent an officer to be attached to David Henderson to help him in the requisitioning.

I am afraid he is rather bitter against the English generally. I asked him how the dog was and he said it was the only thing that kept him on good terms with England. I asked him if I could not be classed in the same category as the dog. He laughed and said "Yes, I have got one Englishman and one Scotchman on my side". Referring in the latter case to the Aberdeen Terrier.

Luncheon. Lyttons, Mr. Gardner Sinclair, and Prince Arthur of Connaught[1] and Captain Sinclair his A.D.C.

I told Lady Lytton — who has rather grand ideas of bringing out their children and servants and taking a big apartment — that I did not think she would be well advised in doing this. She said she thought I was in favour of that. I told her I had been two months ago but that things have altered very much since then and I strongly advised her to take nothing for a longer period than 3 months and not to go to the expense of bringing out her family. I think she is disappointed, as I am quite sure she had made up her mind to stay here and possibly succeed me.

Had a discussion with Lionel Earle,[2] Henderson and others with regard to the buildings. The French Officer came who is to be attached by Clemenceau and they are to settle with him all details. Lionel Earle rather pompous as usual.

Dinner. The Grammonts. Lady Curzon, who had come in the afternoon and George Curzon who arrived very late for Dinner having been motoring 10 hours from Bruges.

B. Pembroke left, I am sorry to say, for England.

In the night I am told that people came and sang "God Save the King" outside the Embassy but as I sleep on the other side and was very sound asleep I never heard a sound, but it is evident people are beginning to get very excited.

Notes to 9 November

1. Prince Arthur of Connaught (1883–1938). Major and Lieutenant-Colonel Scots Greys, 1907–20.
2. Lionel Earle (1866–1948). Permanent Secretary to the Office of Works, 1912–33.

Sunday, 10th November

Dr. Benes came to see me as I had received a communication from the Government at home asking him to take steps to prevent the difficulties which are now existing with the Czechs in Siberia. He has promised to do what he can.

Went to see Clemenceau. I must say he is very good. He keeps me thoroughly "au courant" with everything that is going on. Showed me copies of all the telegrams he had been sending and received. He was in tremendous form.

Northcliffe then came with Onslow to see me about Propaganda in Enemy Countries. He says that he thinks that the time has come when it ought to stop and be on the same basis as it was before but that Onslow should remain and should do all he can to do propaganda work in any German territory we may occupy. He (Northcliffe) does not propose to go on unless as he says he gets a proper understanding with the Prime Minister in writing. I quite agree with him. I also think that Lytton's job could perfectly come to an end in a short time and be done simply by somebody attached to me for this work in the Chancery.

Luncheon. People in the House. The Lyttons, Lady D'Abernon,[1] Johnny Du Cane, and Charlie Winn and Billy Lambton. The latter I am sorry to say not only no better but seems to me if anything to have gone back.

After luncheon Victoria and I picked up Capel and we played a three ball match 9 holes. I was two up on Capel and two up on Victoria.

In the evening Brig-General and Lady Edwina Lewin came to tea. We had a long crack over old times.

Dined with Princesse de Chimay. Very amusing Dinner. Comte and Comtesse de Beaumont, Comte and Comtesse Boisgelin, the Capels, Madame Hennessy, Mlle de Saintsauveur, and Ralph Lambton. Everybody in a great state of excitement. We all expected any moment to hear that the armistice had been signed, but nothing came in.

Notes to 10 November

1. Lady D'Abernon (d.1954). Daughter of Earl of Feversham. Married Lord D'Abernon (British ambassador in Berlin, 1920–26) in 1890.

Monday, 11th November

Heard first thing that armistice had been signed at 5 a.m.

Clemenceau telephoned me to come down to see him. Very nice of him as he so arranged it that I was there with Foch and was the first one of the Allies to congratulate them both. Foch very much moved though I feel in his heart of hearts he regrets the armistice coming quite as soon as it did as he told both of us that within another fortnight the German Army would have been completely surrounded and would have been obliged to lay down their arms.

Most interesting when I was there, Clemenceau sent for some high authority with reference to the taking over of Alsace and Lorraine. They have got of course all the old arrondissements marked out and they are going simply to call them by their numbers as before 1870 and appoint the various Préfets, Governors, etc. It has been decided that the English are to occupy Cologne.

Of course Clemenceau is a little anxious as regards the state of Germany now and whether there is a stable Government who can carry out not only the terms of armistice but with whom we can make Peace.

Went out in the streets for a bit. Paris beginning to get very excited and I should think tonight there will be tremendous scenes.

General Bliss very kindly came to see me to congratulate the British Army. He too is alarmed at the situation in Germany and is I think very critical of the President though he did not actually mention his name. He says that he thinks 5 weeks valuable time has been lost and he was perfectly certain the Germans would have given us 5 weeks ago everything they have given us now and that then we might have had a stable Government to deal with.

Luncheon. Colonel and Mrs. House, M. and Mme Klotz, Lionel Earle, the Curzons, Reggie Pembroke, Madame Hennessy and ourselves. Everybody in a great state of excitement. House proposed the King's health after luncheon for which I thanked him and proposed that of the Allies, but neither of us with any speeches.

George Curzon was extremely troublesome with reference to a place for the Debate. I had absolutely failed to get him one and he was very pompous and said it was a disgraceful thing and as a member of the War Cabinet he ought to have one and expected me I think to go off myself and see that he got one. However luckily after luncheon Klotz said he would get him in and took him off. He had to wait an hour and three quarters before the actual speeches began.

Meanwhile we all waited for the Blues Band which played men from our Leave Club down to the Embassy followed by a gigantic crowd. They played the National Anthems in front here. Miss Decima Moore dressed in the Union Jack headed the procession which was rather amusing. A great deal of enthusiasm and the whole of the crowd joining in the singing of the Marseillaise.

I then went down to the Chamber. Great enthusiasm but I was a little disappointed as Clemenceau made no allusion of any sort or kind to the Allies which personally I think was a great omission on his part. He himself had a great ovation. He contented himself with reading the terms of the armistice which were loudly cheered, especially the parts concerning Alsace and Lorraine and the giving up of the submarines. The Deputies then joined in doing what I believe has never been done before, singing the Marseillaise, everybody joining in, which was really rather a fine ending. I sat between the Spanish and American Ambassadors. Sharp spoke to me about Northcliffe and said that he was doing an infinity of harm. That he was setting the tone to the Yellow Press everywhere and assuming an authority which nobody wished him to have and which apparently Carson[1] and Dillon alone were men enough to fight. I do not know how the two would like to be coupled together but he was so emphatic as to the danger that I think it is worth recording. Quinones on the other hand spoke to me about Spain and he is extremely anxious as to the position though he says it has improved considerably in the last week or so. Bolshevism is very prevalent and Maura is making the most of it. He said he could come and see me the next day and tell me all about it but I could see that he was gravely anxious as to the position.

Got back to find that Victoria with Lady D'Abernon had managed to squeeze into the Courtyard and had shaken hands with Clemenceau as he came out. Both of them in an intense state of excitement over it.

Sir Esmé Howard[2] came to tea. Also Lady D'Abernon.

In the evening dined with the American Ambassador and had a talk with House who the more I see of him the more I like. Very quiet, very decided and evidently bent on keeping the peace.

Victoria wanted to go down the Boulevards but I restrained her as it was bitterly cold.

I forgot to mention that I asked the Band after playing here to go round to the Place de la Concorde and play in front of the Strasbourg Statue. I believe it had an enormous success. I got the Embassy illuminated and I am glad to say it was the only building in Paris that was.

Notes to 11 November

1. Sir Edward Carson (1854–1935). Baron Carson, 1921. Leader of Ulster Unionists. First Lord of the Admiralty, December 1916–July 1917; Minister without Portfolio, July 1917–January 1918.
2. Esmé Howard (1863–1939). Baron Howard, 1930. British Minister in Sweden, 1913–19.

Index

Numbers in *italics* indicate where an individual is identified in the text.

Fisher, Victor 285, *286n*
Fitzgerald, Evelyn 317, *317n*, 318
Fitzgerald, Percy 6
Fletcher, Alan 8, *8n*, 11, 19, 37, 38, 77, 176, 295, 299, 300, 309, 330
Fleuriau, Aimé-Joseph de 136, *138n*
Flynn, Abbé 13
Foch, Ferdinand xxi, 3, *3n*, 15, 16, 17, *17n*, 19, 27, 30, 50, 52, 54, 56, 61, 68, 73, 75, 76, 78, 86, 90, 96, 103, 114, 120, 124, 128, 129, 136, 137, 140, 145, 147, 148, 150, 152, 153, 158, 161, 170, 172–3, 176, 186, 188, 189, 202, 238, 244–5, 248, 252, 255, 257, 260, 261, 269, 273, 290, 292, 297, 298, 299, 318, 321, 325, 326, 328, 329; confidence of 54–5; contempt for Henry Wilson 237; and German armistice 262, 284, 287, 335; quarrel with Haig 293–4, 295–6, 298; on Robertson 55, 256–7; as supreme commander 162, 171, 210; and tanks 189
Folkestone 101
Fontainebleau 228, 229
food taxes xiii
Forbes, Angela 9, 40
Forster, Harry 204
Forwood, Sir William 212, *213n*
Foster, Carnaby 46
Fouquet, Nicolas 228, *230n*
Fournier, Admiral François-Ernest 41, *42n*, 227
Fourteen Points 255, 258n, 264, 279, 289, 299, 300, 302, 315, 321
Fowke, Sir George 44, *45n*, 240, 241, 242
Fowler 281, 282
France; army losses 114; domestic politics of xxviii, xxix, 13, 20, 22, 23, 27, 29, 31, 38, 46, 59–60, 62, 68–9, 81, 93–4, 127, 145, 150–1, 169, 186–7; industrial destruction of 263–4, 265; peace feeling in 23
Franco-American relations 165, 273–4
Franco-Italian relations 146, 191
Franklin-Bouillon, Henri 13, *14n*, 92, 94, 106, 127
Frazier, Arthur 74, *75n*, 123, 137, 243, 244, 278, 279, 291, 298
free trade xi, 313
freedom of the seas 251, 255, 258n, 260, 263, 284, 301, 315, 316, 328, 330
French, Sir John 12n, 42, *43n*, 57n, 115, 277
Furse, Sir William 33, 35, *35n*, 229

Gabriac, comte de 253
Gallipoli 36
Galway Castle 235
Garstin, William 75, *75n*
Gaulois, Le 26, 26n, 95
Geddes, Auckland *18n*, 304
Geddes, Eric 4, *4n*, 10, 17, 18n, 196, 200, 203, 209, 302, 315, 318–19
General Election (1900) 124n; (1906) xi; (1910) xii; (1918) 43n, 123, 127, 198, 209, 270–1, 285, 303, 312, 314
Geneva 302
George V xx, xxiv, xxv, 17, 63n, 91, 94, 97, 98n, 126, 127, 129n, 144n, 158, 161–2, 225, 286n, 336
Georges, Col. Alphonse-Joseph 19, *20n*, 163, 165, 171, 273, 294
Georges-Picot, François 226, *227n*
Géraud, André 9, 13, *14n*, 92
Germany; armistice with xxx, 246, 251, 255, 257, 270–1, 273, 277, 288–9, 294, 300, 307, 308, 315–6, 318, 327–8, 329, 333, 335–6; army, condition of 77–8, 103, 113, 158, 162, 164, 177, 199, 335; Bolshevism in 274, 277; capitulation of 281; colonies of 263, 264, 266, 301, 306, 331; losses of 55, 114; naval mutiny of 323, 326n, 328; peace terms with 68, 263, 294n, 332n; spring offensive of (1918) xxv, xxviii, 55, 57n, 154n; war aims of 68
Gibraltar 188
Giordini 290
Gladstone, William E. 85n, 286n
Gladstone Dock 295

Glasgow 285
Godley, Gen. Alexander 111, *112n*, 121, 122, 177
Goeben and Breslau incident 131, 131n
Goff, Sir Park 42, *43n*
Gompers, Samuel 224, *225n*, 279, 285
Goodwin, Gen. William 65, *66n*
Gordon, Maj.-Gen. Alex 37, *39n*
Gorton 25n
Gosford, Louise 46
Gotha bomber 25, 25n
Gouin, Edouard 34, 209, 228
Gouin, Mme 228
Gouraud, Gen. Henri 225, *226n*
Goût, Jean 309, *311n*
Graham, Lady Evelyn 285
Graham, Maj. Henry 285, *286n*
Grahame, Sir George 5, 6, *6n*, 20, 33, 45, 47, 70, 76, 81, 97, 98, 101, 104, 122, 141, 142, 190, 197, 204, 243, 272
Grammont, comte de 119, 134, 143, 197, 317, 334
Grammont, comtesse Renée de 143
Grand National xiv, 177, 178n
Grant, Lt-Col. Charles 15–16, *16n*, 17, 50, 54, 55, 104, 106, 111, 165, 190, 202, 212, 255, 273, 325, 326
Great Eastern Railway 224
Greece 46, 53n, 72, 74n, 81, 82, 83n, 99, 159, 261; intervention of 36; troops of 52, 61, 246, 262; War of Independence 301n
Green, Maj. Edward 104, 143, 278
Greig, Louis 286, *286n*, 288, 288n, 293
Grey, Sir Edward 46, *46n*
Griscom, Col. Lloyd 299, *301n*
Grosclaude, Etienne 201, *202n*
Guiche, duc de 121, 167, 247, 268, 294, 298, 316
Guillaumat, Gen. Marie-Adolphe 51, *52n*, 61, 64, 81, 82, 83, 112, 173, 200, 245, 249, 249n, 280; on Salonika 51–2, 113, 172, 220, 227
Guillemin, Jean 72, *74n*, 253–4
Gunzburg, Baron Jacques de 284, *285n*
Gwynne, Bishop 109
Gwynne, H. A. xvi, xxiii, xxvi, 109, *109n*

Hadfield, Lady 7, 8
Hague, The 41, 41n, 65n, 180, 279n, 317; Prisoners of War Conference at 332
Haig, Sir Douglas xvi, xix, xx, xxi, xxii, xxiii, xxiv, 12, 12n, 18, 20, 27, 38, 39n, 44, 54, 56, 66, 75, 77, 78, 83, 84, 92, 101, 107, 117, 123, 124, 128, 129, 130, 137, 141, 144, 145, 146, 147, 148, 149, 153, 161, 162, 176, 178, 179, 181, 188, 193, 200, 202, 210, 222, 233, 240, 241n, 252, 267, 269, 277, 287, 299, 301, 302, 306, 320, 329; and armistice terms 295, 297; on Derby xviii; and Home Command 38; qualities of 256; quarrel with Foch 293–4, 295–6, 298, 300; relations with Foch 30, 37; on tanks 147
Hall, Henry 154, *156n*, 156, 167, 174, 188, 248, 249
Haller, Gen. Joseph 223, *224n*, 280
Hallowes, Gen. Henry 192, *193n*
Halsbury, Earl of 270, *271n*
Hamburg 71
Hamilton, Claud 143, *144n*, 190
Hamilton, Ronald 64, *65n*
Hankey, Col. Maurice xxiv, 37, *39n*, 80n, 205n, 244, 247, 249, 282n, 301, 303
Hanover Square 264, 266n
Harcourt, Lewis 156, *157n*
Hardinge, Alexander 129, *129n*, 131, 132, 133, 138, 143
Hardinge, Sir Arthur 53, *54n*, 166
Hardinge, Lady 53
Hardinge, Lord (Charles) xxvi, 42, *43n*, 160; as ambassador in Paris 43n
Harriman, Miss Bordon 294
Harrow 331
Hartington, Charles 30, *30n*, 31
Hartington, Marquess of 5, *5n*, 73, 77, 104, 106, 158, 176
Harvard Club 262